Advanced Rails

Other resources from O'Reilly

Related titles

Ajax on Rails
Learning Ruby
Rails Cookbook™
RESTful Web Services

Ruby on Rails: Up and Running
Ruby Pocket Reference
Test Driven Ajax (on Rails)

oreilly.com

oreilly.com is more than a complete catalog of O'Reilly books. You'll also find links to news, events, articles, weblogs, sample chapters, and code examples.

oreillynet.com is the essential portal for developers interested in open and emerging technologies, including new platforms, programming languages, and operating systems.

Conferences

O'Reilly brings diverse innovators together to nurture the ideas that spark revolutionary industries. We specialize in documenting the latest tools and systems, translating the innovator's knowledge into useful skills for those in the trenches. Visit *conferences.oreilly.com* for our upcoming events.

Safari Bookshelf (*safari.oreilly.com*) is the premier online reference library for programmers and IT professionals. Conduct searches across more than 1,000 books. Subscribers can zero in on answers to time-critical questions in a matter of seconds. Read the books on your Bookshelf from cover to cover or simply flip to the page you need. Try it today for free.

Advanced Rails

Brad Ediger

O'REILLY®

Beijing · Cambridge · Farnham · Köln · Paris · Sebastopol · Taipei · Tokyo

Advanced Rails
by Brad Ediger

Copyright © 2008 Brad Ediger. All rights reserved.
Printed in the United States of America.

Published by O'Reilly Media, Inc., 1005 Gravenstein Highway North, Sebastopol, CA 95472.

O'Reilly books may be purchased for educational, business, or sales promotional use. Online editions are also available for most titles (*safari.oreilly.com*). For more information, contact our corporate/institutional sales department: (800) 998-9938 or *corporate@oreilly.com*.

Editor: Mike Loukides
Production Editor: Rachel Monaghan
Production Services: Octal Publishing, Inc.

Cover Designer: Karen Montgomery
Interior Designer: David Futato
Illustrator: Robert Romano

Printing History:

December 2007:   First Edition.

 This book uses RepKover™, a durable and flexible lay-flat binding.

ISBN-10: 0-596-51032-2
ISBN-13: 978-0-596-51032-9
[C]

Table of Contents

Preface

When I started working with Ruby and Rails in late 2004, there was almost no documentation on the Rails framework. Since then, there has been a tremendous number of books, blogs, and articles written about creating web applications with Rails. But many of them seemed to follow a common pattern: you could create a blog in 15 minutes; a to-do list application was simple. Many of the books I saw devoted an entire chapter to installing Ruby and Rails. Today, there is no lack of resources for the beginning and intermediate Rails developer.

But Rails is clearly useful for much more than toy blogs and to-do lists. The 37signals applications (Basecamp, Highrise, Backpack, and Campfire) are all built with Rails; many of the Internet's high-traffic sites such as Twitter, Penny Arcade, and Yellowpages.com use it. Rails is now used in many high-profile places, yet developers often have to fend for themselves when building such large applications, as the most current and relevant information is often only found spread across various other developers' blogs.

Development and deployment of complex web projects is a multidisciplinary task, and it will always remain so. In this book, I seek to weave together several different topics relevant to Rails development, from the most basic foundations of the Ruby programming language to the development of large Rails applications.

Prerequisites

As its title suggests, *Advanced Rails* is not a book for beginners. Readers should have an understanding of the architecture of the Web, a good command of Ruby 1.8, and experience building web applications with Ruby on Rails. We do not cover installation of Rails, the Rails API, or the Ruby language; working-level experience with all of these is assumed.

I would recommend the following books as a prelude to this one:

- *Programming Ruby,* Second Edition, by Dave Thomas (Pragmatic Bookshelf): Known as "the Pickaxe," this is an excellent introduction to Ruby for programmers, and a comprehensive reference that will serve you for years. Without a doubt the most essential book for Rails developers, no matter what skill level.

- *The Ruby Programming Language*, by David Flanagan and Yukihiro Matsumoto (O'Reilly): Scheduled to be released in January 2008, this book is a comprehensive introduction and reference to Ruby 1.8 as well as 1.9. It does an excellent job of covering even the most difficult aspects of Ruby while still being accessible to programmers learning it.

- *Best of Ruby Quiz* by James Edward Gray II (Pragmatic Bookshelf): 25 selected quizzes from the Ruby Quiz (*http://www.rubyquiz.com/*); includes both the quizzes and a discussion of their solutions. Solving programming puzzles and sharing solutions with others is a great way to hone your Ruby skills.

- *Agile Web Development with Rails,* Second Edition, by Dave Thomas and David Heinemeier Hansson (Pragmatic Bookshelf): The best and most comprehensive book for learning Ruby on Rails. The second edition covers Rails 1.2, but most concepts are applicable to Rails 2.0.

- *Rails Cookbook*, by Rob Orsini (O'Reilly): This contains "cookbook-style" solutions to common problems in Rails, each one of which may be worth the price of the book in time saved. Also worth reading are the similar books *Rails Recipes* by Chad Fowler and *Advanced Rails Recipes* by Mike Clark and Chad Fowler (Pragmatic Bookshelf).

Many varied subjects are covered in this book; I make an effort to introduce subjects that may be unfamiliar (such as decentralized revision control) and provide references to external resources that may be useful. Each chapter has a "Further Reading" section with references that clarify or expand on the text.

I take a bottom-up approach to the concepts in this book. The first few chapters cover the mechanics of metaprogramming in Ruby and the internals of Rails. As the book progresses, these concepts assimilate into larger concepts, and the last several chapters cover the "big-picture" concepts of managing large Rails software development projects and integrating Rails into other systems.

This book is written for Rails 2.0. At the time of this writing, Rails 2.0 has been released as a release candidate, but not in its final form. Details are subject to change, but the concepts and techniques discussed in this book should be valid for Rails 2.0.

Conventions Used in This Book

The following typographical conventions are used in this book:

Plain text

> Indicates menu titles, menu options, menu buttons, keyboard accelerators (such as Alt and Ctrl), plugins, gems, and libraries.

Italic

> Indicates new terms, URLs, email addresses, filenames, file extensions, pathnames, directories, controls, and Unix utilities.

Constant width

> Indicates commands, options, switches, variables, attributes, keys, functions, types, classes, namespaces, methods, modules, properties, parameters, values, objects, events, event handlers, interfaces, XML tags, HTML tags, macros, the contents of files, or the output from commands.

Constant width italic

> Shows text that should be replaced with user-supplied values.

Constant width bold

> Used to highlight portions of code.

 This icon signifies a tip, suggestion, or general note.

 This icon indicates a warning or caution.

Using Code Examples

This book is here to help you get your job done. In general, you may use the code in this book in your programs and documentation. You do not need to contact us for permission unless you're reproducing a significant portion of the code. For example, writing a program that uses several chunks of code from this book does not require permission. Selling or distributing a CD-ROM of examples from O'Reilly books *does* require permission. Answering a question by citing this book and quoting example code does not require permission. Incorporating a significant amount of example code from this book into your product's documentation *does* require permission.

We appreciate, but do not require, attribution. An attribution usually includes the title, author, publisher, and ISBN. For example: "*Advanced Rails*, by Brad Ediger. Copyright 2008 Brad Ediger, 978-0-596-51032-9."

If you feel your use of code examples falls outside fair use or the permission given above, feel free to contact us at *permissions@oreilly.com*.

How to Contact Us

Please address comments and questions concerning this book to the publisher:

O'Reilly Media, Inc.
1005 Gravenstein Highway North
Sebastopol, CA 95472
800-998-9938 (in the United States or Canada)
707-829-0515 (international or local)
707-829-0104 (fax)

We have a web page for this book, where we list errata, examples, and any additional information. You can access this page at:

http://www.oreilly.com/catalog/9780596510329

To comment or ask technical questions about this book, send email to:

bookquestions@oreilly.com

For more information about our books, conferences, Resource Centers, and the O'Reilly Network, see the web site:

http://www.oreilly.com

Safari® Books Online

 When you see a Safari® Books Online icon on the cover of your favorite technology book, that means the book is available online through the O'Reilly Network Safari Bookshelf.

Safari offers a solution that's better than e-books. It's a virtual library that lets you easily search thousands of top tech books, cut and paste code samples, download chapters, and find quick answers when you need the most accurate, current information. Try it for free at *http://safari.oreilly.com*.

Acknowledgments

No book is created without the help of many people. I owe a great debt of gratitude to the many who helped create this work. Without their help and support, these ideas would still be rattling around in my head.

Mike Loukides, my editor at O'Reilly, was instrumental in creating the idea for this book. He helped me understand the type of book I really wanted to write, and provided the encouragement needed to turn sketches of ideas into prose. Mike's extensive knowledge of the industry, the authorship process, and computer science in general were invaluable.

I had an amazing team of technical reviewers, who caught many of my errors in the manuscripts. Thanks are due to James Edward Gray II, Michael Koziarski, Leonard Richardson, and Zed Shaw for their revisions. Any remaining errors were originated and perpetuated on my own. (Should you find one of these errors, we'd love to hear about it at *http://www.oreilly.com/catalog/9780596510329/errata/.*)

The production department at O'Reilly was very professional and accommodating of my odd schedule; Keith Fahlgren, Rachel Monaghan, Rob Romano, Andrew Savikas, Marlowe Shaeffer, and Adam Witwer all helped make this book usable and attractive.

I have many friends and colleagues who offered advice, support, criticism, and review. Thanks to Erik Berry, Gregory Brown, Pat Eyler, James Edward Gray II, Damon Hill, Jim Kane, John Lein, Tim Morgan, Keith Nazworth, Rob Norwood, Brian Sage, Jeremy Weathers, and Craig Wilson for your input. Thanks also to Gary and Jean Atkins, who, although they know nothing about Rails or software development, never failed to ask me about my book's progress and offer encouragement.

Others provided inspiration through their books and writings online, as well as discussions on mailing lists: François Beausoleil, David Black, Avi Bryant, Jamis Buck, Ryan Davis, Mauricio Fernández, Eric Hodel, S. Robert James, Jeremy Kemper, Rick Olson, Dave Thomas, and *why the lucky stiff*.

None of this would have been possible without Ruby or Rails. Thanks to Yukihiro Matsumoto (Matz) for creating such a beautiful language, to David Heinemeier Hansson for creating such a fun framework, and to the Ruby and Rails committers and communities for maintaining them.

Thanks to my parents for their continual support.

Finally, thanks to my wonderful wife, Kristen, who put up with a year-long writing process. She encouraged me to write a book when I thought it impossible, and supported me every step of the way.

## CHAPTER 1

Foundational Techniques

Simplicity is prerequisite for reliability.
—Edsger W. Dijkstra

Since its initial release in July 2004, the Ruby on Rails web framework has been steadily growing in popularity. Rails has been converting PHP, Java, and .NET developers to a simpler way: a model-view-controller (MVC) architecture, sensible defaults ("convention over configuration"), and the powerful Ruby programming language.

Rails had somewhat of a bad reputation for a lack of documentation during its first year or two. This gap has since been filled by the thousands of developers who use, contribute to, and write about Ruby on Rails, as well as by the Rails Documentation project (*http://railsdocumentation.org/*). There are hundreds of blogs that offer tutorials and advice for Rails development.

This book's goal is to collect and distill the best practices and knowledge embodied by the community of Rails developers and present everything in an easy-to-understand, compact format for experienced programmers. In addition, I seek to present facets of web development that are often undertreated or dismissed by the Rails community.

What Is Metaprogramming?

Rails brought metaprogramming to the masses. Although it was certainly not the first application to use Ruby's extensive facilities for introspection, it is probably the most popular. To understand Rails, we must first examine the parts of Ruby that make Rails possible. This chapter lays the foundation for the techniques discussed in the remainder of this book.

Metaprogramming is a programming technique in which code writes other code or introspects upon itself. The prefix *meta-* (from Greek) refers to abstraction; code that uses metaprogramming techniques works at two levels of abstraction simultaneously.

Metaprogramming is used in many languages, but it is most popular in dynamic languages because they typically have more runtime capabilities for manipulating code as data. Though reflection is available in more static languages such as C# and Java, it is not nearly as transparent as in the more dynamic languages such as Ruby because the code and data are on two separate levels at runtime.

Introspection is typically done on one of two levels. *Syntactic introspection* is the lowest level of introspection—direct examination of the program text or token stream. Template-based and macro-based metaprogramming usually operate at the syntactic level.

Lisp encourages this style of metaprogramming by using *S-expressions* (essentially a direct translation of the program's abstract syntax tree) for both code and data. Metaprogramming in Lisp heavily involves *macros*, which are essentially templates for code. This offers the advantage of working on one level; code and data are both represented in the same way, and the only thing that distinguishes code from data is whether it is evaluated. However, there are some drawbacks to metaprogramming at the syntactic level. Variable capture and inadvertent multiple evaluation are direct consequences of having code on two levels of abstraction in the source evaluated in the same namespace. Although there are standard Lisp idioms for dealing with these problems, they represent more things the Lisp programmer must learn and think about.

Syntactic introspection for Ruby is available through the ParseTree library, which translates Ruby source into S-expressions.* An interesting application of this library is Heckle,† a test-testing framework that parses Ruby source code and mutates it, changing strings and flipping `true` to `false` and vice versa. The idea is that if you have good test coverage, any mutation of your code should cause your unit tests to fail.

The higher-level alternative to syntactic introspection is *semantic introspection*, or examination of a program through the language's higher-level data structures. Exactly how this looks differs between languages, but in Ruby it generally means working at the class and method level: creating, rewriting, and aliasing methods; intercepting method calls; and manipulating the inheritance chain. These techniques are usually more orthogonal to existing code than syntactic methods, because they tend to treat existing methods as black boxes rather than poking around inside their implementations.

Don't Repeat Yourself

At a high level, metaprogramming is useful in working toward the *DRY principle* (Don't Repeat Yourself). Also referred to as "Once and Only Once," the DRY principle dictates that you should only need to express a particular piece of information once in a system. Duplication is usually unnecessary, especially in dynamic

---

* *http://www.zenspider.com/ZSS/Products/ParseTree/*
† *http://rubyforge.org/projects/seattlerb*

languages like Ruby. Just as functional abstraction allows us to avoid duplicating code that is the same or nearly the same, metaprogramming allows us to avoid duplicating similar concepts when they recur throughout an application.

Metaprogramming is primarily about simplicity. One of the easiest ways to get a feel for metaprogramming is to look for repeated code and factor it out. Redundant code can be factored into functions; redundant functions or patterns can often be factored out through the use of metaprogramming.

Design patterns cover overlapping territory here; patterns are designed to minimize the number of times you have to solve the same problem. In the Ruby community, design patterns have acquired something of a negative reputation. To some developers, patterns are a common vocabulary for describing solutions to recurring problems. To others, they are overengineered.

To be sure, patterns can be overapplied. However, this need not be the case if they are used judiciously. Design patterns are only useful insofar as they reduce cognitive complexity. In Ruby, some of the fine-grained patterns are so transparent that it would be counterintuitive to call them "patterns"; they are really idioms, and most programmers who "think in Ruby" use them without thinking. Patterns should be thought of as a vocabulary for describing architecture, not as a library of prepackaged implementation solutions. Good Ruby design patterns are vastly different from good C++ design patterns in this regard.

In general, metaprogramming should not be used simply to repeat code. You should always evaluate the options to see if another technique, such as functional abstraction, would better suit the problem. However, in a few cases, repeating code via metaprogramming is the best way to solve a problem. For example, when several very similar methods must be defined on an object, as in ActiveRecord helper methods, metaprogramming can be used.

Caveats

Code that rewrites itself can be very hard to write and maintain. The programming devices you choose should always serve your needs—they should make your life easier, not more difficult. The techniques illustrated here should be more tools in your toolbox, not the only tools.

Bottom-Up Programming

Bottom-up programming is a concept borrowed from the Lisp world. The primary concept in bottom-up programming is building abstractions from the lowest level. By writing the lowest-level constructs first, you are essentially building your program on top of those abstractions. In a sense, you are writing a domain-specific language in which you build your programs.

This concept is extremely useful in ActiveRecord. After creating your basic schema and model objects, you can begin to build abstractions on top of those objects. Many Rails projects start out by building abstractions on the model like this, before writing a single line of controller code or even designing the web interface:

```ruby
class Order < ActiveRecord::Base
  has_many :line_items

  def total
    subtotal + shipping + tax
  end

  def subtotal
    line_items.sum(:price)
  end

  def shipping
    shipping_base_price + line_items.sum(:shipping)
  end

  def tax
    subtotal * TAX_RATE
  end
end
```

Ruby Foundations

This book relies heavily on a firm understanding of Ruby. This section will explain some aspects of Ruby that are often confusing or misunderstood. Some of this may be familiar, but these are important concepts that form the basis for the metaprogramming techniques covered later in this chapter.

Classes and Modules

Classes and modules are the foundation of object-oriented programming in Ruby. Classes facilitate encapsulation and separation of concerns. Modules can be used as *mixins*—bundles of functionality that are added onto a class to add behaviors in lieu of multiple inheritance. Modules are also used to separate classes into namespaces.

In Ruby, every class name is a constant. This is why Ruby requires class names to begin with an uppercase letter. The constant evaluates to the *class object*, which is an object of the class Class. This is distinct from the *Class object*, which represents the actual class Class.* When we refer to a "class object" (with a lowercase C), we mean any object that represents a class (including Class itself). When we refer to the "Class object" (uppercase C), we mean the class Class, which is the superclass of all class objects.

---

* If that weren't confusing enough, the Class object has class Class as well.

The class `Class` inherits from `Module`; every class is also a module. However, there is an important distinction. Classes cannot be mixed in to other classes, and classes cannot extend objects; only modules can.

Method Lookup

Method lookup in Ruby can be very confusing, but it is quite regular. The easiest way to understand complicated situations is to visualize the data structures that Ruby creates behind the scenes.

Every Ruby object[*] has a set of fields in memory:

`klass`
> A pointer to the class object of this object. (It is `klass` instead of `class` because the latter is a reserved word in C++ and Ruby; if it were called `class`, Ruby would compile with a C compiler but not with a C++ compiler. This deliberate misspelling is used everywhere in Ruby.)

`iv_tbl`
> "Instance Variable Table," a hashtable containing the instance variables belonging to this object.

`flags`
> A bitfield of Boolean flags with some status information, such as the object's taint status, garbage collection mark bit, and whether the object is frozen.

Every Ruby class or module has the same fields, plus two more:

`m_tbl`
> "Method Table," a hashtable of this class or module's instance methods.

`super`
> A pointer to this class or module's superclass.

These fields play a huge role in method lookup, and it is important that you understand them. In particular, you should pay close attention to the difference between the `klass` and `super` pointers of a class object.

The rules

The method lookup rules are very simple, but they depend on an understanding of how Ruby's data structures work. When a message is sent to an object,[†] the following steps occur:

---

[*] Except immediate objects (`Fixnum`s, symbols, `true`, `false`, and `nil`); we'll get to those later.

[†] Ruby often co-opts Smalltalk's message-passing terminology: when a method is called, it is said that one is *sending a message*. The *receiver* is the object that the message is sent to.

1. Ruby follows the receiver's klass pointer and searches the m_tbl of that class object for a matching method. (The target of a klass pointer will always be a class object.)

2. If no method is found, Ruby follows that class object's super pointer and continues the search in the superclass's m_tbl.

3. Ruby progresses in this manner until the method is found or the top of the super chain is reached.

4. If the method is not found in any object on the chain, Ruby invokes method_ missing on the receiver of the original method. This starts the process over again, this time looking for method_missing rather than the original method.

These rules apply universally. All of the interesting things that method lookup involves (mixins, class methods, and singleton classes) are consequences of the structure of the klass and super pointers. We will now examine this process in detail.

Class inheritance

The method lookup process can be confusing, so we'll start simple. Here is the simplest possible class definition in Ruby:

```
class A
end
```

This code generates the following data structures in memory (see Figure 1-1).

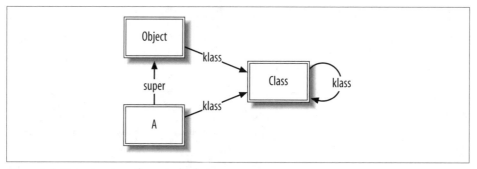

Figure 1-1. Data structures for a single class

The double-bordered boxes represent class objects—objects whose klass pointer points to the Class object. A's super pointer refers to the Object class object, indicating that A inherits from Object. For clarity, from now on we will omit default klass pointers to Class, Module, and Object where there is no ambiguity.

The next-simplest case is inheritance from one class. Class inheritance simply follows the super pointers. For example, we will create a B class that descends from A:

```
class B < A
end
```

The resulting data structures are shown in Figure 1-2.

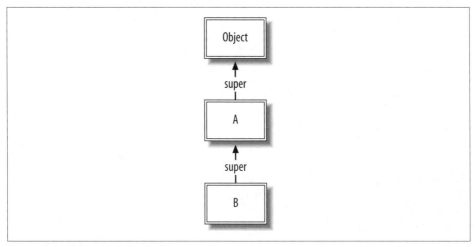

Figure 1-2. One level of inheritance

The super keyword always delegates along the method lookup chain, as in the following example:

```
class B
  def initialize
    logger.info "Creating B object"
    super
  end
end
```

The call to super in `initialize` will follow the standard method lookup chain, beginning with A#initialize.

Class instantiation

Now we get a chance to see how method lookup is performed. We first create an instance of class B:

```
obj = B.new
```

This creates a new object, and sets its klass pointer to B's class object (see Figure 1-3).

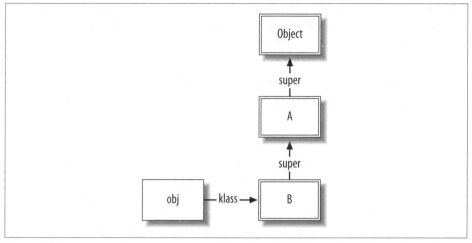

Figure 1-3. Class instantiation

The single-bordered box around obj represents a plain-old object instance. Note that each box in this diagram is an object instance. However, the double-bordered boxes represent objects that are instances of the Class class (hence their klass pointer points to the Class object).

When we send obj a message:

```
obj.to_s
```

this chain is followed:

1. obj's klass pointer is followed to B; B's methods (in m_tbl) are searched for a matching method.

2. No methods are found in B. B's super pointer is followed, and A is searched for methods.

3. No methods are found in A. A's super pointer is followed, and Object is searched for methods.

4. The Object class contains a to_s method in native code (rb_any_to_s). This is invoked, yielding a value like "#<B:0x1cd3c0>". The rb_any_to_s method examines the receiver's klass pointer to determine what class name to display; therefore, B is shown even though the method invoked resides in Object.

Including modules

Things get more complicated when we start mixing in modules. Ruby handles module inclusion with ICLASSes,* which are proxies for modules. When you include a

---

* ICLASS is Mauricio Fernández's term for these proxy classes. They have no official name but are of type T_ICLASS in the Ruby source.

module into a class, Ruby inserts an ICLASS representing the included module into the including class object's super chain.

For our module inclusion example, let's simplify things a bit by ignoring B for now. We define a module and mix it in to A, which results in data structures shown in Figure 1-4:

```
module Mixin
  def mixed_method
    puts "Hello from mixin"
  end
end

class A
  include Mixin
end
```

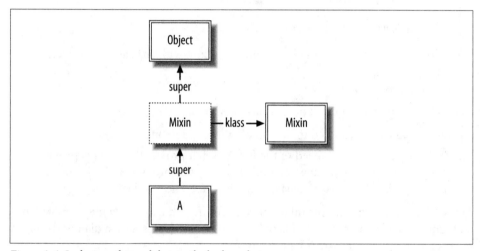

Figure 1-4. Inclusion of a module into the lookup chain

Here is where the ICLASS comes into play. The super link pointing from A to Object is intercepted by a new ICLASS (represented by the box with the dashed line). The ICLASS is a proxy for the Mixin module. It contains pointers to Mixin's iv_tbl (instance variables) and m_tbl (methods).

From this diagram, it is easy to see why we need proxy classes: the same module may be mixed in to any number of different classes—classes that may inherit from different classes (thus having different super pointers). We could not directly insert Mixin into the lookup chain, because its super pointer would have to point to two different things if it were mixed in to two classes with different parents.

When we instantiate A, the structures are as shown in Figure 1-5:

```
objA = A.new
```

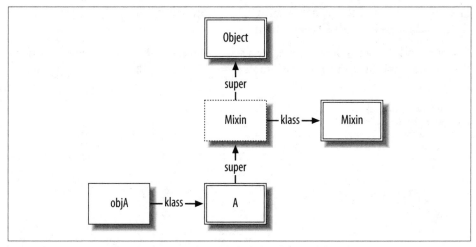

Figure 1-5. Method lookup for a class with an included module

We invoke the `mixed_method` method from the mixin, with `objA` as the receiver:

```
objA.mixed_method
# >> Hello from mixin
```

The following method-lookup process takes place:

1. `objA`'s class, `A`, is searched for a matching method. None is found.
2. `A`'s super pointer is followed to the ICLASS that proxies `Mixin`. This proxy object is searched for a matching method. Because the proxy's `m_tbl` is the same as `Mixin`'s `m_tbl`, the `mixed_method` method is found and invoked.

Many languages with multiple inheritance suffer from the *diamond problem*, which is ambiguity in resolving method calls on objects whose classes have a diamond-shaped inheritance graph, as shown in Figure 1-6.

Given this diagram, if an object of class `D` calls a method defined in class `A` that has been overridden in both `B` and `C`, there is ambiguity about which method should be called. Ruby resolves this by linearizing the order of inclusion. Upon a method call, the lookup chain is searched linearly, including any ICLASSes that have been inserted into the chain.

First of all, Ruby does not support multiple inheritance; however, multiple modules can be mixed into classes and other modules. Therefore, `A`, `B`, and `C` must be modules. We see that there is no ambiguity here; the method chosen is the latest one that was inserted into the lookup chain:

```
module A
  def hello
    "Hello from A"
  end
end
```

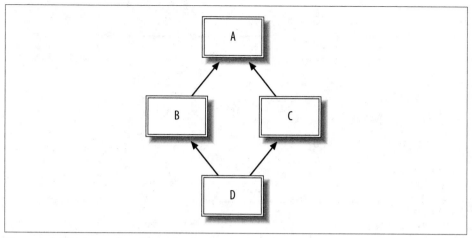

Figure 1-6. The diamond problem of multiple inheritance

```ruby
module B
  include A
  def hello
    "Hello from B"
  end
end

module C
  include A
  def hello
    "Hello from C"
  end
end

class D
  include B
  include C
end

D.new.hello # => "Hello from C"
```

And if we change the order of inclusion, the result changes correspondingly:

```ruby
class D
  include C
  include B
end

D.new.hello # => "Hello from B"
```

In this last example, where B is included last, the object graph looks like Figure 1-7 (for simplicity, pointers to Object and Class have been elided).

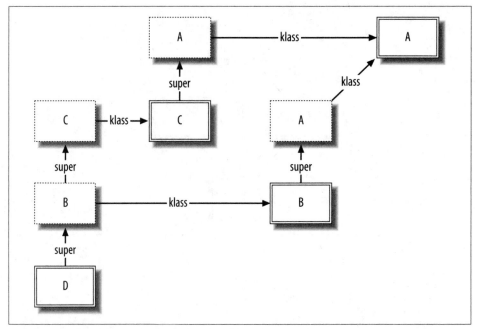

Figure 1-7. Ruby's solution for the diamond problem: linearization

The singleton class

Singleton classes (also *metaclasses* or *eigenclasses*; see the upcoming sidebar, "Single-ton Class Terminology") allow an object's behavior to be different from that of other objects of its class. You've probably seen the notation to open up a singleton class before:

```
class A
end

objA = A.new
objB = A.new
objA.to_s # => "#<A:0x1cd0a0>"
objB.to_s # => "#<A:0x1c4e28>"

class <<objA # Open the singleton class of objA
  def to_s; "Object A"; end
end

objA.to_s # => "Object A"
objB.to_s # => "#<A:0x1c4e28>"
```

The class <<objA notation opens objA's singleton class. Instance methods added to the singleton class function as instance methods in the lookup chain. The resulting data structures are shown in Figure 1-8.

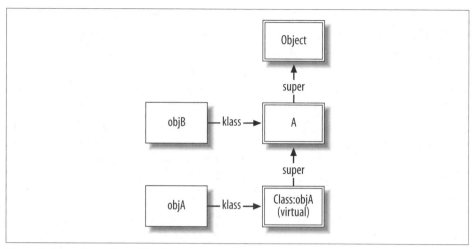

Figure 1-8. Singleton class of an object

Singleton Class Terminology

The term *metaclass* is not particularly accurate when applied to singleton classes. Calling a class "meta" implies that it is somehow more abstract than an ordinary class. This is not the case; singleton classes are simply classes that belong to a particular instance.

True metaclasses are found in languages such as Smalltalk that have a rich metaobject protocol. Smalltalk's metaclasses are classes whose instances are classes. By parallel, Ruby's only metaclass is Class, because all Ruby classes are instances of Class.

A somewhat popular alternate term for a singleton class is *eigenclass*, from the German *eigen* ("its own"). An object's singleton class is its eigenclass (its own class).

The objB instance is of class A, as usual. And if you ask Ruby, it will tell you that objA is also of class A:

```
objA.class # => A
```

However, something different is going on behind the scenes. Another class object has been inserted into the lookup chain. This object is the singleton class of objA. We refer to it as "Class:objA" in this documentation. Ruby calls it a similar name: #<Class:#<A:0x1cd0a0>>. Like all classes, the singleton class's klass pointer (not shown) points to the Class object.

The singleton class is marked as a *virtual class* (one of the flags is used to indicate that a class is virtual). Virtual classes cannot be instantiated, and we generally do not see them from Ruby unless we take pains to do so. When we ask Ruby for objA's class, it traverses the klass and super pointers up the hierarchy until it finds the first nonvirtual class.

Therefore, it tells us that objA's class is A. This is important to remember: an object's class (from Ruby's perspective) may not match the object pointed to by klass.

Singleton classes are called singleton for a reason: there can only be one singleton class per object. Therefore, we can refer unambiguously to "objA's singleton class" or Class:objA. In our code, we can assume that the singleton class exists; in reality, for efficiency, Ruby creates it only when we first mention it.

Ruby allows singleton classes to be defined on any object except Fixnums or symbols. Fixnums and symbols are *immediate values* (for efficiency, they're stored as themselves in memory, rather than as a pointer to a data structure). Because they're stored on their own, they don't have klass pointers, so there's no way to alter their method lookup chain.

You can open singleton classes for true, false, and nil, but the singleton class returned will be the same as the object's class. These values are singleton instances (the only instances) of TrueClass, FalseClass, and NilClass, respectively. When you ask for the singleton class of true, you will get TrueClass, as the immediate value true is the only possible instance of that class. In Ruby:

```
true.class # => TrueClass
class << true; self; end # => TrueClass
true.class == (class << true; self; end) # => true
```

Singleton classes of class objects

Here is where it gets complicated. Keep in mind the basic rule of method lookup: first Ruby follows an object's klass pointer and searches for methods; then Ruby keeps following super pointers all the way up the chain until it finds the appropriate method or reaches the top.

The important thing to remember is that *classes are objects, too.* Just as a plain-old object can have a singleton class, class objects can also have their own singleton classes. Those singleton classes, like all other classes, can have methods. Since the singleton class is accessed through the klass pointer of its owner's class object, the singleton class's instance methods are class methods of the singleton's owner.

The full set of data structures for the following code is shown in Figure 1-9:

```
class A
end
```

Class A inherits from Object. The A class object is of type Class. Class inherits from Module, which inherits from Object. The methods stored in A's m_tbl are instance methods of A. So what happens when we call a class method on A?

```
A.to_s # => "A"
```

The same method lookup rules apply, with A as the receiver. (Remember, A is a constant that evaluates to A's class object.) First, Ruby follows A's klass pointer to Class. Class's m_tbl is searched for a function named to_s. Finding none, Ruby follows Class's super pointer to Module, where the to_s function is found (in native code, rb_mod_to_s).

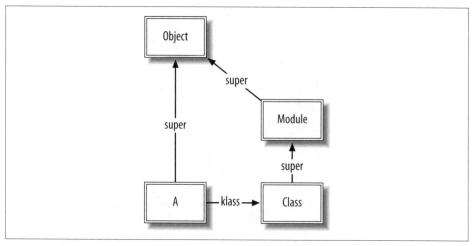

Figure 1-9. Full set of data structures for a single class

This should not be a surprise. There is no magic here. Class methods are found in the exact same way as instance methods—the only difference is whether the receiver is a class or an instance of a class.

Now that we know how class methods are looked up, it would seem that we could define class methods on any class by defining instance methods on the Class object (to insert them into Class's m_tbl). Indeed, this works:

```
class A; end

# from Module#to_s
A.to_s # => "A"

class Class
  def to_s; "Class#to_s"; end
end

A.to_s # => "Class#to_s"
```

That is an interesting trick, but it is of very limited utility. Usually we want to define unique class methods on each class. This is where singleton classes of class objects are used. To open up a singleton class on a class, simply pass the class's name as the object to the singleton class notation:

```
class A; end
class B; end

class <<A
  def to_s; "Class A"; end
end

A.to_s # => "Class A"
B.to_s # => "B"
```

The resulting data structures are shown in Figure 1-10. Class B is omitted for brevity.

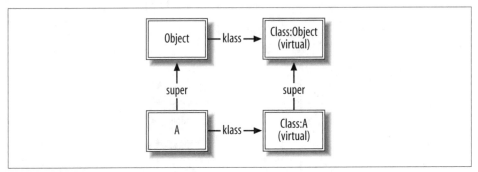

Figure 1-10. Singleton class of a class

The to_s method has been added to A's singleton class, or Class:A. Now, when A.to_s is called, Ruby will follow A's klass pointer to Class:A and invoke the appropriate method there.

There is one more wrinkle in method definition. In a class or module definition, self always refers to the class or module object:

```
class A
  self # => A
end
```

So, inside A's class definition, class <<A can also be written class <<self, since inside that definition A and self refer to the same object. This idiom is used everywhere in Rails to define class methods. This example shows all of the ways to define class methods:

```
class A
  def A.class_method_one; "Class method"; end

  def self.class_method_two; "Also a class method"; end

  class <<A
    def class_method_three; "Still a class method"; end
  end

  class <<self
    def class_method_four; "Yet another class method"; end
  end
end

def A.class_method_five
  "This works outside of the class definition"
end

class <<A
  def A.class_method_six
    "You can open the metaclass outside of the class definition"
  end
end
```

```
# Print the result of calling each method in turn
%w(one two three four five six).each do |number|
  puts A.send(:"class_method_#{number}")
end

# >> Class method
# >> Also a class method
# >> Still a class method
# >> Yet another class method
# >> This works outside of the class definition
# >> You can open the metaclass outside of the class definition
```

This also means that inside a singleton class definition—as in any other class definition—self refers to the class object being defined. When we remember that the value of a block or class definition is the value of the last statement executed, we can see that the value of class <<objA; self; end is objA's singleton class. The class <<objA construct opens up the singleton class, and self (the singleton class) is returned from the class definition.

Putting this together, we can open up the Object class and add an instance method to every object that returns that object's singleton class:

```
class Object
  def metaclass
    class <<self
        self
    end
  end
end
```

This method forms the basis of Metaid, which is described shortly.

Method missing

After all of that confusion, method_missing is remarkably simple. There is one rule: if the whole method lookup procedure fails all the way up to Object, method lookup is tried again, looking for a method_missing method rather than the original method. If the method is found, it is called with the same arguments as the original method, with the method name prepended. Any block given is also passed through.

The default method_missing function in Object (rb_method_missing) raises an exception.

Metaid

why the lucky stiff has created a tiny library for Ruby metaprogramming called *metaid.rb*. This snippet is useful enough to include in any project in which metaprogramming is needed:[*]

---

[*] "Seeing Metaclasses Clearly." *http://whytheluckystiff.net/articles/seeingMetaclassesClearly.html*

```
class Object
  # The hidden singleton lurks behind everyone
  def metaclass; class << self; self; end; end
  def meta_eval &blk; metaclass.instance_eval &blk; end

  # Adds methods to a metaclass
  def meta_def name, &blk
    meta_eval { define_method name, &blk }
  end

  # Defines an instance method within a class
  def class_def name, &blk
    class_eval { define_method name, &blk }
  end
end
```

This library defines four methods on every object:

metaclass
> Refers to the singleton class of the receiver (self).

meta_eval
> The equivalent of class_eval for singleton classes. Evaluates the given block in the context of the receiver's singleton class.

meta_def
> Defines a method within the receiver's singleton class. If the receiver is a class or module, this will create a class method (instance method of the receiver's singleton class).

class_def
> Defines an instance method in the receiver (which must be a class or module).

Metaid's convenience lies in its brevity. By using a shorthand for referring to and augmenting metaclasses, your code will become clearer rather than being littered with constructs like class << self; self; end. The shorter and more readable these techniques are, the more likely you are to use them appropriately in your programs.

This example shows how we can use Metaid to examine and simplify our singleton class hacking:

```
class Person
  def name; "Bob"; end
  def self.species; "Homo sapiens"; end
end
```

Class methods are added as instance methods of the singleton class:

```
Person.instance_methods(false)          # => ["name"]
Person.metaclass.instance_methods -
  Object.metaclass.instance_methods     # => ["species"]
```

Using the methods from Metaid, we could have written the method definitions as:

```
Person.class_def(:name) { "Bob" }
Person.meta_def(:species) { "Homo sapiens" }
```

Variable Lookup

There are four types of variables in Ruby: global variables, class variables, instance variables, and local variables.* Global variables are stored globally, and local variables are stored lexically, so neither of them is relevant to our discussion now, as they do not interact with Ruby's class system.

Instance variables are specific to a certain object. They are prefixed with one @ symbol: @price is an instance variable. Because every Ruby object has an iv_tbl structure, any object can have instance variables.

Since a class is also an object, a class can have instance variables. The following code accesses an instance variable of a class:

```
class A
  @ivar = "Instance variable of A"
end

A.instance_variable_get(:@ivar) # => "Instance variable of A"
```

Instance variables are always resolved based on the object pointed to by self. Because self is A's class object in the class A ... end definition, @ivar belongs to A's class object.

Class variables are different. Any instance of a class can access its class variables (which start with @@). Class variables can also be referenced from the class definition itself. While class variables and instance variables of a class are similar, they're not the same:

```
class A
  @var = "Instance variable of A"
  @@var = "Class variable of A"

  def A.ivar
    @var
  end

  def A.cvar
    @@var
  end
end

A.ivar # => "Instance variable of A"
A.cvar # => "Class variable of A"
```

In this code sample, @var and @@var are stored in the same place: in A's iv_tbl. However, they are different variables, because they have different names (the @ symbols are included in the variable's name as stored). Ruby's functions for accessing instance variables and class variables check to ensure that the names passed are in the proper format:

```
A.instance_variable_get(:@@var)
# ~> -:17:in `instance_variable_get': `@@var' is not allowed as an instance
    variable name (NameError)
```

---

* There are also constants, but they shouldn't vary. (They can, but Ruby will complain.)

Class variables can be somewhat confusing to use. They are shared all the way down the inheritance hierarchy, so subclasses that modify a class variable will modify the parent's class variable as well.

```
>> class A; @@x = 3 end
=> 3
>> class B < A; @@x = 4 end
=> 4
>> class A; @@x end
=> 4
```

This may be useful, but it may also be confusing. Generally, you either want class instance variables—which are independent of the inheritance hierarchy—or the class inheritable attributes provided by ActiveSupport, which propagate values in a controlled, well-defined manner.

Blocks, Methods, and Procs

One powerful feature of Ruby is the ability to work with pieces of code as objects. There are three classes that come into play, as follows:

Proc

A Proc represents a code block: a piece of code that can be called with arguments and has a return value.

UnboundMethod

This is similar to a Proc; it represents an instance method of a particular class. (Remember that class methods are instance methods of a class object, so UnboundMethods can represent class methods, too.) An UnboundMethod must be bound to a class before it can be invoked.

Method

Method objects are UnboundMethods that have been bound to an object with UnboundMethod#bind. Alternatively, they can be obtained with Object#method.

Let's examine some ways to get Proc and Method objects. We'll use the Fixnum#+ method as an example. We usually invoke it using the dyadic syntax:

```
3 + 5 # => 8
```

However, it can be invoked as an instance method of a Fixnum object, like any other instance method:

```
3.+(5) # => 8
```

We can use the Object#method method to get an object representing this instance method. The method will be bound to the object that method was called on, 3.

```
add_3 = 3.method(:+)
add_3 # => #<Method: Fixnum#+>
```

This method can be converted to a Proc, or called directly with arguments:

```
add_3.to_proc # => #<Proc:0x00024b08@-:6>
add_3.call(5) # => 8
# Method#[] is a handy synonym for Method#call.
add_3[5] # => 8
```

There are two ways to obtain an unbound method. We can call instance_method on the class object:

```
add_unbound = Fixnum.instance_method(:+)
add_unbound # => #<UnboundMethod: Fixnum#+>
```

We can also unbind a method that has already been bound to an object:

```
add_unbound == 3.method(:+).unbind # => true
add_unbound.bind(3).call(5) # => 8
```

We can bind the UnboundMethod to any other object of the same class:

```
add_unbound.bind(15)[4] # => 19
```

However, the object we bind to *must* be an instance of the same class, or else we get a TypeError:

```
add_unbound.bind(1.5)[4] # =>
# ~> -:16:in `bind': bind argument must be an instance of Fixnum (TypeError)
# ~>      from -:16
```

We get this error because + is defined in Fixnum; therefore, the UnboundMethod object we receive must be bound to an object that is a kind_of?(Fixnum). Had the + method been defined in Numeric (from which both Fixnum and Float inherit), the preceding code would have returned 5.5.

Blocks to Procs and Procs to blocks

One downside to the current implementation of Ruby: blocks are not always Procs, and vice versa. Ordinary blocks (created with do...end or { }) must be attached to a method call, and are not automatically objects. For example, you cannot say code_block = { puts "abc" }. This is what the Kernel#lambda and Proc.new functions are for: converting blocks to Procs.[*]

```
block_1 = lambda { puts "abc" } # => #<Proc:0x00024914@-:20>
block_2 = Proc.new { puts "abc" } # => #<Proc:0x000246a8@-:21>
```

There is a slight difference between Kernel#lambda and Proc.new. Returning from a Proc created with Kernel#lambda returns the given value to the calling function; returning from a Proc created with Proc.new attempts to return *from* the calling function, raising a LocalJumpError if that is impossible. Here is an example:

```
def block_test
  lambda_proc = lambda { return 3 }
  proc_new_proc = Proc.new { return 4 }
```

---

[*] Kernel#proc is another name for Kernel#lambda, but its usage is deprecated.

```
    lambda_proc.call # => 3
    proc_new_proc.call # =>

    puts "Never reached"
end

block_test # => 4
```

The return statement in lambda_proc returns the value 3 from the lambda. Conversely, the return statement in proc_new_proc returns from the calling function, block_test— thus, the value 4 is returned from block_test. The puts statement is never executed, because the proc_new_proc.call statement returns from block_test first.

Blocks can also be converted to Procs by passing them to a function, using & in the function's formal parameters:

```
def some_function(&b)
  puts "Block is a #{b} and returns #{b.call}"
end

some_function { 6 + 3 }
# >> Block is a #<Proc:0x00025774@-:7> and returns 9
```

Conversely, you can also substitute a Proc with & when a function expects a block:

```
add_3 = lambda {|x| x+3}
(1..5).map(&add_3) # => [4, 5, 6, 7, 8]
```

Closures

Closures are created when a block or Proc accesses variables defined outside of its scope. Even though the containing block may go out of scope, the variables are kept around until the block or Proc referencing them goes out of scope. A simplistic example, though not practically useful, demonstrates the idea:

```
def get_closure
  data = [1, 2, 3]
  lambda { data }
end
block = get_closure
block.call # => [1, 2, 3]
```

The anonymous function (the lambda) returned from get_closure references the local variable data, which is defined outside of its scope. As long as the block variable is in scope, it will hold its own reference to data, and that instance of data will not be destroyed (even though the get_closure function returns). Note that each time get_closure is called, data references a different variable (since it is function-local):

```
block = get_closure
block2 = get_closure

block.call.object_id # => 76200
block2.call.object_id  # => 76170
```

A classic example of closures is the make_counter function, which returns a counter function (a Proc) that, when executed, increments and returns its counter. In Ruby, make_counter can be implemented like this:

```
def make_counter(i=0)
  lambda { i += 1 }
end

x = make_counter
x.call # => 1
x.call # => 2

y = make_counter
y.call # => 1
y.call # => 2
```

The lambda function creates a closure that closes over the current value of the local variable i. Not only can the variable be accessed, but its value can be modified. Each closure gets a separate instance of the variable (because it is a variable local to a particular instantiation of make_counter). Since x and y contain references to different instances of the local variable i, they have different state.

Metaprogramming Techniques

Now that we've covered the fundamentals of Ruby, we can examine some of the common metaprogramming techniques that are used in Rails.

Although we write examples in Ruby, most of these techniques are applicable to any dynamic programming language. In fact, many of Ruby's metaprogramming idioms are shamelessly stolen from either Lisp, Smalltalk, or Perl.

Delaying Method Lookup Until Runtime

Often we want to create an interface whose methods vary depending on some piece of runtime data. The most prominent example of this in Rails is ActiveRecord's attribute accessor methods. Method calls on an ActiveRecord object (like person.name) are translated at runtime to attribute accesses. At the class-method level, ActiveRecord offers extreme flexibility: Person.find_all_by_user_id_and_active(42, true) is translated into the appropriate SQL query, raising the standard NoMethodError exception should those attributes not exist.

The magic behind this is Ruby's method_missing method. When a nonexistent method is called on an object, Ruby first checks that object's class for a method_missing method before raising a NoMethodError. method_missing's first argument is the name of the method called; the remainder of the arguments correspond to the arguments passed to the method. Any block passed to the method is passed through to method_missing. So, a complete method signature is:

```
def method_missing(method_id, *args, &block)
  ...
end
```

There are several drawbacks to using `method_missing`:

- It is slower than conventional method lookup. Simple tests indicate that method dispatch with `method_missing` is at least two to three times as expensive in time as conventional dispatch.

- Since the methods being called never actually exist—they are just intercepted at the last step of the method lookup process—they cannot be documented or introspected as conventional methods can.

- Because all dynamic methods must go through the `method_missing` method, the body of that method can become quite large if there are many different aspects of the code that need to add methods dynamically.

- Using `method_missing` restricts compatibility with future versions of an API. Once you rely on `method_missing` to do something interesting with undefined methods, introducing new methods in a future API version can break your users' expectations.

A good alternative is the approach taken by ActiveRecord's `generate_read_methods` feature. Rather than waiting for `method_missing` to intercept the calls, ActiveRecord generates an implementation for the attribute setter and reader methods so that they can be called via conventional method dispatch.

This is a powerful method in general, and the dynamic nature of Ruby makes it possible to write methods that replace themselves with optimized versions of themselves when they are first called. This is used in Rails routing, which needs to be very fast; we will see that in action later in this chapter.

Generative Programming: Writing Code On-the-Fly

One powerful technique that encompasses some of the others is *generative programming*—code that writes code.

This technique can manifest in the simplest ways, such as writing a shell script to automate some tedious part of programming. For example, you may want to populate your test fixtures with a sample project for each user:

```
brad_project:
  id: 1
  owner_id: 1
  billing_status_id: 12

john_project:
  id: 2
  owner_id: 2
  billing_status_id: 4

...
```

If this were a language without scriptable test fixtures, you might be writing these by hand. This gets messy when the data starts growing, and is next to impossible when the fixtures have strange dependencies on the source data. Naïve generative programming would have you writing a script to generate this fixture from the source. Although not ideal, this is a great improvement over writing the complete fixtures by hand. But this is a maintenance headache: you have to incorporate the script into your build process, and ensure that the fixture is regenerated when the source data changes.

This is rarely, if ever, needed in Ruby or Rails (thankfully). Almost every aspect of Rails application configuration is scriptable, due in large part to the use of internal domain-specific languages (DSLs). In an internal DSL, you have the full power of the Ruby language at your disposal, not just the particular interface the library author decided you should have.

Returning to the preceding example, ERb makes our job a lot easier. We can inject arbitrary Ruby code into the YAML file above using ERb's <% %> and <%= %> tags, including whatever logic we need:

```
<% User.find_all_by_active(true).each_with_index do |user, i| %>
<%= user.login %>_project:
  id: <%= i %>
  owner_id: <%= user.id %>
  billing_status_id: <%= user.billing_status.id %>

<% end %>
```

ActiveRecord's implementation of this handy trick couldn't be simpler:

```
yaml = YAML::load(erb_render(yaml_string))
```

using the helper method erb_render:

```
def erb_render(fixture_content)
  ERB.new(fixture_content).result
end
```

Generative programming often uses either Module#define_method or class_eval and def to create methods on-the-fly. ActiveRecord uses this technique for attribute accessors; the generate_read_methods feature defines the setter and reader methods as instance methods on the ActiveRecord class in order to reduce the number of times method_missing (a relatively expensive technique) is needed.

Continuations

Continuations are a very powerful control-flow mechanism. A continuation represents a particular state of the call stack and lexical variables. It is a snapshot of a point in time when evaluating Ruby code. Unfortunately, the Ruby 1.8 implementation of continuations is so slow as to be unusable for many applications. The upcoming Ruby 1.9 virtual machines may improve this situation, but you should not expect good performance from continuations under Ruby 1.8. However, they are useful constructs, and continuation-based web frameworks provide an interesting alternative to frameworks like Rails, so we will survey their use here.

Continuations are powerful for several reasons:

- Continuations are just objects; they can be passed around from function to function.

- Continuations can be invoked from anywhere. If you hold a reference to a continuation, you can invoke it.

- Continuations are re-entrant. You can use continuations to return from a function multiple times.

Continuations are often described as "structured GOTO." As such, they should be treated with the same caution as any kind of GOTO construct. Continuations have little or no place inside application code; they should usually be encapsulated within libraries. I don't say this because I think developers should be protected from themselves. Rather, continuations are general enough that it makes more sense to build abstractions around them than to use them directly. The idea is that a programmer should think "external iterator" or "coroutine" (both abstractions built on top of continuations) rather than "continuation" when building the application software.

Seaside[*] is a Smalltalk web application framework built on top of continuations. Continuations are used in Seaside to manage session state. Each user session corresponds to a server-side continuation. When a request comes in, the continuation is invoked and more code is run. The upshot is that entire transactions can be written as a single stream of code, even if they span multiple HTTP requests. This power comes from the fact that Smalltalk's continuations are serializable; they can be written out to a database or to the filesystem, then thawed and reinvoked upon a request. Ruby's continuations are nonserializable. In Ruby, continuations are in-memory only and cannot be transformed into a byte stream.

Borges (*http://borges.rubyforge.org/*) is a straightforward port of Seaside 2 to Ruby. The major difference between Seaside and Borges is that Borges must store all current continuations in memory, as they are not serializable. This is a huge limitation that unfortunately prevents Borges from being successful for web applications with any kind of volume. If serializable continuations are implemented in one of the Ruby implementations, this limitation can be removed.

The power of continuations is evident in the following Borges sample code, which renders a list of items from an online store:

```
class SushiNet::StoreItemList < Borges::Component

  def choose(item)
    call SushiNet::StoreItemView.new(item)
  end
```

---

[*] *http://seaside.st/*

```
def initialize(items)
  @batcher = Borges::BatchedList.new items, 8
end

def render_content_on(r)
  r.list_do @batcher.batch do |item|
    r.anchor item.title do choose item end
  end

  r.render @batcher
end

end # class SushiNet::StoreItemList
```

The bulk of the action happens in the render_content_on method, which uses a BatchedList (a paginator) to render a paginated list of links to products. But the fun happens in the call to anchor, which stores away the call to choose, to be executed when the corresponding link is clicked.

However, there is still vast disagreement on how useful continuations are for web programming. HTTP was designed as a stateless protocol, and continuations for web transactions are the polar opposite of statelessness. All of the continuations must be stored on the server, which takes additional memory and disk space. Sticky sessions are required, to direct a user's traffic to the same server. As a result, if one server goes down, all of its sessions are lost. The most popular Seaside application, DabbleDB (*http://dabbledb.com/*), actually uses continuations very little.

Bindings

Bindings provide context for evaluation of Ruby code. A binding is the set of variables and methods that are available at a particular (lexical) point in the code. Any place in Ruby code where statements may be evaluated has a binding, and that binding can be obtained with Kernel#binding. Bindings are just objects of class Binding, and they can be passed around as any objects can:

```
class C
  binding # => #<Binding:0x2533c>
  def a_method
    binding
  end
end
binding # => #<Binding:0x252b0>
C.new.a_method # => #<Binding:0x25238>
```

The Rails scaffold generator provides a good example of the use of bindings:

```
class ScaffoldingSandbox
  include ActionView::Helpers::ActiveRecordHelper
  attr_accessor :form_action, :singular_name, :suffix, :model_instance
```

```
    def sandbox_binding
      binding
    end

    # ...
  end
```

ScaffoldingSandbox is a class that provides a clean environment from which to render a template. ERb can render templates within the context of a binding, so that an API is available from within the ERb templates.

```
part_binding = template_options[:sandbox].call.sandbox_binding
# ...
ERB.new(File.readlines(part_path).join,nil,'-').result(part_binding)
```

Earlier I mentioned that blocks are closures. A closure's binding represents its state—the set of variables and methods it has access to. We can get at a closure's binding with the Proc#binding method:

```
def var_from_binding(&b)
  eval("var", b.binding)
end

var = 123
var_from_binding {} # => 123
var = 456
var_from_binding {} # => 456
```

Here we are only using the Proc as a method by which to get the binding. By accessing the binding (context) of those blocks, we can access the local variable var with a simple eval against the binding.

Introspection and ObjectSpace: Examining Data and Methods at Runtime

Ruby provides many methods for looking into objects at runtime. There are object methods to access instance variables. These methods break encapsulation, so use them with care.

```
class C
  def initialize
    @ivar = 1
  end
end

c = C.new
c.instance_variables             # => ["@ivar"]
c.instance_variable_get(:@ivar)  # => 1

c.instance_variable_set(:@ivar, 3) # => 3
c.instance_variable_get(:@ivar)  # => 3
```

The Object#methods method returns an array of instance methods, including singleton methods, defined on the receiver. If the first parameter to methods is false, only the object's singleton methods are returned.

```
class C
  def inst_method
  end

  def self.cls_method
  end
end

c = C.new

class << c
  def singleton_method
  end
end

c.methods - Object.methods # => ["inst_method", "singleton_method"]
c.methods(false) # => ["singleton_method"]
```

Module#instance_methods returns an array of the class or module's instance methods. Note that instance_methods is called on the class, while methods is called on an instance. Passing false to instance_methods skips the superclasses' methods:

```
C.instance_methods(false) # => ["inst_method"]
```

We can also use Metaid's metaclass method to examine C's class methods:

```
C.metaclass.instance_methods(false) # => ["new", "allocate", "cls_method",
                                          "superclass"]
```

In my experience, most of the value from these methods is in satisfying curiosity. With the exception of a few well-established idioms, there is rarely a need in production code to reflect on an object's methods. Far more often, these techniques can be used at a console prompt to find methods available on an object—it's usually quicker than reaching for a reference book:

```
Array.instance_methods.grep /sort/ # => ["sort!", "sort", "sort_by"]
```

ObjectSpace

ObjectSpace is a module used to interact with Ruby's object system. It has a few useful module methods that can make low-level hacking easier:

- Garbage-collection methods: define_finalizer (sets up a callback to be called just before an object is destroyed), undefine_finalizer (removes those callbacks), and garbage_collect (starts garbage collection).
- _id2ref converts an object's ID to a reference to that Ruby object.
- each_object iterates through all objects (or all objects of a certain class) and yields them to a block.

As always, with great power comes great responsibility. Although these methods can be useful, they can also be dangerous. Use them judiciously.

An example of the proper use of ObjectSpace is found in Ruby's Test::Unit framework. This code uses ObjectSpace.each_object to enumerate all classes in existence that inherit from Test::Unit::TestCase:

```
test_classes = []
ObjectSpace.each_object(Class) {
  | klass |
  test_classes << klass if (Test::Unit::TestCase > klass)
}
```

ObjectSpace, unfortunately, greatly complicates some Ruby virtual machines. In particular, JRuby performance suffers tremendously when ObjectSpace is enabled, because the Ruby interpreter cannot directly examine the JVM's heap for extant objects. Instead, JRuby must keep track of objects manually, which adds a great amount of overhead. As the same tricks can be achieved with methods like Module.extended and Class.inherited, there are not many cases where ObjectSpace is genuinely necessary.

Delegation with Proxy Classes

Delegation is a form of composition. It is similar to inheritance, except with more conceptual "space" between the objects being composed. Delegation implies a "has-a" rather than an "is-a" relationship. When one object delegates to another, there are two objects in existence, rather than the one object that would result from an inheritance hierarchy.

Delegation is used in ActiveRecord's associations. The AssociationProxy class delegates most methods (including class) to its target. In this way, associations can be lazily loaded (not loaded until their data is needed) with a completely transparent interface.

DelegateClass and Forwardable

Ruby's standard library includes facilities for delegation. The simplest is DelegateClass. By inheriting from DelegateClass(klass) and calling super(instance) in the constructor, a class delegates any unknown method calls to the provided instance of the class klass. As an example, consider a Settings class that delegates to a hash:

```
require 'delegate'
class Settings < DelegateClass(Hash)
  def initialize(options = {})
    super({:initialized_at => Time.now - 5}.merge(options))
  end
```

```
  def age
    Time.now - self[:initialized_at]
  end
end

settings = Settings.new :use_foo_bar => true

# Method calls are delegated to the object
settings[:use_foo_bar] # => true
settings.age # => 5.000301
```

The Settings constructor calls super to set the delegated object to a new hash. Note the difference between composition and inheritance: if we had inherited from Hash, then Settings would *be* a hash; in this case, Settings *has* a hash and delegates to it. This composition relationship offers increased flexibility, especially when the object to be delegated to may change (a function provided by SimpleDelegator).

The Ruby standard library also includes Forwardable, which provides a simple interface by which individual methods, rather than all undefined methods, can be delegated to another object. ActiveSupport in Rails provides similar functionality with a cleaner API through Module#delegate:

```
class User < ActiveRecord::Base
  belongs_to :person

  delegate :first_name, :last_name, :phone, :to => :person
end
```

Monkeypatching

In Ruby, all classes are open. Any object or class is fair game to be modified at any time. This gives many opportunities for extending or overriding existing functionality. This extension can be done very cleanly, without modifying the original definitions.

Rails takes advantage of Ruby's open class system extensively. Opening classes and adding code is referred to as *monkeypatching* (a term from the Python community). Though it sounds derogatory, this term is used in a decidedly positive light; monkeypatching is, on the whole, seen as an incredibly useful technique. Almost all Rails plugins monkeypatch the Rails core in some way or another.

Disadvantages of monkeypatching

There are two primary disadvantages to monkeypatching. First, the code for one method call may be spread over several files. The foremost example of this is in ActionController's process method. This method is intercepted by methods in up to five different files during the course of a request. Each of these methods adds another feature: filters, exception rescue, components, and session management. The end result is a net gain: the benefit gained by separating each functional component into a separate file outweighs the inflated call stack.

Another consequence of the functionality being spread around is that it can be difficult to properly document a method. Because the function of the process method can change depending on which code has been loaded, there is no good place to document what each of the methods is adding. This problem exists because the actual identity of the process method changes as the methods are chained together.

Adding Functionality to Existing Methods

Because Rails encourages the philosophy of separation of concerns, you often will have the need to extend the functionality of existing code. Many times you will want to "patch" a feature onto an existing function without disturbing that function's code. Your addition may not be directly related to the function's original purpose: it may add authentication, logging, or some other important cross-cutting concern.

We will examine several approaches to the problem of cross-cutting concerns, and explain the one (method chaining) that has acquired the most momentum in the Ruby and Rails communities.

Subclassing

In traditional object-oriented programming, a class can be extended by inheriting from it and changing its data or behavior. This paradigm works for many purposes, but it has drawbacks:

- The changes you want to make may be small, in which case setting up a new class may be overly complex. Each new class in an inheritance hierarchy adds to the mental overhead required to understand the code.

- You may need to make a series of related changes to several otherwise-unrelated classes. Subclassing each one individually would be overkill and would separate functionality that should be kept together.

- The class may already be in use throughout an application, and you want to change its behavior globally.

- You may want to add or remove a feature at runtime, and have it take effect globally. (We will explore this technique with a full example later in the chapter.)

In more traditional object-oriented languages, these features would require complex code. Not only would the code be complex, it would be tightly coupled to either the existing code or the code that calls it.

Aspect-oriented programming

Aspect-oriented programming (AOP) is one technique that attempts to solve the issues of cross-cutting concerns. There has been much talk about the applicability of AOP to Ruby, since many of the advantages that AOP provides can already be obtained through metaprogramming. There is a Ruby proposal for cut-based AOP,[*] but it may be months or years before this is incorporated.

In cut-based AOP, cuts are sometimes called "transparent subclasses" because they extend a class's functionality in a modular way. Cuts act as subclasses but without the need to instantiate the subclass rather than the parent class.

The Ruby Facets library (*facets.rubyforge.org*) includes a pure-Ruby cut-based AOP library.[†] It has some limitations due to being written purely in Ruby, but the usage is fairly clean:

```ruby
class Person
  def say_hi
    puts "Hello!"
  end
end

cut :Tracer < Person do
  def say_hi
    puts "Before method"
    super
    puts "After method"
  end
end

Person.new.say_hi
# >> Before method
# >> Hello!
# >> After method
```

Here we see that the Tracer cut is a transparent subclass: when we create an instance of Person, it is affected by Tracer without having to know about Tracer. We can also change Person#say_hi without disrupting our cut.

For whatever reason, Ruby AOP techniques have not taken off. We will now introduce the standard way to deal with separation of concerns in Ruby.

Method chaining

The standard Ruby solution to this problem is *method chaining*: aliasing an existing method to a new name and overwriting its old definition with a new body. This new body usually calls the old method definition by referring to the aliased name (the equivalent of calling super in an inherited overriden method). The effect is that a feature can be patched around an existing method. Due to Ruby's open class nature, features can be added to almost any code from anywhere. Needless to say, this must be done wisely so as to retain clarity.

---

[*] *http://wiki.rubygarden.org/Ruby/page/show/AspectOrientedRuby*
[†] *http://facets.rubyforge.org/api/more/classes/Cut.html*

There is a standard Ruby idiom for chaining methods. Assume we have some library code that grabs a `Person` object from across the network:

```
class Person
  def refresh
    # (get data from server)
  end
end
```

This operation takes quite a while, and we would like to time it and log the results. Leveraging Ruby's open classes, we can just open up the `Person` class again and monkeypatch the logging code into `refresh`:

```
class Person
  def refresh_with_timing
    start_time = Time.now.to_f
    retval = refresh_without_timing
    end_time = Time.now.to_f
    logger.info "Refresh: #{"%.3f" % (end_time-start_time)} s."
    retval
  end

  alias_method :refresh_without_timing, :refresh
  alias_method :refresh, :refresh_with_timing
end
```

We can put this code in a separate file (perhaps alongside other timing code), and, as long as we require it after the original definition of `refresh`, the timing code will be properly added around the original method call. This aids in separation of concerns because we can separate code into different files based on its functional concern, not necessarily based on the area that it modifies.

The two `alias_method` calls patch around the original call to `refresh`, adding our timing code. The first call aliases the original method as `refresh_without_timing` (giving us a name by which to call the original method from `refresh_with_timing`); the second method points `refresh` at our new method.

This paradigm of using a two `alias_method` calls to add a feature is common enough that it has a name in Rails: `alias_method_chain`. It takes two arguments: the name of the original method and the name of the feature.

Using `alias_method_chain`, we can now collapse the two `alias_method` calls into one simple line:

```
alias_method_chain :refresh, :timing
```

Modulization

Monkeypatching affords us a lot of power, but it pollutes the namespace of the patched class. Things can often be made cleaner by modulizing the additions and inserting the module in the class's lookup chain. Tobias Lütke's Active Merchant Rails plugin uses this approach for the view helpers. First, a module is created with the helper method:

```
module ActiveMerchant
  module Billing
    module Integrations
      module ActionViewHelper
        def payment_service_for(order, account, options = {}, &proc)
          ...
        end
      end
    end
  end
end
```

Then, in the plugin's *init.rb* script, the module is included in `ActionView::Base`:

```
require 'active_merchant/billing/integrations/action_view_helper'
ActionView::Base.send(:include,
  ActiveMerchant::Billing::Integrations::ActionViewHelper)
```

It certainly would be simpler in code to directly open `ActionView::Base` and add the method, but this has the advantage of modularity. All Active Merchant code is contained within the `ActiveMerchant` module.

There is one caveat to this approach. Because any included modules are searched for methods after the class's own methods are searched, you cannot directly overwrite a class's methods by including a module:

```
module M
  def test_method
    "Test from M"
  end
end

class C
  def test_method
    "Test from C"
  end
end

C.send(:include, M)
C.new.test_method # => "Test from C"
```

Instead, you should create a new name in the module and use alias_method_chain:

```
module M
  def test_method_with_module
    "Test from M"
  end
end

class C
  def test_method
    "Test from C"
  end
end
```

```
# for a plugin, these two lines would go in init.rb
C.send(:include, M)
C.class_eval { alias_method_chain :test_method, :module }

C.new.test_method # => "Test from M"
```

Functional Programming

The paradigm of *functional programming* focuses on values rather than the side effects of evaluation. In contrast to imperative programming, the functional style deals with the values of expressions in a mathematical sense. Function application and composition are first-class concepts, and mutable state (although it obviously exists at a low level) is abstracted away from the programmer.

This is a somewhat confusing concept, and it is often unfamiliar even to experienced programmers. The best parallels are drawn from mathematics, from which functional programming is derived.

Consider the mathematical equation $x = 3$. The equals sign in that expression indicates equivalence: "x is equal to 3." On the contrary, the Ruby statement x = 3 is of a completely different nature. That equals sign denotes assignment: "assign 3 to x." In a functional programming language, equals usually denotes equality rather than assignment. The key difference here is that functional programming languages specify *what* is to be calculated; imperative programming languages tend to specify *how* to calculate it.

Higher-Order Functions

The cornerstone of functional programming, of course, is functions. The primary way that the functional paradigm influences mainstream Ruby programming is in the use of *higher-order functions* (also called *first-class functions*, though these two terms are not strictly equivalent). Higher-order functions are functions that operate on other functions. Higher-order functions usually either take one or more functions as an argument or return a function.

Ruby supports functions as mostly first-class objects; they can be created, manipulated, passed, returned, and called. Anonymous functions are represented as Proc objects, created with Proc.new or Kernel#lambda:

```
add = lambda{|a,b| a + b}
add.class # => Proc
add.arity # => 2

# call a Proc with Proc#call
add.call(1,2) # => 3

# alternate syntax
add[1,2] # => 3
```

The most common use for blocks in Ruby is in conjunction with iterators. Many programmers who come to Ruby from other, more imperative-style languages start out writing code like this:

```
collection = (1..10).to_a
for x in collection
  puts x
end
```

The more Ruby-like way to express this is using an iterator, Array#each, and passing it a block. This is second nature to seasoned Ruby programmers:

```
collection.each {|x| puts x}
```

This method is equivalent to creating a Proc object and passing it to each:

```
print_me = lambda{|x| puts x}
collection.each(&print_me)
```

All of this is to show that functions are first-class objects and can be treated as any other object.

Enumerable

Ruby's Enumerable module provides several convenience methods to be mixed in to classes that are "enumerable," or can be iterated over. These methods rely on an each instance method, and optionally the <=> (comparison or "spaceship") method. Enumerable's methods fall into several categories.

Predicates

These represent properties of a collection that may be true or false.

all?
: Returns true if the given block evaluates to true for all items in the collection.

any?
: Returns true if the given block evaluates to true for any item in the collection.

include?(x), member?(x)
: Returns true if x is a member of the collection.

Filters

These methods return a subset of the items in the collection.

detect, find
: Returns the first item in the collection for which the block evaluates to true, or nil if no such item was found.

select, find_all
: Returns an array of all items in the collection for which the block evaluates to true.

reject

    Returns an array of all items in the collection for which the block evaluates to false.

grep(*x*)

    Returns an array of all items in the collection for which x === item is true. This usage is equivalent to select{|item| x === item}.

Transformers

These methods transform a collection into another collection by one of several rules.

map, collect

    Returns an array consisting of the result of the given block being applied to each element in turn.

partition

    Equivalent to [select(&block), reject(&block)].

sort

    Returns a new array of the elements in this collection, sorted by either the given block (treated as the <=> method) or the elements' own <=> method.

sort_by

    Like sort, but yields to the given block to obtain the values on which to sort. As array comparison is performed in element order, you can sort on multiple fields with person.sort_by{|p| [p.city, p.name]}. Internally, sort_by performs a Schwartzian transform, so it is more efficient than sort when the block is expensive to compute.

zip(*others*)

    Returns an array of tuples, built up from one element each from self and others:

```
puts [1,2,3].zip([4,5,6],[7,8,9]).inspect
# >> [[1, 4, 7], [2, 5, 8], [3, 6, 9]]
```

    When the collections are all of the same size, zip(*others*) is equivalent to ([self]+*others*).transpose:

```
puts [[1,2,3],[4,5,6],[7,8,9]].transpose.inspect
# >> [[1, 4, 7], [2, 5, 8], [3, 6, 9]]
```

    When a block is given, it is executed once for each item in the resulting array:

```
[1,2,3].zip([4,5,6],[7,8,9]) {|x| puts x.inspect}
# >> [1, 4, 7]
# >> [2, 5, 8]
# >> [3, 6, 9]
```

Aggregators

These methods aggregate or summarize the data.

inject(*initial*)

> Folds an operation across a collection. Initially, yields an accumulator (*initial* provides the first value) and the first object to the block. The return value is used as the accumulator for the next iteration. Collection sum is often defined thus:

```
module Enumerable
  def sum
    inject(0){|total, x| total + x}
  end
end
```

> If no initial value is given, the first iteration yields the first two items.

max

> Returns the maximum value in the collection, as determined by the same logic as the sort method.

min

> Like max, but returns the minimum value in the collection.

Other

each_with_index

> Like each, but also yields the 0-based index of each element.

entries, to_a

> Pushes each element in turn onto an array, then returns the array.

The Enumerable methods are fun, and you can usually find a customized method to do exactly what you are looking for, no matter how obscure. If these methods fail you, visit Ruby Facets (*http://facets.rubyforge.org*) for some inspiration.

Enumerator

Ruby has yet another little-known trick up its sleeve, and that is Enumerator from the standard library. (As it is in the standard library and not the core language, you must require "enumerator" to use it.)

Enumerable provides many iterators that can be used on any enumerable object, but it has one limitation: all of the iterators are based on the each instance method. If you want to use some iterator other than each as the basis for map, inject, or any of the other functions in Enumerable, you can use Enumerator as a bridge.

The signature of Enumerator.new is Enumerator.new(*obj*, *method*, **args*), where *obj* is the object to enumerate over, *method* is the base iterator, and *args* are any arguments that the iterator receives. As an example, you could write a map_with_index function (a version of map that passes the object and its index to the given block) with the following code:

```
require "enumerator"
module Enumerable
  def map_with_index &b
    enum_for(:each_with_index).map(&b)
  end
end
```

```
puts ("a".."f").map_with_index{|letter, i| [letter, i]}.inspect
# >> [["a", 0], ["b", 1], ["c", 2], ["d", 3], ["e", 4], ["f", 5]]
```

The enum_for method returns an Enumerator object whose each method functions like the each_with_index method of the original object. That Enumerator object has already been extended with the instance methods from Enumerable, so we can just call map on it, passing the given block.

Enumerator also adds some convenience methods to Enumerable, which are useful to have. Enumerable#each_slice(*n*) iterates over slices of the array, *n*-at-a-time:

```
(1..10).each_slice(3){|slice| puts slice.inspect}
# >> [1, 2, 3]
# >> [4, 5, 6]
# >> [7, 8, 9]
# >> [10]
```

Similarly, Enumerable#each_cons(*n*) moves a "sliding window" of size *n* over the collection, one at a time:

```
(1..10).each_cons(3){|slice| puts slice.inspect}
# >> [1, 2, 3]
# >> [2, 3, 4]
# >> [3, 4, 5]
# >> [4, 5, 6]
# >> [5, 6, 7]
# >> [6, 7, 8]
# >> [7, 8, 9]
# >> [8, 9, 10]
```

Enumeration is getting a facelift in Ruby 1.9. Enumerator is becoming part of the core language. In addition, iterators return an Enumerator object automatically if they are not given a block. In Ruby 1.8, you would usually do the following to map over the values of a hash:

```
hash.values.map{|value| ... }
```

This takes the hash, builds an array of values, and maps over that array. To remove the intermediate step, you could use an Enumerator:

```
hash.enum_for(:each_value).map{|value| ... }
```

That way, we have a small Enumerator object whose each method behaves just as hash's each_value method does. This is preferable to creating a potentially large array and releasing it moments later. In Ruby 1.9, this is the default behavior if the iterator is not given a block. This simplifies our code:

```
hash.each_value.map{|value| ... }
```

Examples

Runtime Feature Changes

This example ties together several of the techniques we have seen in this chapter. We return to the Person example, where we want to time several expensive methods:

```
class Person
  def refresh
    # ...
  end

  def dup
    # ...
  end
end
```

In order to deploy this to a production environment, we may not want to leave our timing code in place all of the time because of overhead. However, we probably want to have the option to enable it when debugging. We will develop code that allows us to add and remove features (in this case, timing code) at runtime without touching the original source.

First, we set up methods wrapping each of our expensive methods with timing commands. As usual, we do this by monkeypatching the timing methods into Person from another file to separate the timing code from the actual model logic:[*]

```
class Person
  TIMED_METHODS = [:refresh, :dup]
  TIMED_METHODS.each do |method|
    # set up _without_timing alias of original method
    alias_method :"#{method}_without_timing", method

    # set up _with_timing method that wraps the original in timing code
    define_method :"#{method}_with_timing" do
      start_time = Time.now.to_f
      returning(self.send(:"#{method}_without_timing")) do
        end_time = Time.now.to_f
```

---

[*] This code sample uses variable interpolation inside a symbol literal. Because the symbol is defined using a double-quoted string, variable interpolation is just as valid as in any other double-quoted string: the symbol :"sym#{2+2}" is the same symbol as :sym4.

```
          puts "#{method}: #{"%.3f" % (end_time-start_time)} s."
        end
      end
    end
  end
```

We add singleton methods to Person to enable or disable tracing:

```
class << Person
  def start_trace
    TIMED_METHODS.each do |method|
      alias_method method, :"#{method}_with_timing"
    end
  end

  def end_trace
    TIMED_METHODS.each do |method|
      alias_method method, :"#{method}_without_timing"
    end
  end
end
```

To enable tracing, we wrap each method call in the timed method call. To disable it, we simply point the method call back to the original method (which is now only accessible by its _without_timing alias).

To use these additions, we simply call the Person.trace method:

```
p = Person.new
p.refresh # => (...)

Person.start_trace
p.refresh # => (...)
# -> refresh: 0.500 s.

Person.end_trace
p.refresh # => (...)
```

Now that we have the ability to add and remove the timing code during execution, we can expose this through our application; we could give the administrator or developer an interface to trace all or specified functions without restarting the application. This approach has several advantages over adding logging code to each function separately:

- The original code is untouched; it can be changed or upgraded without affecting the tracing code.

- When tracing is disabled, the code performs exactly as it did before tracing; the tracing code is invisible in stack traces. There is no performance overhead when tracing is disabled.

However, there are some disadvantages to writing what is essentially self-modifying code:

- Tracing is only available at the function level. More detailed tracing would require changing or patching the original code. Rails code tends to address this by making methods small and their names descriptive.
- Stack traces do become more complicated when tracing is enabled. With tracing, a stack trace into the `Person#refresh` method would have an extra level: `#refresh_with_timing`, then `#refresh_without_timing` (the original method).
- This approach may break when using more than one application server, as the functions are aliased in-memory. The changes will not propagate between servers, and will revert when the server process is restarted. However, this can actually be a feature in production; typically, you will not want to profile all traffic in a high-traffic production environment, but only a subset of it.

Rails Routing Code

The Rails routing code is perhaps some of the most conceptually difficult code in Rails. The code faces several constraints:

- Path segments may capture multiple parts of the URL:
  — Controllers may be namespaced, so the route `":controller/:action/:id"` can match the URL `"/store/product/edit/15"`, with the controller being `"store/product"`.
  — Routes may contain `path_info` segments that destructure multiple URL segments: the route `"page/*path_info"` can match the URL `"/page/products/top_products/15"`, with the `path_info` segment capturing the remainder of the URL.
- Routes can be restricted by conditions that must be met in order for the route to match.
- The routing system must be bidirectional; it is run forward to recognize routes and in reverse to generate them.
- Route recognition must be fast because it is run once per HTTP request. Route generation must be lightning fast because it may be run tens of times per HTTP request (once per outgoing link) when generating a page.

 Michael Koziarski's new `routing_optimisation` code in Rails 2.0 (*actionpack/lib/action_controller/routing_optimisation.rb*) addresses the complexity of Rails routing. This new code optimizes the simple case of generation of named routes with no extra `:requirements`.

Because of the speed needed in both generation and recognition, the routing code modifies itself at runtime. The ActionController::Routing::Route class represents a single route (one entry in *config/routes.rb*). The Route#recognize method rewrites itself:

```
class Route
  def recognize(path, environment={})
    write_recognition
    recognize path, environment
  end
end
```

The recognize method calls write_recognition, which processes the route logic and creates a compiled version of the route. The write_recognition method then overwrites the definition of recognize with that definition. The last line in the original recognize method then calls recognize (which has been replaced by the compiled version) with the original arguments. This way, the route is compiled on the first call to recognize. Any subsequent calls use the compiled version, rather than having to reparse the routing DSL and go through the routing logic again.

Here is the body of the write_recognition method:

```
def write_recognition
  # Create an if structure to extract the params from a match if it occurs.
  body = "params = parameter_shell.dup\n#{recognition_extraction * "\n"}\nparams"
  body = "if #{recognition_conditions.join(" && ")}\n#{body}\nend"

  # Build the method declaration and compile it
  method_decl = "def recognize(path, env={})\n#{body}\nend"
  instance_eval method_decl, "generated code (#{__FILE__}:#{__LINE__})"
  method_decl
end
```

The local variable body is built up with the compiled route code. It is wrapped in a method declaration that overwrites recognize. For the default route:

```
map.connect ':controller/:action/:id'
```

write_recognition generates code looking like this:

```
def recognize(path, env={})
  if (match = /(long regex)/.match(path))
    params = parameter_shell.dup
    params[:controller] = match[1].downcase if match[1]
    params[:action] = match[2] || "index"
    params[:id] = match[3] if match[3]
    params
  end
end
```

The `parameter_shell` method returns the default set of parameters associated with the route. This method body simply tests against the regular expression, populating and returning the `params` hash if the regular expression matches. If there is no match, the method returns `nil`.

Once this method body is created, it is evaluated in the context of the route using `instance_eval`. This overwrites that particular route's `recognize` method.

Further Reading

Minero AOKI's *Ruby Hacking Guide* is an excellent introduction to Ruby's internals. It is being translated into English at *http://rhg.rubyforge.org/*.

Eigenclass (*http://eigenclass.org/*) has several more technical articles on Ruby.

Evil.rb is a library for accessing the internals of Ruby objects. It can change objects' internal state, traverse and examine the `klass` and `super` pointers, change an object's class, and cause general mayhem. Use with caution. It is available at *http://rubyforge.org/projects/evil/*. Mauricio Fernández gives a taste of Evil at *http://eigenclass.org/hiki.rb?evil.rb+dl+and+unfreeze*.

Jamis Buck has a very detailed exploration of the Rails routing code, as well as several other difficult parts of Rails, at *http://weblog.jamisbuck.org/under-the-hood*.

One of the easiest-to-understand, most well-architected pieces of Ruby software I have seen is Capistrano 2, also developed by Jamis Buck. Not only does Capistrano have a very clean API, it is extremely well built from the bottom up. If you haven't been under Capistrano's hood, it will be well worth your time. The source is available via Subversion from *http://svn.rubyonrails.org/rails/tools/capistrano/*.

Mark Jason Dominus's book *Higher-Order Perl* (Morgan Kaufmann Publishers) was revolutionary in introducing functional programming concepts into Perl. When *Higher-Order Perl* was released in 2005, Perl was a language not typically known for its functional programming support. Most of the examples in the book can be translated fairly readily into Ruby; this is a good exercise if you are familiar with Perl. James Edward Gray II has written up his version in his "Higher-Order Ruby" series, at *http://blog.grayproductions.net/categories/higherorder_ruby*.

The Ruby Programming Language, by David Flanagan and Yukihiro Matsumoto (O'Reilly), is a book covering both Ruby 1.8 and 1.9. It is due out in January 2008. The book includes a section on functional programming techniques in Ruby.

CHAPTER 2

ActiveSupport and RailTies

*[Programs] must be written for people to read, and
only incidentally for machines to execute.*
—H. Abelson and G. Sussmann
  *Structure and Interpretation of Computer
  Programs, MIT Press, 1985*

We continue in our bottom-up view of Rails by examining the pieces that form the
basis for Rails. ActiveSupport is a library that provides generic, reusable functions
that are not specific to any one part of Rails. We can use many of these methods ourselves when writing our application code. RailTies is the other half, containing parts
that glue Rails together in a Rails-specific way. Although we will not usually use Rail-
Ties functions in our own code, it is important and instructive to examine them.

Most of this chapter is nonsequential; feel free to skip around. However, in accor-
dance with our bottom-up approach to Rails, later chapters will build on this material.

Ruby You May Have Missed

It is very easy to overlook some of Ruby's more useful methods. The best way to find
them is to read code. Here are some of the more obscure, but helpful, ones.

Array

- `Array#*` can operate as `Array#join` (if given a string or stringlike argument); it also does
  repetition:

      [1, 2, 3] * "; " # => "1; 2; 3"

      [0] * 5 # => [0, 0, 0, 0, 0]

- `Array#pack` and `String#unpack` are useful for working with binary files. *why the lucky
  stiff* uses `Array#pack` to stuff a series of numbers into a BMP-formatted sparkline graph
  without any heavy image libraries, in 13 lines of code (*http://redhanded.hobix.com/
  inspect/sparklinesForMinimalists.html*).

Dir

- `Dir.[]` is shorthand for `Dir.glob`:
    ```
    Dir["/s*"] # => ["/scripts", "/srv", "/selinux", "/sys", "/sbin"]
    ```

Enumerable

- `Enumerable#all?` returns `true` if the given block returns a `true` value for all items in the enumerable. Similarly, `Enumerable#any?` returns `true` if the block returns a `true` value for any item.
    ```
    (1..10).all?{|i| i > 0 && i < 15} # => true

    (1..10).any?{|i| i*i == 9} # => true
    (1..10).any?{|i| i*i == 8} # => false
    ```
- `Enumerable#grep` filters an enumerable against another object using `===`, affording all of the usual flexibility of the `===` method:
    ```
    [1, 2, 3].methods.grep(/^so/) # => ["sort!", "sort", "sort_by"]

    [1, :two, "three", 4].grep(Fixnum) # => [1, 4]
    ```
- `Enumerable#sort_by` sorts the enumerable by the value of the given block, by performing a Schwartzian transform[*] on the data. It builds up a set of input elements, each stored with the result of applying the block to that element. Because the block should return the same value when called with the same input, it only needs to be called once per input. Thus, *O(n)* calculations are done rather than *O(n lg n)*.

    However, the `sort_by` technique is counterproductive when key calculation is inexpensive; in such cases, `Enumerable#sort` should be called with a custom comparison as a block.

File

- `File.join(*parts)` is a platform-independent way to join path segments:
    ```
    File.join("..", "test.rb") # => "../test.rb"
    ```
- `File.open` can take a block, which will automatically close the file when exited.

Hash

- `Hash.new` accepts a block, which provides a way to calculate a default value if the hash has none. This is useful for caching. The first time a cached method is called with a particular set of arguments, the block is invoked; it calculates the value and stores it in the hash for future access. ActiveSupport has an implementation of hash caching in *caching_tools.rb*, which generates hashes like this:
    ```
    Hash.new do |as, a|
      as[a] = Hash.new do |bs, b|
    ```

---

[*] Named after Randal Schwartz, who popularized the map-sort-unmap technique in Perl.

```
        bs[b] = slow_method(a, b)
      end
    end
```

- Hash#delete removes a value from the hash and returns it. This is useful for stripping out keyword arguments from a hash before passing it along somewhere.

Kernel

- Kernel#Array tries to coerce its argument into an array:

```
Array([1,2,3]) # => [1, 2, 3]
Array(1..3)    # => [1, 2, 3]
Array(1)       # => [1]
```

Module

- Module#remove_method removes a method from the specified class. Module#undef_method, on the other hand, actively prevents that method from being invoked on the class; it inserts a special entry into the m_tbl that stops method lookup.

Proc

- Proc#[] is shorthand for Proc.call.

```
p = lambda{|x| x * 2}
p[3] # => 6
```

String

- String#%(args) interpolates the arguments into itself in the manner of sprintf. To provide more than one value for interpolation, you must supply an array.

```
"%.5f" % Math::PI # => "3.14159"
```

```
"%.5f, %.5f" % [Math::PI, Math::E] # => "3.14159, 2.71828"
```

- String#[](regex) returns the portion of the string that matches the given regular expression. If there is no matching portion, nil is returned.

```
"asdf"[/sd/] # => "sd"
"asdf"[/^sd/] # => nil
"asdf"[/d(.)/,1] # => "f"
```

- String#scan(regex) collects all of the regular expression's matches against the string into an array. If the pattern has captures, each element of the array is itself an array of captured text.

```
"asdf".scan(/[a-e]/) # => ["a", "d"]
"hello ruby; hello regex".scan(/hello (\w+)/) # => [["ruby"], ["regex"]]
```

How to Read Code

As implied by the quote introducing this chapter, the primary purpose of source code should not be expressing implementation to a computer; it should be expressing meaning to people. Programming languages are an incredibly expressive and terse medium for the concepts programmers talk about. Proposals to make programming languages more English-like inevitably fail not because of poor implementation but because there is an inherent impedance mismatch between the domains of English language and computer programming.

Thus, computer programming languages should be compared not by their levels of raw power (any Turing-complete language trivially satisfies this requirement) or speed of execution (for most applications, speed is not critical) but by their programmer efficiency—the speed at which a programmer can accurately translate his thoughts into code.

Closely related to programmer efficiency is maintainer efficiency: the ability of a maintainer (who may be the original developer, 12 months later) to read the code and deduce what is going on. Perl is often criticized for being "write-only"; it is easy to write code that is nearly unreadable to future developers. Such code would have high programmer efficiency at the cost of maintainer efficiency.[*]

Ruby wins on both fronts: most Ruby code is easy to write and read, once you know the basic syntax and semantics.[†] Still, diving into any large project such as Rails is difficult. Here, we discuss ways to begin reading a codebase.

How to Locate Code

One disadvantage of the dynamic nature of Ruby is that there is little opportunity for development-time reflection on Ruby code. When using a more static language, IDEs can infer the type of variables, and from that deduce the methods available to those variables. Thus, they can offer assistance in coding by suggesting variable and method names. In Ruby, in principle the only way to know the methods available to an object is to evaluate the expression returning that object's value. This is clearly impractical due to side effects of evaluation or differences in development and execution environment. The effect is that it is impossible to write a general code-completion-style IDE for Ruby.

In practice, this is usually not a problem. Ruby follows a development style that is closer to Lisp than to C/C++. Developers interact with their application while creating it, and usually answer questions about the state of the system by asking

---

[*] I don't mean to bash Perl here. It is very possible to write structured, easily readable code in Perl. But it takes some self-discipline.

[†] For some amusing counterexamples, see *http://iorcc.blogspot.com/*.

questions of it while it is running. There are some methods to find information via static examination of the code, though:

- A good text editor will help you cull through large amounts of source.
  - — TextMate (*http://macromates.com/*) is the semi-official editor of the Ruby on Rails core team. It has great facilities for search (including search by regular expressions) and comes with some pretty impressive Ruby and Rails features. It supports projects (entire source trees managed as one unit). However, it is available for Mac OS X only and costs € 39 at the time of this writing.
  - — Vim (*http://vim.org/*) is an incredible open source text editor available for just about every platform. It has a long learning curve, but it is extremely powerful. If you use Vim with Rails, do yourself a favor and install the vim-ruby package (*http://rubyforge.org/projects/vim-ruby/*).
- In conjunction with a good text editor, you should familiarize yourself with command-line tools for text processing. Regular expressions (used with the tool of your choice such as sed, Perl, or egrep) provide a more powerful query language for finding patterns within large bodies of source.
- Search the Web. The popularity of Rails has created a fury of bloggers who write about Ruby and Rails, and they usually fill in the gaps where the official documentation is lacking. Google Code Search[*] indexes thousands of open source projects, and has useful features such as search by regular expression.

Reading the Call Stack

Most Rails developers are familiar with reading a stack trace when debugging exceptions. It can be very helpful to know the sequence in which framework and application functions were called when something goes wrong. But what if we are just curious? It doesn't make sense to raise an exception just to generate a readable backtrace. Luckily, we have some tools at our disposal to analyze the call stack in running code, nondestructively.

The first such tool is Ruby's standard Kernel#caller method, which gives us a simple backtrace as an array of strings:

```
#!/usr/local/bin/ruby1.8.4

# use the pretty-printer; call stacks can be huge
require 'pp'

class Test
  def foo
    bar
  end
```

---

[*] *http://www.google.com/codesearch*

```
  def bar
    pp caller
    'baz'
  end
end

puts Test.new.foo
```

This gives us the call stack:

```
["./call_stack1.8.4.rb:8:in `foo'", "./call_stack1.8.4.rb:17"]
baz
```

However, this method is clunky. There is very little information that we can use programmatically; this is mainly for informational use. A more flexible stack trace mechanism comes from Mauricio Fernández's call_stack library,* which hooks entry and exit of every method, providing that information at the request of the global call_stack method. This library was developed because Ruby 1.8.5 broke the old implementation of Binding.of_caller (which relied on a bug in 1.8.4). However, call_stack works on 1.8.4 as well. We get much more information through call_stack:

```
#!/usr/local/bin/ruby

require 'rubygems'
require 'call_stack'
require 'pp'

class Test
  def foo
    bar
  end

  def bar
    pp call_stack(-1)
    "baz"
  end
end

call_stack_on

puts Test.new.foo

call_stack_off
```

The call_stack_on and call_stack_off functions add and remove the hook functions that keep track of function execution, so you must call call_stack_on before starting to capture frames. The call_stack function yields an array of stack frames; each frame is an array containing [*class_name*, *method_name*, *filename*, *line*, *binding*, *language*]. This code prints:

---

* *http://eigenclass.org/hiki.rb?call_stack*

```
[[:unknown, :unknown, "./call_stack1.8.5.rb", 18, nil, nil],
 [Test, :foo, "./call_stack1.8.5.rb", 9, #<Binding:0x13c8ba0>, :Ruby],
 [Test, :bar, "./call_stack1.8.5.rb", 13, #<Binding:0x13c8b78>, :Ruby]]
baz
```

The first line of that backtrace corresponds to the call_stack_on method. A warning: since call_stack works by hooking every method call and return, it slows execution even when the data collected is not being used.

We can use call_stack to our advantage to trace the flow of execution through a Rails request. After installing the call_stack gem, place these two lines at the end of *environment.rb*:

```
require 'call_stack'
call_stack_on
```

Then, you can place the following line in an action to log a stack trace with the class name and function name for each stack frame:

```
logger.info(call_stack(-1).map{|frame| "#{frame[0]} : #{frame[1]}"} * "\n")
```

Debugging Ruby and Rails

Ruby ships with a built-in debugger, rdebug. However, Kent Sibilev has improved upon this and released his own Ruby debugging library, *ruby-debug*. This is a full-featured Ruby debugger that also includes breakpoint support for Rails.

 Rails used to have built-in debugging support, based on Binding.of_ caller, that exploited a Ruby 1.8.4 bug. When the bug was fixed in Ruby 1.8.5, the breakpointer broke and we had to rely on third-party utilities to debug Rails applications.

To start using ruby-debug, install it with gem:

```
$ sudo gem install ruby-debug
```

When installed, ruby-debug installs an rdebug binary that is called just like the Ruby executable. To debug simple Ruby scripts, just run your scripts with rdebug rather than ruby. This is an extremely helpful way to examine the path Ruby takes to execute a script.

We can see an example of this with a simple time-reporting script based on Ruby Reports: *http://rubyreports.org/*. This script reads a CSV file and generates a simple PDF based on it:

time_report.rb

```
#!/usr/local/bin/ruby

require "rubygems"
require "ruport"
```

```
table = Table('time.csv')
table.to_pdf(:file => 'time.pdf')
```

We load up this script under ruby-debug:

```
$ rdebug time_report.rb
./time_report.rb:3 require "rubygems"
(rdb:1)
```

The debugger breaks at the first line of Ruby code. We will skip over the require statements with next (abbreviated n; it is the equivalent of "step over" in other debuggers). We can also just hit the Return key to repeat the last command:

```
./time_report.rb:3 require "rubygems"
(rdb:1) n
./time_report.rb:4 require "ruport"
(rdb:1)
./time_report.rb:6 table = Table('time.csv')
(rdb:1)
```

Now we are at the first interesting line of code. We can "step into" Ruport's code (follow the function call downward) with step or s:

```
./time_report.rb:6 table = Table('time.csv')
(rdb:1) s
/usr/local/lib/ruby/gems/1.8/gems/ruport-1.2.0/lib/ruport/data/table.rb:805 table=
(rdb:1)
```

Now we are in Ruport's library code, but we don't have enough context to know what is going on. Using the list (l) command, we show the context from the source:

```
(rdb:1) l
[800, 809] in .../gems/ruport-1.2.0/lib/ruport/data/table.rb
    800    #    # accepts all Data::Table.load options, including block
    801    #
    802    #    t = Table("foo.csv")
    803    #    t = Table("bar.csv", :has_names => false)
    804    def Table(*args,&block)
=>  805      table=
    806      case(args[0])
    807      when Array
    808        opts = args[1] || {}
    809        Ruport::Data::Table.new(f={:column_names => args[0]}.
                                       merge(opts),&block)
```

The backtrace (bt) command shows the series of stack frames in which we are nested:

```
(rdb:1) bt
--> #0 .../gems/ruport-1.2.0/lib/ruport/data/table.rb:805
       in 'Table'
    #1 ./time_report.rb:6
(rdb:1)
```

And we can step through the code until we have satisfied our curiosity, at which point we use cont (c) to exit the debugger and allow the program's execution to continue:

```
(rdb:1) n
.../gems/ruport-1.2.0/lib/ruport/data/table.rb:806 case(args[0])
(rdb:1)
.../gems/ruport-1.2.0/lib/ruport/data/table.rb:807 when Array
(rdb:1)
.../gems/ruport-1.2.0/lib/ruport/data/table.rb:810 when /\.csv/
(rdb:1) c
$
```

The debugger has many other commands and features. Breakpoints can be set and cleared on arbitrary lines or methods, and they can be conditional:

```
(rdb:1) break table.rb:805 if args.first =~ /\.csv/
Set breakpoint 1 at table.rb:805
(rdb:1) c
Breakpoint 1 at table.rb:805
.../gems/ruport-1.2.0/lib/ruport/data/table.rb:805 table=
(rdb:1)
```

The irb command (still experimental) will start up an interactive Ruby session within the context of the current code, allowing you to examine the environment:

```
.../gems/ruport-1.2.0/lib/ruport/data/table.rb:805 table=
(rdb:1) irb
>> pp args
["time.csv"]
=> nil
>>
```

The help command will show you information on the available command language—there are several more commands and options available.

Debugging Rails with ruby-debug

Now that we understand the basics of the debugger console, we can see how it integrates with Rails. The process is quite simple and easy; ruby-debug is built to be used with Rails with virtually no setup.

1. Require the ruby-debug library from *config/environments/development.rb* so that it is only loaded in the development environment:

   ```
   require 'ruby-debug'
   ```

2. Insert a call to debugger anywhere you want to stop the application's execution and drop into the debugger.

   ```
   class SignupController < ApplicationController

     def check_for_service
       debugger
       @query = params[:q]
       (...)
   ```

3. Start up the Rails server. The debugger only works with WEBrick and Mongrel, because the running code still has access to the tty under those servers.

Under FastCGI, the worker processes would not be able to interact with the console.

```
$ script/server
=> Booting Mongrel (use 'script/server webrick' to force WEBrick)
=> Rails application starting on http://0.0.0.0:3000
=> Call with -d to detach
=> Ctrl-C to shutdown server
** Starting Mongrel listening at 0.0.0.0:3000
** Starting Rails with development environment...
** Rails loaded.
** Loading any Rails specific GemPlugins
** Signals ready.  TERM => stop. USR2 => restart.  INT => stop (no restart).
** Rails signals registered.  HUP => reload (without restart).  It might not
   work well.
** Mongrel available at 0.0.0.0:3000
** Use CTRL-C to stop.
```

4. Interact with your application as needed to trigger the debugger. The request will hang in the browser, and the server console will drop into the debugger console and show the line of code it is paused on:

```
app/controllers/signup_controller.rb:5 @query = params[:q]
(rdb:1)
```

Since we called the debugger from within the controller, our debugger console has full access to the controller's lexical environment (the binding from which debugger was called). Thus, we can examine request parameters and step through code just as in the previous example. We have the full set of ruby-debug commands available:

```
app/controllers/signup_controller.rb:5 @query = params[:q]
(rdb:1) pp params
{"commit"=>"Check for Service",
 "action"=>"check_for_service",
 "q"=>"Nevada, MO",
 "controller"=>"signup"}
(rdb:1) n
app/controllers/signup_controller.rb:6 if @query
(rdb:1)
app/controllers/signup_controller.rb:7 @result = Geocoder.geocode @query
(rdb:1)
app/controllers/signup_controller.rb:8 if @result
(rdb:1) pp @result
{:point=>
  #<GeoRuby::SimpleFeatures::Point:0x32c2d08
    @m=0.0,
    @srid=4326,
    @with_m=false,
    @with_z=false,
    @x=-94.359055,
    @y=37.842806,
    @z=0.0>,
 :address=>"Nevada, MO, USA"}
```

Finally, when we leave the debugger with cont (c), the request continues loading in the web browser, and our debugger console becomes a server console again.

```
(rdb:1) c
Rendered /layouts/_nav (0.00012)
Rendered /layouts/_footer (0.00008)
Completed in 39.54861 (0 reqs/sec) | Rendering: 0.01811 (0%) | DB: 0.15506 (0%)
  | 200 OK [http://localhost/signup/check_for_service]
```

Where to Start

Pick something interesting

Don't discount the importance of finding something you like and running with it. This approach has several advantages. It keeps you looking at aspects that interest you, while taking you across the basic components, such as ActiveSupport, that you will need to know. You will also pick up the idioms that other Rails programmers use, and you will probably learn something new in the process.

Learn to love global search. Find an interesting method and search Rails for all of the places that method is called.

Start at the top

The end of this chapter will explain how Rails initialization works. These functions provide good entry points for studying the Rails source. You can start from Initializer and trace a request down through a sequence of calls to your application, following the same path that Ruby takes when executing your code.

Read the Tests

Rails has an extremely comprehensive set of tests. In fact, the tests are sometimes more helpful than the official documentation, because the tests specify proper behavior through code. The tests provide credible, proven examples of how to work with the library in question. Since many of the tests are written in a Test-Driven Development (test-first) style, they often provide more implementation details than the documentation does.

For example, this code from ActiveRecord's *binary_test.rb* proves that ActiveRecord is binary-clean:

```
def setup
  Binary.connection.execute 'DELETE FROM binaries'
  @data = File.read(BINARY_FIXTURE_PATH).freeze
end

# ...
```

```
def test_load_save
  bin = Binary.new
  bin.data = @data

  assert @data == bin.data, 'Newly assigned data differs from original'

  bin.save
  assert @data == bin.data, 'Data differs from original after save'

  db_bin = Binary.find(bin.id)
  assert @data == db_bin.data, 'Reloaded data differs from original'
end
```

Stay Current

Rails is a moving target: people continually contribute patches, and the core team is always looking for ways to improve. The best way to stay on top of the fast-paced changes is to monitor the Rails Trac timeline (*http://dev.rubyonrails.org/timeline*). An RSS feed is available.

Also keep an eye on the ruby-core and rails-core mailing lists, which detail changes being made to the Ruby and Rails core, respectively.

ActiveSupport

ActiveSupport is the library of utility methods that Rails uses. We examine them in detail here for two reasons. First, they can be useful to our application code—we can directly use many of these libraries and methods to our advantage when writing Rails applications. Secondly, we can learn many things about Ruby programming by dissecting these parts. They are small and relatively easy to digest.

Dependencies   *dependencies.rb*

Dependencies autoloads missing constants by trying to find the file associated with the constant. When you attempt to access a nonexistent constant, such as Message, Dependencies will try to find and load *message.rb* from any directory in Dependencies.load_paths.

Dependencies defines Module#const_missing and Class#const_missing, which both proxy to Dependencies.load_missing_constant(const_parent, const_id). That method searches the load paths for a file with the appropriate name; if found, Dependencies loads the file and ensures that it defined the appropriate constant.

Alternatively, Rails will create an empty module to satisfy nesting in the case of nested models and controllers. If a directory named *app/models/store/* exists, Store will be created as an empty module, by the following process:

1. Some piece of code references the undefined constant Store.

2. Ruby calls const_missing.

3. const_missing calls Dependencies.load_missing_constant(Object, :Store).

4. load_missing_constant attempts to find and load *store.rb* somewhere in its list of load paths (Dependencies.load_paths). It fails to find such a file.

5. load_missing_constant sees that *app/models/store* exists and is a directory. It creates a module, assigns it to the appropriate constant, and returns.

Deprecation
deprecation.rb

The ActiveSupport::Deprecation module provides a method by which old APIs are marked for removal. At its core, it is just a fancy warning mechanism. When old APIs are used, they generate a warning in development or test mode. Deprecation warnings are invoked through the ActiveSupport::Deprecation.warn(message, callstack) method. The ActiveSupport::Deprecation.silence method silences those warnings for the duration of the provided block.

The deprecate class method provides an easy way to mark a method as deprecated while still making it available. It decorates the given method with the deprecation warning.

```
def find_first(conditions = nil, orderings = nil, joins = nil) # :nodoc:
  find(:first, :conditions => conditions, :order => orderings, :joins => joins)
end
deprecate :find_first => "use find(:first, ...)"
```

ActiveSupport::Deprecation.behavior is a Proc that is called when a deprecation warning is triggered. It takes two arguments: the deprecation message and the callstack. It can be replaced to modify the default behavior. By default, in the test environment, deprecation warnings print to the standard error stream. In development, they go to the logger. In production, deprecation warnings are silenced.

Deprecated instance variables

ActionController defines a set of objects that are made available to controllers. These objects used to be publicly available instance variables; this usage is now deprecated. For example, the session object (available to controllers through the session and session= methods) used to be accessible as @session. This creates a problem: how do we intercept access to these deprecated instance variables? Ruby isn't so helpful as to provide us a hook that informs us upon instance variable access.

Rails uses a neat trick: a proxy class. The protected objects were moved out of those instance variables and moved into "internal" instance variables (which begin with an underscore). The old instance variables were replaced with instances of ActiveSupport::Deprecation::DeprecatedInstanceVariableProxy, which proxies to the real objects. When a method is called on these proxies (such as @session.id), a warning is generated before delegating the call to the real object. This is a common Ruby trick that is used in several other places in Rails—replacing a standard object with a proxy object that responds in a special way to certain methods.

Inflector

The Inflector module provides a set of simple transformations on English words to facilitate ActiveRecord's manipulations of class and table names. Following the policy of "convention over configuration," for example, a model class named Message would correspond to a table name of messages.

The core of Inflector is the pluralization rules, contained in *inflections.rb*. The default set of rules is fairly broad, but additional rules can be added easily in *config/initializers/inflections.rb* or a similar configuration file, after the framework loads:

```
Inflector.inflections do |inflect|
  inflect.plural /^(ox)$/i, '\1\2en'
  inflect.singular /^(ox)en/i, '\1'

  inflect.irregular 'octopus', 'octopi'

  inflect.uncountable "equipment"
end
```

Inflector.inflections yields a singleton instance of the inflections object. Rules are prepended to the list of inflections, so these rules will override the default as long as they are loaded after the Rails framework. Another consequence of the load order is that the rules should be ordered from most general to most specific within a block; the last appropriate inflection rule seen will be used.

The regular expression captures and backreferences ensure that initial capitals are handled correctly; the initial letters (upper- or lowercase) are captured with a case-insensitive regex and substituted into the replacement. The irregular and uncountable rules take care of that work for us:

```
"ox".pluralize        # => "oxen"
"Ox".pluralize        # => "Oxen"
"Octopus".pluralize   # => "Octopi"
"Equipment".pluralize # => "Equipment"
```

Inflector's module methods, which actually perform the transformations, are proxied from the core extensions to String and Integer; they are usually not called directly on the Inflector module object.* See the respective sections in the Core Extensions documentation later in the chapter for more information.

JSON

JSON (JavaScript Object Notation, pronounced "Jason") is a lightweight subset of JavaScript's notation for literal objects (hash tables) used for data interchange on the Web. ActiveSupport::JSON provides encoders for most basic Ruby data types. The encoders are proxied by the Object#to_json method, added by Core Extensions.

```
(1..5).to_json # => "[1, 2, 3, 4, 5]"
{:a => 1, :b => [2, 3]}.to_json # => "{b: [2, 3], a: 1}"
```

---

* "*thing*".pluralize reads better than Inflector.pluralize("*thing*").

The JSON library protects against circular references, which cannot be encoded into JSON:

```
a = {}
b = {:a => a}
a[:b] = b
a # => {:b=>{:a=>{...}}}

a.to_json
# !> ActiveSupport::JSON::CircularReferenceError: object references itself
```

Whiny Nil   *whiny_nil.rb*

The extensions to NilClass are an ingenious part of ActiveSupport. They are designed to help trap unexpected nil values as early as possible, and to provide more sensible error messages to the developer when nil is encountered.

Without these extensions, calling one of Array's instance methods on an object that happened to be nil would generate a standard NoMethodError if NilClass did not also contain the method. This could be frustrating to track down, especially if the method was called from deep in the framework.

Whiny Nil intercepts those NoMethodErrors with method_missing and makes a suggestion about the type of object the developer may have been expecting (either Array or ActiveRecord::Base), based on the name of the method called.

```
nil.sort
# !> NoMethodError: You have a nil object when you didn't expect it!
# !> You might have expected an instance of Array.

nil.save
# !> NoMethodError: You have a nil object when you didn't expect it!
# !> You might have expected an instance of ActiveRecord::Base.
```

The Whiny Nil extensions also redefine NilClass#id, which raises an error. Without this extension, nil.id would return 4 (Ruby's immediate representation of nil, the same as nil.object_id). This would be confusing when chaining methods together. Under the Whiny Nil system, this raises a more informative exception:

```
nil.id
# !> RuntimeError: Called id for nil, which would mistakenly be 4 --
# !> if you really wanted the id of nil, use object_id
```

The Whiny Nil system can be turned off in the Rails configuration by setting config.whiny_nils to false.

Core Extensions

The Core Extensions are ActiveSupport's collection of extensions to Ruby's core classes and modules. They are basic design patterns solving problems that are encountered often in Ruby. These methods are one level below the Rails API; they are the internal functions that Rails uses. However, we describe them here because they are extremely useful during the process of building a Rails application. The core extensions are low-level utility methods for Ruby; they do not make the impossible possible, but they do help to simplify application code.

Array

Conversions

- Array#to_sentence joins the array's elements and converts to a string:
    ```
    %w(Larry Curly Moe).to_sentence # => "Larry, Curly, and Moe"
    ```
- Array#to_s(:db) collects an array of ActiveRecord objects (or other objects that respond to the id method) into a SQL-friendly string.
- Array#to_xml converts an array of ActiveRecord objects into XML. This is usually used to implement REST-style web services. It relies on the contained objects' implementation of to_xml (such as ActiveRecord::XmlSerialization.to_xml).
    ```
    render :xml => Product.find(:all).to_xml
    ```
    Note that render(:xml => ...) and render(:json => ...) are new synonyms for render(:text => ...) that change the response's MIME type appropriately.

Grouping

- Array#in_groups_of(size, fill_with) groups elements of an array into fixed-size groups:
    ```
    (1..8).to_a.in_groups_of(3) # => [[1, 2, 3], [4, 5, 6], [7, 8, nil]]
    (1..8).to_a.in_groups_of(3, 0) # => [[1, 2, 3], [4, 5, 6], [7, 8, 0]]
    (1..8).to_a.in_groups_of(3, false) # => [[1, 2, 3], [4, 5, 6], [7, 8]]
    ```
- Array#split splits an array on a value or the result of a block:
    ```
    (1..8).to_a.split(4) # => [[1, 2, 3], [5, 6, 7, 8]]
    (1..8).to_a.split {|i| i == 2} # => [[1], [3, 4, 5, 6, 7, 8]]
    ```

Option processing

- Array#extract_options! removes and returns the last array item if it is a hash; otherwise, it returns an empty hash. This supports the common pattern of using a hash as the last argument to provide keyword arguments to a method:
    ```
    def example(*args)
      options = args.extract_options!
      "#{args.inspect} :: #{options.inspect}"
    end

    example 1                # => "[1] :: {}"
    example 1, 2             # => "[1, 2] :: {}"
    example 1, 2, :a => 3    # => "[1, 2] :: {:a=>3}"
    ```

Random selection

- Array#rand returns an element selected at random from the array:
    ```
    (1..10).map{ (1..10).to_a.rand } # => [2, 7, 7, 7, 7, 1, 10, 10, 2, 5]
    ```

Blank

ActiveSupport adds the blank? instance method to all objects. This method returns true for the empty string, a string consisting only of whitespace, false, nil, [], or {}. This provides an easy shortcut to test for missing values—for example, a string can be tested with s.blank? rather than (s.nil? || s.empty?).

Class Attribute Accessors

ActiveSupport extends the Class class to provide friendly attribute accessors specific to a Class object. These attribute accessors (cattr_reader, cattr_writer, and cattr_accessor) mirror the attr_reader, attr_writer, and attr_accessor methods on Module. They define accessors at both the class and instance level.

```ruby
class C
  cattr_accessor :log
  self.log = ""

  def initialize
    log << "#{self.inspect} created\n"
  end
end

3.times {C.new}

puts C.log
# >> #<C:0x10a7d6c> created
# >> #<C:0x10a78d0> created
# >> #<C:0x10a7894> created
```

These methods use class variables instead of instance variables:

```ruby
C.log == (class C; @@log; end) # => true
```

There are also module-level attribute accessors: mattr_reader, mattr_writer, and mattr_accessor.

Class Inheritable Attributes

Inheritable attributes are attributes defined on a class object (as with class attribute accessors). However, the attributes and their values are cloned to children when the class is subclassed. There are three flavors of inheritable attributes: normal, array, and hash. As with class attribute accessors, accessor methods are defined at both the class and instance level, so they can be accessed from instances of the class.

Class inheritable attributes support the inheritance structure used by ActiveRecord. Attributes such as connection specifications can be defined in ActiveRecord::Base, and they will be passed on to subclasses, while they can still be overridden in the subclasses if needed.

The accessors are defined just as with regular class attributes:

```
class Parent
  class_inheritable_array :log
  self.log = []

  def initialize
    super
    log << "#{self.inspect} created"
  end
end

Parent.new

Parent.log # => ["#<Parent:0x10a07c4> created"]
```

The attributes and their values are inherited to children. This attribute inheritance only happens at the time of class inheritance. After the child class has inherited from the parent class, the attributes are separate and do not interact.

```
class Child < Parent
end

Parent.log # => ["#<Parent:0x10a07c4> created"]
Child.log # => ["#<Parent:0x10a07c4> created"]

Parent.new
Child.new

Parent.log # => ["#<Parent:0x10a07c4> created", "#<Parent:0x109fd9c> created"]
Child.log # => ["#<Parent:0x10a07c4> created", "#<Child:0x109fd88> created"]
```

Date and Time

Conversions

core_ext/date/conversions.rb, core_ext/time/conversions.rb

- `Date#to_time`, `Date#to_time(:utc)`, `Date#to_date`, `Time#to_date`, `Time#to_time`: These methods allow you to use dates and times in a roughly interchangeable way.
- `Date#to_s(`*format*`)` formats a date in one of several formats (Table 2-1). The `:default` format is used if no format is specified.
- `Time#to_s(`*format*`)` formats a date and time in one of several formats (Table 2-2). The `:default` format is used if no format is specified.

Table 2-1. Date formats

Format	Example
:default	2006-12-28
:short	28 Dec
:long	December 28, 2006

Table 2-2. Time formats

Format	Example
:default	Thu Dec 28 13:12:23 CST 2006
:db	2006-12-28 13:12:23
:time	13:12
:short	28 Dec 13:12
:long	December 28, 2006 13:12
:rfc822	Thu, 28 Dec 2006 13:12:23 -0600

Conversions from Numeric

core_ext/numeric/time.rb

ActiveSupport adds support methods to the `Numeric` class to support calculations on dates and times. Numbers can be added to and subtracted from `Time` objects; the numbers are treated as seconds. ActiveSupport's conversion methods convert numbers to seconds. Both singular and plural time units are supported.

```
1               == 1.second
60.seconds      == 1.minute
60.minutes      == 1.hour
24.hours        == 1.day
7.days          == 1.week
2.weeks         == 1.fortnight
30.days         == 1.month
365.25.days     == 1.year


Time.now             # => Thu Dec 28 13:30:39 CST 2006
Time.now - 3.days    # => Mon Dec 25 13:30:39 CST 2006
3.days.ago           # => Mon Dec 25 13:30:39 CST 2006
5.hours.from_now     # => Thu Dec 28 18:30:39 CST 2006
```

Time calculations

core_ext/time/calculations.rb

- `Time.days_in_month(month, year)` returns the number of days in the provided month. Year is optional, but if provided, the function will take leap years into account.

    ```
    Time.days_in_month(2) # => 28
    Time.days_in_month(2, 2003) # => 28
    Time.days_in_month(2, 2004) # => 29
    ```

- `Time#change(options)` resets one or more components of the time. The hour, min, sec, and usec options cascade downward—for example, if the hour but not the minute is specified, the minute will be set to zero.

    ```
    t = Time.now
    t # => Thu Dec 28 13:39:18 CST 2006
    t.change(:min => 31, :sec => 12) # => Thu Dec 28 13:31:12 CST 2006
    t.change(:hour => 12) # => Thu Dec 28 12:00:00 CST 2006
    ```

- The ago and since methods, formerly operating on `Time`, now operate on `ActiveSupport::Duration` objects, to support exact time values. Methods such as `Fixnum#months` and `Fixnum#year` now return `ActiveSupport::Duration` objects:

```
1.month # => 1 month
1.month.ago # => Mon Sep 24 23:57:04 -0500 2007
1.month.since(1.year.ago) # => Fri Nov 24 23:57:04 -0600 2006
```

The addition of ActiveSupport::Duration fixes many subtle problems with time calculations, because it stores durations as exact values (years, months, days, hours, minutes, and seconds). Prior to its addition, errors could easily accumulate, as some
duration functions assumed 30-day months and 365.25-day years.

- Time#advance adds the specified (exact) values to the given time:

```
t = Time.now            # => Wed Oct 24 23:50:11 -0500 2007
t.advance :days => 1    # => Thu Oct 25 23:50:11 -0500 2007
t.advance :months => 1  # => Sat Nov 24 23:50:11 -0600 2007
t.advance :years => 1   # => Fri Oct 24 23:50:11 -0500 2008
```

- Convenient shorthand methods, listed below (all are instance methods of Time that
  take no arguments):

  — last_year and next_year

  — last_month and next_month

  — beginning_of_week (aliased as monday and at_beginning_of_week) and next_week

  — beginning_of_day (aliased as midnight, at_midnight, and at_beginning_of_day) and
    end_of_day

  — beginning_of_month (also at_beginning_of_month) and end_of_month (also at_end_
    of_month)

  — beginning_of_quarter (at_beginning_of_quarter)

  — beginning_of_year (at_beginning_of_year)

  — yesterday, tomorrow

Enumerable   *core_ext/enumerable.rb*

- Enumerable#group_by groups the values into a hash based on the result of a block.

```
(1..5).to_a.group_by {|x| x%3} # => {0=>[3], 1=>[1, 4], 2=>[2, 5]}
```

- Enumerable#index_by indexes values based on the result of a block. It differs from
  group_by in that it only keeps one value per index key.

```
(1..5).to_a.index_by {|x| x%3} # => {0=>3, 1=>4, 2=>5}
```

- Enumerable#sum returns the sum of the values (or the result of mapping the given block
  over the values, if a block is given). The optional first argument provides a value to use
  if the enumerable is empty.

```
(1..5).to_a.sum # => 15
(1..5).to_a.sum {|x| x ** 2} # => 55
```

This makes statistical calculations easy:

```
module Enumerable
  def mean
    (sum.to_f) / length
  end

  def variance
    m = mean
```

```
      sum {|x| (x-m)**2} / length
    end

    def standard_deviation
      variance ** 0.5
    end
  end

  "%.2f" % [1,2,3,4,5].standard_deviation # => "1.41"
```

Exception

Four methods are added to Exception for more intuitive stack traces:

- clean_message runs the exception message through Pathname.clean_within, which cleans any pathnames contained within the message (removes extra slashes and resolves . and .. paths).

- clean_backtrace runs the entire backtrace through Exception::TraceSubstitutions and Pathname.clean_within, to clean the pathnames. TraceSubstitutions is used by Action-View's templates to hide certain unsightly parts of the backtrace when template compilation fails.

- application_backtrace returns the set of frames belonging to the Rails application, excluding those that are part of the Rails framework.

- framework_backtrace returns the set of frames that are part of the Rails framework. Together with application_backtrace, this is used on the default Rails rescue pages in the development environment.

File

File.atomic_write atomically writes to a file; it creates a temporary file, yields it to a block for writing, and then renames it to the destination. The advantage over a standard write is that the destination file does not exist in a half-written state at any point.

```
  File.atomic_write('important_file') do |important_file|
    important_file.write data
  end
```

Float

Float#round rounds a floating-point number to the specified decimal place:

```
  Math::PI           # => 3.14159265358979
  Math::PI.round     # => 3
  Math::PI.round(1)  # => 3.1
  Math::PI.round(2)  # => 3.14
  Math::PI.round(3)  # => 3.142
```

Hash

Conversions

core_ext/hash/conversions.rb

Many methods are provided to convert back and forth between hashes and XML representation. These are useful for round-tripping a hash to and from XML for web services.

- Hash#to_xml converts a single-level hash to XML:

  ```
  {:a => "One", :b => "Two", :int => 1, :opt => false}.to_xml
  ```

  yields:

  ```
  <?xml version="1.0" encoding="UTF-8"?>
  <hash>
    <a>One</a>
    <b>Two</b>
    <int type="integer">1</int>
    <opt type="boolean">false</opt>
  </hash>
  ```

- Hash.from_xml creates a hash from the provided XML document. Note that the root element is included in the hash.

  ```
  xml = <<EOXML
  <?xml version="1.0" encoding="UTF-8"?>
  <hash>
    <a>One</a>
    <b>Two</b>
  </hash>
  EOXML

  Hash.from_xml(xml)["hash"] # => {"a"=>"One", "b"=>"Two"}
  ```

Option processing

core_ext/hash/diff.rb, core_ext/hash/keys.rb, core_ext/hash/reverse_merge.rb,
core_ext/hash/slice.rb, core_ext/hash/except.rb

Rails uses hashes to provide keyword arguments to many methods. This is mostly due to a bit of syntactic sugar on Ruby's part; if a hash is passed as a function's last argument, the brackets can be omitted, resembling keyword arguments. However, Ruby has no native keyword argument support, so Rails has to provide some supporting features. ActiveSupport powers this option processing with extensions on the Hash class.

- Hash#diff(other) collects a hash with key/value pairs that are in one hash but not another.

  ```
  a = {:a => :b, :c => :d}
  b = {:e => :f, :c => :d}
  a.diff(b) # => {:e=>:f, :a=>:b}
  ```

- Hash#stringify_keys (which returns a copy) and Hash_stringify_keys! (which modifies the receiver in place) convert the hash's keys to strings. Hash#symbolize_keys and Hash#symbolize_keys! convert the keys to symbols. The symbolize methods are aliased as to_options and to_options!.

```
h = {:a => 123, "b" => 456}

h.stringify_keys # => {"a"=>123, "b"=>456}
h.symbolize_keys # => {:a=>123, :b=>456}
```

- Hash#assert_valid_keys(:key1, ...) raises an ArgumentError if the hash contains keys not in the argument list. This is used to ensure that only valid options are provided to a keyword-argument-based function.

- Hash#reverse_merge and Hash#reverse_merge! (in-place) work like Hash#merge, but in reverse order; in the case of duplicate keys, existing tuples beat those in the argument. This can be used to provide default arguments to a function.

```
options = {:a => 3, :c => 5}
options.reverse_merge!(:a => 1, :b => 4)
options # => {:a=>3, :b=>4, :c=>5}
```

- Hash#slice returns a new hash with only the keys specified. Inversely, Hash#except returns a new hash excluding the specified keys:

```
options = {:a => 3, :b => 4, :c => 5}
options.slice(:a, :c) # => {:c=>5, :a=>3}
options.except(:a) # => {:b=>4, :c=>5}
```

Hash#slice and Hash#except also come in in-place versions, respectively: Hash#slice! and Hash#except!.

HashWithIndifferentAccess

core_ext/hash/indifferent_access.rb

A HashWithIndifferentAccess is a hash whose elements can be accessed with either string or symbol keys:

```
options = {:a => 3, :b => 4}.with_indifferent_access

options.class # => HashWithIndifferentAccess
options[:a] # => 3
options["a"] = 100
options[:a] # => 100
```

HashWithIndifferentAccess is primarily used to offer a nice API to users, for example, so that a developer can write params[:user] or params["user"]. The stringify_keys or symbolize_keys methods should be used in option processing.

However, HashWithIndifferentAccess also fixes a class of security exploits in Rails. In Ruby 1.8, symbols are not garbage collected, so a params hash purely keyed on symbols (as it used to be) could lead to a denial-of-service attack. A malicious client could leak memory and exhaust the symbol table by issuing many requests with unique parameter names. Incidentally, Ruby 1.9 will obviate the need for HashWithIndifferentAccess, because symbols and strings will be treated identically (:aoeu == 'aoeu').

Integer

- `Integer#multiple_of?(number)`, `Integer#even?`, and `Integer#odd?` test for divisibility.

```
3.even? # => false
3.odd? # => true
3.multiple_of? 3 # => true
```

- `Integer#ordinalize` converts an integer to an ordinal number.

```
puts (1..10).map {|i| i.ordinalize}.to_sentence
# >> 1st, 2nd, 3rd, 4th, 5th, 6th, 7th, 8th, 9th, and 10th
```

Kernel

Daemonize

Normally, when a process is attached to a console and that console exits, the program terminates. `Kernel#daemonize` is used to detach a Ruby process from the console, allowing it to persist even if the console goes away. A typical daemon process will use `daemonize` as in the following example:

```
# server setup; process options

daemonize # detach from tty

loop do
  # wait for request
  # process request
end
```

Sending `SIGTERM` to a daemonized process kills it.

Reporting

The top-level methods in this file control console messages that might be displayed.

- `silence_warnings` turns warnings off for the duration of the block. `enable_warnings` turns warnings on for the duration of the block.
- `silence_stream(stream)` silences the given stream (usually `STDOUT` or `STDERR`) for the duration of the block.
- `suppress(*exception_classes)` ignores errors of the specified classes during the execution of the block.

Module

Aliasing

- alias_method_chain(*target*, *feature*) wraps a method in a new function, usually to add a new feature. This mechanism was discussed in Chapter 1. The method call:

  ```
  alias_method_chain :target, :feature
  ```

  is equivalent to:

  ```
  alias_method :target_without_feature, :target
  alias_method :target, :target_with_feature
  ```

  One consequence is that the target_with_feature method must exist before the alias_method_chain call. Punctuation (at the end of ?, !, and = methods) is properly moved to the end of the method names.

- alias_attribute(*new_name*, *old_name*) aliases an ActiveRecord attribute to a new name, adding the getter, setter, and predicate (for example, person.name?) methods.

Delegation

The delegate method provides a simple way to delegate one or more methods to an object:

```
class StringProxy
  attr_accessor :target
  delegate :to_s, :to => :target
  def initialize(target)
    @target = target
  end
end

proxy = StringProxy.new("Hello World!")
proxy.to_s # => "Hello World!"
proxy.target = "Goodbye World"
proxy.to_s # => "Goodbye World"
```

More detailed control over delegation can be obtained with Delegator from the standard library.

Introspection

- Module#included_in_classes iterates over all classes (using ObjectSpace), collecting the classes and modules in which the receiver is included.

  ```
  Enumerable.included_in_classes.include? Array   # => true
  Enumerable.included_in_classes.include? String  # => true
  Enumerable.included_in_classes.include? Numeric # => false
  ```

- Module#parent and Module#parents inspect the module namespace hierarchy:

  ```
  module A
    module B
      class C
      end
    end
  end
  ```

```
A::B::C.parent # => A::B
A::B.parent    # => A
A.parent       # => Object

A::B::C.parents # => [A::B, A, Object]
```

Numeric Conversions

These methods convert byte expressions, such as 45.megabytes, into the equivalent number of bytes (45.megabytes == 47_185_920). As with numeric conversions to time units, both singular and plural units are accepted (1.kilobyte or 3.kilobytes). Valid units are bytes, kilobytes, megabytes, gigabytes, terabytes, petabytes, and exabytes.

Object

instance_exec

The instance_exec method allows us to evaluate a block in the context of an instance. It is like instance_eval, except it allows arguments to be passed into the block. An implementation is in *object/extending.rb*.

The instance_exec implementation uses the Proc#bind implementation from *proc.rb*. This method allows Procs to be treated like UnboundMethods; they can be bound to an object and invoked as methods. The implementation is instructive:

```
class Proc #:nodoc:
  def bind(object)
    block, time = self, Time.now
    (class << object; self end).class_eval do
      method_name = "__bind_#{time.to_i}_#{time.usec}"
      define_method(method_name, &block)
      method = instance_method(method_name)
      remove_method(method_name)
      method
    end.bind(object)
  end
end
```

The class_eval block is evaluated in the context of the object's singleton class, so the method created is specific to that object. A method with a (hopefully) unique name is created, using the Proc as the method body. The instance_method method grabs the newly created method object as an UnboundMethod from the class. Because we hold a reference to the method, we can safely remove it from the singleton class using remove_method, and the method will remain in existence (anonymously). The last line in the class_eval returns the method from the class_eval; the method is then bound to the given object and returned.

This definition of instance_exec is a Ruby 1.8 workaround. In Ruby 1.9, instance_exec is a native method. Also note that this implementation is not threadsafe. It tries to be as safe as possible, qualifying the method names down to the microsecond and putting them in the respective objects' singleton classes, but it will still fail if called twice on the same object during the same microsecond.

Miscellaneous methods

- Object#returning lets you perform some operations on an object and then return it. It is usually used to encapsulate some incidental operations on an object in a block:

```
returning(Person.new) do |p|
  p.name = "Brad"
end # => #<Person:0x1e33b4 @name="Brad">
```

- Object#with_options provides a way to factor out redundant options on multiple method calls. It is usually seen in routing code:

```
map.with_options(:controller => "person") do |person|
  person.default "", :action => "index"
  person.details "/details/:id", :action => "details"
end
```

The with_options call yields an OptionMerger, which is a proxy that forwards all of its method calls to the context (which, in this example, is the original map). The options provided are merged into the method call's last hash argument, so the effect of the person.default call is the same as:

```
map.default "", :action => "index", :controller => "person"
map.details "/details/:id", :action => "details", :controller => "person"
```

There is no magic here that makes this specific to Rails routes; you can use this with any method that takes a hash of Rails-style keyword arguments as the last parameter. The proxy object passed into the with_options block delegates any unknown method calls to the target.

Range

- Range#include? checks to see whether a range completely includes another range:

```
(1..10).include?(3..5)  # => true
(1..10).include?(3..15) # => false
```

- Range#overlaps? checks to see whether a range overlaps another range:

```
>> (1..10).overlaps?(3..15)  # => true
>> (1..10).overlaps?(13..15) # => false
```

String

Inflector

The methods in this file delegate to the Inflector.

- String#singularize and String#pluralize do what you would think. Corner cases are more or less supported; you can add custom rules that override the defaults.

```
"wug".pluralize    # => "wugs"
"wugs".singularize # => "wug"
"fish".pluralize   # => "fish"
```

- String#camelize is used to convert file names to class names; String#underscore does the opposite.

```
"action_controller/filters".camelize   # => "ActionController::Filters"
"ActionController::Filters".underscore # => "action_controller/filters"
```

- String#tableize converts class names to table names (as in ActiveRecord). String#classify converts table names to class names.

  ```
  "ProductCategory".tableize     # => "product_categories"
  "product_categories".classify # => "ProductCategory"
  ```

- String#constantize tries to interpret the given string as a constant name. This is useful for looking up classes returned from String#classify.

  ```
  "ProductCategory".constantize rescue "no class" # => "no class"
  class ProductCategory; end
  "ProductCategory".constantize # => ProductCategory
  ```

String i18n

These files provide interfaces to ActiveSupport::Multibyte for support for multibyte characters. These methods depend on the current value of the $KCODE global variable, which determines the character encoding in use. $KCODE can take on the following values.

$KCODE	Encoding
e, E	EUC
s, S	Shift-JIS
u, U	UTF-8
a, A, n, N	ASCII (default)

In Rails 1.2, $KCODE is automatically set to u, enabling the multibyte operations.

- String#chars returns an instance of ActiveSupport::Multibyte::Chars, which proxies for the String class. Chars defines methods that work properly under Unicode (assuming the proper $KCODE setting), and proxies methods it doesn't know about to String:

  ```
  str = "今日は世界"

  $KCODE = "a"
  str # => "\344\273\212\346\227\245\343\201\257\344\270\226\347\225\214"
  str.length  # => 15
  str.chars.class # => ActiveSupport::Multibyte::Chars
  str.chars.length # => 15

  $KCODE = "u"
  str # => "今日は世界"
  str.length # => 15
  str.chars.length # => 5
  ```

  String#each_char yields each character in turn to the block:

  ```
  $KCODE = "u"
  "今日は世界".each_char {|c| puts c}
  # >> 今
  # >> 日
  # >> は
  # >> 世
  # >> 界
  ```

Miscellaneous methods

- String#at(position) returns the character at the specified position. This is an easy way around the fact that Ruby's String#[] returns a character code rather than a string in Ruby 1.8:

```
"asdf"[0]        # => 97
"asdf"[0] == ?a  # => true
"asdf".at(0)     # => "a"
```

- String#from, String#to, String#first, and String#last work just as their names suggest. As usual, negative indices count from the end of the string:

```
"asdf".from(1)        # => "sdf"
"asdf".to(1)          # => "as"
"asdf".from(1).to(-2) # => "sd"

"asdf".first       # => "a"
"asdf".last        # => "f"
"asdf".first(2)    # => "as"
"asdf".last(2)     # => "df"
```

- String#to_time (defaults to UTC), String#to_time(:local), and String#to_date are easy ways to delegate to ParseDate:

```
"1/4/2007".to_date.to_s # => "2007-01-04"

"1/4/2007 2:56 PM".to_time(:local).to_s # => "Thu Jan 04 14:56:00 CST 2007"
```

- String#starts_with?(prefix) and String#ends_with?(suffix) test whether a string starts with or ends with another string.

```
"aoeu".starts_with?("ao") # => true
"aoeu".starts_with?("A")  # => false
"aoeu".ends_with?("eu")   # => true
"aoeu".ends_with?("foo")  # => false
```

Symbol#to_proc

ActiveSupport defines only one extension to Symbol, but it is a powerful one: the ability to convert a symbol to a Proc using Symbol#to_proc. This idiom is used all over Rails now. Code such as this:

```
(1..5).map {|i| i.to_s } # => ["1", "2", "3", "4", "5"]
```

becomes this, using Symbol#to_proc:

```
(1..5).map(&:to_s) # => ["1", "2", "3", "4", "5"]
```

The & symbol tells Ruby to treat the symbol :to_s as a block argument; Ruby knows that the argument should be a Proc and tries to coerce it by calling its to_proc method. Active-Support supplies a Symbol#to_proc method that returns just such a Proc; when called, it invokes the specified method on its first argument.

TimeZone

Instances of TimeZone are value objects[*] representing a particular time zone (an offset from UTC and a name). They are used to perform conversions between different time zones:

```
Time.now          # => Thu Oct 25 00:10:52 -0500 2007
# UTC-05
TimeZone[-5].now # => Thu Oct 25 00:10:52 -0500 2007
TimeZone[-5].adjust(1.month.ago) # => Tue Sep 25 00:10:52 -0500 2007
```

RailTies

RailTies is the set of components that wire together ActiveRecord, ActionController, and ActionView to form Rails. We will examine the two most important parts of RailTies: how Rails is initialized and how requests are processed.

Rails Configuration

The Rails::Configuration class, defined in *initializer.rb*, holds the configuration attributes that control Rails. It has several general Rails attributes defined as attributes on the Configuration class, but there is a little cleverness in the framework class stubs. The five class stubs (action_controller, action_mailer, action_view, active_resource, and active_record) act as proxies to the class attributes of their respective Base classes. In this way, the configuration statement:

```
config.action_controller.perform_caching = true
```

is the same as:

```
ActionController::Base.perform_caching = true
```

except with a unified configuration syntax.

Application Initialization in 20 Easy Steps

initializer.rb

Rails::Initializer is the main class that handles setting up the Rails environment within Ruby. Initialization is kicked off by *config/environment.rb*, which contains the block:

```
Rails::Initializer.run do |config|
  # (configuration)
end
```

---

[*] A *value object* is an object representing a value, whose identity is defined by that value only. In other words, two objects compare as equal if and only if they have the same state.

Rails::Initializer.run yields a new Rails::Configuration object to the block. Then run creates a new Rails::Initializer object and calls its process method, which takes the following steps in order to initialize Rails:

1. check_ruby_version: Ensures that Ruby 1.8.2 or above (but not 1.8.3) is being used.

2. set_load_path: Adds the framework paths (RailTies, ActionPack,* ActiveSupport, ActiveRecord, Action Mailer, and Action Web Service) and the application's load paths to the Ruby load path. The framework is loaded from *vendor/rails* or a location specified in RAILS_FRAMEWORK_ROOT.

3. require_frameworks: Loads each framework listed in the frameworks configuration option. If the framework path was not specified in RAILS_FRAMEWORK_ROOT and it does not exist in *vendor/rails*, Initializer will assume the frameworks are installed as RubyGems.

4. set_autoload_paths: Sets the autoload paths based on the values of the load_paths and load_once_paths configuration variables. These determine which paths will be searched to resolve unknown constants. The load_paths option is the same one that provided the application's load paths in step 2.

5. load_environment: Loads and evaluates the environment-specific (development, production, or test) configuration file.

6. initialize_encoding: Sets $KCODE to u for UTF-8 support throughout Rails.

7. initialize_database: If ActiveRecord is being used, sets up its database configuration and connects to the database server.

8. initialize_logger: Sets up the logger and sets the top-level constant RAILS_DEFAULT_LOGGER to the instance. If logger is specified in the configuration, it is used. If not, a new logger is created and directed to the log_path specified. If that fails, a warning is displayed and logging is redirected to standard error.

9. initialize_framework_logging: Sets the logger for ActiveRecord, ActionController, and Action Mailer (if they are being used) to the logger that was just set up.

10. initialize_framework_views: Sets the view path for ActionController and Action Mailer to the value of the view_path configuration item.

11. initialize_dependency_mechanism: Sets Dependencies.mechanism (which determines whether to use require or load to load files) based on the setting of the cache_classes configuration item.

12. initialize_whiny_nils: If the whiny_nils configuration item is true, adds the Whiny Nil extensions (that complain when trying to call id or other methods on nil) to NilClass.

---

* ActionPack = ActionController + ActionView.

13. `initialize_temporary_directories`: Sets ActionController's temporary session and cache directories if they exist in the filesystem.

14. `initialize_framework_settings`: Transforms the framework-specific configuration settings into method calls on the frameworks' Base classes. For example, consider the configuration option:

    `config.active_record.schema_format = :sql`

    The `config.active_record` object is an instance of `Rails::OrderedOptions`, which is basically an ordered hash (ordered to keep the configuration directives in order). During initialization, the `initialize_framework_settings` method transforms it into the following:

    `ActiveRecord::Base.schema_format = :sql`

    This offers the advantage that the `Configuration` object doesn't have to be updated every time a framework adds or changes a configuration option.

15. `add_support_load_paths`: Adds load paths for support functions. This function is currently empty.

16. `load_plugins`: Loads the plugins from paths in the `plugin_paths` configuration item (default *vendor/plugins*). If a plugins configuration item is specified, load those plugins respecting that load order. Plugins are loaded close to the end of the process so that they can override any already loaded component.

17. `load_observers`: Instantiates ActiveRecord observers. This is done after plugins so that plugins have an opportunity to modify the observer classes.

18. `initialize_routing`: Loads and processes the routes. Also sets the controller paths from the `controller_paths` configuration item.

19. `after_initialize`: Calls any user-defined `after_initialize` callback. These callbacks are defined in the configuration block by `config.after_initialize { ... }`.

20. `load_application_initializers`: Loads all Ruby files in *RAILS_ROOT/config/initializers* and any of its subdirectories. Old framework initialization that may previously have been contained in *config/environment.rb* can now properly be broken out into separate initializers.

Now the framework is ready to receive requests.

Request Dispatch

dispatcher.rb, *fcgi_handler.rb*, *webrick_server.rb*

The `Dispatcher` class is the outside world's interface to Rails. Web servers dispatch a request to Rails by calling `Dispatcher.dispatch(cgi, session_options, output)`. Rails processes the given CGI request and presents the output to the given location (which defaults to standard output). Rails can be reset by calling `Dispatcher.reset_application!` to process multiple requests.

There are many ways to serve a Rails application. *fcgi_handler.rb* contains the FastCGI handler (RailsFCGIHandler) that shims between a FastCGI-speaking server (Apache, lighttpd, or even IIS) and Rails. *webrick_server.rb* is a server based on WEBrick that can serve Rails.

But the preferred application server for both development and deployment is Zed Shaw's Mongrel.[*] Mongrel contains its own Rails handler that calls the Dispatcher methods directly, using its own CGI wrapper. Of course, more information can be found in Mongrel's source itself.

Further Reading

Diomidis Spinellis's book *Code Reading: The Open Source Perspective* (Addison-Wesley) offers advice on how to approach large codebases, particularly those of open source software.

The Ruby Facets core library[†] is another collection of code that aims to provide utility methods for Ruby. This library covers some of the same ground as the Core Extensions, but also provides additional extensions.

If you need more complicated manipulations to the English language than the Inflector class allows, look to the Ruby Linguistics project.[‡]

---

[*] *http://mongrel.rubyforge.org/*
[†] *http://facets.rubyforge.org/*
[‡] *http://www.deveiate.org/projects/Linguistics*

## CHAPTER 3

Rails Plugins

> *Civilization advances by extending the number of*
> *important operations which we can perform*
> *without thinking of them.*
> —Alfred North Whitehead

Ruby on Rails is very powerful, but it cannot do everything. There are many features that are too experimental, out of scope of the Rails core, or even blatantly contrary to the way Rails was designed (it is opinionated software, after all). The core team cannot and would not include everything that anybody wants in Rails.

Luckily, Rails comes with a very flexible extension system. Rails plugins allow developers to extend or override nearly any part of the Rails framework, and share these modifications with others in an encapsulated and reusable manner.

About Plugins

Plugin Loading

By default, plugins are loaded from directories under *vendor/plugins* in the Rails application root. Should you need to change or add to these paths, the plugin_paths configuration item contains the plugin load paths:

```
config.plugin_paths += [File.join(RAILS_ROOT, 'vendor', 'other_plugins')]
```

By default, plugins are loaded in alphabetical order; attachment_fu is loaded before http_authentication. If the plugins have dependencies on each other, a manual loading order can be specified with the plugins configuration element:

```
config.plugins = %w(prerequisite_plugin actual_plugin)
```

Any plugins not specified in config.plugins will not be loaded. However, if the last plugin specified is the symbol :all, Rails will load all remaining plugins at that point. Rails accepts either symbols or strings as plugin names here.

```
config.plugins = [ :prerequisite_plugin, :actual_plugin, :all ]
```

The plugin locator searches for plugins under the configured paths, recursively. Because a recursive search is performed, you can organize plugins into directories; for example, *vendor/plugins/active_record_acts* and *vendor/plugins/view_extensions*.

The actual plugin locating and loading system is extensible, and you can write your own strategies. The locator (which by default is `Rails::Plugin::FileSystemLocator`) searches for plugins; the loader (by default `Rails::Plugin::Loader`) determines whether a directory contains a plugin and does the work of loading it.

To write your own locators and loaders, examine *railties/lib/rails/plugin/locator.rb* and *railties/lib/rails/plugin/loader.rb*. The locators (more than one locator can be used) and loader can be changed with configuration directives:

```
config.plugin_locators += [MyPluginLocator]
config.plugin_loader = MyPluginLoader
```

Installing Rails Plugins

Plugins are most often installed with the built-in Rails plugin tool, `script/plugin`. This plugin tool has several commands:

discover/source/unsource/sources

> The plugin tool uses an ad-hoc method of finding plugins. Rather than requiring you to specify the URL of a plugin repository, `script/plugin` tries to find it for you. One way it does this is by scraping the "Plugins" page of the Rails wiki[*] for source URLs. This can be triggered with the `discover` command.
>
> The source and unsource commands add and remove source URLs, respectively. The sources command lists all current source URLs.

install/update/remove

> These commands install, update, and uninstall plugins. They can take an HTTP URL, a Subversion URL (`svn://` or `svn+ssh://`), or a bare plugin name, in which case the list of sources is scanned.

`script/plugin install` takes an option, `-x`, that directs it to manage plugins as Subversion externals. This has the advantage that the directory is still linked to the external repository. However, it is a bit inflexible—you cannot cherry-pick changes from the upstream repository. We will examine some better options later.

RaPT

RaPT (*http://rapt.rubyforge.org/*) is a replacement for the standard Rails plugin installer, script/plugin. It can be installed with gem `install rapt`.

The first advantage that RaPT has is that it can search for plugins from the command line. (The second advantage is that it is extremely fast, because it caches everything.)

---

[*] *http://wiki.rubyonrails.org/rails/pages/Plugins*

The `rapt search` command looks for plugins matching a specified keyword. To search for plugins that add calendar features to Rails, change to the root directory of a Rails application and execute:

```
$ rapt search calendar
Calendar Helper
  Info: http://agilewebdevelopment.com/plugins/show/98
  Install: http://topfunky.net/svn/plugins/calendar_helper
Calendariffic 0.1.0
  Info: http://agilewebdevelopment.com/plugins/show/743
  Install: http://opensvn.csie.org/calendariffic/calendariffic/
Google Calendar Generator
  Info: http://agilewebdevelopment.com/plugins/show/277
  Install: svn://rubyforge.org//var/svn/googlecalendar/plugins/googlecalendar
dhtml_calendar
  Info: http://agilewebdevelopment.com/plugins/show/333
  Install: svn://rubyforge.org//var/svn/dhtmlcalendar/dhtml_calendar
Bundled Resource
  Info: http://agilewebdevelopment.com/plugins/show/166
  Install: svn://syncid.textdriven.com/svn/opensource/bundled_resource/trunk
DatebocksEngine
  Info: http://agilewebdevelopment.com/plugins/show/356
  Install: http://svn.toolbocks.com/plugins/datebocks_engine/
datepicker_engine
  Info: http://agilewebdevelopment.com/plugins/show/409
  Install: http://svn.mamatux.dk/rails-engines/datepicker_engine
```

One of these could then be installed with, for example, `rapt install datepicker_engine`.

Piston

In Rails, plugins are perhaps the most common use of code supplied by an external vendor (other than the Rails framework itself). This requires some special care where version control is concerned. Managing Rails plugins as Subversion externals has several disadvantages:

- The remote server must be contacted on each update to determine whether anything has changed. This can incur quite a performance penalty if the project has many externals. In addition, it adds an unneeded dependency; problems can ensue if the remote server is down.

- The project is generally at the mercy of code changes that happen at the remote branch; there is no easy way to cherry-pick or block changes that happen remotely. The only flexibility Subversion affords is the ability to lock to a certain remote revision.

- Similarly, there is no way to maintain local modifications to a remote branch. Any needed modifications can only be kept in the working copy, where they are unversioned.

- No history is kept of how external versions relate to the local repository. If you want to update your working copy to last month's version, nobody knows what version the external code was at.

To solve these problems, François Beausoleil created Piston,[*] a program to manage vendor branches in Subversion. Piston imports the remote branch into the local repository, only synchronizing when requested. As a full copy of the code exists inside the project's repository, it can be modified as needed. Any changes made to the local copy will be merged when the project is updated from the remote server.

Piston is available as a gem; install it with `sudo gem install --include-dependencies piston`.

To install a plugin using Piston, you need to manually find the Subversion URL of the repository. Then, simply import it with Piston, specifying the repository URL and the destination path in your working copy:

```
$ piston import http://svn.rubyonrails.org/rails/plugins/deadlock_retry \
    vendor/plugins/deadlock_retry
Exported r7144 from 'http://svn.rubyonrails.org/rails/plugins/deadlock_retry/'
to 'vendor/plugins/deadlock_retry'

$ svn ci
```

The `svn ci` is necessary because Piston adds the code to your working copy. To Subversion, it is as if you wrote the code yourself—it is versioned alongside the rest of your application. This makes it very simple to patch the vendor branch for local use; simply make modifications to the working copy and check them in.

When the time comes to update the vendor branch, `piston update vendor/plugins/deadlock_retry` will fetch all changes from the remote repository and merge them in. Any local modifications will be preserved in the merge. `piston update` can be called without an argument; in that case, it will recursively update any Piston-controlled directories under the current one.

Piston-controlled directories can be locked to their current version with `piston lock` and unlocked with `piston unlock`. And for current `svn:externals` users, existing directories managed with `svn:externals` can be converted to Piston all at once with `piston convert`.

Piston is also good for managing edge Rails, along with any patches you may apply. To import Rails from the edge, with all of the features of Piston:

```
$ piston import http://svn.rubyonrails.org/rails/trunk vendor/rails
```

Decentralized version control

Piston effectively creates one layer between a remote repository and the working copy. Decentralized version control systems take this model to its logical conclusion: every working copy is a repository, equally able to share changes with other repositories. This can be a much more flexible model than normal centralized version control systems. We examine decentralized version control systems in more detail in Chapter 10.

---

[*] *http://piston.rubyforge.org/*

Plugins and other vendor code can be managed very well with a decentralized version control system. These systems afford much more flexibility, especially in complicated situations with multiple developers and vendors.

A tool is available, hgsvn,* which will migrate changes from a SVN repository to a Mercurial repository. This can be used to set up a system similar to Piston, but with much more flexibility. One repository (the "upstream" or "incoming") can mirror the remote repository, and other projects can cherry-pick desired patches from the upstream and ignore undesired ones. Local modifications suitable for the upstream can be exported to patches and sent to the project maintainer.

Writing Plugins

Once you know how to extend Rails by opening classes, it is easy to write a plugin. First, let's look at the directory structure of a typical plugin (see Figure 3-1).

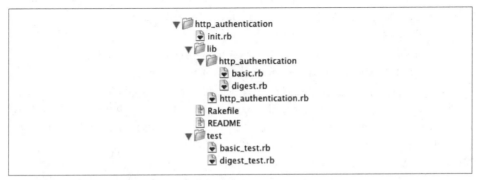

Figure 3-1. Directory structure of a typical plugin

There are several files and directories involved in a Rails plugin:

about.yml (not shown)
> This is the newest feature of Rails plugins—embedded metadata. Right now, this feature works only with RaPT. The command rapt about *plugin_name* will give a summary of the plugin's information. In the future, more features are expected; right now, it exists for informational purposes. Metadata is stored in the *about.yml* file; here is an example from acts_as_attachment:

```
author: technoweenie
summary: File upload handling plugin.
homepage: http://technoweenie.stikipad.com
plugin: http://svn.techno-weenie.net/projects/plugins/acts_as_attachment
license: MIT
version: 0.3a
rails_version: 1.1.2+
```

---

* *http://cheeseshop.python.org/pypi/hgsvn*

init.rb

This is a Ruby file run upon initialization of the plugin. Typically, it will require files from the *lib/* directory. As many plugins patch core functionality, *init.rb* may extend core classes with extensions from the plugin:

```
require 'my_plugin'
ActionController::Base.send :include, MyPlugin::ControllerExtensions
```

The send hack is needed here because Module#include is a private method and, at least for now, send bypasses access control on the receiver.[*]

install.rb (not shown)

This hook is run when the plugin is installed with one of the automated plugin installation tools such as script/plugin or RaPT. It is a good idea not to do anything mission-critical in this file, as it will not be run if the plugin is installed manually (by checking out the source to a directory under *vendor/plugins*).

A typical use for the *install.rb* hook is to display the contents of the plugin's *README* file:

```
puts IO.read(File.join(File.dirname(__FILE__), 'README'))
```

lib/

This is the directory in which all of the plugin code is contained. Rails adds this directory to the Ruby load path as well as the Rails Dependencies load path.

For example, assume you have a class, MyPlugin, in *lib/my_plugin.rb*. Since it is in the Ruby load path, a simple require 'my_plugin' will find it. But since Dependencies autoloads missing constants, you could also load the file simply by referring to MyPlugin in your plugin.

MIT-LICENSE (or other license file; not shown)

All plugins, no matter how small, should include a license. Failure to include a license can prevent people from using your software—no matter how insignificant the plugin may be, it is against the law for someone else to distribute your code without your permission.

For most projects, the MIT license (under which Rails itself is released) is sufficient. Under that license, anyone can redistribute your software freely, provided that they include a copy of the license (preserving your copyright notice). Including the *MIT-LICENSE* file in the plugin is important in this case, as it makes compliance automatic.

Rakefile

This is the core Rake task definition file for the plugin. Usually it is used to launch tests for the plugin itself or package the plugin for distribution.

---

[*] In Ruby 1.9, Object#send will not automatically ignore access control on the receiving object, although the new method Object#send! will.

README

It is helpful to provide a short explanation here of the plugin's purpose, usage, and any special instructions. A hook can be included in *install.rb* (described earlier) to print this file upon plugin installation.

test/

This folder contains the plugin's tests. These tests are run using Rake, without loading Rails. Any tests written in this folder must stand alone—they must either mock out any required Rails functionality or actually load the Rails framework. We will explore both of these options later.

uninstall.rb (not shown)

This is the uninstall hook, run when a plugin is removed by tools such as `script/plugin` or RaPT. Unless you have a very pressing need, the use of this file is discouraged. Like *install.rb*, *uninstall.rb* is not always used—many people simply delete the plugin directory without thought.

Of course, you should feel free to add any folders required by your plugin. Use `File.dirname(__FILE__)` in *init.rb* to refer to your plugin's directory as installed. None of these files are specifically required; for example, a simple plugin may do all of its work in *init.rb*.

You can generate a plugin skeleton with a built-in Rails generator:

```
$ script/generate plugin my_plugin
```

This generates a skeleton in *vendor/plugins/my_plugin* with sample files, a fill-in-the-blanks MIT license, and instructions.

Plugin Examples

To illustrate the flexibility and design of a typical Rails plugin, we will examine some of the plugins available from the rubyonrails.org Subversion repository. Most of these plugins are used fairly commonly; many of them are used in 37signals applications. Consider them the "standard library" of Rails. They are all available from *http://svn.rubyonrails.org/rails/plugins/*.

Account Location

Plugins can be very simple in structure. For example, consider David Heinemeier Hansson's `account_location` plugin. This plugin provides controller and helper methods to support using part of the domain name as an account name (for example, to support customers with domain names of `customer1.example.com` and `customer2.example.com`, using `customer1` and `customer2` as keys to look up the account information). To use the plugin, include `AccountLocation` in one or more of your controllers, which adds the appropriate instance methods:

```
class ApplicationController < ActionController::Base
  include AccountLocation
end

puts ApplicationController.instance_methods.grep /^account/
=> ["account_domain", "account_subdomain", "account_host", "account_url"]
```

Including the AccountLocation module in the controller allows you to access various URL options from the controller and the view. For example, to set the @account variable from the subdomain on each request:

```
class ApplicationController < ActionController::Base
  include AccountLocation
  before_filter :find_account

  protected

  def find_account
    @account = Account.find_by_username(account_subdomain)
  end
end
```

The account_location plugin has no *init.rb*; nothing needs to be set up on load, as all functionality is encapsulated in the AccountLocation module. Here is the implementation, in *lib/account_location.rb* (minus some license text):

```
module AccountLocation
  def self.included(controller)
    controller.helper_method(:account_domain, :account_subdomain,
      :account_host, :account_url)
  end

  protected

  def default_account_subdomain
    @account.username if @account && @account.respond_to?(:username)
  end

  def account_url(account_subdomain = default_account_subdomain,
      use_ssl = request.ssl?)
    (use_ssl ? "https://" : "http://") + account_host(account_subdomain)
  end

  def account_host(account_subdomain = default_account_subdomain)
    account_host = ""
    account_host << account_subdomain + "."
    account_host << account_domain
  end

  def account_domain
    account_domain = ""
    account_domain << request.subdomains[1..-1].join(".") +
      "." if request.subdomains.size > 1
    account_domain << request.domain + request.port_string
  end
```

```
    def account_subdomain
      request.subdomains.first
    end
  end
```

The `self.included` method is a standard idiom for plugins; it is triggered after the module is included in a class. In this case, that method marks the included instance methods as Rails helper methods, so they can be used from a view.

Finally, remember that `Dependencies.load_paths` contains the `lib` directories of all loaded plugins, so the act of mentioning `AccountLocation` searches for *account_location.rb* among those `lib` directories. Because of this, you do not need to require anything in order to use the plugin—just drop the code into *vendor/plugins*.

SSL Requirement

The `ssl_requirement` plugin allows you to specify certain actions that must be protected by SSL. This plugin conceptually divides actions into three categories:

SSL Required
> All requests to this action must be protected by SSL. If this action is requested without SSL, it will be redirected to use SSL. Actions of this type are specified with the `ssl_required` class method.

SSL Allowed
> SSL is allowed on this action but not required. Actions of this type are specified by the `ssl_allowed` class method.

SSL Prohibited
> SSL is not allowed for this action. If an action is not marked with `ssl_required` or `ssl_allowed`, SSL requests to that action will be redirected to the non-SSL URL.

In typical Rails fashion, the methods that specify SSL requirements are a declarative language. They specify *what* the requirements are, not *how* to enforce them. This means that the code reads very cleanly:

```
class OrderController < ApplicationController
  ssl_required :checkout, :payment
  ssl_allowed :cart
end
```

Like the `account_location` plugin, the `ssl_requirement` plugin is enabled by including a module. The `SslRequirement` module contains the entire SSL requirement logic:

```
module SslRequirement
  def self.included(controller)
    controller.extend(ClassMethods)
    controller.before_filter(:ensure_proper_protocol)
  end

  module ClassMethods
    def ssl_required(*actions)
```

```
      write_inheritable_array(:ssl_required_actions, actions)
    end

    def ssl_allowed(*actions)
      write_inheritable_array(:ssl_allowed_actions, actions)
    end
  end

  protected

  def ssl_required?
    (self.class.read_inheritable_attribute(:ssl_required_actions) || []).
      include?(action_name.to_sym)
  end

  def ssl_allowed?
    (self.class.read_inheritable_attribute(:ssl_allowed_actions) || []).
      include?(action_name.to_sym)
  end

  private

  def ensure_proper_protocol
    return true if ssl_allowed?

    if ssl_required? && !request.ssl?
      redirect_to "https://" + request.host + request.request_uri
      return false
    elsif request.ssl? && !ssl_required?
      redirect_to "http://" + request.host + request.request_uri
      return false
    end
  end
end
```

Again, the SslRequirement.included method is triggered when SslRequirement is included in a controller class. The included method does two things here. First, it extends the controller with the SslRequirement::ClassMethods module, to include the ssl_required and ssl_allowed class methods. This is a common Ruby idiom for adding class methods, and it is required because module methods of an included module do not become class methods of the including class. (In other words, ssl_required and ssl_allowed could not be module methods of SslRequirement, because they would not be added as class methods of the controller class.)

The second thing that SslRequirement.included does is to set up a before_filter on the controller to enforce the SSL requirement. This filter redirects to the proper http:// or https:// URL, depending on the logic declared by the class methods.

HTTP Authentication

The final plugin we will examine is the http_authentication plugin, which allows you to protect certain actions in an application by HTTP Basic authentication (currently, Digest authentication is stubbed out but not implemented).

The HTTP Authentication plugin is very straightforward; the most common interface is the ActionController class method authenticate_or_request_with_http_basic, typically used in a before_filter on protected actions. That method takes as parameters an authentication realm and a login procedure block that verifies the given credentials. If the login procedure returns true, the action is allowed to continue. If the login procedure returns false, the action is blocked and an HTTP 401 Unauthorized status code is sent, with instructions on how to authenticate (a WWW-Authenticate header). In that case, the browser will typically present the user with a login and password and allow three tries before displaying an "Unauthorized" page.

The following is a typical use of the HTTP Authentication plugin:

```
class PrivateController < ApplicationController
  before_filter :authenticate

  def secret
    render :text => "Password correct!"
  end

  protected

  def authenticate
    authenticate_or_request_with_http_basic do |username, password|
      username == "bob" && password == "secret"
    end
  end
end
```

Notice that, unlike the two plugins described earlier, here we did not have to include anything in the PrivateController—the authenticate_or_request_with_http_basic method was already provided for us. This is because the plugin added some methods to ActionController::Base (of which ApplicationController is a subclass).

One way to include methods like this is direct monkeypatching. The plugin could have directly written the methods into ActionController::Base:

```
class ActionController::Base
  def authenticate_or_request_with_http_basic(realm = "Application",
                                              &login_procedure)
    authenticate_with_http_basic(&login_procedure) ||
      request_http_basic_authentication(realm)
  end
```

```
def authenticate_with_http_basic(&login_procedure)
  HttpAuthentication::Basic.authenticate(self, &login_procedure)
end

def request_http_basic_authentication(realm = "Application")
  HttpAuthentication::Basic.authentication_request(self, realm)
end
end
```

This works for small plugins, but it can get clunky. The better solution, chosen by this plugin, is to first create a module named for the plugin (sometimes including the developer's name or company to reduce the chance of namespace collisions). Here is the abridged code for the HTTP Authentication plugin's class methods:

```
module HttpAuthentication
  module Basic
    extend self
    module ControllerMethods
      def authenticate_or_request_with_http_basic(realm = "Application",
                                                  &login_procedure)
        authenticate_with_http_basic(&login_procedure) ||
          request_http_basic_authentication(realm)
      end

      def authenticate_with_http_basic(&login_procedure)
        HttpAuthentication::Basic.authenticate(self, &login_procedure)
      end

      def request_http_basic_authentication(realm = "Application")
        HttpAuthentication::Basic.authentication_request(self, realm)
      end
    end
  end
end
```

Now, the methods are self-contained within `HttpAuthentication::Basic::ControllerMethods`. A simple statement in the plugin's *init.rb* file adds the methods to `ActionController::Base`:

```
ActionController::Base.send :include,
  HttpAuthentication::Basic::ControllerMethods
```

Testing Plugins

Like the rest of Rails, plugins have very mature testing facilities. However, plugin tests usually require a bit more work than standard Rails tests, as the tests are designed to be run on their own, outside of the Rails framework. Some things to keep in mind when writing tests for plugins:

- Unlike in the Rails plugin initializer, when running tests, load paths are not set up automatically, and Dependencies does not load missing constants for you. You need to manually set up the load paths and require any parts of the plugin that you will be testing, as in this example from the HTTP Authentication plugin:

```
$LOAD_PATH << File.dirname(__FILE__) + '/../lib/'
require 'http_authentication'
```

- Similarly, the plugin's *init.rb* file is not loaded, so you must set up anything your tests need, such as including your plugin's modules in the TestCase class:

```
class HttpBasicAuthenticationTest < Test::Unit::TestCase
  include HttpAuthentication::Basic

  # ...
end
```

- You must usually recreate (mock or stub) any Rails functionality involved in your test. In the case of the HTTP Authentication plugin, it would be too much overhead to load the entire ActionController framework for the tests. The functionality being tested is very simple, and requires very little of ActionController:

```
def test_authentication_request
  authentication_request(@controller, "Megaglobalapp")
  assert_equal 'Basic realm="Megaglobalapp"',
               @controller.headers["WWW-Authenticate"]
  assert_equal :unauthorized, @controller.renders.first[:status]
end
```

To support this limited subset of ActionController's features, the test's setup method creates a stub controller:

```
def setup
  @controller = Class.new do
    attr_accessor :headers, :renders

    def initialize
      @headers, @renders = {}, []
    end

    def request
      Class.new do
        def env
          {'HTTP_AUTHORIZATION' =>
            HttpAuthentication::Basic.encode_credentials("dhh", "secret") }
        end
      end.new
    end

    def render(options)
      self.renders << options
    end
  end.new
end
```

The `Class.new do ... end.new` syntax creates an instance of an anonymous class with the provided class definition. A more verbose, named, equivalent would be:

```
class MyTestController
  # class definition...
end
@controller = MyTestController.new
```

- Sometimes, dependencies are complicated enough so as to require actually loading a full framework. This is the case with the SSL Requirement plugin, which actually loads `ActionController` and sets up a controller for testing purposes. First, the code loads `ActionController` (this either requires RUBYOPT="rubygems" and a suitable gem version of `ActionController`, or setting the ACTIONCONTROLLER_PATH environment variable to a copy of the `ActionController` source):

```
begin
  require 'action_controller'
rescue LoadError
  if ENV['ACTIONCONTROLLER_PATH'].nil?
    abort <<MSG
Please set the ACTIONCONTROLLER_PATH environment variable to the directory
containing the action_controller.rb file.
MSG
  else
    $LOAD_PATH.unshift << ENV['ACTIONCONTROLLER_PATH']
    begin
      require 'action_controller'
    rescue LoadError
      abort "ActionController could not be found."
    end
  end
end
```

Then, the test code loads `ActionController`'s `test_process`, which affords access to `ActionController::TestRequest` and `ActionController::TestResponse`. After that, logging is silenced and routes are reloaded:

```
require 'action_controller/test_process'
require 'test/unit'
require "#{File.dirname(__FILE__)}/../lib/ssl_requirement"

ActionController::Base.logger = nil
ActionController::Routing::Routes.reload rescue nil
```

Finally come the test controller and test case—these follow much the same format as Rails functional tests, as we have done all of the setup manually.

```
class SslRequirementController < ActionController::Base
  include SslRequirement

  ssl_required :a, :b
  ssl_allowed :c

  # action definitions...
end
```

```
class SslRequirementTest < Test::Unit::TestCase
  def setup
    @controller = SslRequirementController.new
    @request    = ActionController::TestRequest.new
    @response   = ActionController::TestResponse.new
  end

  # tests...
end
```

The Deadlock Retry plugin, another standard Rails plugin designed to retry dead-locked database transactions, provides a good example of how to stub out an ActiveRecord model class:[*]

```
class MockModel
  def self.transaction(*objects, &block)
    block.call
  end

  def self.logger
    @logger ||= Logger.new(nil)
  end

  include DeadlockRetry
end
```

This allows simple features to be tested without introducing a database dependency:

```
def test_error_if_limit_exceeded
  assert_raise(ActiveRecord::StatementInvalid) do
    MockModel.transaction { raise ActiveRecord::StatementInvalid,
                            DEADLOCK_ERROR }
  end
end
```

Testing Plugin Database Dependencies

The semantics of some plugins makes them difficult to test without relying on a database. But while you would like your tests to run everywhere, you cannot depend on a particular DBMS being installed. Additionally, you want to avoid requiring your users to create a test database in order to test a plugin.

Scott Barron has come up with a clever solution, which he uses in his acts_as_state_machine plugin[†] (a plugin to assign states to ActiveRecord model objects, such as pending, shipped, and refunded orders). The solution is to allow the user to test with any DBMS, and fall back to SQLite (which is widely installed) if none is chosen.

---

[*] I would call this a stub, not a mock object, though some do not make the distinction. A stub tends to be "dumb" and has no test-related logic—it only serves to reduce external dependencies. A mock is much smarter and has knowledge of the test environment. It may keep track of its own state or know whether it is "valid" with respect to the test cases that interact with it.

† *http://elitists.textdriven.com/svn/plugins/acts_as_state_machine/trunk*

To make this work, a set of test model objects and corresponding fixtures are included in the plugin's *test/fixtures* directory. The plugin also includes a database schema backing the models (*schema.rb*) and some statements in *test_helper.rb* that load the fixtures into the database. The full test directory structure is shown in Figure 3-2.

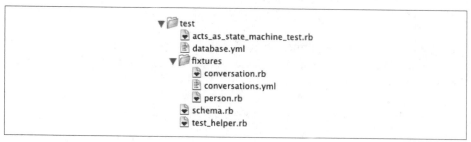

Figure 3-2. Plugin testing directory structure

The first piece of the puzzle is the *database.yml* file, which includes not only configuration blocks for standard DBMSs, but also for SQLite and SQLite3, which save their database in a local file:

```
sqlite:
  :adapter: sqlite
  :dbfile: state_machine.sqlite.db
sqlite3:
  :adapter: sqlite3
  :dbfile: state_machine.sqlite3.db
# (postgresql and mysql elided)
```

The schema files, fixtures, and models are self-explanatory; they are a Ruby schema file, YAML fixtures, and ActiveRecord model classes, respectively. The real magic happens in *test_helper.rb*, which ties everything together.

The test helper first sets up Rails load paths and loads ActiveRecord. Then it loads *database.yml* and instructs ActiveRecord to connect to the database (defaulting to SQLite):

```
config = YAML::load(IO.read(File.dirname(__FILE__) + '/database.yml'))
ActiveRecord::Base.logger = Logger.new(File.dirname(__FILE__) + "/debug.log")
ActiveRecord::Base.establish_connection(config[ENV['DB'] || 'sqlite'])
```

Next, the schema file is loaded into the database:

```
load(File.dirname(__FILE__) + "/schema.rb") if
  File.exist?(File.dirname(__FILE__) + "/schema.rb")
```

Finally, the plugin's fixture path is set as TestCase's fixture path and added to the load path so that models in that directory will be recognized:

```
Test::Unit::TestCase.fixture_path = File.dirname(__FILE__) + "/fixtures/"
$LOAD_PATH.unshift(Test::Unit::TestCase.fixture_path)
```

Now, the test (*acts_as_state_machine_test.rb*) can reference ActiveRecord classes and their fixture data just as in a standard Rails unit test.

Further Reading

Geoffrey Grosenbach has a two-part article on Rails plugins, including some information on writing plugins. The two parts are available from the following:

http://nubyonrails.com/articles/the-complete-guide-to-rails-plugins-part-i
http://nubyonrails.com/articles/the-complete-guide-to-rails-plugins-part-ii

CHAPTER 4

Database

All non-trivial abstractions, to some degree, are leaky.
—Joel Spolsky

For many developers, Rails starts with the database. One of the most compelling features of Rails is ActiveRecord, the object-relational mapping (ORM) layer. ActiveRecord does such a good job of hiding the gory details of SQL from the programmer that it almost seems like magic.

However, as Joel Spolsky says, all abstractions are leaky. There is no perfectly transparent ORM system, and there never will be, due to the fundamentally different nature of the object-oriented and relational models. Ignore the underlying database at your own peril.

Database Management Systems

The Rails community has been built around the MySQL database management system (DBMS*) for years. However, there are still a lot of misconceptions surrounding DBMSs, especially when used with Rails. While MySQL has its place, it is certainly not the only option. In the past few years, support for other databases has vastly grown. I encourage you to keep an open mind throughout this chapter, and weigh all criteria before making a decision on a DBMS.

Rails supports many DBMSs; at the time of this writing, DB2, Firebird, FrontBase, MySQL, OpenBase, Oracle, PostgreSQL, SQLite, Microsoft SQL Server, and Sybase are supported. You will probably know if you need to use a DBMS other than the ones mentioned here. Check the RDoc for the connection adapter for any caveats specific to your DBMS; some features such as migrations are only supported on a handful of connection adapters.

---

* Informally, DBMSs are often referred to as "databases." Consistent with industry practices, in this book "database management system" refers to the software package or installation thereof, while "database" refers to the actual data set being managed.

PostgreSQL

I list PostgreSQL* first because it is my platform of choice. It is one of the most advanced open source databases available today. It has a long history, dating back to the University of California at Berkeley's Ingres project from the early 1980s. In contrast to MySQL, Postgres has supported advanced features such as triggers, stored procedures, custom data types, and transactions for much longer.

PostgreSQL's support for concurrency is more mature than MySQL's. Postgres supports multiversion concurrency control (MVCC), which is even more advanced than row-level locking. MVCC can isolate transactions, using timestamps to give each concurrent transaction its own snapshot of the data set. Under the *Serializable* isolation level, this prevents such problems as dirty reads, nonrepeatable reads, and phantom reads.† See the upcoming sidebar, "Multiversion Concurrency Control," for more information about MVCC.

One advantage that PostgreSQL may have in the enterprise is its similarity to commercial enterprise databases such as Oracle, MS SQL Server, or DB2. Although Postgres is not by any means a clone or emulation of any commercial database, it will nevertheless be familiar to programmers and DBAs who have experience with one of the commercial databases. It will also likely be easier to migrate an application from Postgres to (say) Oracle than from MySQL to Oracle.

PostgreSQL has an unfortunate reputation for being slow. It got this reputation because the default configuration is optimized for performance on a tiny machine. Therefore, it will perform fairly consistently out of the box on a server with as little as 64 MB of RAM or as much as 64 GB. Like any database, Postgres must be tuned for any serious use. The official documentation at *http://www.postgresql.org/docs/* has lots of great information on performance tuning.

One disadvantage of using PostgreSQL is that it has a smaller community around it. There are more developers, especially in the Rails world, working with MySQL. There are more tested solutions built around MySQL than PostgreSQL. The company behind MySQL, MySQL AB, provides commercial support for its product. There is no such centralized support structure for Postgres, as there is no single company behind PostgreSQL; however, there are several companies that specialize in Postgres consulting and provide support contracts.

---

* Technically pronounced "post-gres-Q-L," and usually just called "Postgres." This is a contender for the least intuitive name in computing today. It has its roots in PostgreSQL's long-ago predecessor, Postgres, which did not support SQL.

† For a detailed look at how Postgres handles concurrency, including a summary of the potential problems and how Postgres handles them, see the documentation at *http://www.postgresql.org/docs/8.2/interactive/transaction-iso.html*.

Multiversion Concurrency Control

Multiversion concurrency control (MVCC) is one of the most powerful ways to achieve isolation between concurrent database transactions. MVCC gives each transaction a snapshot of the data it accesses, as the data existed at the start of the transaction. The transaction performs actions on the data, which are logged with timestamps. When the transaction commits, the DBMS checks the logs to ensure there are no conflicts with other transactions; if the transaction can be performed successfully, it is applied to the database at once, atomically.

The alternative to MVCC is row-level locking, which is used by MySQL's InnoDB storage engine. Row-level locking locks only those rows affected by an update during a transaction (as opposed to page- or table-level locking, which are more coarse). The primary advantage that MVCC has over locking is that MVCC does not block readers. Since all update transactions are applied atomically, the database is always in a consistent state. Pending transactions are stored as logs alongside the database to be written upon commit, rather than being applied to the database in the middle of the transaction. The most significant consequence of this is that reads never block, since they are read from the database, which is always consistent.

It is important to realize that isolation for concurrent transactions usually trades off against performance. MVCC uses more storage space than locking because it has to store a snapshot for each in-progress transaction. And though MVCC never blocks reads, the DBMS may roll back update transactions if they cause a conflict.

MySQL

The MySQL DBMS is controversial. Some hold it to be a toy, while others consider it to be a good foundation for web applications. Nevertheless, MySQL is the dominant DBMS in use for Rails web applications today, and it has improved greatly between versions 3 and 5.

Part of the Rails scalability mantra is "shared nothing": each application server should be able to stand on its own. Thus, you can throw five of them behind a load balancer and it doesn't matter if a user is served by different servers throughout the course of a session. However, the bottleneck is the database. A big assumption of this shared-nothing architecture is that the application servers all share a database. If you use a database that doesn't have great support for concurrency, you will have problems.

Old versions of MySQL had some fairly serious issues, many revolving around the issue of data integrity and constraints. The problem was not so much that the issues existed as that MySQL's developers seemed to have an attitude of "you aren't going to need it." Even transactions are not supported with the default storage engine (MyISAM) to this day. In versions prior to 5.0, there were many bugs that would silently discard incorrect data rather than raising an error. To be fair, new versions of MySQL are addressing a lot of its issues. I would still recommend PostgreSQL as a general rule where speed is not the primary criterion, since it has had enterprise-level features for much longer. If you use MySQL, take these recommendations:

- Use version 5.0 or later. Many of the issues that existed with previous versions have been fixed or improved in 5.0 and newer versions.

- Use InnoDB for absolutely anything where data integrity or concurrency matter. MyISAM, the default engine on most MySQL installations, does not support features that most RDBMSs consider essential: foreign key constraints, row-level locking, and transactions. In most business environments, these features are non-negotiable. InnoDB is a journaled storage engine that is much more resilient to failures. Rails does the right thing here and defaults to the InnoDB storage engine when creating tables.

  Unfortunately, InnoDB can be much slower than MyISAM, and the table sizes are usually several times larger. MyISAM is usually faster when reads vastly outnumber writes or vice versa, while InnoDB is generally faster when reads and writes are balanced. It all comes down to the requirements of the specific application; these are general rules. You should always benchmark with your real data, and an accurate sample of queries and statements you will be issuing, in a realistic environment.

  There are a few exceptions to this guideline: MyISAM may be a better choice if you need full-text indexing (which is only supported on MyISAM tables at this time). In addition, if raw speed of reads or writes is the primary concern, MyISAM can help. For example, a logging server for web analytics might use MyISAM tables: you want to be able to dump logs into it as fast as possible, and reads are performed far less often than writes.

- Set the SQL mode to TRADITIONAL. This can be accomplished with the following command:

  ```
  SET GLOBAL sql_mode='TRADITIONAL';
  ```

  This will make MySQL a little bit more strict, raising errors on incorrect data rather than silently discarding it.

MySQL does have some clear advantages over PostgreSQL in some situations. On the whole, MySQL tends to be faster. For many web applications, query speed may be the most important factor. MySQL also has more stable, tested replication and clustering options available. MySQL is also somewhat better at handling binary data stored in the database (we discuss this at length later in the chapter). For many web applications, MySQL may be a clear win.

SQLite

SQLite is a minimalist database that is excellent for small projects. Although it does not support many fancy features, it is a great choice for projects that will not grow very large. It supports ACID transactions* out of the box. SQLite is a library that is linked into your program; there is no server process to speak of. The library code residing in your application's process space accesses a database file.

SQLite provides no concurrency, as there is no server process to enforce the ACID properties. Therefore, it uses file-level locking: the entire database file is locked at the filesystem level during a transaction. Still, for many small applications, it fits the bill perfectly. It is a good replacement for data that may have been stored in flat files, as it supports most of the SQL-92 standard and would be easy to migrate to a more traditional DBMS as needs grow.

Microsoft SQL Server

Though Rails grew up in the Linux/Unix world, it has developed great community support for the Windows platform as well. Not only are Microsoft SQL Server database connections supported in Rails, there are also provisions for connecting to SQL Server from a Linux-based systems as well, using the FreeTDS library.†

From a Windows client, the standard approach is to use Ruby-DBI (a Ruby database-independent adapter) with ADO. The configuration looks like this:

```
development:
  adapter: sqlserver
  host: server_name
  database: my_db
  username: user
  password: pass
```

Your configuration may vary, depending on the version of SQL Server and the ADO libraries you have installed. Once the database configuration is in place, the standard ActiveRecord API methods can be used to manipulate data.

Oracle

Rails supports Oracle versions 8i, 9i, and 10g through the ruby-oci8 library,‡ which supports the OCI8 API. Windows, Linux, and OS X are supported as clients. The connection configuration is fairly standard, using oci as the connection adapter name.

---

* ACID stands for Atomic, Consistent, Isolated, and Durable, which are necessary properties for transactional integrity within a database. See http://en.wikipedia.org/wiki/ACID for a full definition and explanation.

† Instructions are at http://wiki.rubyonrails.org/rails/pages/HowtoConnectToMicrosoftSQLServerFromRailsOnLinux; FreeTDS is available from http://www.freetds.org/.

‡ http://rubyforge.org/projects/ruby-oci8/

However, the Oracle client library still maps net service names to connection speci-fications, so the `host` parameter provides a service name rather than a physical hostname:

```
development:
  adapter: oci
  host: ORCL
  username: user
  password: pass
```

The `ORCL` in the preceding configuration corresponds to an entry in the *TNSNAMES. ORA* file, which will look something like this:

```
ORCL =
  (DESCRIPTION =
    (ADDRESS_LIST =
      (ADDRESS = (PROTOCOL = TCP)(HOST = srv)(PORT = 1521))
    )
    ...
  )
```

Alternatively, you can provide the connection specification on one line with the Rails database configuration:

```
development:
  adapter: oci
  host: (DESCRIPTION = (ADDRESS_LIST = (...)))
  username: user
  password: pass
```

The connection setup is the hardest part. Once the database is connected, Rails sup-ports Oracle connections just as it does connections to any other DBMS. Stored pro-cedures and other Oracle-specific syntax are available through the standard methods that expose an SQL interface, such as `ActiveRecord::Base.find_by_sql`.

Large/Binary Objects

Sooner or later, many web applications must deal with the issue of LOB (large object) data. LOB data may be small, but it is usually large compared to other attributes being stored (tens of kilobytes to hundreds of gigabytes or larger). The defin-ing characteristic of LOB data, however, is that the application has no knowledge of the semantics of the internal structure of the data.

The canonical example is image data; a web application usually has no need to know the data in a JPEG file representing a user's avatar as long as it can send it to the client, replace it, and delete it when needed.

LOB storage is usually divided into CLOB (character large object) for text data and BLOB (binary large object) for everything else. Some DBMSs separate the two as sep-arate data types. CLOB types can often be indexed, collated, and searched; BLOBs cannot.

Database Storage

The DBA types among us might prefer database storage of large objects. From a theoretical standpoint, storing binary data in the database is the most clean and straightforward solution. It offers some immediate advantages:

- All of your application data is in the same place: the database. There is only one interface to the data, and one program is responsible for managing the data in all its forms.

- You have greater flexibility with access control, which really helps when working with large-scale projects. DBMS permitting, different permissions may be assigned to different tables within the same database.

- The binary data is not tied to a physical file path; when using filesystem storage, you must update the file paths in the referring database if you move the storage location.

There are many practical considerations, though, depending on your DBMS's implementation of large objects.

PostgreSQL

PostgreSQL has some downright weird support for binary data. There are two ways to store binary data in a PostgreSQL database: the BYTEA data type and large objects.

The BYTEA[*] type is the closest thing PostgreSQL has to a BLOB type—just a sequence of bytes—but it is really terrible for large amounts of binary data. The protocol for shuttling BYTEA types back and forth from the database requires escaping all non-printable bytes, so a single null byte would be encoded as the ASCII string \000 (4 bytes). Needless to say, this causes unnecessary expansion of the data. In addition, it is impossible to stream data from the database to the web browser without running it through an unescape filter. Pulling a 2 MB binary file from the database usually means streaming somewhere around 6 MB of data through the unescape code.[†] The naïve method runs all of the data through Ruby strings, where it balloons tremendously in memory. A better option would be to have the postgres C library handle quoting and unquoting, but this is a lot of work and still suboptimal. Up to 1 GB of data can be stored in a BYTEA column.

The other option is large objects. The large object features in PostgreSQL work well enough, but they are also a little bit clunky. Files are kept in the pg_largeobject system catalog in small pages.[‡] A pointer is kept in the referring table to the OID (object ID) of the file. Up to 2 GB of data may be stored in a large object. This method is fast, and has good APIs, but there are drawbacks. There is no per-table or per-object access control;

---

[*] Short for "byte array."

[†] Assuming fairly uniform binary data, the BYTEA quoting rules lead to an average expansion ratio of 1:2.9.

[‡] The size is defined in LOBLKSIZE. It defaults to 2 KB.

the `pg_largeobject` catalog is global to the database, and accessible by anyone with permission to connect to the database. The large object mechanism is also slightly deprecated in favor of in-table storage, as the TOAST storage technique allows values of up to 1 GB in length to be stored directly as attributes within the table.

My recommendation is to use filesystem storage for all binary objects if you use PostgreSQL. Although the database might be the more proper place for this type of data, it just does not work well enough yet. If you have to use the database, large objects actually perform pretty well. Avoid BYTEA at all costs.

MySQL

MySQL does a fairly good job with binary data. LOB-type columns (including the TEXT types) can store up to 4 GB of data, using the LONGBLOB type. Actual storage and performance depend on the wire protocol being used, buffer size, and available memory. Storage is efficient, using up to 4 bytes to store the data length, followed by the binary data itself. However, MySQL suffers from issues similar to PostgreSQL with streaming data, and it is always more awkward for a web application to stream data from the database than from the filesystem.

Oracle

Oracle supports the BLOB data type, for objects up to 4 GB. It is supported by a fairly mature API, and can be used directly from Rails.

Oracle also provides the BFILE type, which is a pointer to a binary file on disk. Consider it a formalization of the filesystem storage method discussed below. This may prove to be of value in some situations.

Filesystem Storage

The reality is that filesystem storage is the best option, as a general rule. Filesystems are optimized to handle large amounts of binary and/or character data, and they are fast at it. The Linux kernel has syscalls such as `sendfile( )` that work on physical files. There are hundreds of third-party utilities that you can only leverage when using physical files:

- Image processing is arguably the most popular application for storing binary data. Programs like ImageMagick are much easier to use in their command-line form, operating on files, rather than getting often-problematic libraries like RMagick to work with Ruby.
- Physical files can be shared with NFS or AFS, put on a MogileFS host, or otherwise clustered. Achieving high availability or load balancing with database large objects can be tricky.
- Any other utility that works on files will have to be integrated or otherwise modified to work from a database.

Why Is Filesystem Storage So Fast?

The short answer is that web servers are optimized for throwing binary files down a TCP socket. And the most common thing you do with binary files is throw them down a TCP socket.

Long answer: the secret to this performance, under Linux and various BSDs, is the kernel sendfile( ) syscall (not to be confused with X-Sendfile, discussed later). The sendfile( ) function copies data quickly from a file descriptor (which represents an open file) to a socket (which is connected to the client). This happens in kernel mode, not user mode—the entire process is handled by the operating system. The web server doesn't even have to think about it. When sendfile( ) is invoked, the process looks a bit like Figure 4-1.

On the other hand, Rails is necessarily involved with the whole process when reading data from the database. The file must be passed, chunk by chunk, from the database to Rails, which creates a response and sends the whole thing (including the file) to the web server. The web server then sends the response to the client. Using sendfile( ) would be impossible here because the data does not exist as a file. The data must be buffered in memory, and the whole operation runs in user mode. The entire file is processed several times by user-mode code, which is a much more complicated process, as shown in Figure 4-2.

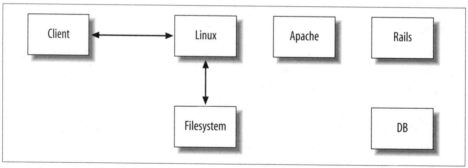

Figure 4-1. Serving files using sendfile()

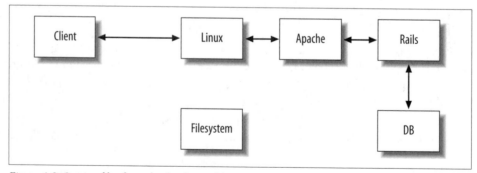

Figure 4-2. Serving files from the database

Sending Data with X-Sendfile

Often you will need to send a file to the client for download after doing some processing in Rails. The most common example is an access-controlled file—you need to verify that the logged-in user has the appropriate level of access before sending the file, for example. The easy way to do this is with the send_file or send_data API calls, which stream data from the server to the client:

```
class DataController < ApplicationController
  before_filter :check_authenticated

  def private_document
    file = File.find params[:id]
    send_file file.path if file
  end

end
```

This method is easy, but it is slow if you are sending static files. Rails reads the file and streams it byte-by-byte to the client. The X-Sendfile protocol makes this easy and fast, by allowing Rails to do its processing but then offloading the "heavy lifting" to the web server (which may offload that processing to the operating system kernel, as described previously).

The X-Sendfile protocol is a very simple standard, first introduced in the Lighttpd web server, which directs the web server to send a file from the filesystem to the client rather than a response generated by the application server. Because the web server is optimized for throwing files at the client, this usually yields a decent speed improvement over reading the file into memory and sending it from Rails with the send_file or send_data API calls.

Because the web server requires access to the file in order to send it to the client, you must use filesystem large object storage. In addition, the files to be sent must have permissions set so as to be accessible to the web server. However, the files should be outside of the web root, lest someone guess a filename and have free access to your private files.

X-Sendfile uses the X-Sendfile HTTP header pointing to the server's path to the file to send, in conjunction with the other standard HTTP headers. A typical response using X-Sendfile would look something like this:

```
X-Sendfile: /home/rails/sample_application/private/secret_codes_69843.zip
Content-Type: application/octet-stream
Content-Disposition: attachment; file="secret_codes.zip"
Content-Length: 654685
```

Assuming the web server is properly configured, it will ignore any response body and stream the file from disk to the client.

From Rails, you can set the response headers by modifying the `response.headers` hash:

```
response.headers['X-Sendfile'] = file_path
response.headers['Content-Type'] = 'application/octet-stream'
response.headers['Content-Disposition'] = "attachment; file=\"#{file_name}\""
response.headers['Content-Length'] = File.size(file_path)
```

Web server configuration

Of course, the front end web server must be properly configured to recognize and process the X-Sendfile header. Mongrel does not support X-Sendfile, as it assumes you will proxy to it from a server more capable of serving static content.

If you are using Lighttpd, it has X-Sendfile support built in. For Lighttpd/FastCGI, just enable the `allow-x-send-file` option in the server configuration:

```
fastcgi.server = (
  ".fcgi" => (
    "localhost" => (
      ...
      "allow-x-send-file" => "enable",
      ...
    )
  )
)
```

If you are using Apache 2, things are a little more complicated (although not by much). You have to install the `mod_xsendfile` module[*] into Apache. There are two configuration flags, both accepting on/off values, which can then be used to control X-Sendfile behavior:

XSendFile
: Determines whether the X-Sendfile header is processed at all.

XsendFileAllowAbove
: Determines whether that header can send files above the path of the request. It defaults to off for security reasons.

Both of these configuration options can be used in any configuration context, down to the *.htaccess* file (per-directory). Best practice dictates that you should only specify XSendFile on in the narrowest possible context. Having X-Sendfile unnecessarily enabled is a security risk, as it allows a server application to send any file that the web server can access to the client.

To my knowledge, there is no way to use X-Sendfile on Apache 1.3 at this time.

---

[*] *http://celebnamer.celebworld.ws/stuff/mod_xsendfile/*

Serving Static Files

One advantage of filesystem storage is that as long as the file data doesn't need to be protected with access control or otherwise acted upon dynamically, you can leverage your static web servers to serve that data. By exporting the storage path via NFS (or a caching filesystem such as AFS to conserve bandwidth), you can share the application's files with the static servers on your content distribution network. This completely removes the load from the application servers and provides a more scalable solution.

Managing Uploads in Rails

Most applications that use large objects must deal with uploads. This can be tricky in any framework, but Rails handles most of the details and there are some best practices to guide you with the rest.

Attachment plugins

One of the easiest ways to handle Rails uploads is to use one of the popular plugins for upload processing. The standard plugin used to be Rick Olson's acts_as_attachment (*http://svn.techno-weenie.net/projects/plugins/acts_as_attachment/*). Many Rails developers are familiar with its interface, and for quite a while it was the standard way to handle uploaded data. However, there were a few factors that made it unsuitable for many applications:

- It is tied to RMagick (and therefore ImageMagick) for image processing. ImageMagick is notoriously difficult to install, primarily because it depends on many backend libraries for processing different image formats. At the time acts_as_attachment was written, ImageMagick was the best option. Now, however, there is a lighter alternative, ImageScience, based on the FreeImage library.

- The entire attachment data must be read into memory and converted to a Ruby string. For large files, this is expensive—Rails passes the application a TempFile, which is slurped into a String. If using filesystem storage, the string is then written back out into a file!

- There is no support for alternative storage methods such as Amazon's S3.

Luckily, there is an alternative. Rick has rewritten acts_as_attachment to resolve these issues. The rewrite is called attachment_fu, and it is publicly available at *http://svn.techno-weenie.net/projects/plugins/attachment_fu/*.

The attachment_fu library supports all of acts_as_attachment's options and more. It can use RMagick as a processor, but it also supports MiniMagick (a lightweight alternative to RMagick that still wraps ImageMagick) and ImageScience. It can store attachments in a database, the filesystem, or S3 out of the box. It also has great facilities for expansion; it is easy to write your own processor or storage backend. A typical use of attachment_fu looks like this:

```
class UserAvatar < ActiveRecord::Base
  belongs_to :user
  has_attachment :content_type => :image,
                 :max_size => 100.kilobytes,
                 :storage => :file_system,
                 :resize_to => [100, 100]
end
```

Attachment_fu is almost completely backward-compatible with acts_as_attachment. Simply change the acts_as_attachment method call to has_attachment. Of course, complete API documentation is provided with the plugin as RDoc.

Rolling your own

The attachment plugins are powerful, but they cannot do everything. If you do decide to do your own upload processing, here are some things to take into account:

- You must validate the uploaded data. What constitutes a valid file upload? Are there restrictions on the size of the uploaded data (minimum or maximum size)? Must the uploaded file have a certain MIME type or extension?

- Rails can hand you any of several different types of objects, depending on what was uploaded and its size. James Edward Gray II has an article[*] on how to correctly and efficiently handle all cases.

- Ensure that files can be cloned properly when the associated record is cloned. (In the case of filesystem storage, this should just be a FileUtils.cp call.)

- Make sure that you delete the file from storage when the record is deleted. This can be done with an after_destroy callback on the model. In the case of database storage, you may find it more efficient to use a trigger or rule.

Upload progress

One feature that many applications require is upload progress notification: showing the user a progress bar that indicates how much of the file has been uploaded. This is surprisingly hard and server-dependent, but there are tools to make it easier. For simplicity, we will restrict discussion in this section to the Mongrel application server.

Mongrel serializes Rails requests; at any given time, a single Mongrel process can only execute one Rails request. This is required because ActionController is not thread-safe. But upload progress requires two simultaneous requests: the upload itself as well as AJAX requests to check its progress. How do we reconcile this?

The answer is that Mongrel is very conservative about what it locks; it only serializes requests while they are actually executing controller code. While the file is being transferred, Mongrel buffers it into memory, but during that time it allows other

---

[*] http://cleanair.highgroove.com/articles/2006/10/03/mini-file-uploads

requests to complete. When the file transfer completes, Mongrel processes that Rails request all at once, only locking during the time the Rails code executes.

The `mongrel_upload_progress` gem hooks into Mongrel to provide a shared variable that the multiple requests can use to communicate about the status of file uploads. This variable is accessible to the Rails handler as `Mongrel::Uploads`. A simple Rails action (called via AJAX) calls `Mongrel::Uploads.check(upload_id)` to check the status and update the client.

Though all of this complication makes it possible to use just one Mongrel process, most moderately trafficked applications will require multiple Mongrels. All actual Rails requests are still serialized, so the number of requests being processed in Rails concurrently is limited to the number of Mongrel processes. However, the shared-memory solution used previously does not work with more than one Mongrel—each Mongrel is a separate process and they have no shared memory.

The solution is to use DRb (Distributed Ruby). A background process is started as a shared repository for upload status. Each upload handler notifies the background process of its status via DRb as it receives blocks from the file. The Rails handlers can then query the common backend for the status of any file, regardless of which Mongrel handled the original upload or status request.

The upload progress gem can be installed with `gem install mongrel_upload_progress`. A sample Rails application illustrating how to use the gem is located at *http://svn.techno-weenie.net/projects/mongrel_upload_progress/*. The official Mongrel upload progress documentation is available at *http://mongrel.rubyforge.org/docs/upload_progress.html*.

Advanced Database Features

Among Rails programmers, advanced database features are often a point of contention. Some contend that constraints, triggers, and procedures are essential; some shun them completely, saying that intelligence belongs in the application only. I am sympathetic to the argument that all business logic belongs in the application; it is nearly impossible to make agile changes to changing requirements when logic is split between two locations. Still, I believe that constraints, triggers, and even stored procedures have their place in enterprise applications. In order to explain why, we'll have to examine a distinction that comes up often in relation to this debate: the difference between application and integration databases.

Application Versus Integration Databases

Martin Fowler differentiates between application databases and integration databases.* The basic distinction is that an integration database is shared among many applications, while an application database "belongs" to the one application using it.

---

* *http://www.martinfowler.com/bliki/DatabaseStyles.html*

In this sense, "application" can mean one program or multiple programs within an application boundary (the same logical application). Usually this distinction refers to how the schema is organized; in Rails, integration databases are often referred to as databases with "legacy schemas." In application databases, integration can still be performed through messaging at the application layer rather than the database layer.

Rails is opinionated about how your database schemas should be structured: the primary key should be id, foreign keys should be thing_id, and table names should be plural. This is not database bigotry; Rails has to choose a sensible default for the "convention over configuration" paradigm to be effective. It is relatively painless to change almost any of these defaults. Rails plays nice with integration databases.

Many Rails developers shun integration databases as unnecessary; they maintain that all integration should be done at the application layer. Some take that a step further and state that data integrity checking belongs in the application only, to keep all business logic in the same place. Although this might be ideal, the real world is not always that nice. Even if all integration can be done at the application level, there are still plenty of valid reasons to use database constraints.

In addition, most databases in the enterprise tend to become integration databases over time. Databases that are useful for one purpose are often appropriated for another use. Sometimes you have a database that isn't under your control, and you want to use the data without performing a full ETL (extract, transform, load). Even running a small script against your database without using the ActiveRecord model, or maintaining the database manually through a console client such as mysql or psql, means you have something accessing your database outside of your domain model. If the validations in the domain are the only way to ensure that the data is consistent, this may lead to problems.

Constraints

Database-level constraints provide a way to explicitly specify an application's implicit assumptions about its data. There are two types of constraints, which should not be confused:

Business logic
> "A manager may not manage more than five employees." The key characteristic of business logic constraints is that they could conceivably change throughout the lifetime of the database. Business logic constraints should never be in the database, barring a very good reason to the contrary.

Integrity
> "U.S. Social Security numbers, when provided, must contain exactly nine digits." Integrity constraints define the nature of the data being represented. Admittedly, "the nature of the data" is a somewhat nebulous concept; the meaning will differ between databases. Integrity constraints must reside in the database, if for no other reason than to provide a last-level sanity check on the data.

As with any other area of data modeling, there are gray areas. An example would be "an employee's salary must be positive," which could conceivably go either way.* The advantage of constraints is that they narrow the domain of possible results the database can generate. When you know the DBMS for an online store can never output a negative price for a product, you can sum the prices for the line items belonging to an order without worrying about invalid prices. Though the line is drawn in different places for different applications, the basic principle is this: *the database should not enforce business logic, but it should enforce consistency and integrity.*

Regardless of differences of opinion on check constraints, one type of constraint is non-negotiable: foreign-key constraints. If a foreign-key relationship is required, an unassociated record is semantically meaningless and must not be allowed to happen. It only makes practical sense to formalize that association.

The only truly robust way to ensure that a database maintains integrity over years as it accumulates data (as databases tend to do) is to declare appropriate constraints on the data. Unless you can say for certain that *every* application or person accessing the database will do so through the domain model (going through all associated validations) every time, the only sensible option is to treat the database as an integration database.

There is a bonus to providing constraints: typically, the more constraints provided on a database, the better job the query optimizer can do at creating a query plan.

A common complaint about database constraints is that they require you to specify semantic information in two places: your database and your application code (you usually want to trap invalid data in your application's validations before attempting to insert it into your database, even if the database would catch the error anyway). The DrySQL library† goes a long way toward removing this duplication. It infers the schema relationships and validation rules from the database's types and constraints, so they don't have to be specified in the application. DrySQL works with all of the major DBMSs: PostgreSQL 8 and up, MySQL 5 and up, SQL Server, Oracle, and DB2.

With DrySQL installed, you can simply require the library in the environment configuration file:

```
require 'drysql'
```

Then, all that is needed is to inform ActiveRecord of the mapping between tables and model classes (even that is not necessary if the tables are named according to the defaults):

```
class Client
  set_table_name "customers"
end
```

---

* I would probably keep that one at the application level, because it contains the business rule that no employee's salary is zero. However, "an employee's salary must be non-negative" would most likely be an integrity constraint, as it is nearly inconceivable that you would "pay" an employee a negative salary.

† *http://drysql.rubyforge.org/*

If the table had been named `clients`, you would not even need the `set_table_name` call. The relationships and constraints will be inferred from the `customers` table's constraints.

Composite Keys

Composite keys, primary keys made up of two or more attributes, are best avoided. Not only are they harder to manage than simple primary keys, they are usually more fragile. The motivation for using composite keys is usually based in some inherently unique aspect of the data, which means the composite key will be meaningful (tied to the data) rather than meaningless (tied to the database only). It is usually much more resilient to assign a meaningless primary key used only within the database. That way, data integrity is internal to the database rather than being tied to an external system or process.

As an example, consider a database that tracks U.S. members by their driver's license numbers. A candidate key would be {*Issuing state*, *License number*}. One immediate advantage of a meaningless key is that integer values are easier to represent than lists; it is easier to refer to a record as `12345` than as [`IL,1234`]. This makes foreign keys much simpler, and it simplifies web services and other protocols used for interoperability.

But the most basic problem is that a primary key is usually treated as a unique, stable identifier for a record. A composite key may not actually be unique in practice and may even change. If you were to use the preceding composite key, you should be prepared to answer questions like:

- What happens when a member moves or has a new license number issued?
- What happens if some inherent characteristic of the key changes? For example, how would you handle it if license numbers were always 9 digits and changed to 10? This is a problem in general with keying off of meaningful data.
- Are you prepared to have every record with a duplicate or missing key rejected? Or might it be desirable to have the system hold invalid data for a time until it is corrected?

There are some valid situations for using composite keys, though. A good example is in multimaster replication. One big problem in asynchronous multimaster replication is synchronizing primary key sequences. If you insert two records at roughly the same time to two master servers, there must be some mechanism to ensure that the two servers issue different values for the primary keys on each record, lest problems ensue when the records are replicated.

The composite-key solution to the problem of multimaster sequences is to issue each server an ID and use that as part of the key; then each server can maintain its own sequence independently of the others. The two records could have primary keys of {*ServerA, 5*} and {*ServerB, 5*} and there would be no conflict. Note that this is a legitimate use of composite keys, since the keys are meaningless (relative to the data being stored in attributes).

For situations such as this, Dr Nic Williams has made composite keys work with ActiveRecord. The `composite_primary_keys` gem is available at *http://compositekeys. rubyforge.org/*.

As an example, consider the multimaster sequence problem discussed previously. We have an `Order` model that is replicated between two servers using multimaster replication. We must use a composite key to ensure unique primary keys regardless of which server an order is created on. First, we install the gem:

```
gem install composite_primary_keys
```

Then, we have to require this library in our application. From Rails, we can include this statement at the end of our environment.rb:

```
require 'composite_primary_keys'
```

The next step is to call the `set_primary_keys(*keys)` method to inform ActiveRecord that we will be using composite keys:

```
class Order < ActiveRecord::Base
  set_primary_keys :node_id, :order_id
end
```

After setting up the composite key, most ActiveRecord operations take place as usual, with the exception that primary keys are now represented by an array rather than an integer.

```
Order.primary_key      # => [:node_id, :order_id]
Order.primary_key.to_s # => "node_id,order_id"
Order.find 1, 5        # => #<Order:0x1234567 @attributes={"node_id"=>"1",
                                                           "order_id"=>"5"}>
```

Even associations work normally; you only have to specify the foreign key explicitly on both sides of the association. To demonstrate this, we can add a `LineItem` model that belongs to a corresponding `Order`.

```
class Order < ActiveRecord::Base
  set_primary_keys :node_id, :order_id
  has_many :line_items, :foreign_key => [:order_node_id, :order_id]
end

class LineItem < ActiveRecord::Base
  set_primary_keys :node_id, :line_item_id
  belongs_to :order, :foreign_key => [:order_node_id, :order_id]
end
```

Note that as in regular associations, the foreign keys are the same on both sides of the association, as there is only one foreign key that defines the relationship (even though, in this case, the foreign key is composed of two attributes). This can be confusing if you don't consider the way the relationship is represented in the schema, because the `foreign_key` option defined in Order's has_many :line_items statement actually refers to attributes of `LineItem`.

As a final touch, we can set things up so that we don't have to worry about the keys at all in code. Remember that the original reason for using composite keys was to allow us to use independent sequences on each database server. First, we create those sequences in SQL when creating the tables. The way we set this up is DBMS-specific; the PostgreSQL syntax would be:

```
CREATE SEQUENCE orders_order_id_seq;
CREATE TABLE orders(
  node_id integer not null,
  order_id integer not null default nextval('orders_order_id_seq'),
  (other attributes)
  PRIMARY KEY (node_id, order_id)
);

CREATE SEQUENCE line_items_line_item_id_seq;
CREATE TABLE line_items(
  node_id integer not null,
  line_item_id integer not null default nextval('line_items_line_item_id_seq'),

  -- FK to orders
  order_node_id integer not null,
  order_id integer not null,

  (other attributes)
  PRIMARY KEY (node_id, line_item_id)
);
```

When we execute this DDL on all database nodes and enable replication between them, each node has its own sequence independent of the others. Now we just have to make sure that each node uses its own node ID. We could either do this in the database with column defaults (if we can use different DDL for each node) or in the application with a before_create callback (if each application accesses only one node).

Triggers, Rules, and Stored Procedures

Now we're in dangerous territory. Let it be known that you should probably have a good reason to use triggers, rules, or stored procedures for anything terribly complicated. That is not to say that they have no purpose; they can be lifesavers. But they should be used to address a specific problem or concern, such as the following:

- A complicated process that involves searching through lots of data (such as OLAP or log analysis) can be much faster if offloaded to the database server. As always, profiling is key; premature optimization can cost you execution speed, not just developer time.

- Concerns that have little to do with the application logic, such as audit logs, can usually be safely moved to the database as triggers.

- PostgreSQL can use rules to create updateable views. Unfortunately, this is currently the only way to get updateable views.

- When using Postgres large objects, you should use a trigger to delete the large object when the corresponding record (containing the LOB's OID) is deleted. Consider this a form of referential integrity.

- Extended or non-native types will use stored procedures for access. PostGIS, a geospatial database for Postgres, uses functions to manage spatial data and indexes.

- The TSearch2 library, integrated into PostgreSQL 8.3 and later, uses functions to access full-text indexing functions.

Some applications use stored procedures for all data access, in order to enforce access control. This is definitely not the Rails way. Although it can be made to work, it will be more difficult than directly accessing tables and views. Views provide sufficient access control for most enterprise applications; only use stored procedures if you have to. ActiveRecord can transparently use updateable views as if they were concrete tables.

Examples

Large object deletion

Since PostgreSQL's large objects are decoupled from their associated record, it is useful to set up a simple rule to delete them when the corresponding record is deleted. The rule can be implemented as follows:

```
-- (table name is 'attachments'; LOB OID is 'file_oid')

CREATE RULE propagate_deletes_to_lob AS
  ON DELETE TO attachments
  DO ALSO SELECT lo_unlink(OLD.file_oid) AS lo_unlink
```

Data partitioning

PostgreSQL has a very powerful rule system that can rewrite incoming queries in many ways. One use for this rule system is to implement partitioning, where data from one table is federated into one of several tables depending on some condition. Consider a database of real estate listings. For historical purposes, we may want to keep listings that have expired, been sold, or been removed from the system. However, most of the data being used on a day-to-day basis is derived from listings that are current and for sale.

In addition, the datasets of "current listings" and "all listings" will have differing data needs; the former is likely to be used transactionally while the latter is probably used analytically. It makes sense to store these separately, as they may have different characteristics.

First, we assume that we already have listing data in a table called listings, and it has a status column representing the status of the listing. We create the two tables, current_listings and non_current_listings, which inherit from the main table. This way, we can say SELECT * FROM listings and Postgres will include the data from the two inherited tables automatically.

```
CREATE TABLE current_listings (CHECK (status = 'C'))
  INHERITS (listings);
CREATE TABLE non_current_listings (CHECK (status != 'C'))
  INHERITS (listings);
```

Next, we create rules that rewrite inserts on the parent table to inserts on the proper child:

```
CREATE RULE listings_insert_current AS
  ON INSERT TO listings WHERE (status = 'C')
  DO INSTEAD INSERT INTO current_listings VALUES(NEW.*);
CREATE RULE listings_insert_non_current AS
  ON INSERT TO listings WHERE (status != 'C')
  DO INSTEAD INSERT INTO non_current_listings VALUES(NEW.*);
```

Now that the rules are set up, we move the existing data in listings to the proper subtable:

```
INSERT INTO current_listings SELECT * FROM listings WHERE STATUS = 'C';
INSERT INTO non_current_listings SELECT * FROM listings WHERE STATUS != 'C';
DELETE FROM listings;
```

We know that the DELETE statement is safe because no new data has been inserted into the listings table, thanks to the rewrite rules. This is why it is important that the partition conditions are a proper partitioning such as status = 'C' and status != 'C' (non-overlapping and completely covering all possibilities). This ensures that every row is inserted into one of the child tables, not the parent. Note that this would not be a proper partitioning if the status column allowed NULL values, as both conditions would be false.

Now we can insert and select data against listings as if it were one table, while PostgreSQL transparently handles the partitioning and works with the proper partition. This is a very simple example. In particular, we need to implement rules for UPDATE and DELETE queries before using this scheme. This method can easily be extended to many partitions, even on complicated conditions.

Connecting to Multiple Databases

Occasionally, you will have the need to connect to several different databases from one application. This is useful for migrating from an old schema to a new one. It is also helpful if you have differing data requirements within one application; perhaps some data is more critical and is stored on a high-availability database cluster. In any case, it is easy in Rails. First, specify multiple database environments in the *database.yml* configuration file:

```
legacy:
  adapter: mysql
  database: my_db
  username: user
  password: pass
  host: legacy_host

new:
  adapter: mysql
  database: my_db
  username: user
  password: pass
  host: new_host
```

Then, you can simply refer to these configuration blocks from the ActiveRecord class definition using the `ActiveRecord::Base.establish_connection` method:

```
class LegacyClient < ActiveRecord::Base
  establish_connection "legacy"
end

class Client < ActiveRecord::Base
  establish_connection "new"
end
```

This approach also works with multiple Rails environments. Just specify each environment in the *database.yml* file as usual:

```
legacy_development:
  # ...

legacy_test:
  # ...

legacy_production:
  # ...

new_development:
  # ...

new_test:
  # ...

new_production:
  # ...
```

Then, use the `RAILS_ENV` constant in the database configuration block name:

```
class LegacyClient < ActiveRecord::Base
  establish_connection "legacy_#{RAILS_ENV}"
end

class Client < ActiveRecord::Base
  establish_connection "new_#{RAILS_ENV}"
end
```

You can go one step further and DRY this code up by using class inheritance to define which database an `ActiveRecord` class belongs to:

```
class LegacyDb < ActiveRecord::Base
  self.abstract_class = true
  establish_connection "legacy_#{RAILS_ENV}"
end

class NewDb < ActiveRecord::Base
  self.abstract_class = true
  establish_connection "new_#{RAILS_ENV}"
end

class LegacyClient < LegacyDb
end

class Client < NewDb
end
```

The `self.abstract_class = true` statements tell ActiveRecord that the `LegacyDb` and `NewDb` classes cannot be instantiated themselves; since they represent database connections, they are not backed by concrete tables in the database.

Magic Multi-Connections

Dr Nic Williams's Magic Multi-Connections gem (*http://magicmodels.rubyforge.org/magic_multi_connections/*) allows you to connect to different databases concurrently from the same application. This is very useful when using one master and several read-only slaves serving the same models. The syntax is transparent; it uses module namespaces and imports the models (`ActiveRecord::Base` subclasses) into the namespaces.

For a single-master situation, you could define another database connection in *database.yml* for the read slave:

```
read_slave:
  adapter: postgresql
  database: read_only_production
  username: user
  password: pass
  host: read_slave_host
```

This database is backed by a module, which mirrors the ActiveRecord classes using this database connection:

```
require 'magic_multi_connections'
module ReadSlave
  establish_connection :read_slave
end
```

Now, all pre-existing models can be accessed through the `read_slave` connection by prefixing the model class with `ReadSlave::`.

```
# use the read-only connection
@user = ReadSlave::User.find(params[:id])

# write to the master (can't use @user.update_attributes because it would
# try to write to the read slave)
User.update(@user.id, :login => "new_login")
```

Caching

If you have far more reads than writes, model caching may help lighten the load on the database server. The standard in-memory cache these days is *memcached*.* Developed for LiveJournal, memcached is a distributed cache that functions as a giant hashtable. Because of its simplicity, it is scalable and fast. It is designed never to block, so there is no risk of deadlock. There are four simple operations on the cache, each completing in constant time.

You can actually use memcached in several different places in Rails. It is available as a session store or a fragment cache store out of the box, assuming the ruby-memcache gem is installed. It can also be used to store complete models—but remember that this will only be effective for applications where reads vastly outnumber writes. There are two libraries that cover model caching: cached_model and acts_as_cached.

The cached_model library (*http://dev.robotcoop.com/Libraries/cached_model/index. html*) provides an abstract subclass of ActiveRecord::Base, CachedModel. It attempts to be as transparent as possible, just caching the simple queries against single objects and not trying to do anything fancy. It does have the disadvantage that all cached models must inherit from CachedModel. Use of cached_model is dead simple:

```
class Client < CachedModel
end
```

On the other hand, the acts_as_cached plugin (*http://errtheblog.com/post/27*) gives you more specificity over what is cached. It feels more like programming against memcached's API, but there is more power and less verbosity. It has support for relationships between objects, and it can even version each key to invalidate old keys during a schema change. A sample instance of acts_as_cached might look like this:

```
class Client < ActiveRecord::Base
  acts_as_cached

  # We have to expire the cache ourselves upon significant changes
  after_save :expire_me
  after_destroy :expire_me

  protected
```

---

* Pronounced "mem-cache-dee," for "memory cache daemon." Available from *http://danga.com/memcached/*.

```
def expire_me
  expire_cache(id)
end
end
```

Of course, the proper solution for you will depend on the specific needs of the application. Keep in mind that any caching is primarily about optimization, and the old warnings against premature optimization always apply. Optimization should always be targeted at a specific, measured performance problem. Without specificity, you don't know what metric you are (or should be) measuring. Without measurement, you don't know when or by how much you've improved it.

Load Balancing and High Availability

Many applications require some form of load balancing and/or high availability. Though these terms are often used together and they can often be obtained by the same methods, they are fundamentally two different requirements. We define them thus:

Load balancing
> Spreading request load over several systems so as to reduce the load placed on a single system.

High availability
> Resiliency to the failure of one or several constituent components; the ability to continue providing services without interruption despite component failure.

These are completely different things, but they are often required and/or provided together. It is important to understand the difference between them in order to properly analyze the requirements of an application. It is possible to provide load balancing without high availability—for example, consider a group of servers presented to the Internet via round-robin DNS. The load is distributed roughly equally over the group of servers, but the system is certainly not highly available! If one server goes down, DNS will still faithfully distribute requests to it, and every one in *N* requests will go unanswered.

Conversely, high availability can be provided without load balancing. High availability necessitates the use of redundant components, but nothing says that those components must be online and in use. A common configuration is the hot spare: a duplicate server that stays powered up but offline, continually monitoring its online twin, ready to take over if necessary. This can actually be more economical than trying to balance requests between the two servers and keep them in sync.

In this section, we review the primary load balancing and high availability solutions for common database management systems.

MySQL

Replication

MySQL has built-in support for master-slave replication. The master logs all transactions to a *binlog* (binary log). During replication, the binlog is replayed on the slaves, which apply the transactions to themselves. The slaves can use different storage engines, which makes this facility useful for ancillary purposes such as backup or full-text indexing. Master-slave replication works well for load balancing in applications where reads outnumber writes, since all writes must be applied to the master.

However, master-slave replication as described does not provide high availability; there is a single master that is a single point of failure. A slave can be promoted to be the master during failover, but the commands to do this must be executed manually by a custom monitoring script. There is currently no facility for automatically promoting a slave. Additionally, all clients must be able to determine which member is currently the master. The MySQL documentation suggests setting up a dynamic DNS entry pointing to the current master; however, this will introduce another potential failure point.

MySQL cluster

The primary high-availability solution for MySQL is the MySQL Cluster technology, available since version 4.1. Cluster is primarily an in-memory database, though as of version 5, disk storage is supported. The Cluster product is based on the NDB storage engine, backed by data nodes.

MySQL Cluster is designed for localized clusters; distributed clusters are not supported as the protocol used between nodes is not encrypted or optimized for bandwidth usage. The interconnect can use Ethernet (100 Mbps or greater) or SCI (Scalable Coherent Interconnect, a high-speed cluster interconnect protocol). It is most effective for clusters with medium to large datasets; the recommended configuration is 1–8 nodes with 16 GB of RAM each.

Because the majority of the data is stored in memory, the cluster must have enough memory to store as many redundant copies of the full working set as the application dictates. This number is called the *replication factor*. With a replication factor of 2, each piece of data is stored on two separate servers, and you can lose only one server out of the cluster without losing data.

For high availability, at least three physical servers must be used: two data nodes and a management node. The management node is needed to arbitrate between the two data nodes if they become disconnected and out of synchronization with each other. A replication factor of 2 is used, so the two data nodes must each have enough memory to hold the working set, unless disk storage is used.

Since the Cluster software is simply a storage engine, the cluster is accessed through a standard MySQL server with tables defined with the NDB backend. The server accesses the cluster to fulfill requests from the client. The overall architecture is shown in Figure 4-3.

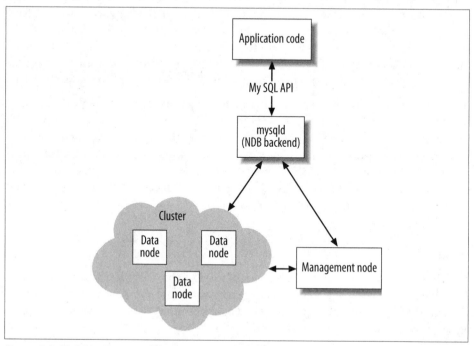

Figure 4-3. MySQL Cluster architecture

Because the mysqld servers only differ from nonclustered servers in their backend, they can be replicated with binlogs just as nonclustered servers can. So, it is possible to achieve long-distance master-slave replication among multiple clusters.

It is also possible to have several mysqld servers accessing the same cluster and serving the same clients for redundancy. In the preceding diagram, the MySQL server is a single point of failure; if it goes down, there is no way for the application to access the cluster. There are three approaches to handling load balancing and failover when multiple MySQL servers are involved:

- Modify the application code to handle failed servers and retry queries to different servers. Each MySQL server will have its own IP address in this scenario.

- Use a separate hardware or software load balancer between the application and the MySQL servers. This will create one Virtual IP address (VIP) that will be directed to one of the physical servers via DNAT. This method is expensive, as you need at least two load balancers for high availability.

- Use a software high-availability solution such as Wackamole (*http://www.backhand.org/wackamole/*). This will expose a pool of virtual IP addresses and ensure that exactly one live server has each IP address at all times. If a server fails, its VIPs are redistributed among those remaining. The pool of VIPs is distributed via a DNS round-robin list, so the application will pick a VIP more or less at random.

PostgreSQL

There are several load-balancing and high-availability options for PostgreSQL. Because there is no single company behind PostgreSQL, the options are provided by different organizations and companies. Each product typically embodies a different replication or clustering paradigm. Some of the options are described in this section.

High availability: Warm standby

Warm standby is a simple way to achieve high availability under PostgreSQL. It takes some configuration, but the configuration is documented well. Warm standby uses the write-ahead log (WAL) that PostgreSQL logs activity to. Changes are written in the WAL prior to being committed, so the database state can be reconstructed even if a transaction is interrupted catastrophically. *Log shipping* is the process of sending the WAL as files from the master to a slave.

Under a warm standby setup, a server is on standby, in restore mode. It is continuously restoring from the primary server, using a restore command that waits for WALs to become available and applies them as soon as they do. If the primary server dies, a monitoring system (which must be provided by the user) designates the standby as the new primary server.

Master-slave replication: Slony-I

Slony-I is a master-slave replication system similar to the replication mechanisms included with MySQL. It supports promoting slaves to masters, but, like MySQL, does not provide any mechanism to detect that nodes have failed.

An upgrade to Slony, Slony-II, is in the very early stages of development now. It plans to provide multimaster synchronous replication for PostgreSQL based on the Spread group-communication framework.

Multimaster replication: PGCluster

PGCluster (*http://pgcluster.projects.postgresql.org/*) is a product that offers multimaster replication and clustering for PostgreSQL. It provides both load balancing and high availability for a database cluster. The software handles failover, and yields a readily available solution if three or more physical servers are used.

PGCluster's replication style is synchronous; updates are propagated to all servers before the update transaction succeeds. Thus, it should only be used in environments where all master servers are at the same location and are always connected. Asynchronous replication, in which changes are propagated to other servers some time after the transaction commits, is generally considered a hard problem. Asynchronous replication is also application-specific, as the proper way to handle conflicts between two committed transactions depends on the application's needs.

Oracle

Oracle's clustering product is Oracle Real Application Clusters (RAC). In contrast to the shared-nothing clustering solutions available for other DBMSs, RAC is a *shared-everything* clustering product. In RAC, multiple Oracle instances access a shared database cluster. The shared-everything architecture depends on a common data store such as a storage area network (SAN).

Oracle supports many flexible replication options, from simple data-only one-way replication to distributed multimaster replication. These solutions are very powerful but also very complicated.

Microsoft SQL Server

Like Oracle, SQL Server has extensive features supporting both replication and clustering. SQL Server even supports "merge replication," which is essentially asynchronous multimaster replication. Of course, both the clustering and replication options require large amounts of configuration.

There is no out-of-the-box load-balancing solution for SQL Server yet; once you have a replicated database, you still must write application code so as to direct requests to the appropriate server.

LDAP

LDAP, the Lightweight Directory Access Protocol, is a database system optimized for user directory information. It is most often used in large organizations, integrated with the enterprise authentication and email systems. However, it is a database in its own right. We do not have space to cover LDAP in detail, but there are many resources available for working with LDAP in Rails.

ActiveLDAP

The ActiveLDAP library (*http://ruby-activeldap.rubyforge.org/*) is an almost drop-in replacement for ActiveRecord that uses LDAP instead of an RDBMS as a backend. To use it from Rails, set up a configuration file, *config/ldap.yml*, as follows:

```
development:
  host: (ldap server name)
  port: 389
  base: dc=mycompany,dc=com
  password: my_password

production:
  ...
```

Then, at the bottom of *config/environment.rb*, set up the connection:

```
ldap_path = File.join(RAILS_ROOT,"config","ldap.yml")
ldap_config = YAML.load(File.read(ldap_path))[RAILS_ENV]
ActiveLDAP::Base.establish_connection(ldap_config)
```

To set up ActiveLDAP, just subclass ActiveLDAP::Base and set the LDAP mapping on a class-by-class basis:

```
class Employee < ActiveLDAP::Base
  ldap_mapping :prefix => "ou=Employees"
end
```

LDAP queries can then be executed using the class methods on ActiveLDAP::Base:

```
@dan = Employee.find :attribute => "cn", :value => "Dan"
```

Authenticating with LDAP

One of the most common reasons for using LDAP is to integrate into an existing authentication structure. If an LDAP server is provided for a Windows domain, this will allow the web application to authenticate users against that domain rather than maintaining its own user models separately.

Set up the *ldap.yml* file as described previously (without specifying a password), but do not bind to the LDAP server from *environment.rb*. We will perform the bind as part of the authentication process. The following code is adapted from the Rails wiki:[*]

```
class LdapUser < ActiveLDAP::Base
  ldap_mapping :prefix => (LDAP prefix for your users)

  LDAP_PATH = File.join(RAILS_ROOT,"config","ldap.yml")
  LDAP_CONFIG = YAML.load(File.read(ldap_path))[RAILS_ENV]

  def self.authenticate username, password
    begin
      ActiveLDAP::Base.establish_connection(config.merge(
        :bind_format => "uid=#{username},cn=users,dc=mycompany,dc=com",
        :password => password,
        :allow_anonymous => false
      ))
      ActiveLDAP::Base.close
      return true
```

---

[*] *http://wiki.rubyonrails.org/rails/pages/HowtoAuthenticateViaLdap*

```
      rescue ActiveLDAP::AuthenticationError
        return false
      end
    end
  end
```

Authentication is then very simple:

```
LdapUser.authenticate "my_username", "password" # => true or false
```

Further Reading

Chris Date's *Database in Depth* (O'Reilly) is a very accessible introduction to relational theory aimed at software developers who are experienced in the use of relational databases. It reintroduces readers into the technical foundations behind the relational model.

Theo Schlossnagle's *Scalable Internet Architectures* (Sams) is a short but comprehensive treatment of ways to accomplish scalability (both high availability and load balancing are covered); it covers ground from the smallest two-server failover cluster up to global server load balancing.

Both the MySQL manual (*http://dev.mysql.com/doc/*) and the PostgreSQL manual (*http://www.postgresql.org/docs/*) have a wealth of information about general database topics, as well as specific information pertaining to the use of those DBMSs.

## CHAPTER 5

Security

Given a choice between dancing pigs and security,
users will pick dancing pigs every time.
—Ed Felten and Gary McGraw

Security issues are often overlooked on smaller sites or low-traffic applications; unfortunately, the reach of the Web has expanded to a point where end-to-end security is essential on any public-facing web site. There actually are people with nothing better to do than run a distributed denial-of-service attack on "Aunt Edna's Funny Cat Pictures." Nobody can afford to ignore the dangers that face a site simply as a consequence of being accessible on the Internet.

In this chapter, we will take a top-down approach to examining the various security-related issues that plague web application developers. We start by examining the architectural, application-level principles you should keep in mind. Later, we will get progressively more detailed. We will examine the security-related issues you should keep in mind when working at a lower level in Rails.

Application Issues

First, we will examine some important principles that should guide the design of any web application.

Authentication

The most important guideline in the area of authentication is simple:

Always salt and hash all passwords!

There are very few valid exceptions to this rule, and even fewer apply to web applications. The only possible reason to store passwords in plain text is if they must be provided to an external service in plain text. Even then, the passwords should be symmetrically encrypted with a shared secret, to provide defense in depth.

Let's examine the reasoning behind this rule. Hashing passwords prevents them from being recovered if the database or source code is compromised. Salting them protects them from rainbow attacks.

Salting is the process of ensuring that the same password hashes to different values for different users. Consider the following code, which hashes but does not salt.

```
require 'digest/sha1'

$hashes = {}

def hash(password)
  Digest::SHA1.hexdigest(password)
end

def store_password(login, password)
  $hashes[login] = hash(password)
end

def verify_password(login, password)
  $hashes[login] == hash(password)
end

store_password('alice', 'kittens')
store_password('bob',   'kittens')

$hashes # => {"alice"=>"3efd62ee86d4a141c3e671d86ba1579f934cf04d",
        #     "bob"=>  "3efd62ee86d4a141c3e671d86ba1579f934cf04d"}

verify_password('alice', 'kittens') # => true
verify_password('alice', 'mittens') # => false
verify_password('bob',   'kittens') # => true
```

Although this is more secure than storing the passwords in plain text, it is still insecure; anyone who has the hash file can tell that Alice and Bob have the same password.

More importantly, this scheme is vulnerable to a *rainbow attack*. An attacker can precompute *rainbow tables* by running every word in a dictionary through the hash function. He can then compare each hash in the rainbow table to each hash in the password file. Since a password always hashes to the same value, the attacker obtains all the dictionary passwords in one fell swoop.

This attack can be prevented by salting the passwords when hashing them. Compare the following code:

```
require 'digest/sha1'

$hashes = {}
$salts = {}

def hash(password, salt)
  Digest::SHA1.hexdigest("--#{salt}--#{password}--")
end
```

```
def generate_salt(login)
  Digest::SHA1.hexdigest("--#{Time.now.to_s}--#{login}--")
end

def store_password(login, password)
  salt = $salts[login] = generate_salt(login)
  $hashes[login] = hash(password, salt)
end

def verify_password(login, password)
  $hashes[login] == hash(password, $salts[login])
end

store_password('alice', 'kittens')
store_password('bob',   'kittens')

$hashes # => {"alice"=>"955b034a284ed2405c8f1a275e2191484161b1c5",
        #     "bob"=>  "2f7ef18f0f50efd2b8684c49e85befc95509a74f"}
$salts  # => {"alice"=>"0682a0e26655e234ee45ea6a68af8ebd3e2c0eaf",
        #     "bob"=>  "6116fb3dc0e9824b7c99e81f6dac6c17b7a6257b"}

verify_password('alice', 'kittens') # => true
verify_password('alice', 'mittens') # => false
verify_password('bob',   'kittens') # => true
```

This method ensures that the same password will hash to different values with a high probability. The acts_as_authenticated plugin (*http://technoweenie.stikipad.com/plugins/show/Acts+as+Authenticated*) salts passwords by default.

One common reason that people store passwords as plain text is for password recovery. The reality is that storing and sending passwords in plain text is never a good idea. The proper way to recover passwords is to send an email to the user with a link that includes a randomly generated token. The link takes the user to a page that verifies the token and then allows him to enter a new password.

Password hashing in Rails

In a Rails application, there are some standard best practices for working with hashed passwords. First, the database contains attributes for the hashed password and salt:

```
ActiveRecord::Schema.define do
  add_column :users, :crypted_password, :string
  add_column :users, :salt, :string
end
```

 ActiveRecord::Schema.define is a simple way to use Rails schema definition statements from the Rails console or other Rails code outside of migrations. The full set of schema definition methods (see ActiveRecord::ConnectionAdapters::SchemaStatements) is available inside the block.

The User model has a virtual attribute for the unencrypted password, so that you can set the password using the instance method User#password= and it will be hashed automatically. The hashing is performed by a before_save callback:

```
class User < ActiveRecord::Base
  attr_accessor :password

  before_save :encrypt_password

  protected

  def encrypt_password
    return if password.blank?
    self.salt = Digest::SHA1.hexdigest("--#{Time.now.to_s}--#{login}--") if
      new_record?
    self.crypted_password = encrypt(password)
  end

  def encrypt(password)
    Digest::SHA1.hexdigest("--#{salt}--#{password}--")
  end
end
```

The actual authentication is handled by the User.authenticate class method, which takes a login and password and returns either the corresponding user or nil if the login or password are incorrect.

```
class User < ActiveRecord::Base
  def self.authenticate(login, password)
    u = find_by_login(login)
    u && u.authenticated?(password) ? u : nil
  end

  def authenticated?(password)
    crypted_password == encrypt(password)
  end
end
```

Don't Trust the Client

ActionPack (ActionController plus ActionView) makes a lot of things easier for you as a developer. To do so, it abstracts away a lot of the details of the HTTP request/response cycle. This is usually a good thing: you really don't want to deal with every detail of the CGI protocol. But it is important not to let this abstraction get in the way of writing secure code. One of the foundational principles that you should keep in mind is that you can never trust the information that the web browser (the client) sends you.

This is one area where the leaky abstraction that Rails provides can hurt. It really pays to understand how HTTP works, at least to the point that you know whether a particular piece of information comes from the client, the application framework, or the environment. You can never, ever trust anything that comes from the client, because the client can send whatever data it wants. It can insert fake headers, extra parameters, malformed query strings, or whatever it wants. Here is a short list of the pieces of data that cannot be trusted. This is not a complete list, but it should get you thinking.*

- Form parameters (query string and POST data): the most common mistake made in this area is trusting form parameters provided in an HTTP request. We discuss this later in the chapter.
- Cookies (however, we will see an exception later).
- Referer† header, which contains the URI of the page that the current page was linked from. It was included with the intent of helping webmasters track down broken links. Using it for authentication or security purposes is completely backward.
- User-Agent header, which purportedly identifies the name of the client software that is accessing the page. Like Referer, this is primarily useful for log analysis and should never be used for security purposes.

As an example, we can examine poor security design from another platform. PHP has a configuration option, `register_globals`, which can cause some serious security problems when set. When the option is enabled, variables from the query string are added to the global namespace automatically. The dull but pedagogical example is that of user authentication code, which authenticates the user and then shows some secret information depending on the user's level of access:

```php
<?php
  if(authenticated()) {
    $user_id = get_user_id();
  }
?>

...

<?php
  // Show the secret if the user is authenticated
  if($user_id) {
    echo("Soylent Green is people!");
  }
?>
```

With `register_globals` enabled, a malicious user can just access `index.php?user_id=4` and the `$user_id` variable will be set to 4 from the query string. Since we presume the `authenticated()` function returns `false` (as the user is not a legitimate user), the if

---

* Of course, these only represent vulnerable parts at the HTTP protocol level. Later, we will see how vulnerabilities can expose themselves at higher levels. Vulnerabilities at lower levels, such as TCP session hijacking, are usually not the developer's concern.

† Yes, this is a misspelling, but it is too deeply entrenched in HTTP history to change now. Consider it a lesson to protocol designers.

statement is bypassed. When we get to the part of the code that contains the secret, $user_id is still 4, and the secret is revealed even though the user was never success-fully authenticated.

This design leads to huge security problems because the user has the potential to choose the value of any local variable that you do not explicitly set. Fortunately for all, the register_globals option in PHP has been disabled for some time now by default.

Form processing

We have a similar problem in Rails due to a compromise between security and brev-ity of code. Rails supports mass assignment of form parameters to ActiveRecord objects, so that form fields named person[first_name], person[last_name], and person[email] can be used to build an ActiveRecord Person object with one line of code:

```
person = Person.new params[:person]
```

The params[:person] object is a hash mapping attribute names to values, translated from the form parameters courtesy of ActionController:

```
{:first_name => "John", :last_name => "Smith", :email => "john@example.com"}
```

Those parameters are assigned to the Person object, calling the Person#first_name=, Person#last_name=, and Person#email= setters, respectively. It is just as if we had set them individually:

```
person = Person.new
person.first_name = params[:person][:first_name]
person.last_name  = params[:person][:last_name]
person.email      = params[:person][:email]
```

This is a handy shortcut, but it leaves us vulnerable. Suppose someone submits the form with a field named person[access_level]. Remember, the values that they sub-mit need have no relation to the form we send them. By default, this would call Person#access_level= with the value provided in the form. Clearly, we need to pro-tect against this. We can either use the attr_protected or attr_accessible class methods of ActiveRecord::Base. The attr_protected method specifies which attributes may not be assigned to via mass assignment:

```
class Person < ActiveRecord::Base
  attr_protected :access_level
end
```

Conversely, the attr_accessible method specifies which attributes may be assigned to with mass assignment; any attributes not on the list are blocked. This is prefera-ble when the list of attributes may change, as it represents a "default deny" stance. If new attributes are added to the model, they will be blocked by default.

```
class Person < ActiveRecord::Base
  attr_accessible :first_name, :last_name, :email
end
```

Hidden form fields

Rails makes simple CRUD (create, read, update, delete) operations on a single model object so easy that it is easy to ignore the security implications. Here's an example of how *not* to process a form.

app/models/comment.rb
```
class Comment < ActiveRecord::Base
  belongs_to :user
end
```

app/views/comment/new.rhtml
```
<% form_for :comment do |f| %>
  <%= f.hidden_field :user_id %>
  Comment: <%= f.text_field :comment %>
<% end %>
```

app/controllers/comments_controller.rb
```
class CommentsController < ApplicationController
  def new
    @comment = Comment.new :user_id => get_current_user()
  end

  def create
    # Danger Will Robinson!
    @comment = Comment.create params[:comment]
  end
end
```

This looks innocuous enough, but it has one problem: the hidden field is trusted! By not verifying that the params[:comment][:user_id] value received in the create method is sane, we have just allowed anyone to create a comment attached to an arbitrary user.

Rails can only handle so much for you. The params object is CGI-unescaped and parsed into nested hashes, but that's as much as the framework can do for you. Any time you use the params object, realize that it can contain anything the user wants. If you need any stronger guarantees about the content of the params object, you need to use cryptography.

The implications of this are tremendous: every once in a while, some online store gets in trouble for storing prices as hidden form fields, and not validating them when an order is placed. Someone with at least a minimal knowledge of HTTP then teaches them the "don't trust the client" lesson by ordering a few plasma TVs for a dollar each.

Client-side validation

A corollary of these form-processing principles is that validation should always take place on the server. This is not to discount the importance of client-side validation, but the application must be designed to be secure, no matter what is sent at the HTTP level.

It is perfectly OK to validate data at the client. This is useful because when users make mistakes filling out a form, client-side validation saves a round-trip to the server. But if the only thing keeping invalid data out of your application is a piece of JavaScript, malicious users can simply turn off JavaScript and submit your form.

These two methods of validation represent two different perspectives. Client-side validation (if any) should emphasize usability, while server-side validation should be driven by security.

Cookies

In Rails, there is usually no need to deal with raw cookies. The session abstraction provides a way to store data in a way that looks like a cookie but can be trusted. The session store is usually a server-side data store tied to a unique session identifier in a cookie. Because session IDs are sparse and hard to guess, it is a safe assumption that if a user presents a particular session ID, he has access to that session. And since the application code is the only thing that can access the session store, you can trust that the data you read is the same as what you wrote.

There is a new method of session storage, CookieStore, that is now the default in edge Rails and Rails 2.0. It marshals the entire session into a cookie, rather than key-ing a server-side session from a client-side cookie. The idea is that most sessions are small, usually containing only a user ID and flash message. Cookies work fine for this (they usually have a 4 KB limit). Rails ensures data integrity by signing the cookie with a message authentication code (MAC) and raising a `TamperedWithCookie` exception if the data was modified.

Double-check everything

Here is another mistake that is easy to make in Rails. Because the REST philosophy behind Rails encourages resource-based URIs (each URI represents a particular resource or object), it can be easy to overlook security. This happens often when finding a record from the database by primary key—often it is easy to neglect checking for proper ownership. Here is an example that illustrates that problem:

app/models/message.rb
```
class Message < ActiveRecord::Base
  belongs_to :user
end
```
app/controllers/messages_controller.rb
```
class MessagesController < ApplicationController
  def show
    @message = Message.find params[:id]
  end
end
```

That example would allow anyone to read any message, even messages owned by other users. In this case, you probably want to restrict viewing of messages to the users that own them. The proper way to do that is:

```
def show
  @message = Message.find_by_user_id_and_id(current_user.id,
    params[:id])
end
```

This automatically gives you protection against users viewing messages they don't own, by raising a `RecordNotFound` exception.

Secure Fallback

Now that many Rails applications incorporate some amount of AJAX, fallback is an important concern. Depending on your users' needs, either *graceful degradation* (starting with a full-featured site, then testing and fixing for older browsers) or *progressive enhancement* (starting with minimal features and adding features for newer browsers) may be the catch phrase. In either case, developing for older browsers involves *fallback*, or using a less-preferred option when the preferred option fails. It is important that fallback is secure—otherwise, attackers could force the application into fallback mode in order to subvert its weaknesses.

A typical example of fallback on the Web is using a regular form post when a Java-Script form post fails:

```
<form action="/standard_non_ajax_action"
  onsubmit="do_ajax_submit(); return false;">
  ...
</form>
```

When the user has JavaScript enabled, the `do_ajax_submit()` function is called and the standard form post is canceled. Typically, that function will serialize the parameters, send them to the server, and perform some other action. With Rails' `respond_to` methods, you can actually use the same actions for both standard HTML and Java-Script responses, differentiated by the HTTP Accept header.

There is no specific security guidance here, except to review your code and be sure that an attacker cannot bypass your security by using your non-AJAX methods rather than your AJAX ones. Typically, the AJAX methods are the flashiest, best supported, and best tested. They get the most attention, but it is just as important to pay attention to the non-AJAX interfaces.

Avoid Security Through Obscurity

One principle of security is that security through obscurity is no security at all. Security should be inherent in the system, and not depend on an attacker's ignorance of architecture. This descends from Kerckhoffs' principle in cryptography: a system's security should lie only in its key (rather than in the algorithm). This principle can be paraphrased for web applications: your application should be designed so as to remain secure even if your source code, architecture, and configuration (with the obvious exception of passwords and the like) were published for all to see.

This is not to say that you should publish your routes and system architecture; there is no need to aid an attacker. *Defense in depth* (having multiple redundant layers of security) is an important principle as well. But the guiding principle is never to rely on secrecy for security.

Secure Your Error Messages

Error messages can reveal a lot about the configuration of your servers. Even the default Apache error messages may reveal semi-sensitive information through the server signature line:

Apache/1.3.36 Server at www.example.com Port 80

You don't necessarily want to volunteer this information to a potential attacker. In addition, the HTTP Server header often contains more detailed information, including a list of all server modules that are installed and their versions. You can reduce this information to a minimum with two lines of Apache configuration. Put these at the top level of the Apache configuration file:

```
ServerSignature Off
ServerTokens Prod
```

In Rails, you can also inadvertently expose stack traces and source code on error if you don't ensure that Rails knows which requests are "local." By default, in development mode, the `ActionController::Base.consider_all_requests_local` configuration attribute is set to `true`. This means that every uncaught exception will show a stack trace (with source code), regardless of the source IP address. This is fine for local development, but it is insecure if you have a development server open to the public Internet. The `consider_all_requests_local` directive is disabled by default in production mode.

You can override the default `local_request?` function in your `ApplicationController` if you have more complicated rules regarding what constitutes a local request (such as addresses on the public Internet from which you develop):

```
class ApplicationController
  LOCAL_ADDRS = %w(123.45.67.89 98.76.54.32)
  def local_request?
    LOCAL_ADDRS.include? request.remote_ip
  end
end
```

In any case, try triggering some exceptions on your public servers with a temporary action like this one:

```
class UserController < ApplicationController
  def blam
    raise "If you can read this, your server is misconfigured!"
  end
end
```

This exception should be caught and logged to the Rails development log, but the client should only see a nice "500 Internal Server Error" page.

Whitelist, Don't Blacklist

A general principle of network security is that *whitelists* (lists of what to allow) are more secure than *blacklists* (lists of what to block). This principle descends from a default-deny, or fail-secure, stance. Whitelists err on the side of caution, assuming malice when presented with something they don't understand.

Zed Shaw, creator of the Mongrel web server, is a vocal proponent of this philosophy.* Much of Mongrel's security comes from its default-deny stance. When presented with a protocol violation, Mongrel closes the socket, rather than sticking around and trying to guess what the client meant (possibly getting exploited in the process).

We will revisit this issue in the "Canonicalization: What's in a Name?" section later in the chapter.

Web Issues

Now that we have examined some of the architectural ways that you can protect your application, we will take a look at some of the issues endemic to the Web.

Rails Sessions

Most web frameworks have some form of session management: a persistent server-side storage mechanism for data specific to one client's browsing session. The exact scope of a "browsing session" depends on implementation details and the method of session tracking. Most commonly, a non-persistent cookie is used, so a session consists of all visits to a site before closing the browser. Alternatively, a persistent cookie (one with an explicit expiration date) can be used; this will persist even when the browser is closed. This is useful to remember information (such as a shopping cart) across visits for otherwise anonymous users. Some frameworks such as Seaside provide URL-based (query-string) sessions so that a user may even have multiple sessions active at the same time in different browser windows.

Most of Rails's session storage methods provide the following properties:

Confidentiality
> Nobody except the server can read the data stored in the session.

Integrity
> Nobody except the server, including the client itself, can modify the data stored in the session other than by throwing the session out and obtaining a new one. A corollary is that only the server should be able to create valid sessions.

---

* *http://mongrel.rubyforge.org/docs/security.html*

The traditional session storage methods in Rails are server-side; they store all of the session data on the server, generate a random key, and use that as the session ID. The session ID is not tied to the data other than as an index, so it is safe to present to the client without compromising confidentiality.

Rails uses as much randomness as possible to create the session ID: it takes an MD5 hash of the current time, a random number, the process ID, and a constant. This is important: guessable session IDs allow *session hijacking*. In a session hijacking attack, an attacker sniffs or guesses a session ID from an authenticated user and presents it to the server as his own, thus assuming the authenticated user's session. This is similar to the TCP sequence-number prediction attack, and the mitigation is the same: make the session IDs as random as possible.

Cookie-based sessions

There are many problems with server-side session storage. File-based storage, which marshals the sessions to a local file on the server, is not scalable: to make it work in a cluster, you either need a shared filesystem or a load balancer that supports *sticky sessions* (directing all requests in the same session to one server in the cluster). This can get tricky and is often inefficient. Database-backed sessions solve this problem by keeping session state in a central database. However, this database can become a bottleneck because it must be accessed once for every request that needs session data (such as for user authentication). The DRb session store is not widely used and requires running yet another server process.

There is a solution to these problems. Most Rails sessions are lightweight: they usually contain little more than a user ID (if authenticated) and possibly a flash message. This means that they can be stored on the client rather than the server. The Rails CookieStore does just this: instead of storing the session on the server and storing its ID on the client in a cookie, it stores the entire session in a cookie.

Of course, security must be taken into account. Remember the all-important rule: never trust the client. If we just marshaled data into a string and placed it in a cookie, we would have no way to prevent the client from tampering with the session. The user could simply send the cookie corresponding to the session data user_id=1 and trick the server into thinking that he was logged in as the user with ID 1.

To counter this, the CookieStore signs each cookie with an HMAC (keyed-hash message authentication code), which is essentially a hash of the cookie data along with a secret key. The client cannot forge or modify sessions because he cannot generate valid signatures across the modified data. The server checks the hash on each request and raises a TamperedWithCookie exception if the hash does not match the data. This is the standard way to store data with an untrusted client while still assuring integrity.

In Rails 2.0, the CookieStore is now the default session store. The CookieStore requires a secret key or phrase and session cookie key to be defined; it will raise an exception if either of these are missing. These options can be set alongside other session options in *config/environment.rb*:

```
config.action_controller.session = {
  :session_key => "_myapp_session",
  :secret => "Methinks it is like a weasel"
}
```

There are a few limitations to the CookieStore:

- In most cases, cookies are limited to 4 KB each. The CookieStore will raise a CookieOverflow exception if the data and HMAC overflow this limit. This is not an error you want to get in production (as it requires architectural changes to remedy), so make sure your session data will be well below this limit.

- The entire session and HMAC are calculated, transmitted, and verified on each request and response. The CookieStore is smart enough not to retransmit the cookie if it has not changed since the last request, but the client must transmit all cookies on each request.

- Unlike the server-side session stores, the CookieStore allows the client to read all session data. This is not usually an issue, but it can be a problem in certain cases. Some applications require sensitive user data (such as account numbers or credit card numbers) to be hidden even after a user is logged in, for extra security. Also consider that the data may be stored as plain text in the browser cache on the client. Sensitive data should be stored on the server, not in the session.

- The CookieStore is vulnerable to replay attacks: since the cookies do not incorporate a nonce,* a user who has a valid session can replay that session at any later time, and convince the server that it is current. Never store transient data, such as account balances, in the session.

Cross-Site Scripting

Cross-site scripting (XSS, to avoid confusion with Cascading Style Sheets and Content Scramble System) is one of the most common vulnerabilities in web applications created recently. "Web 2.0"-style applications are particularly vulnerable due to the shifting emphasis toward user-generated content.

XSS usually is made possible because of inadequate escaping of user-entered code, particularly in blog posts, comments, and other user-generated content. In an XSS attack, an attacker inserts code, particularly JavaScript, into a third-party site (the target) in such a way that the browser treats it as part of the target page for security purposes.

---

* A *nonce*, or "number used once," is a random value generated by the server that the client must include with its request. Because the nonce is different on each request, the server can ensure that the same request is not sent twice.

In many cases, this is desirable: a blog will allow users to comment on entries, in some cases adding their own HTML. This can expose a vulnerability: if script tags are not filtered out before displaying the content, they are exposed to viewers as if part of the third-party site. This can bypass browser security policies, as browsers usually restrict scripts' access permissions based on the origin of the code. If the code appears to be coming from the target site, it can access information (e.g., cookies) belonging to the target site.

Mitigation

Defending against XSS vulnerabilities can be either very easy or very difficult. If the application in question does not allow untrusted users to enter HTML, defending against XSS is easy. In this case, each HTML character must be escaped before output. The Rails h( ) method escapes all special HTML characters for you:

```
<% @post.comments.each do |comment| %>
  <li><%=h comment.text %></li>
<% end %>
```

On occasion, there is debate over whether to store content that must be escaped for display in its plain-text or escaped forms. The advantage of storing data escaped is that you never forget to escape it for display; the advantage of storing it unescaped is that it is in its "natural" state. Cal Henderson makes a good point regarding this: you never know when you might have to escape data in a different manner for display elsewhere, so data should usually be stored in its plain-text form. An exception might be made for Unicode: it is usually important to ensure that data stored in a Unicode encoding is well-formed, lest it cause problems in processing. In situations like this, it is usually best to check for well-formedness at both ingress and egress.

Of course, things are rarely this simple. The reason XSS attacks are still so common is that often developers want their untrusted users to be able to enter arbitrary HTML, just not the "verboten tags" and "verboten attributes"—those that can execute scripts. And filtering them out is harder than it might seem (see the section "Canonicalization: What's in a Name?," later in the chapter, for the reason why).

Rails provides some help here, through the sanitize( ) method. This method removes form and script tags, elides the onSomething attributes, and kills any URIs with the "javascript:" scheme. The default set of prohibited tags and attributes may be sufficient to block execution of arbitrary script. This method is used just like h( ):

```
<% @post.comments.each do |comment| %>
  <li><%=sanitize comment.html %></li>
<% end %>
```

However, you should be very, very careful when using blacklisting such as this. There are too many edge cases to be absolutely sure that every piece of potentially malicious code is blocked. Rails security experts advise against the use of blacklisting.[*]

---

[*] See *http://www.rorsecurity.info/2007/08/17/dont-use-strip_tags-strip_links-and-sanitize/*.

Whitelisting

Instead, whitelisting is a good option. Rick Olson has created a whitelisting plugin, white_list (*http://svn.techno-weenie.net/projects/plugins/white_list/*), that is the preferred method for preventing cross-site scripting attacks. It is based on a more sound philosophy (only allowing that which is explicitly allowed), and it has more extensive tests than the Rails blacklisting helpers. The basic helper usage is very similar to the other sanitizing methods; after installing the plugin, the whitelisting filter can be applied as follows:

```
<%= white_list @post.body %>
```

The white_list plugin has a default set of tags, attributes, and URI schemes that are allowed, and by default the <script> tag is never allowed:

```
WhiteListHelper.bad_tags   = %w(script)

WhiteListHelper.tags       = %w(strong em b i p code pre tt output samp kbd
                                var sub sup dfn cite big small address hr
                                br div span h1 h2 h3 h4 h5 h6 ul ol li dt
                                dd abbr acronym a img blockquote del ins
                                fieldset legend)

WhiteListHelper.attributes = %w(href src width height alt cite datetime
                                title class)

WhiteListHelper.protocols  = %w(ed2k ftp http https irc mailto news gopher
                                nntp telnet webcal xmpp callto feed)
```

These default options can be changed or augmented by changing those variables from a configuration file:

```
WhiteListHelper.tags.merge %w(table td th)
WhiteListHelper.tags.delete 'div'
WhiteListHelper.attributes.merge %w(id class style)
```

Cross-Site Request Forgery

Cross-site request forgery (CSRF) is an obscure class of web attacks that exploit the trust a web server places in a session cookie. Unfortunately, although the attack is obscure, it is very real, and you must protect against it. This is the typical case in security: the defender must defend against all possible points of attack, but the attacker only has to pick his favorite one. Luckily, Rails provides tools to defend against CSRF attacks, provided that you use a little common sense.

The basic flaw leading to a CSRF vulnerability is that a poorly designed site trusts HTTP requests that come in with the proper authentication cookie, without taking steps to ensure that the user actually authorized the action. In a CSRF attack, the attacker's site convinces your browser to request some URI from the target site (the vulnerable application), via one of several methods. Assume that you are already authenticated to the target site, and it verifies that authentication through a cookie.

Since a browser holding a cookie for the target site will send that cookie with each request, the server receives the request and the cookie and performs the action.

A sample CSRF attack takes place as follows. This process is illustrated in Figure 5-1.

1. The client receives code from the attacker, via either a compromised server or a script or image tag placed by the attacker on a third-party web site (possibly via XSS). The code references a URI of the target application that performs some action.

2. The client requests that URI from the target application, sending the authentication cookie (because the client is already authenticated to the target). The target then performs the action on the client's behalf, even though the end user did not authorize the action.

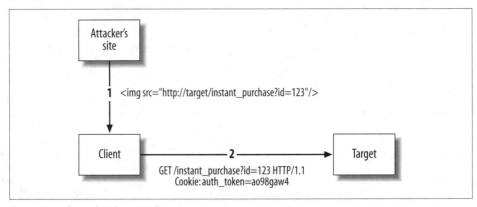

Figure 5-1. Cross-Site Request Forgery

CSRF mitigation

The first and foremost way to defend against CSRF is to use the proper HTTP verbs. This has been the mantra of the Rails core team since before Rails 1.0. GET and HEAD requests should be *safe*: they can be called without changing server state. GET, HEAD, PUT, and DELETE should be *idempotent*: calling them once or 100 times should have the same effect. (They are defined this way so that a client, unsure if a request has completed, can retry the same request with no ill effects.)

So, the primary problem with the preceding example is that it used a verb that should be safe (GET) with an action that caused side effects (instant_purchase). If the action had in fact been free of side effects, there would have been no problem. No confidential information could be leaked directly, as the response went directly from the target to the client. The basic problem is that the wrong HTTP verb was used. We will revisit this discussion in Chapter 7, when we discuss the REST architectural style.

However, cross-site request forgery is not limited to GET requests. There are several ways for an attacker to create a POST request using JavaScript, including XmlHttpRequest and creating and posting hidden forms. Using the proper HTTP actions alone is not sufficient to defend your application.

In this case, secret form tokens are helpful. The idea is to generate a token for each session that is included as a hidden field in every form. The token is an HMAC (hash message authentication code) of the session ID. This gives the token two important properties:

- It is hard or impossible for an attacker to generate a valid token given only the session ID, so the token certifies that the server generated the session ID.
- The token changes with each session.

A valid token corresponding to the current session ID must be included with each request that has side effects. If the token is not present or invalid, the action is canceled. This prevents the attack, because the attacker has no way to include a valid token with the client's request to the target application.

Rails 2.0 now incorporates request forgery protection by default. Actions with methods other than GET are checked for a valid token. The form helpers have been extended to add a token based on a secret key and the session to each generated form. By default, it tries to do the right thing. See the documentation on ActionController::RequestForgeryProtection::ClassMethods for detailed information.

The most important thing that needs to be done if not using cookie-based sessions is to set a secret:

```
class ApplicationController < ActionController::Base
  protect_from_forgery :secret => 'application-secret-283039@4%dX963'
end
```

If you are using cookie-based session storage, ActionController generates a secret for you anyway; you may omit the secret parameter. Note that it is important that the session cookie is a true nonpersistent session cookie—that is, it disappears after the session is over. If the session cookie is persistent, the token ID will be the same each session and CSRF attacks will still be possible.

Canonicalization: What's in a Name?

The term *canonicalization* refers to the process of conforming input to an expected representation. Loosely, *canonicalization issues* are problems that arise because the same resource can be referenced in different ways.

Canonicalization often comes up when working with filesystem paths. On a Unix-like system, you'd expect the paths */home/joeuser*, *~joeuser*, and */var/log/../../home/joeuser* to reference the same path, even though they are composed of different characters.

You would need some form of path normalization if you wanted to compare these paths. More importantly, you would want to know that */var/www/public/../config/database.yml* is most definitely not within */var/www/public*, lest you try to serve it as plain text to the client. As bad as that is, it is much worse when allowing a user to upload files.

The double-dot problem (known as a *directory traversal attack*) is one of the oldest, most basic canonicalization problems around, but it persists to this day. Path normalization is easy in Ruby using the `File.expand_path` method, and this should *always* be used as a final test for any files opened based on user input:

```
name = params[:filename]

base_path = File.expand_path(File.join(RAILS_ROOT, "public"))
file_path = File.join(base_path, name)

if File.expand_path(file_path).starts_with?(base_path)
  data = File.read(file_path)
else
  raise "Access denied"
end
```

Another approach to preventing directory traversal is to blacklist paths containing characters such as `../`. However, this is very, very hard to do right. Path components can be URI-encoded, and it is difficult to predict how many levels of decoding will be performed before hitting the filesystem. With the advent of Unicode and its many encodings, there are myriad ways one set of characters can be represented to a web application. Far better to check the thing you actually care about (whether or not the file is in the right directory) than to check something incidental to it (whether or not any "funny" characters were used in the pathname).

SQL Injection

SQL injection is an attack against programs that do not take proper precautions when accessing a SQL-based database. A standard example of vulnerable code is:

```
search = params[:q]
Person.find_by_sql %(SELECT * FROM people WHERE name = '#{search}%')
```

Of course, all someone has to do is search for "`'; DROP TABLE people; --`", which yields the following statement:

```
SELECT * FROM people WHERE name = ''; DROP TABLE people; --%';
```

Everything after the `--` is treated as a SQL comment (otherwise, the attempt might cause a SQL error). First, the `SELECT` statement is executed; then the `DROP TABLE` statement causes havoc. Ideally, the database user that executes that statement should not have `DROP TABLE` privileges, but SQL injection is always damaging. There are plenty of other attack vectors.

Another typical example of SQL injection is a query such as "' OR 1 = 1; --", which yields:

```
SELECT * FROM people WHERE name = '' OR 1 = 1; --%';
```

This query would return all records from the people table. This can have security implications, especially when this sort of code is found in authentication systems.

For applications written against the standard APIs, Rails is amazingly well protected against SQL injection attacks. All of the standard finders and dynamic attribute finders sanitize single attribute arguments, but there is only so much that they can do. Remember the cardinal rule: *never interpolate user input into a SQL string.*

Most of the Rails finders that accept SQL also accept an array, so you can turn code like "SELECT * FROM people WHERE name = '#{search_name}'" into ["SELECT * FROM people WHERE name = ?", search_name] nearly anywhere. (Note the lack of quoting around the question mark; Rails interprets the type of search_name and quotes it appropriately.) The user-provided name value will have any special SQL characters escaped, so you don't have to worry about it.

For any situations where you need to do this quoting yourself, you can steal the private sanitize_sql method from ActiveRecord::Base (just don't tell anyone):

```
class << ActiveRecord::Base
  public :sanitize_sql
end

name = %(O'Reilly)
puts ActiveRecord::Base.sanitize_sql([%(WHERE name = ?), name])
# >> WHERE name = 'O''Reilly'
```

Ruby's Environment

No analysis of Rails security would be complete without examining the environment that Ruby lives in.

Using the Shell

The Kernel.system method is useful for basic interaction with system services through the command line. As with SQL, though, it is important to ensure that you know exactly what is being passed, especially if it comes from an external source.

The best way to protect against malicious user input making it to the shell is to use the multiparameter version of system, only passing the command name in the first parameter. The subsequent parameters are shell-escaped and passed in, which makes it much harder to slip something into the command line unnoticed:

```
def svn_commit(message)
  system("/usr/local/bin/svn", "ci", "-m", message)
end
```

The message passed in to that method will always be the third parameter to svn, no matter what kind of shell metacharacters it contains.

Object Tainting

Tainting is an idea that came to Ruby from Perl. Because data that comes from the outside is not to be trusted, why not force it not to be trusted by default? Any data read from the environment or outside world is marked as tainted. Depending on the current value of a special Ruby global, $SAFE, certain operations are prohibited on tainted data. Objects may only (officially) be untainted by calling their untaint method.

This is a good idea that, because of implementation details, has not gained much traction in the Rails community. It can become a pain to deal with every piece of data that was derived from user input. There is one Rails plugin, safe_erb, which leverages tainting to ensure that all user-supplied data is HTML-escaped before being displayed again. Request parameters and cookies are tainted upon each request, and an error is raised if tainted data is attempted to be rendered. (The Ruby tainting facility is not used other than as a flag on the objects, because anything more would require a $SAFE level greater than zero, which is Rails-unfriendly.) This reduces the possibility of cross-site scripting attacks. The plugin is available at *http://agilewebdevelopment.com/plugins/safe_erb*.

Further Reading

The HTTP/1.1 specification, RFC 2616, has some guiding principles for security at the HTTP level (*http://www.w3.org/Protocols/rfc2616/rfc2616-sec15.html*).

Current Rails best practices for security are summarized at *http://www.quarkruby.com/2007/9/20/ruby-on-rails-security-guide*. This guide provides "cookbook"-style solutions for many real-world problems such as authentication; mitigating SQL injection, XSS, and CSRF; handling file uploads; and preventing form spam.

## CHAPTER 6

Performance

Premature optimization is the root of all evil (or at least most of it) in programming.
—Donald Knuth (attributed to C. A. R. Hoare)

Performance is an interesting beast. Performance optimization often has a bad reputation because it is often performed too early and too often, usually at the expense of readability, maintainability, and even correctness. Rails is generally fast enough, but it is possible to make it slow if you are not careful.

You should keep the following guidelines in mind when optimizing performance:

Algorithmic improvements always beat code tweaks

It is very tempting to try to squeeze every last bit of speed out of a piece of code, but often you can miss the bigger picture. No amount of C or assembly tweaking will make bubblesort faster than quicksort. Start your optimization from the top down.

As a general rule, maintainability beats performance

Your code should be first easy to read and understand, and only then optimized for speed.

Only optimize what matters

Typically, the code profile has a lopsided distribution: 80% of the time is spent in 20% of the code (for some value of 80% and 20%). It makes sense to spend your limited resources optimizing the sections that will bring the greatest gain in performance.

Measure twice, cut once

The only way to be certain about where your code is spending its time is to measure it. And just as in carpentry, you can waste a lot of time if you make changes without being very sure exactly what those changes should be. In this chapter, we will explore some of the best tools and methods for determining where to cut.

Measurement Tools

Of course, in order to properly measure performance, we need tools. This section is concerned with analysis of Ruby and Rails code, as well as web applications in general. There are a series of tools that can be used to analyze the full Rails stack, from HTTP down to Ruby's internals.

Black-Box Analysis

The most basic high-level measurement you will be interested in is: *in the ideal case, how fast can this server serve requests?* While the answer is a somewhat nebulous value that often bears no relation to actual performance under typical load, it is still useful to compare against itself—for example, when testing caching or deploying a new feature set.

This technique is called *black-box analysis*: we measure how much traffic the server can handle, while treating it as a "black box." For now, we don't really care what's inside the box, only about how fast it can serve requests. We will leave the minutiae of profiling and tweaking until later.

For this stage, we will need a benchmarking utility—but first, a brief diversion into the world of mathematics.

Statistics: The least you need to know

It doesn't take much knowledge of statistics to properly interpret the results of black-box analysis, but there are some things you need to know.

Statistical analysis deals with the results of multiple samples, which in this case correspond to HTTP response times. In Ruby fashion, we will illustrate this with a Ruby array:

```
samples = %w(10 11 12 10 10).map{|x|x.to_f}
```

The average, or *mean*, of these samples is their sum divided by the number of samples. This is straightforward to translate into Ruby—adding a few methods to Enumerable:

```
module Enumerable
  def sum(identity = 0)
    inject(identity) {|sum, x| sum + x}
  end

  def mean
    sum.to_f / length
  end
end
```

This gives us predictable results:

```
samples.sum    # => 53.0
samples.length # => 5
samples.mean   # => 10.6
```

Everyone is familiar with the mean, but the problem is that by itself, the mean is nearly worthless for describing a data set. Consider these two sets of samples:

```
samples1 = %w(10 11 12 10 10  9 12 10 9  9).map{|x|x.to_f}
samples2 = %w( 2 11  6 14 20 21  3  4 8 13).map{|x|x.to_f}
```

These two data sets in fact have the same mean, 10.2. But they clearly represent wildly different performance profiles, as can be seen from their graph (see Figure 6-1).

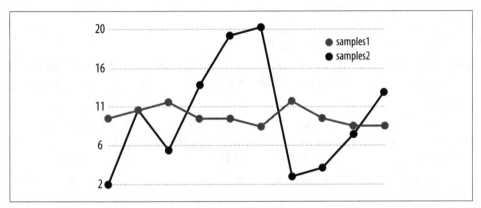

Figure 6-1. Two vastly different response-time profiles with the same mean

We need a new statistic to measure how much the data varies from the mean. That statistic is the *standard deviation*. The standard deviation of a sample is calculated by taking the root mean square deviation from the sample mean. In Ruby, it looks like this:

```
module Enumerable
  def population_stdev
    Math.sqrt( map{|x| (x - mean) ** 2}.mean )
  end
end
```

This code maps over the collection, taking the square of the deviation of each element from the mean. It then takes the mean of those squared values, and takes the square root of the mean, yielding the standard deviation.

However, this is only half the story. What has been introduced so far is the *population standard deviation*, while what we really want is the *sample standard deviation*. Without completely diving into the relevant mathematics, the basic difference between the two is whether the data represent an entire population or only a portion of it.

As our data set represents application response times, from which we want to infer a mean and confidence interval applicable to data points we have not sampled, we want to use the sample standard deviation. Using the population standard deviation on our sample would underestimate our population's actual standard deviation. Here is the Ruby code for the sample standard deviation, which we will use from here on out:

```
module Enumerable
  def stdev
    Math.sqrt( map{|x| (x - mean) ** 2}.sum / (length-1) )
  end
end
```

The standard deviation is a very useful way to get a feel for the amount of variation in a data set. We see that the second set of samples from above has a much larger standard deviation than the first:

```
samples1.stdev # => 1.13529242439509
samples2.stdev # => 6.7954232964384
```

The standard deviation has the same units as the sample data; if the original data were in milliseconds, then the samples have standard deviations of 1.1 ms and 6.4 ms, respectively.

We can use the standard deviations to estimate a *confidence interval*. The confidence interval and mean will give us a good idea for the limits of the data. Assuming a normal distribution,* the following guidelines apply:

- Approximately 68% of the data points lie within one standard deviation (σ) of the mean.
- 95% of the data is within 2σ of the mean.
- 99.7% of the data is within 3σ of the mean.

Using the second rule, we will generate a 95% confidence interval from the statistics we have generated. This Ruby code uses the mean and standard deviation to return a range in which 95% of the data should lie:

```
module Enumerable
  def confidence_interval
    (mean - 2*stdev) .. (mean + 2*stdev)
  end
end

samples1.confidence_interval # => 7.92941515120981..12.4705848487902
samples2.confidence_interval # => -3.39084659287681..23.7908465928768
```

---

* It is reasonable to assume a normal distribution here. We can safely treat series of server response times as i.i.d. random variables; therefore, by the central limit theorem, the distribution will converge to normal given enough samples.

We see that the server that produced the first set of samples will usually (95% of the time) respond in between 8 and 12 ms. On the other hand, the data from the second server varies so wildly as to be nearly meaningless.

When comparing two data sets, it is important to compare not just their means but their standard deviations and confidence intervals as well. It may look as if you have made an improvement, but if the confidence intervals overlap by a significant amount, there is no statistical significance to the result.

Black-box analysis with httperf

Now that we know how to analyze results, we can benchmark a site. The best reference is Zed Shaw's instructions about tuning Mongrel using httperf (*http://mongrel.rubyforge.org/docs/how_many_mongrels.html*). We will not repeat the procedure here, but we will give some caveats:

- Ensure that you have the front end server (usually Apache, lighttpd, or nginx) configured to serve static files. Then do a baseline measurement that requests a static file from the front end web server. You will never get Rails faster than this.

- Run your tests from a machine as close as possible (in network terms) to the server. You want to eliminate latency and *jitter* (variance in latency) from the results.

- Do not run performance tests from your web server. There are too many interactions between the server and the analyzer that will be confounded with your results. Even if CPU utilization is not a problem (such as on a multiprocessor machine), you will not know if I/O contention has skewed the results.

Code Timing

The Ruby standard library includes Benchmark, which can be used to answer simple questions about code performance. The key word here is *simple*: it is all too easy to ignore confounding factors and take the numbers that Benchmark gives you as gospel.

Suppose we want to compare conventional method dispatch to the idiom of using method_missing and then examining the method name to decide what action to take. Here is a simple code example that benchmarks the two options:

```
require 'benchmark'

class Test
  def test_one
    1 + 1
  end

  def method_missing(method_id)
    case method_id
    when :test_unknown: 1 + 1
```

```
      else super
      end
    end
end

t = Test.new

Benchmark.bmbm do |b|
  b.report("Direct method call") do
    1_000_000.times { t.test_one }
  end

  b.report("method_missing") do
    1_000_000.times { t.test_unknown }
  end
end
```

Note what we are not testing: we are not comparing the raw speed of ordinary method dispatch versus a bare call to method_missing. We are comparing an ordinary method call to the standard Ruby practice of using method_missing to answer for one method name. This gives us answers that are more relevant to our question: "How much will method_missing hurt me in this particular piece of code?"

We use the Benchmark.bmbm method, which runs the entire benchmark suite once (the "rehearsal") to minimize startup costs and give the measured code a "warm start." To get the most accurate numbers possible, each trial runs one million method calls.

The Benchmark library starts garbage collection before each run, because garbage collection during the measured run would alter the results. Here is the output of that benchmark on my computer:

```
Rehearsal -------------------------------------------------------
Direct method call    0.350000    0.000000    0.350000 (  0.352929)
method_missing        0.480000    0.000000    0.480000 (  0.476009)
---------------------------------------------- total: 0.830000sec

                          user      system       total         real
Direct method call    0.320000    0.000000    0.320000 (  0.324030)
method_missing        0.480000    0.000000    0.480000 (  0.477420)
```

The rehearsal numbers come first, followed by the actual measurement. We can see that under this environment, the average cost of a normal method call is 320 nanoseconds (0.32 seconds per million calls), while a method_missing call and case statement take 480 nanoseconds. Modulo the accuracy of our measurement, this is a 50% performance penalty for using method_missing. Balanced against the additional power we get from method_missing, this certainly seems to be a good trade.

Benchmark is a powerful tool, but it can quickly amount to guesswork and black magic. There is no use optimizing method dispatch unless it is a bottleneck.[*]

---

[*] Here's a hint: at more than two million method calls per second, method dispatch is probably not your bottleneck.

Don't just go poking around looking for code to benchmark, though. Profilers are much more powerful utilities when you don't know what needs optimization. We will consider them next.

Rails Analyzer Tools

The Rails Analyzer Tools (*http://rails-analyzer.rubyforge.org/*) are a set of utilities that can help profile your Rails application. While Benchmark is Ruby-specific, and httperf will benchmark any web site, the Rails Analyzer Tools were written with Rails in mind.

Production log analyzer

The first tool, the Production Log Analyzer, scans your production logfiles to find the slowest actions in your deployed application. This is very useful for problem solving, but it has a number of downsides. It requires the logs to go through the SyslogLogger (provided with the Rails Analyzer Tools), so you must set this up before the requests come in. The tool also requires a syslogd that supports filtering on program names, which usually means either running BSD or installing syslog-ng. For these reasons, we will not go into detail on its use here. Complete setup instructions are available at *http://rails-analyzer.rubyforge.org/pl_analyze/*.

Action profiler

Once you know which actions are hurting for performance, you need a way to dig deeper. Action Profiler is a library (and a corresponding executable, action_profiler) that glues Rails to a profiler. It profiles a single Rails action through the entire Rails stack and application code so that you can examine where the most time is being spent during that action.

Action Profiler can be used with one of several profiling engines: ZenProfiler, ruby-prof, and Ruby's built-in Profiler class. They will be tried in that order unless one is specified on the command line with the -P option. Here is a sample run of Ruby's Profiler, showing a flat call profile:

```
$ action_profiler -P Profiler ListingController#map
Warmup...
Profiling...
  %   cumulative   self              self     total
 time   seconds   seconds    calls  ms/call  ms/call  name
13.73    0.07      0.07       204     0.34     0.34   ERB::Util.html_escape
11.76    0.13      0.06      1462     0.04     0.08   String#gsub
11.76    0.19      0.06         6    10.00    10.00   AssetTagHelper.
                                                       compute_public_path
 9.80    0.24      0.05        89     0.56     0.67   FormOptionsHelper.
                                                       option_value_selected?
 9.80    0.29      0.05       178     0.28     0.28   Array#<<
 3.92    0.31      0.02        44     0.45     6.36   Array#each
 3.92    0.33      0.02       287     0.07     0.07   Kernel.respond_to?
```

3.92	0.35	0.02	89	0.22	0.45	Array#each_index
3.92	0.37	0.02	89	0.22	0.34	Inflector.humanize
1.96	0.38	0.01	179	0.06	0.06	Kernel.===
1.96	0.39	0.01	67	0.15	0.15	String#concat
1.96	0.40	0.01	16	0.63	0.63	ActionView::Base# template_exists?
1.96	0.41	0.01	613	0.02	0.02	String#to_s
1.96	0.42	0.01	7	1.43	1.43	MonitorMixin.synchronize

(and many more lines...)

These results include the following columns.

Column name	Description
% Time	Percentage of total time spent in only this function.
Cumulative Seconds	Total number of seconds spent in this function, including time spent in functions called by this one.
Self Seconds	Total number of seconds spent in only this function, *excluding* time spent in functions called by this one.
Calls	Total number of calls to this function during the profiling period.
Self ms/call	Average number of milliseconds spent in this function per call, excluding calls to other functions.
Total ms/call	Average number of milliseconds spent in this function per call, including calls to other functions.
Name	Name of the function being profiled.

The generated profile shows that we are spending most of our time in five functions: html_escape (better known as h( )), gsub, compute_public_path, option_value_selected?, and <<. This is hard to improve upon, and in fact this particular action is pretty snappy. There is not much that we can do to reduce time spent in methods like Array#<< except find ways to call them fewer times.

This example demonstrates both the power and weakness of flat profiles. Although they are very useful to get a general idea of which functions are taking the most time, they do not help very much with long-running or complicated programs. Rails applications certainly qualify as complicated—even a simple action can easily have hundreds of lines in the profile. It can be difficult to track down where your expensive functions are being called.

The solution to this complexity is, believe it or not, more complexity—provided we introduce some structure to the data. We will see later in the chapter how a graph profile, though it contains a huge amount of data, can offer better insight into where time is being spent.

Rails Analyzer Tools

The Rails Analyzer Tools are a collection of miscellaneous parts that help with performance tuning. Two of the utilities, bench and crawl, measure "black-box" performance by making rapid-fire HTTP requests to a site. We can already do this, and more, with httperf.

The IOTail library mixes in a `tail_lines` method to `IO` and `StringIO`. This method yields once for each line that is added to an open file, as it is added. This is used in some of the other utility methods from the Rails Analyzer Tools.

The real gem in this library, however, is `rails_stat`. This simple command-line utility takes as arguments the path to a Rails production log and an optional refresh interval, which defaults to 10 seconds. It sits on the logfile, watching for new lines, and summarizes the traffic to the site, refreshing at the given interval until it receives SIGINT (Ctrl-C):

```
$ rails_stat log/production.log
~ 1.4 req/sec, 0.0 queries/sec, 7.9 lines/sec
```

The implementation of `rails_stat` is very simple (it is based on IOTail). This code could be used as the basis for a flexible real-time log analytics system.

Rails Optimization Example

To tie these concepts together, we will look at the process of benchmarking, profiling, and optimizing a Rails action. This example comes from a real application, one that is fairly large and complicated. We have seen pieces of this application before; it is a map-based real estate search application. The application deals heavily with geospatial data, and is based on the PostGIS spatial extensions to PostgreSQL.

We have identified an action to profile: the action that performs the search itself (`POST /searches`). This action is not particularly slow in absolute terms, but it is our most commonly used feature, and any more performance we can get reduces overall latency and makes our application feel snappier.

Profiling an Action

Once we have decided on an action whose performance we want to improve, we can profile it to see where our time is being spent. Jeremy Kemper recently added a new request profiler to Rails, which will be released with the final version of Rails 2.0. Its library is located at *actionpack/lib/action_controller/request_profiler.rb*, and it is accessible through *script/performance/request*. It is a fairly simple wrapper around the ruby-prof library, adding some commonly needed Rails functionality:

- Rather than running a single action, the request profiler runs a specified integration test script, so the test procedure can be arbitrarily complex. This also means that we can profile non-GET requests, which is a must for the action we wish to profile.
- The request profiler can run a script multiple times, while only profiling time actually spent in those actions (not the overhead of starting up the profiler).
- The profiler script opens up both the flat and HTML graph profiles for us; we will see later how both of these are useful.

First, we need to install the ruby-prof gem:

```
$ sudo gem install ruby-prof
```

We need to write an integration script that drives the profiler. As mentioned previously, this script can be arbitrarily complicated, but ours will be a single request. The script uses the same methods as integration scripts, except that the script's execution is wrapped in an integration runner (technically, the script's text is inserted into the runner using instance_eval), so the integration session methods can be called as top-level methods.

test_script.rb
```
post '/searches', :search => {:pclass => 1, :city_id => 149, :subtype => 'HOUSE'}
```

We can drive the profiler with this script. We will also specify the number of trials; this is a fairly long-running action (around half a second on my machine without the profiling overhead), so we will run 10 trials:

```
$ script/performance/request -n 10 test_script.rb
```

This will generate two profiles in the *tmp* directory (and open them using open on OS X). The flat profile, which we have seen before, is *tmp/profile-flat.txt*. The new graph profile, which is much more detailed, is *tmp/profile-graph.html*.

The graph profile is extremely complicated, because it is a linearized version of the call graph for every function that was called during profiling. When opened in a browser, it starts off as shown in Figure 6-2.

We will examine portions of this graph, but a complete description of these fields is beyond the scope of this book. An introduction is available at *http://ruby-prof. rubyforge.org/graph.txt*.

The profile is divided into blocks, which are separated by horizontal lines. Each block in this profile is centered around one function—the one in boldface that has values in the first two columns (*%Total* and *%Self*). If we only look at that one line from each block, we have a fairly standard flat profile, like the one we saw previously from Ruby's Profiler. The *%Total* column indicates the percentage of overall time spent in this method and any methods it calls (and recursively on down); the *%Self* column excludes children and only relates to the current method.

The added value that we receive from the graph profile is the parent and child information in each block. Each function has zero or more parents (functions that called this function) and zero or more children (functions called by this function). Parents are listed above the current function within a block, and children are listed below the current function.

Profile Report

Thread ID	Total Time
2057980	12.69

Thread 2057980

%Total	%Self	Total	Self	Wait	Child	Calls	Name	Line
100.00%	0.00%	12.69	0.00	0.00	12.69	0	**ActionController::RequestProfiler#profile**	**61**
		12.69	0.00	0.00	12.69	1/1	ActionController::RequestProfiler#benchmark	61
		12.69	0.00	0.00	12.69	1/1	<Module::Benchmark>#realtime	307
100.00%	0.00%	12.69	0.00	0.00	12.69	1	**<Module::Benchmark>#measure**	**291**
		0.00	0.00	0.00	0.00	2/2	Struct::Tms#stime	295
		12.69	0.00	0.00	12.69	1/1	Integer#times	21
		0.00	0.00	0.00	0.00	2/2	Struct::Tms#cutime	295
		0.00	0.00	0.00	0.00	1/19731	Class#new	295
		0.00	0.00	0.00	0.00	5/5	Float#-	295
		0.00	0.00	0.00	0.00	2/42	<Class::Time>#now	294
		0.00	0.00	0.00	0.00	2/2	Struct::Tms#cstime	295
		0.00	0.00	0.00	0.00	2/2	<Module::Benchmark>#times	294
		0.00	0.00	0.00	0.00	2/2	Time#to_f	295
		0.00	0.00	0.00	0.00	2/2	Struct::Tms#utime	295
		12.69	0.00	0.00	12.69	1/1	<Class::ActionController::RequestProfiler::Sandbox>#benchmark	21
100.00%	0.00%	12.69	0.00	0.00	12.69	1	**<Module::Benchmark>#realtime**	**306**
		12.69	0.00	0.00	12.69	1/1	<Module::Benchmark>#measure	307
		12.69	0.00	0.00	12.69	10/10	Integer#times	21
100.00%	0.00%	12.69	0.00	0.00	12.69	10	**ActionController::RequestProfiler::Sandbox#dispatch**	**28**
		0.04	0.00	0.00	0.04	10/10	ActionController::Routing::RouteSet#recognize	34
		0.00	0.00	0.00	0.00	40/19731	Class#new	32
		12.65	0.00	0.00	12.65	10/10	<Class::ActionController::Base>#process	35
		12.69	0.00	0.00	12.69	1/1	ActionController::RequestProfiler#benchmark	68
100.00%	0.00%	12.69	0.00	0.00	12.69	1	**<Class::ActionController::RequestProfiler::Sandbox>#benchmark**	**20**
		12.69	0.00	0.00	12.69	1/1	<Module::Benchmark>#realtime	21
					and many more rows...			

Figure 6-2. Beginning of a graph profile

The meaning of the *Calls* column is different for different rows. For the primary row within a block, it simply refers to the total number of calls to the function. For the parent rows, it takes the form calls/total, where calls is the number of times the parent function called the current function and total is the total number of times the current function was called. Note that since all functions calling the current function are parents, the calls values of all parents will sum to the calls value of the current function.

For child rows, the semantics are the same, but they are from the child's point of view. The calls value of a child row is the number of times the current function calls the child function, as a fraction of the total number of times the child function was called. The denominator of this number will be the same as the calls value for the child function's own block. This gives a picture of how much impact the current function has on the child, relative to the child's other callers.

Optimizing and Reprofiling

Now, we will examine the profile to find areas of our code that are slow. There are two main columns we need to watch while scanning the profile:

%Self

> This value represents the amount of time spent in this method only (excluding time spent in its children), relative to total profiling time. If one method is doing an inordinate amount of work, it will have a proportionally higher *%Self* value.

Calls

> This column shows the number of calls made to this function during the profiling period. All of the optimization in the world on one method will not help if the method is being called too many times. Again, algorithmic optimizations are always the place to start; then, individual bits of code can be tweaked if more performance is needed.

A good place to start is the flat profile, as it is sorted by the *%Self* column, highest first. (The graph profile is sorted by *%Total* instead.) The beginning of our flat profile looks like this:

```
Thread ID: 2057980
Total: 12.69


%self    total    self    wait    child    calls   name
9.93     2.06     1.26    0.00    0.80     2730    GeoRuby::SimpleFeatures::
                                                     HexEWKBParser#decode_hex

6.86     1.43     0.87    0.00    0.56     4430    Array#each_index
4.65     1.82     0.59    0.00    1.23     4230    Array#each-1
2.68     0.34     0.34    0.00    0.00     132130  Hash#[]=
2.68     0.34     0.34    0.00    0.00     156540  Fixnum#==
2.60     0.38     0.33    0.00    0.05     77550   String#gsub
```

Most of these values are fairly reasonable (we are doing a lot of necessary data processing in Ruby, and it is reasonable that Array#each_index would be a significant component of this). However, we are spending a lot of time in GeoRuby::SimpleFeatures::HexEWKBParser#decode_hex. The *%Self* value of 9.93 means that we are spending nearly 10% of the total request time inside this method. We should investigate this by looking for that method's block in the graph profile (see Figure 6-3).

%Total	%Self	Total	Self	Wait	Child	Calls	Name
		2.06	1.26	0.00	0.80	2730/2730	GeoRuby::SimpleFeatures::HexEWKBParser#parse
16.23%	9.93%	2.06	1.26	0.00	0.80	2730	**GeoRuby::SimpleFeatures::HexEWKBParser#decode_hex**
		0.10	0.10	0.00	0.00	70980/156540	Fixnum#==
		0.00	0.00	0.00	0.00	1/84	Proc#call
		0.15	0.15	0.00	0.00	68250/68250	String#hex
		0.19	0.19	0.00	0.00	70980/87410	String#length
		0.19	0.19	0.00	0.00	68250/71580	String#<<
		0.15	0.15	0.00	0.00	70980/70980	String#slice!
		0.02	0.02	0.00	0.00	2730/3030	Kernel#clone

Figure 6-3. The decode_hex method dominates our request time

Now, we may want to examine the source of these calls to decode_hex. This function has only one caller, HexEWKBParser#parse. Clicking on that line takes us to its own block (see Figure 6-4).

%Total	%Self	Total	Self	Wait	Child	Calls	Name
		3.46	0.02	0.00	3.44	2730/2730	<Class::GeoRuby::SimpleFeatures::Geometry>#from_hex_ewkb
27.27%	0.16%	3.46	0.02	0.00	3.44	2730	**GeoRuby::SimpleFeatures::HexEWKBParser#parse**
		2.06	1.26	0.00	0.80	2730/2730	GeoRuby::SimpleFeatures::HexEWKBParser#decode_hex
		1.38	0.06	0.00	1.32	2730/2730	GeoRuby::SimpleFeatures::EWKBParser#parse

Figure 6-4. Tracing upward through the call stack

Following this chain of callers upward, we find that these calls are coming from the spatial_adapter plugin that we use to interface with the PostGIS database. These functions are doing a particularly computationally intensive form of type casting; they are converting the hex strings coming from PostGIS to Ruby objects such as points and polygons (EWKB is the *extended well-known binary* format that PostGIS uses to represent geometrical objects).

The decode_hex function is pure Ruby. It could probably be rewritten with C, OCaml, or another high-performance extension language, which would likely improve performance substantially. However, we should be considering algorithmic improvements first.

The first thing that catches my eye about this profile is the number of calls. On the data set being used, our test query returns slightly fewer than 100 geospatial objects. So why are we decoding geospatial objects 2,730 times? After some investigation, we find this note in the spatial adapter's code:

> Because ActiveRecord keeps only the string values directly returned from the database, it translates from these to the correct types every time an attribute is read (using the code returned by this method), which is probably OK for simple types, but might be less than efficient for geometries. Also, you cannot modify the geometry object returned directly or your change will not be saved.

So, every time we reference a geospatial column (via Listing#location), it is being decoded again from the string representation. We can do better than that. We will keep a cache of the last-seen string value (the EWKB value from PostGIS), as well as its corresponding geometry (the Ruby object). This is done by inserting the following code into the Listing class:

```
class Listing
  # Cache location information
  # AR wants to cast the HexEWKB string to a Geometry on each access,
  # let's not do that
  def location
    string = location_before_type_cast
    return @location_geometry if string == @location_string

    @location_string = string
    @location_geometry = super
```

```
    end

    # Invalidate cache when new location is assigned
    def location=(val)
      @location_geometry = @location_string = nil
      super
    end

    # Invalidate cache when record is reloaded
    def reload
      @location_geometry = @location_string = nil
      super
    end
  end
```

Now that we have made a substantial change, it is time to reprofile and see how the numbers compare. After running the profiler again, we see that we have managed to push that method a few notches down the list:

```
Thread ID: 2057980
Total: 11.21

  %self   total   self   wait   child   calls  name
   8.56    1.38   0.96   0.00    0.42    4430  Array#each_index
   7.76    2.07   0.87   0.00    1.20    4230  Array#each-1
   4.19    0.74   0.47   0.00    0.27    1040  GeoRuby::SimpleFeatures::
                                               HexEWKBParser#decode_hex
```

We have cut the number of calls to decode_hex from 2,730 to 1,040. (This number is still higher than 100 because there is another spatial class that we have not optimized yet.) In addition, we have cut the total time spent in decode_hex from 1.26 seconds to 0.47 seconds without optimizing the actual function at all. When we benchmark these different versions of the application, we will see what kind of an impact the optimizations have on the action as a whole.

Next, we notice from the preceding flat profile that we are spending the most time in Array#each_index and Array#each-1 (the ruby-prof syntax indicating the first-level recursive call to Array#each). These are more complicated to track down, primarily because they have many callers (Array#each is used in many places).

The optimization process for this problem was fairly difficult, and we do not show it here; it was a fairly boring and highly application-specific optimization. (It involved rewriting a complicated clustering algorithm to build up the same data set using fewer intermediate data structures.) But the change did result in a small improvement in the profile, as well as the overall running time:

```
Thread ID: 2057980
Total: 10.7

  %self   total   self   wait   child   calls  name
   7.94    1.38   0.85   0.00    0.53    4430  Array#each_index
   5.23    1.77   0.56   0.00    1.21    4230  Array#each-1
```

```
3.64    0.40    0.39    0.00    0.01    133960    Hash#[]=
3.55    0.70    0.38    0.00    0.32      1040    GeoRuby::SimpleFeatures::
                                                  HexEWKBParser#decode_hex
```

Source Control and Optimization

Source control is our friend during the optimization process. The application uses Mercurial, a distributed version-control system, which makes it very easy to test large, complicated changes and then pull all, some, or no changes back into the main codebase, depending on their performance improvement. In this case, we used source control to run benchmarks on several different optimizations after the fact, to see how much of an improvement each one made.

We followed the following (simplified) process with Mercurial:

1. Clone the main trunk repository to a new repository and copy over any necessary nonversioned configuration files (such as *config/database.yml*).

   ```
   $ hg clone trunk performance-testing
   $ cp trunk/config/database.yml performance-testing/config/
   ```

2. In the new repository, repeat the profile-optimize-test cycle and check in each change.

   ```
   $ cd performance-testing
   (make changes, test)
   $ hg ci
   ```

3. If the performance improvements were successful, pull the changes back into the main repository.[a]

   ```
   $ cd ../trunk
   $ hg pull -u ../performance-testing
   $ hg up
   ```

We examine the distributed version-control paradigm in more detail in Chapter 10.

---

[a] The Mercurial Queues extension (also called MQ; its use is detailed at *http://www.selenic.com/mercurial/wiki/index.cgi/MqExtension*) makes this process much more straightforward, and makes it easier to cherry-pick or throw away individual changes (even while working in the main repository). However, it is far beyond this book's scope.

Benchmarking

Now that we have made optimizations, we should see how they affect the actual performance of our application. We saved this section for later so that we could compare the two optimizations to each other; in reality, you should benchmark after each optimization to be sure that each change has the desired effect.

We will be comparing the performance of the three versions of the application:

- No optimization (the control)
- The Listing#location optimization
- The rewrite of the clustering algorithm

The benchmarking tool we will be using is Railsbench (*http://railsbench.rubyforge.org/*) by Stefan Kaes. This provides some very convenient tools for benchmarking Rails applications and visualizing the results. Railsbench has a slightly complicated installation procedure. First, install the gem:

```
$ sudo gem install railsbench
```

Next, you should add the directory containing the Railsbench scripts to your PATH, and make them executable. This can be done as follows:

```
$ eval `railsbench path`
$ sudo railsbench postinstall
```

Railsbench looks for some environment variables to know where the Rails application is and where its data should go, so we need to export those:

```
$ export RAILS_ROOT=.
$ export RAILS_PERF_DATA=.
```

Now Railsbench is installed and ready to run. But first, there are some changes we need to make to the application. We install the Railsbench code into our application:

```
$ railsbench install
```

That command provides us with a few files that are used for benchmarking:

config/benchmarks.rb

>   Railsbench configuration. Use this file to provide Rails with custom session data, if needed.

config/benchmarks.yml

>   Defines the set of benchmarks that can be run; each one has a name, URI, HTTP method, and optional POST data. Most of this file can be generated automatically from the application's routes; we will do this as our next step.

config/environments/benchmarking.rb

>   This is a separate Rails environment used for benchmarking. When created, it is a copy of the *production.rb* file, but it can be customized to meet the benchmark's needs.

Railsbench has a command to generate the *config/benchmarks.yml* file based on the application's routes. We will run this to create the basic version of the file.

```
$ railsbench generate_benchmarks
```

We delete actions from this file that we do not need to benchmark (such as named routes generated automatically by map.resources, some of which are unused). And we modify the searches_create benchmark, changing the method to post and adding the POST data we need:

```
searches_create:
    uri:            /searches/
    action:         create
    controller:     searches
    method:         post
    post_data:      "search[pclass]=1&search[city_id]=149&search[subtype]=HOUSE"
```

There is one last change we must make. By default, all Rails environments except production have a log level of :debug. We want to set the benchmarking environment's log level to :info, so that we don't confound the benchmarking results with I/O issues from heavy log traffic. Add the following line to *config/environments/benchmarking.yml*:

```
config.log_level = :info
```

Running the benchmark

Now we can run the benchmarks. We use the Railsbench perf_run command, which takes as an argument the number of requests to make on each trial. We specify the benchmark from *benchmarks.yml* with the -bm= option, and we specify 20 trials with the RAILS_PERF_RUNS variable:

```
$ RAILS_PERF_RUNS=20 perf_run 100 -bm=searches_create
benchmarking 20 runs with options 100 -bm=searches_create

perf data file: ./perf_run.searches_create.txt
    requests=100, options=-bm=searches_create

loading environment              2.43529

page request                   total  stddev%   r/s    ms/r
searches_create              44.70490  0.4030  2.24  447.05

all requests                 44.70490  0.4030  2.24  447.05
```

 Railsbench can benchmark multiple actions during the same run. We are only benchmarking one action here, so we can just look at the searches_create line in this table for our information. The last line is just a summary.

The data shows us that we averaged 2.24 requests per second (447.05 milliseconds per request). Each of 20 trials involves 100 requests, so the mean runtime for each trial was 44.705 seconds. The standard deviation for that figure was 0.4030% of the mean, or 0.180 seconds. (Thus, 95% of the trials should fall between 44.34 seconds and 45.06 seconds, two standard deviations away from the mean.)

perf_run saves its raw data for this run in *perf_run.searches_create.txt*, and we will feed that file into other utilities for analysis. Between each benchmark, we store this file away for comparison across the different versions under test.

Interpreting the results

Railsbench includes a utility called perf_comp that will compare results between different runs of perf_run. When run with two arguments (the two data files to be compared), it will give a summary of each and a comparison between them. Here is the comparison between the first benchmark (the control) and the second (with the Listing#location cache improvement):

```
$ perf_comp a/perf_run.searches_create.txt b/perf_run.searches_create.txt
perf data file 1: a/perf_run.searches_create.txt
  requests=100, options=-bm=searches_create

perf data file 2: b/perf_run.searches_create.txt
  requests=100, options=-bm=searches_create

page                   c1 real   c2 real  c1 r/s  c2 r/s  c1 ms/r  c2 ms/r  c1/c2
searches_create        44.70490  43.13935   2.2     2.3    447.05   431.39   1.04

all requests           44.70490  43.13935   2.2     2.3    447.05   431.39   1.04
```

This is mostly information we have seen before. The interesting bit of information is the far-right number in the table (1.04): the ratio of the old runtime to the new. In this case, we see that the cache optimization afforded us a 4% improvement in overall runtime on this action. This is a decent performance improvement, for an action that is already fairly well optimized.

Compare that to the second optimization, the refactoring:

```
$ perf_comp b/perf_run.searches_create.txt c/perf_run.searches_create.txt
perf data file 1: b/perf_run.searches_create.txt
  requests=100, options=-bm=searches_create

perf data file 2: c/perf_run.searches_create.txt
  requests=100, options=-bm=searches_create

page                   c1 real   c2 real  c1 r/s  c2 r/s  c1 ms/r  c2 ms/r  c1/c2
searches_create        43.13935  42.79449   2.3     2.3    431.39   427.94   1.01

all requests           43.13935  42.79449   2.3     2.3    431.39   427.94   1.01
```

This change only resulted in a performance gain of 1%, which is probably not worth pursuing for performance's sake alone. (In this case, the code under question was in desperate need of a rewrite, so this was a net gain anyway.)

We should also compare the actual ranges that the trial times fall into, to be sure that these results have statistical significance. To visualize this, I instrumented the Railsbench PerfInfo class to show the actual trial times (not just the mean and standard deviation), and piped the data through R.[*] The result is shown in Figure 6-5.

This box-and-whisker plot shows the median value (the heavy line), the first and third quartile (into which the middle half of the data points fall; represented by the box), and the complete range (the brackets). From this, we see that the first optimization was a clear winner; the ranges of values do not even overlap.

The second optimization is not as clear-cut; there is still significant overlap between the two ranges of observations. If there is any performance gain, it is likely marginal, as it is overshadowed by the inherent variability of the response times.

[*] R (*http://www.r-project.org/*) is a language for statistical computing.

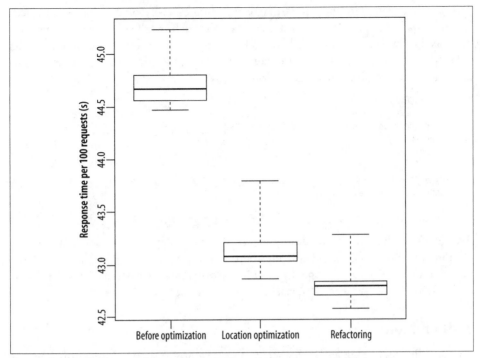

Figure 6-5. Performance comparison between the control and two optimized versions

ActiveRecord Performance

Object-relational mapping systems provide such a high-level environment for working with data that it is easy to forget about efficiency until it becomes a problem. Here are some common problems and solutions for ActiveRecord development.

Diving into SQL

When faced with a problem that doesn't map neatly to the given abstractions, most programmers have an instinct to jump down a level. When using ActiveRecord, this means using raw SQL.

For security as well as performance, it is important to understand the SQL that is being generated from the commands you issue. ActiveRecord provides a useful abstraction, but if you are not careful, it will bite you.

The simplest way to drop into raw SQL is to use `ActiveRecord::Base.find_by_sql`. This is a very flexible method that returns the same results as `find(:all, ...)`, but allows you to specify custom SQL. It will even sanitize an array for you:

```
Person.find_by_sql ["SELECT * FROM people WHERE name LIKE ?", "#{name}%"]
```

The problem with find_by_sql is that it instantiates every object that is returned. This is usually fine, but sometimes it can be too much overhead. To avoid this, you may need to bypass ActiveRecord and talk directly with the connection adapter. This is fairly easy, but you can make it easier by bolting some convenience methods onto ActiveRecord to sanitize the query automatically:

```
class <<ActiveRecord::Base
  def select_values(sql)
    connection.select_values(sanitize_sql(sql))
  end
end

sql = %(SELECT id FROM people WHERE last_name = ?)
last_name = %(O'Reilly)

Person.select_values [sql, last_name] # => ["12", "42"]
```

Because ActiveRecord is not doing any of the work here, the values come across without any type conversion (as strings here). The complete list of methods available through the connection adapter (the ActiveRecord::Base.connection object) is listed in the RDoc for ActiveRecord::ConnectionAdapters::DatabaseStatements.

1+N Problem

The so-called *1+N problem* is characteristic of the problems that you can run into if you are not aware of your tools. It is best illustrated with an example.

Assume that we are using the following model, which splits off a person's login into a separate User model:[*]

```
class Person < ActiveRecord::Base
  has_one :user
end

class User < ActiveRecord::Base
  belongs_to :person
end
```

If you want to find the usernames of all people from Illinois, you might write this code:

```
logins_from_illinois = []
Person.find_all_by_state('IL').each do |person|
  logins_from_illinois << person.user.login
end
```

Not only is this iterative code bad style in Ruby, it can be inefficient. Even the functional version suffers from the same problem:

```
logins_from_illinois = Person.find_all_by_state('IL').
  map{|p| p.user.login}
```

---

[*] This style can be very useful, especially when you need to keep track of many people who may or may not actually be able to log in to a Rails application.

Invoking the user method on each Person object will force a separate load from the database. If the people with IDs 4, 17, 36, and 39 matched the find_all_by_state method, the following queries would be issued:*

```
SELECT * FROM people WHERE state = 'IL';
-- returns people with ID in (4, 17, 36, 39)

SELECT * FROM users WHERE person_id = 4;
SELECT * FROM users WHERE person_id = 17;
SELECT * FROM users WHERE person_id = 36;
SELECT * FROM users WHERE person_id = 39;
```

This is why this problem is called the 1+ N problem. This code issues one query to find the IDs of the objects to retrieve (or the values of a foreign key, as shown here) and N queries to retrieve the actual objects. If there were 1,000 objects matching the query, this method would require 1,001 queries.

This is a very inefficient method of retrieving data. All but the first query return a single row. Most of the time is wasted in constructing N queries, transmitting them to the database server, parsing them (Rails does not use prepared statements, so each statement must be compiled and planned individually), and retrieving the results.

The solution is to use a SQL join for the first and only query:

```
SELECT * FROM people LEFT JOIN users ON people.id = users.person_id
    WHERE people.state = 'IL';
```

That is much faster as it retrieves all needed data in one SQL statement. Rails makes this easy: we can use the :include option to User.find to create a join:

```
logins_from_illinois = User.find(:all, :include => :person,
    :conditions => "people.state = 'IL'").map(&:login)
```

Note the pluralization: in the :include parameter, we use the singular, as it is the name of the association (a User has-one Person). But since the :conditions are directly injected into the SQL statement, the table name is used (... WHERE people. state = 'IL').

Indexing

Another area in which you have to be careful of your database is indexing. Improper indexing is a common problem; indexing is easily overlooked when creating a database, and you often do not see the results until there is a major performance impact on the application.

Unfortunately, this is an area where Rails does not (and cannot) help you. Indexing is quite application-specific. Other than primary keys (which are usually automatically indexed by the database), you must remember to create the necessary indexes yourself.

---

* The actual queries have been simplified for clarity. Most of the Rails database adapters reflect on the database's metadata for information about available tables, columns, and data types.

There is really no substitute for understanding what queries are being sent to the database and how they are being satisfied.

Be sure to think critically about where you need indexes, as well as where you don't need them. In particular, you should omit indexes on tables that are very infrequently read from (such as audit logs). Gratuitous indexes can hurt write performance, as they must be updated when data in the table is changed.

Foreign key indexes

Foreign keys are the most common place where indexes are needed (and often omitted). In fact, MySQL generates an index on the referencing column automatically when a foreign key is created.[*] PostgreSQL does not; you must create all indexes except for those on primary keys manually. Foreign key indexes assist in queries by associations, such as:

```
SELECT * FROM projects WHERE user_id = 123;
```

Without a proper index on user_id, every row in the projects table must be examined. It is standard practice to create an index on most foreign keys. However, there are exceptions. Indexes do not help on attributes of low cardinality—those where there are few unique values. The standard example is an index on the sex column of a person; there are (generally) only two possible values. For a clause such as WHERE sex = 'M', an index lookup would probably take longer than a full table scan.

This concern also applies to lookup tables (type tables) that simply serve to define values for an attribute. If the possible values are small or unevenly distributed, an index might slow things down. An example would be a foreign key into an order status lookup table, as shown in Table 6-1.

Table 6-1. order_status

status_id	status
1	opened
2	billed
3	shipped
4	returned

Other indexes

Foreign keys are just the beginning, however, and they are the easiest thing to get right. The rest is highly application-specific, so you will have to look at the queries you are actually issuing to get a feel for where you need indexes. Indexing can quickly look more like an art than a science.

---

[*] Some would consider this behavior helpful; others consider it presumptuous, as indexes are not always needed on foreign keys.

One complication in indexing decisions is that certain DBMSs (MySQL 4 and earlier, and PostgreSQL 8.0 and earlier) will use at most a single index on each table per query. This means that you should choose your indexes carefully. Consider this query, which shows a list of a user's payments, showing the most recent first:

```
SELECT * FROM payments WHERE user_id = 12345 ORDER BY paid_at DESC;
```

Even if there are separate indexes defined on (user_id) and (paid_at), the best those DBMSs can do is to use the user_id index and manually sort on paid_at, without the help of an index. In order to use an index, you must define one that includes both columns: (user_id, paid_at). This situation happens often when using acts_as_list: many times you want to filter based on a foreign key and then sort by a position column.

Check your DBMS manual for details. Some database systems have further restrictions or hints. For example, on multicolumn indexes, PostgreSQL performs best when the most restrictive condition applies to the leftmost column in the index.

In PostgreSQL, it is also possible to create an index on an expression such as LOWER(last_name). This index would be used, for example, to satisfy clauses like WHERE LOWER(last_name) = 'smith' or ORDER BY LOWER(last_name) ASC. This is a tradeoff: the expression must be calculated for each row when the index is created, but that expression is treated as a constant when querying.

You should take a look at your development log to find common queries that are either being executed too often or take too long. You may find that you have missed an index. Common places where indexes are omitted are the following:

- Columns that need to be sorted: position (when using acts_as_list) or any other natural sort field such as last name, transaction date, or price.

- Lookup fields other than foreign keys: order number, department code, or username.

- Columns that are commonly used in a GROUP BY query—but be careful that the indexed attribute has a high enough cardinality (number of unique values) to make it worth an index.

Full-text indexing

I do not recommend using a DBMS's built-in full-text indexing capability. Many applications will quickly outgrow the limitations of the built-in indexing features. Repopulating a large full-text index can be slow, and it is better to have indexing under your control in situations where the database may grow.

The industry leader in full-text search is Ferret, Dave Balmain's port of Lucene. It is available from *http://ferret.davebalmain.com/trac/*. It has a great reputation and is almost infinitely configurable. It keeps most of Lucene's API, so it will be more familiar to Java programmers.

Jens Krämer's acts_as_ferret library (*http://projects.jkraemer.net/acts_as_ferret/*) makes it quite a bit easier to use Ferret to search an ActiveRecord model. The basic procedure is as follows:

1. Install the Ferret library as a gem:

   ```
   $ sudo gem install ferret
   ```

2. Install acts_as_ferret as a Rails plugin:

   ```
   $ script/plugin install \
       svn://projects.jkraemer.net/acts_as_ferret/tags/stable/acts_as_ferret
   ```

3. Add the acts_as_ferret call to any model that should be indexed. The :remote => true option directs acts_as_ferret to connect to a central Ferret server over DRb; this option is required when using multiple application servers:

   ```
   class Product < ActiveRecord::Base
     acts_as_ferret :fields => [:title, :description, :product_number],
                    :remote => true
   end
   ```

4. Use the find_by_contents class method to query the index:

   ```
   results = Product.find_by_contents "toaster"
   ```

5. If a manual reindex is necessary, use the rebuild_index class method:

   ```
   Product.rebuild_index
   ```

For those of us who are only killing flies, and thus don't need a sledgehammer, Mauricio Fernández has a solution: FTSearch. Although it does not have many of the features that Ferret provides, it is much lighter (about 3% of the size, as measured in lines of code) and it has the most commonly used features. FTSearch is available from *http://eigenclass.org/hiki/ftsearch+repository+accessible*, and Mauricio has a technical description at *http://eigenclass.org/hiki.rb?simple+full+text+search+engine*.

Spatial indexes

Spatial data has a completely different set of requirements than other data, owing primarily to the types of queries that are typically made against it. Even simple spatial queries can turn into expensive computational geometry problems.

All major DBMSs have some sort of module for working with spatial data: PostGIS, MySQL Spatial Extensions, Oracle Spatial, and DB2 Spatial Extender. Most commonly, these modules use R-tree indexes to categorize spatial objects in the database. As with any index, defining R-tree indexes must be done manually and takes some skill. As always, consult your DBMS manual for details.

As usual, there is a lighter-touch option available. The GeoKit library (*http://geokit. rubyforge.org/*) can work with latitude and longitude columns in an ordinary database, doing distance calculations for you. This is great for simple applications that involve a bit of geospatial data, such as store locators (made possible by GeoKit's distance-based ActiveRecord finders and automatic interface to geocoding web services):

```
Store.find :all, :origin => '60685', :within => 10, :order => 'distance asc'
```

Updating index statistics

The query planner maintains statistics on each index to decide which one to use during query planning. While the index is updated whenever the table is modified (as the index always needs to be up to date), the index statistics are only updated at the DBA's request. In PostgreSQL, the command VACUUM ANALYZE table_name is used. In MySQL, the equivalent commands are ANALYZE TABLE table_name and OPTIMIZE TABLE table_name, depending on the storage engine.

It is important to run these commands when the "shape" of the table or index changes substantially—for example, when many rows are inserted or deleted. Under PostgreSQL, the pg_autovacuum daemon can be set up to run maintenance automatically on a periodic basis. This is highly recommended for better performance, and it is automatically enabled starting in PostgreSQL 8.3.

Database Performance Measurement

The first place to look for simple query timing is the Rails development log. By default, the development log lists each SQL query as it is executed, and prepends the query with its execution time in seconds. This is a fine measure relative to other actions and queries on the development machine, but it should not be compared to actions in different environments.

You can diagnose a database bottleneck in a production environment by scanning the production logs. Although the Rails production logs do not list each query, they do list the total time spent in the database for each request:

```
Completed in 0.06189 (16 reqs/sec) | Rendering: 0.04007 (64%) |
    DB: 0.01952 (31%) | 200 OK
```

Using this information, you can find the database-hungry actions in a real-world environment. Then, you can break down the queries that comprise that action and profile each one at the database. This will give you hints about how you might better design your application or database structure to avoid the bottlenecks.

Examining the query plan

Before any SQL query is executed, it must be compiled and planned. The planning process decides on the steps that are taken to answer the query. This includes the selection of indexes and the series of scans, filters, merges, sorts, and other low-level operations that take place to generate the requested data.

All major DBMSs provide powerful tools that show how the query planner has decided to execute a query. In PostgreSQL, the EXPLAIN keyword shows the query plan corresponding to the requested query. The EXPLAIN ANALYZE query syntax is a variant that actually executes the query and returns actual cost values. Here is an example of the first variant:

```
listings_development=> EXPLAIN SELECT min(listing_id) as listing_id,
    count(listing_id) as cluster_size, cluster_id, level
    FROM cluster_ancestors
    WHERE listing_id IN (16466,18320,17948)
    GROUP BY cluster_id, level;

                              QUERY PLAN
----------------------------------------------------------------------------
HashAggregate  (cost=199.48..199.59 rows=7 width=12)
  -> Bitmap Heap Scan on cluster_ancestors  (cost=6.22..198.86 rows=62 width=12)
        Recheck Cond: ((listing_id = 16466) OR (listing_id = 18320) OR
        (listing_id = 17948))
      -> BitmapOr  (cost=6.22..6.22 rows=62 width=0)
          -> Bitmap Index Scan on cluster_ancestors_listing_id_and_level_idx
              (cost=0.00..2.07 rows=21 width=0)
                Index Cond: (listing_id = 16466)
          -> Bitmap Index Scan on cluster_ancestors_listing_id_and_level_idx
              (cost=0.00..2.07 rows=21 width=0)
                Index Cond: (listing_id = 18320)
          -> Bitmap Index Scan on cluster_ancestors_listing_id_and_level_idx
              (cost=0.00..2.07 rows=21 width=0)
                Index Cond: (listing_id = 17948)
(10 rows)
```

The different indentation levels form a tree showing how the data is retrieved from the table and aggregated into a result. Each operation shows a cost estimate, which is roughly related to the number of disk blocks that must be accessed for that operation. The first cost number is the estimated cost to calculate the first row; the second number is the cost to calculate all of the rows. Each step also lists the estimated number of rows returned from that step, as well as the average width, in bytes, of each row. The preceding tree represents the following execution plan (in chronological order):

1. The cluster_ancestors_listing_id_and_level index is scanned for each of the three listing_id values in the WHERE clause. This is an inexpensive scan because it is restricted based on a subset of the index. The query planner estimates that each scan will return 21 rows.

   The index scan is a bitmap scan, so instead of returning the rows themselves, this step just generates a list of the matching rows to be retrieved later. The width is listed as 0 bytes per row because the actual rows are not returned.

2. The BitmapOr step takes the bitwise OR of the three bitmaps returned from the lower steps, effectively returning their union. It returns a bitmap itself, so the width is still 0.

3. The Bitmap Heap Scan uses the bitmap to retrieve the actual rows from the table. The number of rows stays the same, but the width is now 12.

4. A HashAggregate performs the grouping and processes the aggregate functions—the min( ) and count( ) functions in the SELECT clause.

We can see from this example that there are already sufficient indexes on the table, and they are being used properly. This is probably as fast as the query will get given the table size, so there is not much to be gained from more tweaks.

In MySQL, the syntax is the same (without the ANALYZE keyword), but the output is substantially different. MySQL's syntax is more simplistic, but it is arguably easier to understand.

```
mysql> EXPLAIN SELECT * FROM default_en_listingsdb ldb
       INNER JOIN default_en_listingsdbelements ldbe
          ON ldb.listingsdb_id = ldbe.listingsdb_id
       WHERE ldb.listingsdb_id = 141054;
+----+-------------+-------+-------+----------------+----------------+-------+------+
| id | select_type | table | type  | possible_keys  | key            | ref   | rows |
+----+-------------+-------+-------+----------------+----------------+-------+------+
|  1 | SIMPLE      | ldb   | const | PRIMARY        | PRIMARY        | const |    1 |
|  1 | SIMPLE      | ldbe  | ref   | idx_listing_id | idx_listing_id | const |   40 |
+----+-------------+-------+-------+----------------+----------------+-------+------+
2 rows in set (0.35 sec)
```

Rather than defining the steps the database engine takes to fulfill the query, this syntax shows the tables that contribute to the query. As this is a simple inner join, the two tables that comprise the FROM clause are listed, and the select_type of both is SIMPLE (which indicates that they are not components of a union or subquery).

The WHERE clause restricts the first table to one row, referenced by the primary key. The type of that lookup is const, which is the fastest type. The possible_keys column shows the possible indexes that could satisfy the query (PRIMARY), and the key column shows the one that the query planner chose.

The second table, indexed by foreign key, uses a ref lookup on the index, which is fast enough in this case as the number of rows returned (40) is small. If we had not defined the idx_listing_id index, the type would be ALL rather than ref, indicating that the entire table must be scanned.

A basic understanding of your database's query planner is vital to writing good queries and tracking down bad ones. Even for PostgreSQL and MySQL, freely available open source databases, the documentation is very readable and of excellent quality.

Architectural Scalability

One of the hardest parts of building and deploying a web application is growing it. Luckily, Rails was designed with scalability in mind. The Rails scalability mantra is *shared-nothing*—the idea that each application server should stand on its own, not having to coordinate with other application servers to handle a request. The only thing that needs to be shared when scaling upward is the database.*

---

* Some would consider a shared database to be shared-*something*, but I digress.

Nevertheless, there are a few other concerns that you should be aware of when scaling a Rails application. The biggest concerns are the other shared state besides the application data: storage for sessions and cached data.

Sessions

The Rails session infrastructure is built on top of Ruby's `CGI::Session` from the standard library.* `CGI::Session` takes care of the basics of CGI session management. It provides the following session stores, each implemented as a class within `CGI::Session`:

FileStore
> Stores data in a file as plain text. No attempt is made to marshal the data, so you must convert any session data into a `String` first.

MemoryStore
> Stores session data natively in the memory of the Ruby interpreter process.

PStore
> Similar to FileStore, but marshals the data before storing it. This allows you to store any type of data in the session. This is a good option for development, but it is not suitable for a production environment.

Because these options are quite thin and not too suited for large-scale web applications, Rails provides some session managers that are more helpful. In particular, all of these options enable sessions to be shared between different application servers. These implement the same interface as the other `CGI::Session` stores, so they are drop-in replacements. We will examine each one in detail here.

ActiveRecordStore

As its name suggests, the ActiveRecordStore is designed to store sessions in a database via ActiveRecord. However, it is flexible, and does not strictly require ActiveRecord. The standard usage of ActiveRecordStore is very simple if you are already using ActiveRecord—just set the session store in *config/environment.rb*:

```
config.action_controller.session_store = :active_record_store
```

A Rake task is provided to create the database migration for the sessions table: rake db:sessions:create. You do not need to create the ActiveRecord Session class, as the ActiveRecordStore sets one up for you. This class is called `CGI::Session::ActiveRecordStore::Session`, so you can poke around its internals if you need to change anything:

```
CGI::Session::ActiveRecordStore::Session.table_name = 'web_sessions'
```

The ActiveRecordStore uses few features of ActiveRecord, so it will actually work with classes that act like ActiveRecord. This is useful if you are not otherwise using

---

* Standard library documentation is available at *http://www.ruby-doc.org/stdlib/*.

ActiveRecord, or if you are tuning performance and ActiveRecord's advanced features are too heavy.

One such example, SqlBypass, is provided for you. It provides the necessary subset of ActiveRecord to handle sessions. Activate it by manually changing the session class:

```
CGI::Session::ActiveRecordStore.session_class =
    CGI::Session::ActiveRecordStore::SqlBypass
```

Of course, you can easily write your own classes that talk to the session database, and plug them in by this mechanism. The RDoc on CGI::Session::ActiveRecordStore explains the exact requirements.

MemCacheStore

The MemCacheStore is a grown-up version of the DRbStore (a very simple centralized in-memory session store). It uses Danga Interactive's *memcached* daemon to store sessions. (*memcached* is discussed in detail in Chapter 4.) For scalability purposes, memcached is usually preferable to the DRbStore, except in very small settings.

To activate the MemCacheStore, you must install the ruby-memcache gem (gem install ruby-memcache). Then, start up a memcached server on an appropriate machine. This command will tell memcached to use up to 512 MB of RAM, listen on port 11211 (the default memcached port), and daemonize itself:

```
memcached -d -m 512 -p 11211
```

Then, set the Rails session store to the MemCacheStore:

```
config.action_controller.session_store = :mem_cache_store
```

Any options can be set with the session method. For example, you can specify multiple memcached servers to balance requests:

```
class ApplicationController
    session :cache => MemCache.new('10.0.0.13:11211', '10.0.0.14:11211')
end
```

By default, memcached acts as a cache. It takes a -m <MBsize> argument that specifies how much memory to use, and if it hits that limit it will start deleting the oldest records to make room for new ones. This is usually undesirable for session storage. If you use memcached for session storage, ensure that you have enough memory in the cache to hold all current sessions.

Depending on your tolerance for lost sessions, you may want to consider running memcached with the -M option. This option tells memcached to return an error when the memory is full, rather than deleting items from the cache.

Remember that memcached stores data in memory only.[*] If you stop the memcached process, you instantly lose all sessions. There is a new session store,

---

[*] Storing persistent data in memcached is actually a slight abuse of what it was designed for, but it's really darn fast so no one complains.

db_memcache_store, which uses memcached as a cache on top of database sessions, so sessions will not be lost when the memcached server is stopped. It is still slow, but it looks promising. It can be installed as a Rails plugin from *http://topfunky.net/svn/ plugins/db_memcache_store/*.

CookieStore

By default, Rails 2.0 assumes that the session will be small (usually a user ID and any flash data) and stores the entire session in a client-side cookie. This removes a server-side obligation to keep track of sessions, but it introduces some minor security issues. The issues surrounding the cookie session store were discussed in detail in Chapter 5.

Session management

Of course, the ultimate performance enhancement to sessions is not having to use them at all. The session class method allows you to specify actions for which sessions are not needed at all. This can save a decent amount of processing power for actions that are viewed often but do not require the use of a session.

```
class PersonController < ApplicationController
  session :off, :only => [ :list, :show ]
end
```

Caching

Database caching via cached_model and acts_as_cached has been discussed earlier in the book. If your bottleneck is in retrieving records from a database, memcached and those solutions will help.

There is another significant bottleneck in most applications, though, and this one requires more thought. Many applications have rendered pages or parts of rendered pages that, while dynamic, can be cached to some extent. Rails has a few different types of caching methods that allow various levels of granularity when deciding what to cache.

By default, caching is only enabled in production mode, so as not to complicate the debugging process. You can enable caching in development mode with the following line in *config/environments/development.rb*:

```
config.action_controller.perform_caching = true
```

Many Rails plugins are available that modify or improve the standard caching functionality. The Agile Web Development plugins database (*http://agilewebdevelopment. com/plugins*) is the best place to look if you have a specific need.

Page caching

Page caching is conceptually the simplest form of response caching, and it is also the fastest method. However, it is also the least flexible as it caches an entire page. When a page is cached, on first access Rails stores the entire HTML response in a file whose name corresponds to the path used to access the action. For example, the cached response to the path */people/show/12* would be stored in *RAILS_ROOT/public/people/show/12.html*. This enables the web server to answer subsequent requests directly from the file instead of consulting Rails.*

Because the entire page is cached and served from the filesystem, page caching cannot be used if even a small part of the page is dynamic. But it is this same characteristic that makes page caching incredibly fast. Page caching is activated with the caches_page class method:

```
class PersonController < ActionController::Base
  caches_page :list, :show, :new
end
```

Once a page is cached in the filesystem, it must be manually removed if the information becomes stale. Rails has a method, expire_page, which removes the specified page from the page cache. It is not recommended to expire pages directly from the controller, as you must remember to expire at any point where you update the related models. This gets ugly, and it is way too brittle when code changes. Even though caching is a controller-related function, cache expiration is much more of a model-related concern.

Far better is to use *cache sweepers*, which are model observers that expire the appropriate pages when the related model objects change. The sweepers call expire_page as needed. We will cover sweepers later in this chapter.

Do not use page caching if the output depends on any query string parameters. If you do, the page will be cached with the parameters passed to the first request, and subsequent requests will ignore the parameters as they are served from the filesystem.

If you use page caching, be sure that your generated URLs do not end with a trailing slash (*/controller/action/id/*). The route recognizer will function properly in that case, but page caching will be broken because the web server won't find the appropriate file.

Action caching

Where page caching is too generic, there is another option: *action caching*. Action caching still stores the entire HTML response, but it runs the filters first. This is very useful if you have static pages that only authenticated users can see. Performance is worse than page caching, as Rails must process each request.

---

* When serving Rails applications, web servers are configured to first check the */public* directory for a file matching the request. If the file is not found, they pass the request to Rails.

Action caching is triggered by the caches_action method. Here's an example that only allows a page to be viewed on Tuesdays:

```
class UserController < ApplicationController
  before_filter :tuesday?, :only => :happy_tuesday
  caches_action :happy_tuesday

  def happy_tuesday
    render :text => "Happy Tuesday!"
  end

  protected

  def tuesday?
    Time.now.wday == 2
  end
end
```

Action-cached pages are expired with the expire_action method, which is again best called from a cache sweeper. Alternatively, since action caching is implemented on top of fragment caching, you can use the expire_fragment method to expire one or many actions at once. You can even use a regular expression to expire all cached instances of one action (or all actions if you like).

Fragment caching

When the preceding options fail, fragment caching can help. Fragment caching is the most flexible, but least helpful, option. It is designed to store small fragments of the page, but it makes no assumptions about your data. You can store HTML fragments, XML, JSON, or even images in the fragment cache.

Manual access to the fragment cache uses the read_fragment, write_fragment, and expire_fragment methods. This example caches barcode images as they are generated, to avoid generating them every time they are needed:

```
# /barcode/generate/12345
class BarcodeController < ApplicationController
  def generate
    text = params[:id]

    # Retrieve barcode from fragment cache or generate it ourselves
    bc = read_fragment("barcode/generate/#{text}") ||
         write_fragment("barcode/generate/#{text}", Code39.to_jpeg(text))

    # Write the response to the client
    send_data bc, :type => 'image/jpeg', :disposition => 'inline'
  end
end
```

In this example, we assume that the barcode for a particular piece of text never changes, so we don't have to worry about cache expiration. In the real world, we would want to expire old entries so as not to fill up all available RAM or disk space. If we are using memcached as a fragment cache store, we do not have to worry about this; memcached keeps the cache to the size we ask it to by throwing away the oldest entries when it fills up.

Fragment cache stores. Like the various session stores, there are several fragment cache stores that can hold your cached data. The default is the memory store, which is the simplest and requires no options. It stores the fragments in the server's memory space. Each Mongrel or FastCGI listener will have its own fragment cache.

The FileStore, as its name implies, stores fragments in a filesystem directory. When configured, it takes one argument, the path to the cache directory:

```
config.action_controller.fragment_cache_store = :file_store,
    "/var/rails/fragment_cache"
```

The DRbStore (`fragment_cache_store = :drb_store`) requires a running DRb server to store the fragments. It takes a single configuration argument: the URI of the DRb server (`druby://drb_server_name:9192/`). Finally, the MemCacheStore (`:mem_cache_store`) uses a memcached server. Its argument is the hostname or IP address of the server running memcached.

It is technically possible to use the same memcached server for session storage and caching, as session IDs and fragment cache names are not likely to collide (MemCacheStore session keys begin with `session:`). However, this is not recommended. Sessions and fragment caching have fundamentally different needs, and it is not terribly difficult to set up multiple memcached servers (use the `-p` option to specify a port number). I recommend keeping separate concerns separated.

Cache stores have more flexibility than session stores when scaling upward. Though a session must always be reliably available to all of the application servers, you don't lose anything from a fragment cache miss (except a small performance penalty as you have to regenerate the content). Therefore, you could theoretically decide to give each application server its own memory fragment cache. Although this is usually a bad idea (it expands the total amount of memory required), it can make sense if the information to be cached is partitioned along application server boundaries.

Fragment cache helper. The most typical use for fragment caching is in caching an expensive-to-calculate part of a page that must be displayed often. In most cases, there is other dynamic information on the page (even something as simple as a block showing the current user's login name), so the whole page cannot be cached with either page caching or action caching.

There is a Rails helper for caching part of a page. This helper, called cache, abstracts away the details of writing to the cache and checking it. The simplest scenario, where there is at most one cached block per page, looks like this:

```
Welcome, <%=h @username %>.

<% cache do %>
  The prime factors of 1693371614173 are
  <%=h 1693371614173.prime_factors.to_sentence %>.
<% end %>
```

The fragment cache store is presented as a hashtable. Fragments are stored by a string key. The default key scheme uses the path of the current action to index the hash. When cache is called, it calls url_for with the arguments given to cache (if any). This gives the fragment a name like example.com/user/welcome.

Additional options can be given to cache to uniquely identify different fragments within the same action. These options will be passed through to url_for. In particular, you can use this to differentiate between two or more cached fragments on the same page:

```
<% cache(:id => 'one') do %>
  This is cached as example.com/some/action/one.
<% end %>

<% cache(:id => 'two') do %>
  This is cached as example.com/some/action/two.
<% end %>
```

The url_for function is only used here to provide a unique name for the cached fragment; it does not need to map to a real-world route. But sticking to these conventions (the real action name plus an optional action suffix) will avoid collisions with names of unrelated fragments.

Fragment expiration. The expire_fragment method removes a fragment from the cache. It takes either a string or a hash argument, in the same format as the write_fragment and cache methods. If passed a hash, it will run it through url_for and delete the appropriate items from the cache.

Alternatively, expire_fragment can take a regular expression as an argument, and it will delete all pages with keys matching that regexp. This is not recommended. That syntax is not supported with memcached (which cannot iterate over its keys), and for all other fragment cache stores, Rails must iterate over every key and check it against the regular expression. This can slow things down tremendously.

Cache sweepers

As discussed before, cache sweepers are model observers that expire cached pages, actions, and fragments when their model objects change. Sweepers inherit from ActionController::Caching::Sweeper and implement the standard callback methods.

```
class PersonSweeper < ActionController::Caching::Sweeper
  observe Person

  def after_save(record)
    expire_cache(record)
  end

  def after_destroy(record)
    expire_cache(record)
  end

  def expire_cache(record)
    # Actions to take when +record+ is changed or destroyed
    expire_page :controller => 'person', :action => 'show', :id => record.id
    expire_page :controller => 'person', :action => 'list'
  end
end
```

The sweeper must be activated by name from the controller:

```
class PersonController < ApplicationController
  caches_page :list, :show, :new
  cache_sweeper :person_sweeper, :only => [ :create, :update, :destroy ]
end
```

Because sweepers bridge between the model and controller, it makes sense to create a new directory for the caching-related classes. Place the sweeper in *app/cachers*, and add the following line to your *environment.rb* file:[*]

```
config.load_paths += %W(#{RAILS_ROOT}/app/cachers)
```

As long as your files are named according to standard Rails conventions (Person-Sweeper is defined in *person_sweeper.rb*), Rails will autoload the corresponding file when an unknown symbol such as PersonSweeper is first encountered. The load_paths option simply adds to the list of locations that Dependencies searches. We covered Dependencies in detail in Chapter 2.

Other Systems

The remainder of this chapter is a collection of miscellaneous performance tips and solutions to common problems. If you have specific trouble, the Rails wiki (*http://wiki.rubyonrails.com/*) might help. The wiki is disorganized at times, but it has a large amount of relevant information on many topics if you are willing to search.

---

[*] The idea and implementation of this separation of concerns come from Mephisto, which is a good example of a cleanly structured Rails application. The code is available from *http://svn.techno-weenie.net/projects/mephisto/trunk/*.

Choosing the Right Tool

A large part of software development consists of selecting the right tools for the job. This encompasses not only languages but libraries, frameworks, source control, databases, servers, and all of the other tools and materials that go into a completed application.

Leveraging external programs

Sometimes the best way to solve a problem is not to have a problem at all. Chances are, if you have a moderately complicated technical problem, someone else has solved it. 37signals' Basecamp takes this approach when resizing images—rather than dealing with the hassle of installing RMagick, they just shell out to ImageMagick:[*]

```
def thumbnail(temp, target)
  system(
    "/usr/local/bin/convert #{escape(temp)} -resize 48x48! #{escape(target)}"
  )
end
```

Part of the beauty of scripting languages is that they were designed out of necessity, so they have ways to glue disparate parts together. In addition, most scripting languages have a rich set of community-developed libraries available. Though CPAN (Perl's collection of third-party libraries) is the undisputed champion in this arena, Ruby has Rubyforge (*http://rubyforge.org*) and the Ruby Application Archive (*http://raa.ruby-lang.org/*).

Writing inline C code

Writing Ruby extensions in C used to be hard. If you wanted to rewrite performance-sensitive functions, there were many things besides the actual code that you had to deal with. Not so anymore.

Ryan Davis has unleashed an incredible tool, RubyInline,[†] for integrating C with Ruby. This tool allows you to embed C/C++ code as strings directly within an application. The strings are then compiled into native code (only to be recompiled when they change) and installed into your classes. The canonical example, the factorial function, shows just how fast and clean this can be:

```
require 'rubygems'
require 'inline'    # gem install RubyInline
require 'benchmark'

class Test
  # Standard Ruby factorial function
```

---

[*] *http://www.loudthinking.com/arc/000598.html*

[†] *http://www.zenspider.com/ZSS/Products/RubyInline/Readme.html*

```
def factorial(n)
  result = 1
  n.downto(2) { |x| result *= x }
  result
end

# Reimplemented in C (compiled on the fly)
inline do |builder|
  builder.c <<-EOINLINE
    long factorial_c(int max) {
      int i = max,
          result = 1;
      while (i >= 2) { result *= i--; }
      return result;
    }
  EOINLINE
end
end
```

We can then set up a benchmark to compare the two implementations:

```
t = Test.new

Benchmark.bmbm do |b|
  b.report("Ruby factorial") do
    200_000.times { t.factorial(20) }
  end

  b.report("C factorial") do
    200_000.times { t.factorial_c(20) }
  end
end
```

On my machine, the C implementation is extremely fast—more than 25 times the speed of the standard Ruby implementation!

```
                       user      system      total        real
Ruby factorial     2.760000    0.010000    2.770000 (  2.753621)
C factorial        0.110000    0.000000    0.110000 (  0.104440)
```

The best part of RubyInline is that it keeps your code clean. Ruby and C code addressing the same area can be intermingled, rather than being spread across multiple files. And RubyInline handles the type conversion for you—you can deal with ints, longs, and char *s, and they will automatically be converted to and from Ruby types.

ActionMailer

Email delivery can be a difficult and aggravating aspect of a deployed application. The SMTP protocol was not designed to withstand the types of attacks that are being directed at the mail system today, and so delivering mail can be a more complicated process than it may seem.

One common problem is that email delivery via SMTP is quite slow, on the average. In addition, it is an unknown; the time it takes to send one email is highly variable. Even when delivering to an SMTP relay on the local network (which is a good idea for high-volume sites), SMTP delivery is slow.

To counteract this slowness, it is usually desirable to decouple the email sending from the web request/response cycle. It makes sense to allow the user to continue working, even if the server is still trying to send email in the background. One option is to simply fork off a separate OS process, or use a separate interpreter thread (via Thread.new with a block) to send email asynchronously. However, this solution does not scale well, as you must handle any concurrency issues that arise on your own. In addition, you have overhead from starting a new thread or process on each piece of mail. For high-volume mail situations, you want a mailer daemon running a tight loop that can send mail without having to start a worker process.

The scalable option is the Robot Co-op's ar_mailer.* This little library uses the database as an outgoing mail spool. When mail is to be sent, rather than delivering it externally, Rails just dumps it into the database. The separate ar_sendmail process picks it up and sends it along. This way, the application does not get backed up because of slow SMTP performance. ar_sendmail can be run periodically (from cron) or continuously, as a daemon.

Further Reading

Zed Shaw's most famous rant, *Programmers Need To Learn Statistics Or I Will Kill Them All* (*http://www.zedshaw.com/rants/programmer_stats.html*), is an excellent (if a little aggressive) description of the most common misconceptions surrounding performance measurement.

Peepcode has a screencast on benchmarking with httperf at *http://peepcode.com/products/benchmarking-with-httperf*. It is $9 but is worth the cost for anyone involved in performance tuning.

Evan Weaver has a set of MySQL configuration files that are tuned for common Rails situations at *http://blog.evanweaver.com/articles/2007/04/30/top-secret-tuned-mysql-configurations-for-rails*. These are drop-in replacements for the standard *my.cnf* configuration file, and they are much more current than the examples provided with MySQL.

---

* *http://blog.segment7.net/articles/2006/08/15/ar_mailer*

## CHAPTER 7

REST, Resources, and Web Services

There are only two hard things in Computer Science:
cache invalidation and naming things.
—Phil Karlton

The architectural principles of Representational State Transfer, or REST, have been taking the Rails world by storm. The idea behind REST has been around since Roy Fielding first described it in his 2000 doctoral dissertation. However, the ideas have only started to gain traction among Rails developers since David Heinemeier Hansson's presentation of those ideas in 2006 and the subsequent adoption of RESTful principles in Rails 1.2. RESTful design is a new way of thinking about network architecture based on an observation of how the Web works.

What Is REST?

In short, REST is a unifying theory for how "distributed hypermedia" systems (primarily, the World Wide Web) are best organized and structured. The term was coined by Roy Fielding, coauthor of the HTTP specification, in his 2000 doctoral dissertation *Architectural Styles and the Design of Network-Based Software Architectures.*[*] The dissertation extracts a set of principles that are common to network architectures, based on an examination of the structure of the Web and the HTTP protocol. Starting with the "null style," which is the absence of constraints on architecture, Fielding arrives at REST by placing a series of constraints on network architecture:

Client-Server
> The client-server constraint imposes a separation of data storage from user interface and presentation. The most important benefit of this separation is that client and server can exist in separate organizations and be maintained, developed, and scaled independently.

---

[*] Available from *http://www.ics.uci.edu/~fielding/pubs/dissertation/top.htm.*

Stateless

The server may not hold persistent state about its sessions with the client. Each request from client to server is independent and self-contained. This increases verbosity, but aids reliability and scalability. When there is little or no stored context on a server, the system is more resilient to periodic failure, and there are fewer requirements for inter-server coordination when the system is scaled up.

Cache

This step requires the server to indicate whether or not the client may cache a response, and to define parameters for such caching. Providing explicit cache control information allows the client to cache more aggressively, reducing network traffic and increasing performance.

Uniform Interface

A uniform interface is the primary item that distinguishes REST from RPC and other network styles. Forcing the client and server to communicate using a well-known uniform interface pushes the application-specific complexity out of the network layer into the application layer, where it belongs. It allows standardized software components to be reused for vastly different applications, as they speak the same language.

Layered System

Architectures are permitted to be broken down into independent layers (in the sense of the OSI or TCP/IP layered models). Each layer mediates only between the layers immediately adjacent to itself. In this way, layers can evolve or be replaced independently with minimal impact to the remainder of the architecture.

Code-on-Demand

Client software is extensible by retrieving and executing code from a server. This allows clients to expand their capabilities in an ad-hoc manner after an architecture is deployed.

REST is often referred to as an *architectural style*, instead of an architecture. Rather than defining a specific "best" architecture, REST defines principles by which architectures are created and evaluated—it puts constraints on network architecture.

We often use a linguistic analogy to explain REST; in many ways, the REST principles are modeled on human communication. Resource names are "nouns," as they refer to things. It is important to remember the distinction between resources and their names. Just as the word "apple" is not itself an apple, the name http://example.com/person/123 is just a name, not the resource itself. A corollary is that a resource may have many names (though good REST style indicates that this should be kept to a minimum, where possible).

In the same way, HTTP methods are referred to as "verbs" because they specify an action on a resource or its representation.

Fielding's thesis is very general; it actually applies to any "network-based architecture." However, REST is most commonly applied to the World Wide Web and HTTP, and we will constrain our subject of discussion in this chapter to REST's application to HTTP. Necessarily, this will impose constraints and guidelines not derived from Fielding's thesis. Therefore, the principles explained in this chapter are a subset of those of Fielding's REST.

In some ways, REST is simply "HTTP as it was meant to be." As the Web grew in popularity, many of the original design decisions that guided HTTP were ignored. Developers of web applications tended to see things like HTTP verbs and response status codes as incidental to the application, or as a triviality to be dealt with when time allowed. Using HTTP as intended was often seen as unnecessary or arduous. However, in recent years, a return to REST principles indicates that HTTP was good enough after all. Developers are learning these lessons:

- Most, if not all, domains can be fairly easily modeled as sets of CRUD (create, read, update, delete) operations. These operations roughly correspond to HTTP POST, GET, PUT, and DELETE, respectively. In this way, the set of actions is standardized.

- Names corresponding to resources (/person/123) are generally consistent, robust, and understandable. Names corresponding to service endpoints (/personService) tend to be too broad and underspecified, while names corresponding to RPC calls (/person/show/123, when accessed with GET) are redundant.

- Orthogonality wins. Names should identify resources; nothing more or less. Success and failure should be inferred from the HTTP response status, not from an error message within the payload. A resource can have multiple representations, but they should all be identified as originating from the same resource (and their names should reflect that).

The combination of nouns, verbs, and content types is often referred to as the *REST triangle*. Together, the three corners of the triangle define the architecture. A REST-centric design decomposition is often done by deciding on the nouns (identifying and naming things), selecting a uniform set of verbs (easy if you are using HTTP), and choosing content types.

Verbs

Verbs correspond to actions on resources. A verb will either send a representation of a resource from the server to the client or update the resource on the server with information from the client.

In REST, verbs are a constrained territory. While the set of content types is open for revision and expansion, and resource names are infinitely expandable, the set of verbs is fixed. However, the constraints put on the scope of verbs allows them to be universal; any verb can be applied to any noun.

HTTP defines a handful of methods; the set can be expanded by protocols such as WebDAV, but the basic set is sufficient for REST. The four most common methods are GET, PUT, DELETE, and POST; we will examine each of them and their purpose here.

We can form some linguistic analogies as a simplification of the four common verbs. Roughly speaking, this is what they mean, using "this" to refer to the request body, and "there" to refer to the URI acted upon:

- GET: "Give me whatever is there."
- PUT: "Store this there."
- DELETE: "Delete whatever is there."
- POST: "Hey you there, process this."

GET

The GET method transfers a representation of a resource from the server to the client. It is used for read-only access to a resource. GET is by far the most common verb on the Web; it is often the only method used on static web sites.

A common mistake is to use GET for an action that updates a resource. GET is defined as a *safe* method (see the upcoming sidebar, "Safe and Idempotent Methods"); it should be used for retrieval, not updates. Using GET for updates causes many problems because it breaks the assumptions that the client and any proxies may have about the nature of GET requests.

This problem came into the Rails public eye in 2005, when the Google Web Accelerator was released. The Web Accelerator is a proxy that uses the time the user is viewing a page to prefetch the outgoing links from that page, reducing the latency between clicking on a link and seeing the resulting page. Because following a link that updates the server could have catastrophic results (consider prefetching every "Delete" link on a page full of users), the Accelerator only followed standard web links (which use GET).

However, many popular web applications (including 37signals' Backpack) were vulnerable. Many Rails applications were affected, as the Rails "pretty URL" convention dictated URLs like /people/delete/123, rather than the conventions of other web frameworks, which led to URLs like /people.php?action=delete&id=123. The end result was a scramble among web developers to convert all GET links with side effects into POSTs. Later, the Google team added a feature to the Web Accelerator so that it would not prefetch links with query strings, but there was a scramble nevertheless.

However, all of this fuss was but a symptom of the real problem. The problem was not so much that GET links performed actions; it was that HTTP was being used improperly. The contract between clients and servers had been broken. So, when all of the GET /people/delete/123 actions became POST /people/delete/123, it was an improvement, but not by much, as POST is not terribly relevant to a "delete person" action. A more RESTful design would involve an action such as DELETE /people/123.

Safe and Idempotent Methods

One purpose of the HTTP standard is to define the implicit meanings of the various HTTP methods. This is the mental working model that many developers use when working on web applications: GET retrieves a representation, PUT updates a resource, and so on.

But another, more important, purpose of the HTTP specification is to form an explicit contract between the server, the client, and any proxies or caches along the way. This tells each principal what they can and cannot assume about the data they work with. The concepts of safe and idempotent methods fall under this category.

Safe methods are used for retrieval; the purpose of a safe request should never be to perform an update. The HTTP safe methods are GET and HEAD. (HEAD is functionally equivalent to GET, but only returns the response headers, not the body.)

Safety is usually defined at the application level, and the definition of a safe method can change based on application semantics. A GET operation may incur incidental side effects, such as loading query results into a cache or updating a hit counter; the action would still be described as safe. The distinction drawn by the HTTP specification is that safe requests should not incur an obligation on the user's behalf (such as an online payment or creation of a user account). In other words, it must always be the server that decides to perform an update based on a safe request.

GET, HEAD, PUT, and DELETE are *idempotent methods*. The result (response as well as resource state) of an idempotent action is the same, no matter how many times that action is performed (assuming each action is identical and there is otherwise no change to resource state). Idempotent methods may change resource state, but they are not required to (all safe methods are by definition idempotent).

The result of this definition is resiliency; if a client initiates a PUT request and is not sure whether it completed successfully, it can retry the same request with no negative consequences.

PUT

The PUT method updates a resource with the representation provided in the body of the PUT request. If the resource did not exist before the PUT request, the request creates a new one with the given representation.

A common point of confusion is how resource names (URIs) apply to PUT versus POST requests. A PUT request must always be directed toward the URI of the resource in question; even if creating a new resource, the URI must be that of the resource to be created. If the client does not know the URI of the resource (for example, if it is derived from a server-generated ID), a POST request should be used.

DELETE

As its name implies, the DELETE method deletes the resource identified by its URI. If the deletion is carried out (the server may not allow a deletion), subsequent GET queries to the same URI should return a status code of 410 (Gone) or 404 (Not Found).

POST

We list POST last because it is the method of last resort. It is neither safe nor idempotent, so there are few technical restrictions to its power. As such, it is abused for many operations that could better be represented by another verb. Theoretically, POST could be used for every action on the Web without violating the letter of the RFC.

Though POST is powerful, it should not be used where GET, PUT, or DELETE would suffice. The semantics of those three methods are much simpler, and the constraints put on them allow easier caching and scalability. POST can, in theory, be cached via the Cache-Control and Expires headers, but in practice this is rarely implemented.

POST is primarily used in one of two ways: creation of new objects and annotation of existing objects. In either case, the URI of the POST is that of the object's container or parent. The RFC draws an analogy of a directory structure; to create or update an object, you POST to its containing "directory."

To create a resource, its representation is sent via POST to a URI responsible for creating resources of that type. If the request for creation succeeds, the server issues a redirect via the Location header pointing to the URI of the created resource.

When annotating a resource, the POST URI is that of the resource to be annotated (the "parent" of the entity being sent). This is different from a PUT request in that the resource being POSTed to is not being updated with a new representation, but rather annotated with additional information.

Resources

The most foundational concept of REST is the *resource*. The most general definition of a resource is *something with identity*. It really is as simple as that. In popular usage, the term "resource" usually means something that is network-addressable on the Internet, and it is with these types of resources that we will concern ourselves. But a resource can really be anything, tangible or intangible, that can be named. As RFC 2396 explains:*

> A resource can be anything that has identity. Familiar examples include an electronic document, an image, a service (e.g., "today's weather report for Los Angeles"), and a collection of other resources. Not all resources are network "retrievable"; e.g., human beings, corporations, and bound books in a library can also be considered resources.

---

* *http://tools.ietf.org/html/rfc2396*

<div class="sidebar">

Pragmatic REST

REST in Rails is a balance between theoretical purity and pragmatism. The fact is that many browsers do not support the full set of response codes according to the HTTP standard.

Resource creation via POST is a good example of a discrepancy. The correct response to successful creation is a *201 Created* code with a Location header pointing to the created resource. However, most web browsers will not redirect in response to a 2xx-series response. Rails strikes a balance. When rendering HTML, it uses a 3xx-series redirect to satisfy web browsers. When rendering XML, it is assumed that the client will be cognizant of all HTTP response codes, and it uses the appropriate response codes.

We see this in action in a typical scaffolded controller:

```ruby
# POST /products
# POST /products.xml
def create
  @product = Product.new(params[:product])

  respond_to do |format|
    if @product.save
      flash[:notice] = 'Product was successfully created.'
      format.html { redirect_to(@product) }
      format.xml  { render :xml => @product,
                    :status => :created, :location => @product }
    else
      format.html { render :action => "new" }
      format.xml  { render :xml => @product.errors,
                    :status => :unprocessable_entity }
    end
  end
end
```

</div>

Implicit in this definition of resources is that resources have state as well (a resource could have empty state in the degenerate case, but this is atypical). One of the constraints that REST places on interaction with resources is that every RESTful resource has a uniform interface. No client has ad-hoc access (read or write) to a resource's state; it is internal to the resource. All access takes place by transferring *representations* of the resource's state[*] back and forth via a uniform set of methods (in our case, HTTP).

Name opacity

A controversial principle of REST is whether names should be *opaque*. An opaque value, in a network protocol, is a piece of data that the recipient can remember and

---

[*] Hence the name: *Representational State Transfer*.

return, but cannot interpret. The concept of URIs as opaque values originates not with Roy Fielding, but with Tim Berners-Lee:

> The only thing you can use an identifier for is to refer to an object. When you are not dereferencing, you should not look at the contents of the URI string to gain other information.

This is a controversial idea, and the REST community is split over it. URIs have evolved as a hybrid of opaque and transparent names. Particularly with human-friendly ("pretty") URIs, people naturally expect to be able to interpret and modify the URIs that they use. Upon receiving a 404 Not Found for John Smith's index of papers published in 1997 at *http://example.edu/~jsmith/papers/1997/index.html*, it is reasonable to expect *http://example.edu/~jsmith/*, if it exists, to be somehow associated with John Smith.

URIs tend to self-organize into a hierarchy, in no small way due to their provenance as filesystem paths. It is not a good idea to break users' expectations in this regard. Although it may or may not be desirable for clients to always respect name opacity (by only using URIs for dereferencing), it is certainly undesirable for servers to force name opacity by creating inscrutable naming schemes.

Those who believe names should be opaque generally state that relationships between URIs should be mined through links between resources. If a person (or machine) retrieves a list of users (GET /users), the response would contain links to each user in the list (/users/1, /users/2, ...). Commonsense as this may seem, especially for a machine-consumable service, there are prominent RESTful web services (such as Amazon S3, which we will examine later) that do not use links at all.

URI templates, described in an Internet Draft (*http://www.ietf.org/internet-drafts/draft-gregorio-uritemplate-02.txt*), are a promising new hybrid between link-based and hierarchical navigation. A URI template provides a structured pattern for URIs, so that they make sense as hierarchies but can still be treated as opaque:

```
http://example.com/carts/{cart_id}
```

A client application could use this template to generate a URI for a shopping cart. The primary advantage of URI templates is that they are structured; the template can be provided as an input to a web service client, rather than hardcoding the URI into the application.

The bottom line is that opacity as a hard-and-fast rule does not always make sense. Sometimes a graph of data accessed through links makes sense; sometimes a structured naming system might be more fruitful.

The advantages of a structured name system are apparent with algorithmic resources, which represent the results of a calculation. These resources are typically infinite in number, and are accessed through names like http://example.com/search/banana. In this case, it can make more sense to allow both the client and intermediaries to infer semantics from the URI.

Representations and Content Types

Resources on the Web "live" and hold their state at the server, but they are only ever accessed through the representations that they expose. Like Plato's cave, we never see the resource itself; all that we see are the shadows on the wall—the representations of that resource.

Different representations of a resource vary based on their content types. The same resource might be available at /users/1.html, /users/1.xml, and /users/1.js. The formats of these names imply that they are representations of the same resource (again, even if the names are treated as opaque and the client cannot rely on this knowledge, it is a valuable convention).

Selecting a representation

One detail unspecified by REST is how a client requests a particular content type. As many representations may be available from the same resource, how does the server know which one to send?

In practice, the answer is either URI extensions or content negotiation. Extensions are easy to understand and implement: the URI is examined for a filename extension (such as .js, .html, or .xml). The most suitable representation is then selected based on a *type map* (a structure that maps filename extensions to content types). For example, fetching the URI /orders/124.html might return:

```
<!DOCTYPE html PUBLIC "-//W3C//DTD XHTML 1.0 Strict//EN"
  "http://www.w3.org/TR/xhtml1/DTD/xhtml1-strict.dtd">
<html xmlns="http://www.w3.org/1999/xhtml">
  <head>
    <title>Viewing Order #124</title>
  </head>
```

```
<body id="order-124">
  <h1>Order #124</h1>
  <p>Items:</p>
  <ul id="order-124-items">
    <li><a href="/orders/124/items/1">Office Chair, Medium</a></li>
    <li><a href="/orders/124/items/2">Ergonomic Keyboard</a></li>
  </ul>
</body>
</html>
```

But a request to the same resource with a different URI, at /orders/124.xml, might result in a more easily machine-readable XML version:

```
<Order id="124">
  <Items>
    <Item id="1" href="/orders/124/items/1">Office Chair, Medium</Item>
    <Item id="2" href="/orders/124/items/2">Ergonomic Keyboard</Item>
  </Items>
</Order>
```

The JavaScript representation at /orders/124.js might use JSON:

```
{"order": {
  "id": 124,
  "items": [
    {"id": 1, "href": "/orders/124/items/1",
      "description": "Office Chair, Medium"},
    {"id": 2, "href": "/orders/124/items/2",
      "description": "Ergonomic Keyboard"}]
}}
```

Changing content types based on URI extensions is nice and easy, and it plays well with the way we traditionally expect the Web to work. Among other things, it makes the URIs look like filenames again, and behave somewhat like filesystem paths. However, this is not always optimal within the REST model.

All of these are clearly different representations of the same resource, and yet they have different URIs. Many argue that the URI should name only the resource, and not the representation. How would it be possible to use the same name to refer to all of these resources?

The answer is *content negotiation*. This is a part of the HTTP request and response where the client and server negotiate some common parameters so that they can communicate.

As a whole, HTTP content negotiation is very flexible; it can negotiate a representation based on language (through the Accept-Language request header), character encoding (through the Accept-Charset header), content coding (Accept-Encoding), or content type (Accept). It is the latter that we are most concerned with.

Rather than specifying the content type explicitly in the URI, we specify an Accept header in the HTTP request. This header lists the content types we are willing to accept, in decreasing order of priority. Under content negotiation on the preceding service, this request would return the HTML version:

```
GET /orders/124 HTTP/1.1
Host: www.example.com
Accept: text/html, application/xhtml+xml, text/*, image/png, image/*, */*
```

Clients can vary their `Accept` header to request different representations of the requested resource, and the server will try to satisfy the request with any representations it can serve.

Basing the choice of representation on either URI extensions or `Accept` header content negotiation is a valid decision. They each have their benefits and drawbacks, and Rails supports both.

Statelessness

At the network level, HTTP is a stateless protocol. Each client/server interaction repeats some information on each connection to the server. This costs some redundancy, but it pays off in other areas such as scalability. By definition, Fielding's REST is always stateless. The interaction between client and server carries no state at lower or higher levels.

However, there is a difference between resource state and application state. *Resource state* is the internal state that all nontrivial resources carry, and it is essential to a web application. Examples of resource state would include the changes made to a hosted document or the content of a to-do list; without this state, there would be no application.

On the other hand, *application state* (also called *session state*) is the state of the client's interaction with the server. Application state tracks a user or client's progress through an application. Keeping this state on the server violates REST principles as it breaks addressability. An implication of REST is that the representation retrieved from a resource should depend only on that resource's state and the client's request. If the server presents a different representation for the same URI based on the path that the client took to get to that URI, then the URI loses its addressability. It cannot be shared or bookmarked.

At the lower levels, application state includes HTTP cookies, which can break REST in lesser or greater amounts. At the higher levels, web application frameworks (Rails included) often expose a session persistence mechanism. Typically, a repository of session state is kept on the server, indexed by a key that is given in an HTTP cookie to the client.* This is much more self-evidently an application state repository.

---

* Newer versions of Rails default to a cookie-based session store, which stores the entire session, not just an index, in the cookie. This has several advantages, but also some security concerns. I discuss the trade-offs in Chapter 5.

REST maintains that all application state should be kept on the client. This is what is meant by *statelessness*; not that there is no state within the application, but that each request can stand on its own; the client/server session itself maintains no state.

HTTP state

Let's examine how state is typically dealt with in web applications. HTTP provides cookies as a method for servers to persist small amounts of data on the client. Like all protocols in layered systems, HTTP uses lower-level (stateless) primitives to build higher-level (stateful) abstractions. Here, we'll examine the mechanics of that process.

By default, unless sessions are manually disabled, Rails sets up a new session on a client's first interaction with the application. At the HTTP level, it looks like this (irrelevant headers elided):

Client → Server
```
GET / HTTP/1.1
Host: www.example.com
```

 The HTTP Host request header is mandatory in HTTP 1.1. It tells the server which DNS name was used to contact it. This is essential for *name-based virtual hosting*. Thousands of sites may share one IP address, differentiated only by the Host headers sent by clients.

Server → Client
```
HTTP/1.1 200 OK
Content-Type: text/html; charset=utf-8
Set-Cookie: _session_id=6cd3556deb0da54bca060b4c39479839; domain=example.com
```

 In this example, the server explicitly sets the cookie domain to example.com. Without the domain parameter, the cookie's scope would be limited to www.example.com (the domain of the original request) and its subdomains, for security reasons. But since the server set the cookie with the more general domain, it will be shared between requests to example.com, www.example.com, shop.example.com, and the like.

When a client requests a URI from a server, it sends any applicable cookies in the request headers.

Client → Server
```
GET /protected-resource HTTP/1.1
Host: www.example.com
Cookie: _session_id=6cd3556deb0da54bca060b4c39479839
```

By using HTTP cookies, application state is made persistent. This can have its advantages. Sometimes it is used for tracking; it is an easy way to watch a visitor as he progresses through a site. But most often, cookies are used to track user authentication and/or personalization.

From an HTTP perspective, it would seem rather odd that another mechanism would have to be introduced for authentication. HTTP already provides methods for authenticating users, and they work statelessly.

However, the standard HTTP Basic and Digest authentication mechanisms have many problems, and they are rarely used on the public Web. There are several factors affecting their widespread adoption:

- They use the standard browser/operating system controls to prompt for credentials; they cannot be styled.
- They do not easily facilitate logout.
- There is no easy way to request login conditionally, or return different representations based on whether or not the user is logged in.
- HTTP Basic authentication does not really even attempt to hide the username and password when transmitting across the network; in Base64 encoding, they are essentially plain text. Digest authentication is much more secure, but is not universally supported in older browsers.

Thus, a web application requiring authentication usually presents login forms itself and keeps track of user authentication using a cookie. Most implementations of this run contrary to the principles of REST by keeping additional application state outside of the request envelope. The cookie itself is stored and transmitted just like an HTTP authentication request would be, but the difference is that authentication cookies usually gain their validity from being tied to server-side application state.

Why statelessness?

Statelessness, and its application to web sites and web applications, is often a point of contention, even among REST's adherents. Though most developers agree that minimizing the amount of application state carried on the server is a useful goal, it is not always clear to what degree the principles should be carried.

The primary benefit of statelessness is that it enables scalability by allowing application servers to be treated as black boxes from an architectural perspective. In Rails, this is often called *shared-nothing* architecture. If each request is independent of session state, it does not matter whether the subsequent requests in a browsing session are handled by one server or 1,000. In an architecture with 1,000 application servers, the only communication between the servers is made by changing state in the resources themselves (typically through a database or filesystem).

Contrarily, in an environment that requires server-side session state, there are two options. The servers can directly communicate and discuss the session state, which introduces another interface; besides dealing with resource state, servers must also communicate about application state. The other option is *sticky sessions*, directing the load balancer to funnel all requests from the same session to the same application server. This can work well, and it eliminates the need for backend server communication. Avi Bryant (of Seaside fame) endorses this architecture.

However, it eliminates the possibility of high availability (sessions cannot be shared between two servers unless they communicate), and a server that is restarted typically loses its sessions (unless storing them in persistent storage, which negates many advantages of sticky sessions). Neither of these options is terribly RESTful, and so we promote statelessness as far as is practical.

Resourceful session state: An example

So what is the RESTful alternative to holding session state on the server? As with nearly any problem REST developers face, the solution is to *model it as a resource*. With the exception of authentication information (discussed later in the chapter), nearly anything that would be stored in a session could also be factored into a resource.

Consider the example of a shopping cart. A typical, simple, non-RESTful Rails implementation would look something like this:

app/models/cart.rb

```
# A simple Hash that defaults to zero.
# Used to map product IDs to quantities to represent a shopping cart.
class Cart < Hash
  def initialize
    super(0)
  end
end
```

app/controllers/carts_controller.rb

```
class CartsController < ApplicationController
  before_filter :set_cart

  def add_product
    product_id = params[:id]
    quantity = params[:quantity] || 1

    # Increment cart quantity by provided quantity
    session[:cart][product_id.to_i] += quantity.to_i
  end

  def update_quantity
    product_id = params[:id]
    quantity = params[:quantity]

    # Set cart quantity to provided quantity
    session[:cart][product_id.to_i] = quantity.to_i
  end

  def remove_product
    product_id = params[:id]
```

```
        # Remove specified item from cart
        session[:cart].delete product_id.to_i
      end

      def empty
        session[:cart] = Cart.new
      end

      protected

      def set_cart
        session[:cart] ||= Cart.new
      end
    end
```

config/routes.rb

```
    map.add_to_cart '/carts/add_product/:id',
      :controller => 'carts', :action => 'add_product'
    map.update_cart_quantity '/carts/update_quantity/:id',
      :controller => 'carts', :action => 'update_quantity'
    map.remove_product '/carts/remove_product/:id',
      :controller => 'carts', :action => 'remove_product'
    map.empty_cart '/carts/empty',
      :controller => 'carts', :action => 'empty'
```

We are using named routes here so that we gain the benefit of the Rails named URI generators. For non-RESTful Rails applications, named routes are much preferred over the default :controller/:action/:id route, as they decouple URIs from their implementation. For example, the "remove product" action in the views would typically be coded as follows:

```
    link_to "Remove Product",
      remove_product_path(:id => @product.id),
      :method => :post
```

If all links are generated through the Rails named route mechanism, then URIs can be changed simply by changing the template in the routes file, without touching any of the code that links to the page being changed.

Though this is a relatively clean implementation, it still requires the use of persistent session storage on the server. This is not optimal, for the reasons we discussed earlier.

In addition, this code could use some architectural cleanup. Because a resource can be any *thing*, we will choose to model the cart as a resource itself. Rather than URIs affecting the product, which have effects on the cart in the session, we choose URIs that explicitly model their effects on our newly created cart resource. Using some standard RESTful Rails URI conventions, we come up with the following set of actions.

Action	Non-RESTful URI (POST method)	RESTful method and URI
Create cart	(N/A)	POST /carts
Add item	/carts/add_product/123	PUT /carts/4/products/123
Update quantity	/carts/update_quantity/ 123?quantity=2	PUT /carts/4/products/123 line_item[quantity]=2
Remove item	/carts/remove_item/123	DELETE /carts/4/products/123
Empty cart	/carts/empty_cart	DELETE /carts/4

Note that our old code has no action for "create cart," but the new code requires that as an explicit step. This is a consequence of RESTful design; we now realize that the cart resource (along with its child, the cart-product or line-item resource) is a separate resource and should be treated as such. Rather than treating cart creation as a side effect of some other action, we explicitly make cart creation a client-initiated action.

Also notice that the old code has RPC-style URIs; they contain the method name. The new URIs have a more proper separation of concerns. The HTTP method contains the verb or action; the URI contains the name of the object of that action (the resource); and the optional request body contains information pertaining to the resource.

Now that we have decided on a set of URLs for the application, we can start writing code. First, we have identified the types of resources that will be involved. They were implied previously, but we will describe them:

Cart factory (/carts)
> This resource is responsible for generating carts. An empty POST to /carts will create a new cart and return its URI in the HTTP Location header.

Cart (/carts/4)
> Represents a cart; in this model, shopping cart state is kept explicitly in this resource rather than in the user's session.

Line Item (/carts/4/products/123)
> Represents an instance of a product in a user's cart. Subordinate to (nested within) the cart resource.

> These three types of resources are just that—types, not resources themselves. Although there is only one "cart" resource type, there are potentially infinitely many "cart" resources (/carts/4, /carts/5, and so on). This is an important distinction to keep in mind. Typically, resource types will either have cardinality one (such as our "cart factory" type) or infinity (as with our "carts" type).

In Rails, the first two types are handled by the same controller, by convention. Operations on the collection as a whole (such as POST /carts) and on its members (such as

DELETE /carts/4) are traditionally routed through the same controller. The third type, line items, will be routed through a controller nested under the first controller.

First, we write the models corresponding to the newly created Cart and LineItem resource types. Following Rails conventions, we will store these in the database using ActiveRecord:

app/models/cart.rb

```
class Cart < ActiveRecord::Base
  # delete line items on cart destroy
  has_many :line_items, :dependent => :destroy

  def add_product(product_id, quantity)
    quantity ||= 1
    li = line_items.find_or_create_by_product_id(product_id.to_i)
    # Increment the line item's quantity by the provided number.
    LineItem.update_counters li.id, :quantity => quantity
  end

  def update_quantity(product_id, quantity)
    li = line_items.find_by_product_id(product_id.to_i)
    li.update_attributes! :quantity => quantity
  end
end
```

 The ActiveRecord::Base.update_counters method generates one SQL query to update an integer field with the provided delta (positive or negative). This avoids two SQL queries (find and update) in favor of more expressive code like this:

```
LineItem.update_counters 3, :quantity => -1
>> UPDATE line_items SET quantity = quantity - 1 WHERE id = 3
```

app/models/line_item.rb

```
class LineItem < ActiveRecord::Base
  belongs_to :cart
  belongs_to :product

  # Fields:
  #   cart_id integer
  #   product_id integer
  #   quantity integer default(0)
end
```

The structure of the ActiveRecord models parallels our resource architecture. We define two instance methods on Cart, add_product (which adds quantity copies of the product to the cart) and update_quantity (which sets the quantity of the existing product in the cart to the provided quantity). The cart is emptied by deleting the Cart object (which destroys it and its dependent LineItems, thanks to the :dependent => :destroy directive on has_many). Similarly, an item is removed from the cart simply by destroying its corresponding LineItem.

Let's examine the routes that make this work:

config/routes.rb
```
map.resources :carts do |cart|
  cart.resources :products, :controller => 'line_items'
end
```

Because we are conforming to the Rails conventions of how RESTful routes should work, there is very little manual configuration here. We get a lot "for free," just for following the conventions:

- Incoming requests are mapped to the proper controller based not only on the URI but also on the HTTP method used. (Some browsers and proxies do not support HTTP methods other than GET and POST; we will see later how Rails works around this.)

- We get named routes completely for free, including the ability to route to a specific representation such as XML:

```
carts_path                            # => /carts

cart_path(some_cart)                  # => /carts/123
formatted_cart_path(some_cart, :xml)  # => /carts/123.xml

products_path(some_cart)              # => /carts/123/products
product_path(some_cart, some_product) # => /carts/123/products/456
```

- The routing system pre-populates the params hash with the ID variables we need, named appropriately. So, for a request to /carts/123/products/456, the params hash will contain the pairs :cart_id => 123 and :id => 456. We can use a before_filter in the controller to pick these off and retrieve them from the database, cleaning up the controller code.

Later in this chapter, we will explore the Rails RESTful routing system in detail. But now, let's take a look at the controllers that power the cart system. For simplicity, we will ignore any responses that we might render in the real world, and instead focus on sending correct HTTP response codes with no response body. (For this reason, we have left out any kind of "view cart" action also.)

app/controllers/carts_controller.rb
```
class CartsController < ApplicationController
  # POST /carts
  def create
    @cart = Cart.create
    # Return 201 Created to indicate success; point to location of new cart
    render :nothing => true, :status => :created, :location => cart_path(@cart)
  end

  # DELETE /carts/:id
  def destroy
    @cart = Cart.find(params[:id])
    @cart.destroy
    # Return 200 OK to indicate successful delete
    render :nothing => true
```

```
    end
  end
```

The CartsController handles the "create a cart" (POST /carts) and "empty cart" (DELETE /carts/:id) actions. The routing system maps the requests to the corresponding CRUD actions; they use their traditional Rails names (index, show, new, create, edit, update, and destroy).

We take great care to return the proper HTTP response status codes upon success so that the client knows exactly which action was taken. On creation of a cart, we render with a 201 Created status code and use the Location header to point to the newly created cart. On cart deletion, we render a 200 OK to tell the client that the request was successful.

The LineItemsController is slightly more complex, as line item resources are nested within a cart. We use a set of before_filters to retrieve the corresponding records:

app/controllers/line_items_controller.rb
```
class LineItemsController < ApplicationController
  # Nested RESTful routes set params[:cart_id] on each action.
  # Use that param to retrieve the cart.
  before_filter :find_cart

  # For member actions (update, destroy), find the line item
  # by looking at params[:id].
  before_filter :find_line_item, :only => [:update, :destroy]

  # PUT /carts/:cart_id/products/:id
  def update
    # Create line item if it does not exist
    @line_item ||= LineItem.new(:cart_id => params[:cart_id],
                    :product_id => params[:id], :quantity => 1)

    # Update attributes from params
    @line_item.update_attributes params[:line_item]
    render :nothing => true # Status: 200 OK
  end

  # DELETE /carts/:cart_id/products/:id
  def destroy
    @line_item.destroy
    render :nothing => true
  end

  protected

  def find_cart
    @cart = Cart.find params[:cart_id]
  end

  def find_line_item
    @line_item = @cart.line_items.find(params[:id])
  end
end
```

The preceding update method illustrates a difference between REST in theory and RESTful Rails in practice. In Rails, the PUT method is always mapped to update, while REST in general can also use PUT to create resources. We work around this by allowing creation from the update method, to allow us to use the more RESTful design.

Traditionally, Rails would use create for this action, which would require POSTing "product_id=123" to the parent resource at /carts/4/ products. This would be a RESTful design if the server chose the resulting URI (for example, if the LineItem's ID was used instead of a combination of cart and product ID). However, because the client has all of the information about the resource's URI (/carts/4/products/ 123), it should just PUT the resource to that URI.

At first glance, this code may seem to be much more complicated than the original, non-RESTful code. However, we have moved a great deal of functionality out of the framework (removing the dependency on sessions) and made the session state into an explicit set of resources. One of the big advantages that we gain is that the state now has all of the benefits of REST; state items are addressable, and we can now use a stateless server, assisting in scalability. This RESTful architecture is much more uniform than the old architecture, because it uses standard HTTP and CRUD methods instead of custom ones.

Authentication

Many web services and web applications need authentication of their users. Unfortunately, RESTful authentication on the human-readable Web is in a sad state. RESTful HTTP web services designed to be consumed by machines tend to have more options, because the developer of the application can somewhat dictate how the client must connect, even if it involves custom authentication schemes.

For browser-based web sites and web applications, there are fewer options; for an application to be usable by humans on the public Web today, it needs to support the browsers its clients will be using.

There are two methods commonly supported in browsers for HTTP authentication: Basic and Digest. Both are defined and explored in RFC 2617 (*http://tools.ietf.org/ html/rfc2617*). Basic authentication is very simple, but it is insecure. Usernames and passwords are sent in plain text over the network.* Digest authentication is a step up; it uses a challenge/response mechanism for the client to prove it knows the password without sending it over the network.

Digest authentication could technically violate the statelessness principles of REST. The nonce values that the server generates during the authentication process must be

---

* The easiest solution, as with forms-based authentication, is to encrypt the entire login transaction with SSL.

stored for as long as the sessions are valid (if sessions last an hour, the server must hold all newly generated nonces for an hour). This serves to prevent replay attacks; if this information were not kept and verified, an eavesdropper could simply "replay" a sniffed authentication handshake and convince the server that he is the original user.[*]

The problem with keeping any application state on the server is that it hinders scalability. For a pool of 100 application servers to implement HTTP Basic authentication, they need only share the list of valid login/password combinations. But for the same pool to implement Digest authentication, the servers should share a list of issued nonce values to defend against replay attacks.

HTTP authentication is desirable from a RESTful perspective, because it minimizes or eliminates session state kept on the server. There are other options for authentication; perhaps the most common in Rails is to use the session mechanism to store the ID of the currently logged-in user. Typically, this session is indexed by a key that is given to the client. Newer versions of Rails store a server-signed copy of the entire session in a cookie. This is actually more RESTful, but it is vulnerable to some of the same replay attacks as Digest authentication (other Rails session storage is not vulnerable, as a direct consequence of its server-side state). It is of course up to the application developer to draw the boundaries, depending on the application's security needs and the consequences of session replay.

There is another solution that can make HTTP authentication practical. For applications that can handle a JavaScript dependency, Paul James has created an ingenious way to use HTTP authentication with HTML forms. Details are at *http://www.peej.co.uk/ articles/http-auth-with-html-forms.html*. This method uses XMLHttpRequest to try an authentication through HTTP against a remote server. Once the authentication is complete, the credentials are stored as usual in the browser and used on future requests to the protected content. There are a few rough edges with browser support (the logout feature is not supported in Internet Explorer), but otherwise this is a wonderful solution.

Benefits of a RESTful Architecture

In this chapter, we have touched on some of the benefits that a RESTful application architecture can provide, and hopefully you have seen some of those benefits for yourself. Now we will list and explain each of the major benefits that REST strives to achieve.

---

[*] Although RFC 2617 does not mandate any checking of nonce values, it suggests it, subject to the application's need for security against replay attacks.

Conceptual Simplicity

The cornerstone of REST is simplicity. The decision to use a standard set of verbs (whether the HTTP verbs or some other set) virtually eliminates an entire area of discussion. The uniform registration and naming system of MIME types certainly doesn't settle the debate, but it definitely simplifies it.

With those two corners of the REST triangle taken care of, potentially the biggest gray area is in identifying and naming resources. Naming is one area where simplicity really pays off, because it is very easy to get it wrong. However, if you stick with a standard set of verbs and content types religiously, they will help constrain your choice of nouns.

It is very important to define clean, readable, persistent URIs for your resources. The REST FAQ (*http://rest.blueoxen.net/cgi-bin/wiki.pl?RestFaq*) makes a good observation about naming:

> GET is restricted to a single-URL line and that sort of enforces a good design principle that everything interesting on the Web should be URL-addressable. If you want to make a system where interesting stuff is not URL-addressable, then you need to justify that decision.

This is what designers and architects mean when they say "constraints are freeing." The principles of REST were derived from examination of how the Web and other hypertext networks actually work. Rather than being some set of arbitrary restrictions, they embody the way that the Web should act.

By working within the principles of REST, any pain you may feel should be treated as a hint that you might be going against the grain of the Web's natural architecture. It is certainly possible that your particular case is a special one. Certain application domains just do not fit well into the REST paradigm. (REST has been described as "Turing-complete" in a parallel with programming languages. Though any application may be expressed in terms of REST, some may be much more conducive to REST than others.) But trying to push yourself into the REST paradigm forces you to defend any exceptions and special cases, and in doing so you may find that the exceptions were not necessary after all.

Caching and Scalability

REST fits perfectly with the Rails *shared-nothing* philosophy—the idea that the only communication between application servers should be through the database (in REST terms, by "modifying resource state"). We mentioned previously how this assists scalability; the fewer interactions necessary between application servers, the easier it is to scale them horizontally when load dictates.

Caching is well known as a hard problem. Phil Karlton famously called cache invalidation one of the "two hard things in Computer Science." One of the requirements of HTTP caching is *transparency*; the semantics of the information transferred must be the same as if no cache were involved. What this means in practice depends not only on what type of caches are used and where they are placed within a network architecture, but also on the semantics of updates and "freshness" within the application itself.

Because caching behavior is so application-dependent, the decision was made for HTTP to provide mechanisms for caching without specifying actual behavior or client/server responsibility in great detail. As Fielding describes it (in section 6.3.2.6 of his thesis):

> Because REST tries to balance the need for efficient, low-latency behavior with the desire for semantically transparent cache behavior, it is critical that HTTP allow the application to determine the caching requirements rather than hard-code it into the protocol itself. The most important thing for the protocol to do is to fully and accurately describe the data being transferred, so that no application is fooled into thinking it has one thing when it actually has something else. HTTP/1.1 does this through the addition of the Cache-Control, Age, Etag, and Vary header fields.

Section 13 of the HTTP/1.1 specification (RFC 2616) details HTTP's caching behavior.[*] HTTP provides several features for cache control, which interact to provide a framework on which servers, clients, and intermediaries can build a caching policy. These features include the following:

Conditional GET

A conditional GET is an HTTP GET request containing one or more additional header fields specifying conditions under which the requested resource should or should not be sent. It is used in conjunction with the Last-Modified header and/or entity tags, discussed next.

Last-Modified

The Last-Modified response header contains a date/time value indicating the time at which the provided resource was last modified. When a client holds a (potentially old) version of this resource, it can *validate* that version by performing a conditional GET with an If-Modified-Since header set to the time its version was last modified. If the server has a newer version, it will send the new version with an updated Last-Modified header. If there is no newer version, the server will send a 304 Not Modified response with no body, saving time and bandwidth.

Entity tags (ETags)

Entity tags are short labels that serve to identify a particular version of an entity. Typically, they are a hash of the response body; in this way, entities can be compared by exchanging the tag rather than the entire body.

Entity tags, like Last-Modified, also use conditional GET. The client sends a request with an If-No-Match header specifying the ETag of its latest version. If the server calculates a different ETag for the newest version of that resource, it will send

[*] *http://www.w3.org/Protocols/rfc2616/rfc2616-sec13.html*

the entire body. But if the calculated ETag matches the one the client sent, a 304 Not Modified response is returned.

There are many different strategies for calculating entity tags, depending on the application's needs. The simple strategy of hashing the response body works, but it can be inefficient as the server must still generate and hash the response. For dynamic content, this can be extremely inefficient (and it may be more reasonable to use If-Modified-Since and compare it against a timestamp on the source data).

The solution often used for static content is to incorporate the file's inode, as it can be much faster to stat(2) a file than to open it and read its data into memory. This works well, but it cannot be used in clusters where the data resides on separate filesystems among systems in the cluster.

Rails provides transparent ETag support, which we will revisit later in this chapter.

Cache-Control *header*

The HTTP Cache-Control header provides a way to specify cache semantics not covered by other HTTP mechanisms. This header provides the following features, and more:

- Clients can request a response that may be old, but by only up to a certain amount of time (max-age).

- Clients and servers can dictate that certain information never be cached by intermediate shared caches (private), or by any cache (no-cache).

- The caching protocol can be extended without breaking HTTP semantics, if agreed upon by the client and server and implemented thus.

Robustness to Change

Another advantage conferred by RESTful design is that the designs tend to be more resilient to change than RPC-style interfaces. RESTful design drives the architectural decisions into noun territory. Noun selection tends to be domain-driven, while RPC interfaces tend to be more implementation-driven, as they expose their procedures (an implementation detail) as part of the interface. While RPC interfaces often need an extra layer of indirection to separate the interface from the implementation, REST cultivates a separation of interface and implementation by encouraging more abstract interfaces.

Also, because REST distinguishes the idea of "resource" from "representation," it is easy to add new content types representing the same resource as new formats are required. No architectural changes are required, as REST is based on a separation between an abstract resource and its representations.

Uniformity

One of the biggest advantages afforded by the REST guidelines is a uniform interface. The verbs (in our case, the HTTP methods) are universally uniform, across all application domains. Content types, though not universal (they differ across domains), are standardized and relatively well known.

The fact that you are limited to such a small set of methods may seem constraining, but in practice it is not a major concern. Anything you would want to model can easily be framed in terms of the CRUD operations. This way of thinking about the world helps to push essential complexity into one part of an architecture, where it is easily dealt with. Usually, when it seems that you need more than the basic methods, there is another entity lurking in the model, waiting to be extracted.

Content types are standardized in a different way. Content types are usually somewhat application-specific, and so it would make no sense for them to be universal. However, to facilitate communication, content types are usually somewhat standard. In the HTTP world, this means *MIME* (Multipurpose Internet Mail Extensions), an Internet standard that defines a framework for content types. The set of MIME types is extensible, so new applications can define local types and even register them with the IANA once they are in widespread use.

The uniformity that REST provides tremendously aids standardization efforts. When bringing multiple systems together (as happens when developing a standard), the fewer differences there are, the fewer political disagreements. If everyone standardizes on a set of verbs (which are universally standardized when using HTTP), then the only differences that remain are the content types (which are fairly straightforward to standardize within an application domain) and nouns.

Therefore, complying with a RESTful interface helps to reduce the huge problem of standardization to the somewhat more manageable problems of representing data (content types) and naming things (nouns). Though these are still areas where disagreement and politics can interfere, the principles of REST help to focus the discussion by narrowing the topics of discussion.

RESTful Rails

At RailsConf 2006, David Heinemeier Hansson's keynote marked the beginning of the RESTful philosophy becoming mainstream in Rails. The keynote, *Discovering a World of Resources on Rails*,* presented a roadmap for moving Rails 1.2 toward a more RESTful, CRUD-based default.

---

* Presentation slides and video available at *http://www.scribemedia.org/2006/07/09/dhh/*.

One of the key points in the presentation was that resources can be more than things we might think of as "objects"; examples given were relationships between objects, events on objects, and object states. This is an important principle in REST. Rather than adding another method #close on a Case object, it may be more clear to factor out a Closure object if more information about the closure needs to be persisted.

RESTful Routing

From the outside of an application, the most visible change in RESTful Rails is the new routing. Classic Rails routing was based around the default route of /:controller /:action/:id, with any extra parameters usually being carried in the query string. This had advantages of simplicity and uniformity in routing, but it was brittle to change. Refactoring actions from one controller to another required updating all links pointing to that action; they had to be changed from:

```
link_to 'Close', :controller => 'cases', :action => 'close', :id => @case.id
```

to:

```
link_to 'Close', :controller => 'closures', :action => 'create',
                 :id => @case.id
```

The next major innovation in Rails routing was the prevalence of named routes. By associating each URI with a name, you would get an easy way to refactor route URLs without changing the inward links. This provided another layer of abstraction on top of the actual URI parameters:

config/routes.rb
```
map.close_case '/cases/close/:id', :controller => 'cases', :action => 'close'
```
_case.rhtml
```
link_to 'Close', close_case_path(:id => @case.id)
```

Then, when the action moved, you could simply change the route without touching the views:

```
map.close_case '/closures/create/:id', :controller => 'closures',
                                        :action => 'create'
```

This greatly improved maintainability, but it increased verbosity. As there was another layer of abstraction between URIs and actions, there was another file that needed to be maintained, kept in sync with the rest of the code, and consulted when tracing a request's path through the application.

The biggest problem, however, was that these routes tended to be redundant and overly numerous. The problem was not so much that there was one named route for each URI, but that the URIs referred to actions on resources instead of resources. The HTTP phrase "GET /cases/show/1" is redundant. Both HTTP GET and the show action mean "give me this data." According to RESTful principles, that phrase should be "GET /cases/1," where the HTTP verb specifies the action and the URI specifies the object of that action. Thus, Rails *resource routing* was born.

Resource-Based Named Routes

Resource routing encapsulates all of the Rails CRUD actions into one routing statement:

```
map.resources :cases
```

The resources method sets up a series of RESTful named routes. Just with that one statement, you can now use `link_to('View All', cases_path)`, `link_to('Destroy', case_path(@case), :method => :delete)`, and many more. This is more maintainable because there are fewer named routes and they are standardized. It also encourages you to model according to CRUD; you have to think carefully before adding ad-hoc methods to controllers because each special case must be listed separately in the route.

The following table shows the seven standard Rails CRUD actions, their semantics, and the HTTP phrases that they correspond to. It assumes a routing declaration of `map.resources :people`.

HTTP	Rails	Semantics
GET /people	index	Shows a list of all people
GET /people/new	new	Shows a form to create a new person
POST /people	create	Creates a new person; redirects to its URI
GET /people/1	show	Shows a representation of the specified person
GET /people/1/edit	edit	Shows an edit form for the specified person
PUT /people/1	update	Updates the specified person with the provided data
DELETE /people/1	destroy	Removes the specified person

The controller name defaults to the resource name; in this case, the routing code would look for a `PeopleController`. This can be changed; specifying `map.resources :people, :controller => 'members'` would instead look for a `MembersController`.

By default, Rails generates four basic named routes for the `map.resources :people` declaration. The four routes are shown below, along with their corresponding URIs and the parameters that are passed back to the controller in the params hash when the route is recognized.

Note that the URI generators will accept either an ID or an arbitrary object. Such objects will be converted to a URI-friendly ID using #to_param, so anything that responds to #to_param (such as an `ActiveRecord::Base` or `ActiveResource::Base` object) will work.

Named route	URI	Params
people_path	/people	{}
person_path(1) person_path(@person)	/people/1	{:id => 1}

Named route	URI	Params
new_person_path	/people/new	{}
edit_person_path(1) edit_person_path(@person)	/people/1/edit	{:id => 1}

You may occasionally see URIs like /people/1;edit when reading information about RESTful development in Rails. For a time, the semi-colon was a route component separator (Rails 1.2 still uses it), but it has since been removed in Rails 2.0.

These routes are also available in a _url variant that includes the scheme, host, and port. For example, people_path returns /people, while people_url returns http:// localhost:3000/people (of course, with the appropriate scheme, host, and port, depending on that of the incoming request). In addition, there is a hash_for_ variant that returns a hash of parameters ready to be passed into url_for, rather than returning the URI directly as a string:

```
>> app.hash_for_people_path
=> {:action=>"index", :controller=>"people", :only_path=>true,
    :use_route=>"people"}
>> app.hash_for_people_url
=> {:action=>"index", :controller=>"people", :only_path=>false,
    :use_route=>"people"}
```

The app variable is an instance of ApplicationController:: Integration::Session (used for Rails integration testing) that is made available at the Rails console. It can be used to troubleshoot controller issues (such as routing), and even to make mock HTTP requests of the application, just as in integration testing:

```
$ script/console
Loading development environment.
>> app.get '/hello/world'
=> 200
>> app.response.headers
=> {"Status"=>"200 OK", "type"=>"text/html; charset=utf-8",
    "cookie"=>[], "Cache-Control"=>"no-cache",
    "Content-Length"=>13}
>> app.response.body
=> "Hello, world!"
```

Extra query string parameters can be added to the named routes, but in the case of member routes, the member object or ID must be included in the hash as an :id parameter:

```
$ script/console
Loading development environment.
>> app.person_path(1)
=> "/people/1"
>> app.person_path(:id => 1)
```

```
=> "/people/1"
>> app.person_path(:id => 1, :section => 'enrollment')
=> "/people/1?section=enrollment"
```

Similarly, the default collection routes can also take a hash of query string parameters:

```
>> app.people_path(:sort => 'last_name')
=> "/people?sort=last_name"
```

Routes can also be generated with a specific format; any of the formats specified in Mime::Types (discussed later) are valid. There is another series of formatted_ named routes for this purpose:

```
>> app.formatted_person_path(1, :js)
=> "/people/1.js"
>> app.formatted_person_path(1, :xml)
=> "/people/1.xml"
>> app.formatted_people_path(:rss)
=> "/people.rss"
```

This is useful in conjunction with respond_to, which switches responses based on the content type accepted by the client. Note that, like the other named routes, if we want custom query string parameters, we must convert all of the arguments to a hash:

```
>> app.formatted_person_path(:id => 1, :format => :xml,
                             :section => 'enrollment')
=> "/people/1.xml?section=enrollment"
```

Custom resource routes

The REST helpers also have provisions to create custom named routes pertaining either to the collection (the parent resource) or the members of the collection (the children). These are created with the :collection and :member options to map.resources, respectively. Each new route must have a corresponding HTTP verb it is to be used with. The routes directly correspond to actions on the controller. For example, we may have this declaration in *config/routes.rb*:

```
map.resources :people, :collection => { :search => :get },
                       :member => { :deactivate => :post }
```

This sets up search_people_path and deactivate_person_path routes that have restrictions so as only to accept the specified HTTP methods. We can try these out at the console:

```
$ script/console
Loading development environment.
>> app.search_people_path(:query => 'Brian')
=> "/people/search?query=Brian"
>> app.get app.search_people_path(:query => 'Brian')
=> 200
>> app.request.request_uri
=> "/people/search?query=Brian"
>> app.request.params
=> {"query"=>["Brian"]}
```

The named routes will only be recognized given the proper HTTP method; if called with other methods, they will return 404:

```
>> app.deactivate_person_path(1)
=> "/people/1/deactivate"
>> app.post app.deactivate_person_path(1)
=> 200
>> app.get app.deactivate_person_path(1)
=> 404
```

Note that defining custom routes like this can easily deviate from REST. It is easy to overload a resource with many custom methods that may better be factored into resources of their own. For example, rather than POSTing to /people/1/deactivate, the RESTful action would be either to PUT active=0 to /people/1 or to PUT a value of 0 to /people/1/active, depending on whether active was modeled as a separate resource or an attribute of the person resource. It is intentional that custom routes are a bit unpleasant to use, because most of the application domain should be modeled with CRUD and special cases should be the exception rather than the rule.

Nested resource routes

Rails has a provision to specify nested resources when generating named routes. For example, consider a social networking application where each person can have many friends; we can express these resource relationships with the nested route declaration:

```
map.resources :people do |person|
  person.resources :friends
end
```

In this situation, the friends resources are scoped to a particular person. The URI for a friend belonging to a person would look like /people/1/friends/2, and a person's friends could be viewed at /people/1/friends.

The corresponding named routes are simple, with one minor change: they take an extra parameter, for the person_id to which they are scoped. Given that route declaration, we now have the following routes (note that the declaration also includes the base people resources).

Named route	URI	Controller	Params
people_path	/people	people	{}
person_path(1)	/people/1	people	{:id => 1}
friends_path(1)	/people/1/friends	friends	{:person_id => 1}
friend_path(1, 2)	/people/1/friends/2	friends	{:person_id => 1, :id => 2}

Note that we are still in a flat controller namespace. By default, those route declarations will look for PeopleController and FriendsController. If the resources are truly nested, and friends are always scoped to a person, it may make more sense to use controller namespaces. This would involve changing `FriendsController` to `People::FriendsController` and moving it to *app/controllers/people/friends_controller.rb*. Then, the route declaration should be changed to:

```
map.resources :people do |person|
  person.resources :friends, :controller => 'people/friends',
                   :name_prefix => 'person_'
end
```

The `name_prefix` option adds a prefix to the generated routes. In this case, adding that option to the `person.resources` line gives us named routes like `person_friends_path` and `person_friend_path` instead of `friends_path` and `friend_path`, which better reflects the new scoping of our resources.

There is a `path_prefix` option that will add a prefix to the URIs that the route will recognize and generate. This comes with nested routes—you don't have to do anything. The nested routes above could be manually specified as follows:

```
map.resources :people
map.resources :friends, :controller => 'people/friends',
              :name_prefix => 'person_',
              :path_prefix => '/people/:person_id'
```

This usage is not as pretty, but it affords more control over the parameter names your controller is passed. This method makes more sense if the IDs being used in the routes are something other than ActiveRecord numeric primary keys.

Singleton resource routes

Sometimes, there will be an entity that exists as a singleton, such that there will only be one in existence within its containing scope. An example would be a subscription user's account, which contains billing information. This information is modeled as a separate resource from the user's other data. In contrast to the collection resource /users/1/posts and its member /users/1/posts/1, we have the singleton resource /users/1/account.

Rails provides a way to map singleton resources with the `map.resource` statement (in parallel to `map.resources` for collections of resources). The resource name is still singular, but the inferred controller name is plural. Our routing statement for the preceding example would be:

```
map.resources :users do |user|
  user.resource :account
end
```

This code would expect an AccountsController to contain the user account actions. Singleton resources contain the same methods as collection resources, but with no index action.

HTTP	Rails	Semantics
GET /users/1/account/new	new	Shows a form to create user's account
POST /users/1/account	create	Creates the user's account; redirects to its URI
GET /users/1/account	show	Shows account information
GET /users/1/account/edit	edit	Shows an edit form for the account
PUT /users/1/account	update	Updates the account with the provided data
DELETE /users/1/account	destroy	Removes the account

The named routes for singleton resources are similar to those for collections, again missing only the route to the collection.

Named route	URI	Params
account_path(1)	/users/1/account	{:user_id => 1}
new_account_path(1)	/users/1/account/new	{:user_id => 1}
edit_account_path(1)	/users/1/account/edit	{:user_id => 1}

Depending on the application, not all of these routes may be used. For example, if the account is created automatically when the user is created, then the new, create, and destroy actions may not apply.

ActionView Support

The Rails link_to family of helpers can take a :method parameter to define the HTTP method that will be used when a user clicks on the link. For a method of POST, PUT, or DELETE, the helpers generate JavaScript that creates a hidden inline form, sets up the appropriate hidden form field for the _method parameter (as is detailed next in "Method emulation"), and submits it. The handler returns false so that the link's actual target is not followed. For example, the ERb code:

```
<%= link_to 'Delete', person_path(@person), :method => :delete %>
```

creates the following link:

```
<a href="/people/1" onclick="
  var f = document.createElement('form');
  f.style.display = 'none';
  this.parentNode.appendChild(f);
  f.method = 'POST';
  f.action = this.href;
  var m = document.createElement('input');
  m.setAttribute('type', 'hidden');
  m.setAttribute('name', '_method');
  m.setAttribute('value', 'delete');
  f.appendChild(m);
  f.submit();
  return false;
">Delete</a>
```

Although this uses JavaScript to accomplish its primary action, it is still safe (though nonfunctional) in browsers that do not support JavaScript. Those browsers will ignore the onclick action, instead treating the link as a standard GET link. If the link is clicked, the browser will send GET /people/1, which will harmlessly call the show action on that person.

Note that we would not want to fall back to an action that actually calls our delete method, because it is behind a standard HTML link (once the JavaScript is stripped out). As the GET action is presumed to be idempotent and safe, proxy caches and user agents would be permitted to prefetch our link without the user's request. This is the same problem that caused the Google Web Accelerator issues discussed earlier. But the advantage of RESTful design is that we could not name the delete action by URI alone if we wanted to; it requires the resource's URI in conjunction with the DELETE HTTP method, and all of the semantics involved therein.

 In applications where non-JavaScript-aware browsers need to be fully supported, you should use other helpers such as button_to or the standard form helpers. These create HTML constructs with the proper semantics; even user agents that do not support JavaScript respect that <button> or <form> tags are unsafe and should not be followed without the user's interaction.

Method emulation

REST is designed to use a full set of HTTP methods, which at a minimum include GET, PUT, POST, HEAD, and DELETE. Unfortunately, there are a few roadblocks to using these directly. HTML 4 only supports GET and POST as form methods, and of course standard HTML links only request documents via GET (by design). In addition, many proxies, caches, and other intermediaries often only support GET and POST, as the other methods were not in wide use on the Web for many years.

To work around this problem, Rails uses a small hack. Methods other than GET or POST are sent as POST (the catch-all method as it is neither required to be safe nor idempotent). To allow the server to determine the original method, it is stored in a POST variable called _method. The Prototype JavaScript library works in the same way when calling an action via Ajax.Request or Ajax.Updater with a method other than GET or POST.

Content Types

The idea that one resource can have multiple representations in different content types is one of the core principles of REST. It recognizes that different representations of one thing, whether formatted as JavaScript, HTML, XML, ICS, or in any other format, is fundamentally the same resource. Rails has introduced rich support for rendering different responses based on the content type the client wants, via the respond_to method.

The `respond_to` method yields a responder (an instance of `ActionController::MimeResponds::Responder`, usually called `format`), which can respond to various content type methods in order to send different content based on the client's expectations (as defined in the `Accept` request header).

Typical responder methods are `format.html` and `format.xml`, which define responder blocks for HTML and XML requests, respectively. As these are standard Ruby method calls, they can be intermingled with other Ruby code such as conditionals. The block of the first method call matching the request's `Accept` header will be executed. This block usually renders a response in the specified format.

The blocks can also be omitted, in which case the default action is taken (the same action that would have happened had there been no render or redirect calls in the action). For example:

```
respond_to do |format|
  format.html # same as format.html { render }
  format.xml  { render :xml => @product }
end
```

If all format blocks are the default, a list of types can simply be provided to `respond_to` directly, with no block. For example, this code:

```
respond_to do |format|
  format.html
  format.xml
end
```

can be condensed into:

```
respond_to :html, :xml
```

The default Rails route has also changed to accommodate different formats. Where once the default route was `/:controller/:action/:id`, now it is `/:controller/:action/:id.:format`. This passes any provided file extension into the appropriate controller as `params[:format]`. This is what `respond_to` uses internally to decide on a response type.

The set of MIME types that Rails recognizes is defined in *actionpack/lib/action_controller/mime_types.rb*. Each mapping has a set of MIME types, as well as the Rails symbol that is used to denote those types (e.g., `:html` or `:xml`). At the time of this writing, the following types are recognized.

Shortcut	MIME types
all	*/*
text	text/plain
html	text/html, application/xhtml+xml
js	text/javascript, application/javascript, application/x-javascript
css	text/css
ics	text/calendar
csv	text/csv

Shortcut	MIME types
xml	application/xml, text/xml, application/x-xml
rss	application/rss+xml
atom	application/atom+xml
yaml	application/x-yaml, text/yaml
multipart_form	multipart/form-data
url_encoded_form	application/x-www-form-urlencoded
json	application/json, text/x-json

New MIME types can be registered with `Mime::Type.register`. This method takes four arguments: the primary MIME type, the Rails shortcut, a set of synonym MIME types (such as `text/x-json` for JSON text), and a set of synonym file extensions, used to force a format where the client does not send an `Accept` header or sends an improper one.

 The Rails shortcut symbol, such as `rss`, is also taken to be a file extension; a request URI ending in `.rss` will trigger a `format.rss` block. The list of synonym extensions adds to this default extension.

For example, suppose we want to add JPEG format support to an application. We would like to write `format.jpg` in a `respond_to` block to render a JPEG response. This requires mapping the `jpg` format type to the `image/jpeg` type, as well as the `jpg` and `jpeg` extensions. We can do this by simply putting the following in our *config/initializers/mime_types.rb*:

```
Mime::Type.register "image/jpeg", :jpg, [], %w(jpeg)
```

HTTP Caching

Earlier in the chapter, we discussed HTTP's use of conditional `GET` for client-side caching. Under conditional `GET`, the client requests a resource along with an identifier of the client's latest copy, so the server doesn't have to send a resource that the client already has.

One of the most important parts of caching is inexpensively figuring out the identity of a given entity. In order to determine whether an entity is stale, you must compare its content with the canonical version on the server. One trivial way to do this would be to generate and compare the entire response body, but this is ridiculous. It saves no bandwidth, CPU time, or I/O. We need a shorter way to identify an entity.

The HTTP standard provides for Entity Tags (usually called *ETags*, after the HTTP header in which they are provided), which serve to identify the resource that they are attached to. You can compare two resources by comparing their ETag. This is used with conditional `GET`, where the client sends the ETag associated with its latest version in an `If-None-Match` header. The server compares this ETag with that of its latest version; if they match, the client has the latest version and the server renders a simple 304 Not Modified response.

Often, the ETag is a hash of the response body, but it can be anything that is likely to change when the body does. Another common method used for static content is to use some combination of the file's inode number, last-modified time, and size; this is very efficient because all of that information can be determined with a stat(2) syscall. Of course, this method breaks down in clusters (where the static files might span filesystems) or when serving dynamic content.

Rails has built-in support for transparently generating ETags. The method used is the "simplest thing that could possibly work"; it is generic because it makes no assumptions about the structure or semantics of an application. Its implementation is simple enough that it can be shown here:

```
def handle_conditional_get!
  if body.is_a?(String) &&
      (headers['Status'] ? headers['Status'][0..2] == '200' : true) &&
      !body.empty?
    self.headers['ETag'] ||= %("#{Digest::MD5.hexdigest(body)}")
    self.headers['Cache-Control'] = 'private, max-age=0, must-revalidate' if
        headers['Cache-Control'] == DEFAULT_HEADERS['Cache-Control']

    if request.headers['HTTP_IF_NONE_MATCH'] == headers['ETag']
      self.headers['Status'] = '304 Not Modified'
      self.body = ''
    end
  end
end
```

On each request with a 200 OK response, Rails generates an MD5 hash of the response body and sets it as the ETag (unless one has already been set; this allows you to provide custom ETags simply by setting them). It also sets the Cache-control: must-revalidate flag, which instructs caches (including caching user agents, such as web browsers) to revalidate the cache against the ETag, using the If-None-Match header. This ensures that the generated ETags are actually used. Finally, if a response comes in with an If-None-Match header, and its value is the same as the generated ETag, the response body is cleared and rendered with a 304 Not Modified status.

The default Rails ETag mechanism works well and is completely transparent, but it has some drawbacks. The main limitation is that the response body must still be generated (which often means several trips to the database, template rendering, URI generation, and, finally, MD5 hashing) before a decision can be made. If the client's version was actually the latest, all of that work is discarded. Therefore, the default ETag implementation only saves bandwidth, not CPU time or I/O. We must get into more application-specific caching methods in order to avoid rendering a response altogether.

Custom caching

Making cache control more granular requires coupling the caching a bit more with the application. Assaf Arkin's restfully_yours plugin* provides some helper methods for RESTful Rails development, primarily in the domain of cache control. It provides methods to support both conditional GET (which controls caches using If-Modified-Since and If-None-Match) and conditional PUT (which prevents stale updates using If-Unmodified-Since and If-Match).

The first method provided is if_modified, which supports conditional GET. It takes one or more entities as arguments, which are expected to respond to either the updated_at or etag methods (or both).† The updated_at method generates Last-Modified headers, while the etag method generates an ETag header. Any of these methods can be overridden or defined on custom entities, depending on the application's idea of "last update time" or "identity."

This behavior works transparently with ActiveRecord entities. If the ActiveRecord object has timestamps, its updated_at attribute will be used to provide a Last-Modified time. The restfully_yours plugin also provides a default etag method that uses an MD5 hash of either the ActiveRecord ID and lock version if using optimistic locking (this is a cheap way to get a monotonically increasing version number) or all of its attributes otherwise. This saves all but the initial trip to the database to get the attributes and instantiate the ActiveRecord object.

Here is a typical use of this plugin's conditional GET functionality:

```
def show
  @product = Product.find params[:id]
  if_modified @product do
    render
  end
end
```

The if_modified function yields to its block if the provided entity (@product in this case) has been modified from the client's version, as determined by the appropriate request headers. If the entity has not been modified, a 304 Not Modified response will be rendered. This is preferable to the default Rails ETag method because the if_modified decision is made before rendering the body, which may be expensive. The disadvantage is that the list of entities to track must always be passed to if_modified, and they must generate sensible values for updated_at and etag.

The complement to conditional GET is conditional PUT. Both of them use similar request and response headers, but they use them toward different ends. While conditional GET is used to save bandwidth by not resending duplicate response bodies,

---

* Available from *http://labnotes.org/svn/public/ruby/rails_plugins/restfully_yours*.

† updated_on can be used as a synonym for updated_at. In Rails, the _on variants indicate dates, while the _at variants indicate times.

conditional PUT is used to prevent stale updates by making PUT requests conditional on the previous state of the resource.

In other words, a conditional PUT contains an If-Unmodified-Since or If-Match header (the exact opposites of the If-Modified-Since and If-None-Match headers, respectively) with the Last-Modified date or ETag of the last known representation of that resource. If the server's version of the resource (before the requested update) differs from that requested by the client, the update will be aborted and a 412 Precondition Failed response code returned. Typical usage is as follows:

```
def update
  @product = Product.find params[:id]
  if_unmodified @product do
    if @product.update_attributes params[:product]
      redirect_to product_path(@product)
    else
      render
    end
  end
end
```

Now, before updating the product with the provided attributes, the headers will be inspected to ensure that the client and server agree on the resource's state before the update. If they are the same, the PUT will proceed as usual.

Note that the typical application of this code has a race condition between if_unmodified checking the headers and actually performing the update. This is unavoidable from the plugin's standpoint, as it has no idea what you will be doing inside the block.

To ensure that this race condition doesn't cause problems under heavy concurrency, you will need to wrap the entire SELECT/UPDATE series in a database transaction, and run the database under a transaction isolation level that prevents nonrepeatable reads (such as SERIALIZABLE).

HTTP Response Status Codes

One often-overlooked part of HTTP is the rich set of response status codes it defines. The HTTP/1.1 RFC defines many response codes that are appropriate for document-based interactions; this set was enriched by WebDAV with some status codes that filled in the gaps for dynamic web applications (such as 422 Unprocessable Entity, used when the submitted entity is semantically invalid, often as determined by ActiveRecord validations).

HTTP response codes are three-digit numbers with an optional human-readable explanation. The numbers are defined by RFC 2616 (for HTTP/1.1), but the text is only suggested by RFC. The first digit of the numerical code indicates to which of five categories the response belongs. The categories are divided in this way so that a client that does not understand an obscure response code can infer some semantic information about the status (for example, whether the request succeeded or failed, and whether the request should be tried again) by examining the status code's first digit.

1xx: Informational
> These codes are used for protocol negotiations between client and server. This series of status codes is not currently in wide use.

2xx: Success
> A code in the 2xx series indicates that the request completed successfully. The request may have either been processed immediately or accepted for processing.

3xx: Redirection
> These codes indicate that the client must look elsewhere for the requested resource. The new location is provided in the Location response header.

4xx: Client Error
> These codes indicate that the server cannot understand, cannot fulfill, or refuses to fulfill the client's request, apparently due to the client's error.

5xx: Server Error
> 5xx response codes indicate that the server understood the request but is incapable of performing it, temporarily or permanently, due to a server error.

The advantage of using standardized codes, of course, is that everyone (theoretically) uses them and understands them. In particular, Rails uses a rich set of response codes when requesting and providing data over a RESTful interface. ActiveResource, for example, will respond to a 404 by raising `ActiveResource::ResourceNotFound` (a parallel of `ActiveRecord::RecordNotFound`), and to a 422 by raising `ActiveResource::ResourceInvalid` (upon failed validations).

ActiveResource: Consuming RESTful Services

One huge advantage of coding web services RESTfully is that clients can then consume them using a standard interface. ActiveResource is a library, now part of edge Rails, which abstracts RESTful resources using an ActiveRecord-like interface. It fits well into the Rails model of building applications, and as long as the server was built using RESTful Rails conventions, using ActiveResource is nearly transparent.

To demonstrate the power of ActiveResource, we will build a very simple application (nothing more than a scaffolded interface to a set of ActiveRecord objects) to manage a set of products in a fictional store. We will first build this as a basic ActiveRecord application using RESTful principles; then we will use ActiveResource to disconnect the backend web service from the front end interface.

We will be using the `scaffold` generator (formerly `scaffold_resource`) to build some quick RESTful templates for the interface. The use of generators is debated in Rails; some say that they are a useful way to get code up and running, while others say they hide too many details and don't allow enough flexibility. We will not debate the merits here; we simply use the generator to build a simple application without letting the details get in the way.

First, we create the Rails application skeleton:

```
$ rails products_example
      create
      create  app/controllers
      create  app/helpers
      ...
      create  log/production.log
      create  log/development.log
      create  log/test.log
$ cd products_example
```

Then, after setting up our development database information, we use the `scaffold` generator to create the model, controller, and sample templates all at once for the Product model. The generator will set up the appropriate fields in the database if they are provided on the command line:

```
$ script/generate scaffold product \
    name:string description:text price:float quantity:integer \
    created_at:datetime
      exists  app/models/
      exists  app/controllers/
      exists  app/helpers/
      ...
      create  db/migrate
      create  db/migrate/001_create_products.rb
       route  map.resources :products
$ rake db:migrate
== CreateProducts: migrating ===================================================
-- create_table(:products)
   -> 0.0746s
== CreateProducts: migrated (0.0747s) ==========================================
```

 In practice, prices should not be stored as floating-point values; rather, they should be stored as integers in the lowest-common-denominator unit of currency (such as cents when the currency is U.S. dollars). The Money gem by Tobias Lütke (`gem install money`) makes this easier in Rails.

After migrating and tweaking the forms a bit, we have a very simple CRUD application for products. Starting the server with `script/server`, we can see an empty list at *http://localhost:3000/*, as shown in Figure 7-1.

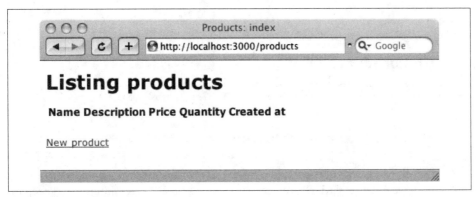

Figure 7-1. Empty product list

We can now enter details for a sample product, which we then see as part of the list. This process is shown in Figures 7-2 and 7-3.

Figure 7-2. Product creation screen

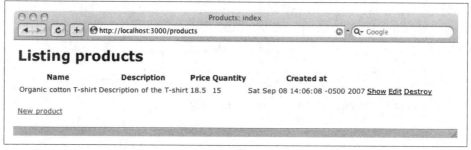

Figure 7-3. List of products

We now have a basic CRUD application that uses a RESTful interface. The templates are written using the RESTful Rails helpers and URL generators. Here is an example from the *New Product* template:

app/views/products/new.erb

```
<h1>New product</h1>

<%= error_messages_for :product %>

<% form_for(:product, :url => products_path) do |f| %>
  <p>
    <b>Name</b><br />
    <%= f.text_field :name %>
  </p>

  ...

<% end %>

<%= link_to 'Back', products_path %>
```

The route definitions can be simplified to one `resources` method call that sets up all of the appropriate method-based routes for the `ProductsController`:

config/routes.rb

```
ActionController::Routing::Routes.draw do |map|
  map.resources :products
end
```

The generated controller is a fairly standard scaffolded controller, which responds to the seven basic CRUD actions with their standard Rails names.

HTTP verb	URI	Rails method
GET	/products	index
GET	/products/1	show
GET	/products/new	new
GET	/products/1/edit	edit

HTTP verb	URI	Rails method
POST	/products	create
PUT	/products/1	update
DELETE	/products/1	destroy

Note that the Rails convention is to create a resource by POSTing to its parent (collection) resource; this is necessary because the server chooses the newly created resource's URI (as it contains an arbitrary ID).

The controller actions make use of the HTTP response codes most appropriate for error messages, success messages, and redirects. Rather than just being useful, as is often the case with human-consumable web applications, status codes are absolutely essential for web services. Client libraries such as ActiveResource rely on them to take the appropriate actions.

One important addition to the old-style Rails scaffolded controllers is the use of respond_to to send a different content type depending on the Accept header and possible format parameters in the URI (such as /products.xml).

app/controllers/products_controller.rb
```
# POST /products
# POST /products.xml
def create
  @product = Product.new(params[:product])

  respond_to do |format|
    if @product.save
      flash[:notice] = 'Product was successfully created.'
      format.html { redirect_to product_url(@product) }
      format.xml  { render :xml => @product, :status => :created,
                            :location => product_url(@product) }
    else
      format.html { render :action => "new" }
      format.xml  { render :xml => @product.errors }
    end
  end
end
```

Here we see the standard use of respond_to; the format.html and format.xml calls are intermingled with standard Ruby controller code. By default, this RESTful controller looks at the Accept header to determine whether to render its responses as HTML or XML. We can add more representations simply by adding a format directive and appropriate templates. For example, using the built-in Rails JSON serialization functions, we can add a simple JSON representation of a newly created object:

```
format.js { render :json => @product.to_json, :status => :created,
                    :location => product_url(@product) }
```

The render :json variant renders the given text and sets the response's content type to text/x-json. We should also present a JSON version of our error codes upon error, in the else block above:

```
format.js { render :json => @product.errors.to_json,
                    :status => :unprocessable_entity }
```

 We send an HTTP response code of 422 Unprocessable Entity here. The 422 code is not in the HTTP/1.1 specification; it was added later by WebDAV. However, it is the most appropriate response code to our situation (the client has submitted a resource that is unprocessable), and even Roy Fielding agreed that 422 is the most appropriate code for this sort of situation. In addition, in Rails 2.0, ActiveResource treats a 422 response as a failed validation.

Now we will turn this simple web application into a client/server application. Here is where the magic happens. We will disconnect the backend (ActiveRecord and database access) from the front end (the user interface). The backend will become the server, and the front end will become the client. The two will talk over HTTP using a RESTful interface.

As the application is already set up to render XML when requested (via an Accept header of text/xml or a format extension of .xml), no changes are needed to the server. We can treat the server as a web service simply by requesting XML over HTTP. The client will require some slight modifications to talk over a RESTful HTTP interface rather than a database connection, but the changes will be very small as ActiveResource was designed to have an ActiveRecord-like interface.

First, we will copy the entire project (the original of which will become the server) into a separate directory, which will become the client:

```
$ cp -R products_example products_example_client
```

As mentioned previously, the server needs no modification at all. We can start it on port 4000, which will become the location at which we access the web service:

```
$ cd products_example_client
$ script/server --port 4000
```

Now we can open up the code for the client and modify it to query *http://localhost: 4000/* for products. We open *app/models/product.rb*, which was a very straightforward ActiveRecord model:

```
class Product < ActiveRecord::Base
end
```

We change this to an equivalently simple ActiveResource model, backed by the web service that we have set up:

```
class Product < ActiveResource::Base
  self.site = "http://localhost:4000/"
end
```

Now we have to fix a small glitch due to differences between ActiveRecord and ActiveResource. Unlike ActiveRecord objects, ActiveResource objects don't know their potential set of attributes when they are initialized (as that would take a web service call to determine). In our client application, the ProductsController#new action sets up an empty Product with the following:

```
@product = Product.new
```

On the server, @product is an ActiveRecord::Base object. That statement fetches some metadata about the products table's columns, their data types, and their constraints. On the other hand, on the client, @product is an ActiveResource::Base object. Initializing it with .new does not contact the server, and therefore it knows nothing about its own attributes.

To resolve this, we will cheat a little. The *app/views/products/new.erb* view accesses the product's attributes with text_field and the like:

```
<% form_for(:product, :url => products_path) do |f| %>
  <p>
    <b>Name</b><br />
    <%= f.text_field :name %>
  </p>

  ...
<% end %>
```

These methods are helpful; they will use the @product object if it is present (and use its attribute values as default values in the text boxes). However, if @product is nil, the helpers will not complain and will just render empty input fields. So, we can get away with not initializing @product at all. Simply comment out the line initializing @product, and the situation will be resolved:

```
# GET /products/new
# GET /products/new.xml
def new
  #@product = Product.new

  respond_to do |format|
    format.html # new.erb
    format.xml  { render :xml => @product }
  end
end
```

Now we start the client's web server on port 3000 (with the web service's web server still running on port 4000):

```
$ cd products_example_client
$ script/server
```

Loading up *http://localhost:3000/products* in the browser, the application looks and behaves the same, but it is backed by a RESTful connection over HTTP rather than a SQL connection.

We can examine the client's log to find a fairly standard-looking request and response:

```
Processing ProductsController#index (for 127.0.0.1 at 2007-09-14
    14:30:36) [GET]
  Session ID: BAh7Bi...
  Parameters: {"action"=>"index", "controller"=>"products"}
Rendering template within layouts/products
Rendering products/index
Completed in 1.02543 (0 reqs/sec) | Rendering: 0.19423 (18%) |
    DB: 0.00000 (0%) | 200 OK [http://localhost/products]
```

But, as you may notice here, there is no "Product Load" entry indicating a database call. If we look at the server's log, we notice that the client issued a GET request from ActiveResource for *http://localhost:4000/products.xml* to load the list of products:

```
Processing ProductsController#index (for 127.0.0.1 at 2007-09-14
    14:30:38) [GET]
  Session ID: 04bc0d4b88c250a9cd50fb481991e2d9
  Parameters: {"format"=>"xml", "action"=>"index",
    "controller"=>"products"}
  Product Load (0.000591)   SELECT * FROM products
Completed in 0.15692 (6 reqs/sec) | Rendering: 0.00255 (1%)
    | DB: 0.00059 (0%) | 200 OK [http://localhost/products.xml]
```

We can see the XML wire protocol that ActiveResource uses by querying the web service directly—just navigate to *http://localhost:4000/products.xml*. The response is generated by the ActiveRecord XmlSerializer, via @products.to_xml:

```
<?xml version="1.0" encoding="UTF-8"?>
<products>
  <product>
    <created-at type="datetime">2007-09-08T14:06:08-05:00</created-at>
    <description>Description of the T-shirt</description>
    <id type="integer">1</id>
    <name>Organic cotton T-shirt</name>
    <price type="float">18.5</price>
    <quantity type="integer">15</quantity>
  </product>
</products>
```

Of course, real-world applications will be more complicated than this. The real problems come from the complexity involved in integrating different systems. In this example, we were greatly assisted by having a monoculture—making Rails talk to Rails is easier than, say, making a J2EE system talk to Rails.

However, the advantage of a RESTful architecture lies in its constraints. Agreeing on RESTful principles narrows the universe of discourse—it pares down the space in which two systems can disagree and still call themselves RESTful. And REST constrains architecture in a way that has been found to be applicable to most applications, so it is a reasonable default for new architectures. The conventions of ActiveResource layer on top of these constraints in a way that is friendly to Rails/ActiveRecord applications, and not very difficult to integrate with other applications.

Action Web Service

Action Web Service (AWS) is a client and server library for SOAP and XML-RPC web services. It used to be the default web service component in Rails, but it has actually since been dropped from Rails 2.0 in favor of ActiveResource and RESTful interfaces.

AWS is still being maintained as a separate library, and is still a good choice for those who need to interoperate with SOAP or XML-RPC applications. It is discouraged for greenfield development, though; current best practices support the use of RESTful HTTP architectures. Thus, we will not go into detail here on its usage. API Documentation for AWS is available at *http://aws.rubyonrails.org/*, and the library itself can be installed as a gem (gem install actionwebservice).

Case Study: Amazon S3

Amazon S3 (Simple Storage Service) is an online file-storage web service provided by Amazon. It is unique among online storage services in several ways:

- It has a no-minimum pricing structure. Storage is billed by the GB-month, bandwidth is billed by the GB, and there is an additional charge per GET, PUT, and LIST request.

- There is no web interface to create objects; the only full mode of access is through the API.

- It is generally agreed that the S3 API is the first large public API that calls itself RESTful and actually lives up to the principles of REST.

- In addition to the rich HTTP web service interface, S3 can serve objects over plain HTTP (without any custom HTTP headers) and BitTorrent. Many organizations use S3 as a storage network for their static content because it can serve images, CSS, and JavaScript just as well as a standard web server.

The full documentation for the S3 API is at *http://aws.amazon.com/s3*. We will now look into the basic architecture of S3, its concepts, and its set of operations.

Concepts and Terminology

S3 is used to store *objects*, which are streams of data with a *key* (a name) and attached metadata. They are like files in many ways. Objects are stored in *buckets*, which also have a key. Buckets are like filesystem directories, with a few differences:

- Bucket names must be unique across the entire S3 system. You cannot pick a bucket name that has already been chosen by someone else.

- Bucket names must be valid DNS names (alphanumeric plus underscore, period, and dash).

- Buckets cannot be nested. There is one level of buckets, which contain objects. However, we can fake such nesting by giving objects keys like `blog/2007/01/05/index.html`. Slash characters, though they often designate hierarchy in URIs, are treated like any other character in object keys. We can even query keys by prefix, so we can ask to list keys starting with `blog/2007/01/05`.

Amazon provides three different URI templates by which objects can be accessed. These are genuine RESTful URIs; they refer to the resources themselves, and nothing else:

- `http://s3.amazonaws.com/bucketkey/objectkey`
- `http://bucketkey.s3.amazonaws.com/objectkey`
- `http://bucketkey/objectkey`

This last URI is an example of a *virtual hosted bucket*; by using a DNS name as a bucket key, and pointing that DNS name at `s3.amazonaws.com.` via a CNAME, S3 will recognize the bucket key from the `Host` header and serve the appropriate object. This makes it possible to serve an entire domain from S3, nearly transparently. If we create a bucket called `images.example.com`, place a JPEG photo in it as an object called `hello.jpg`, and ensure the proper CNAME is set up pointing `images.example.com.` to `s3.amazonaws.com.`, then our image is accessible at *http://images.example.com/hello.jpg* with a standard web browser, just as if we had an HTTP server serving that URI.

Authentication

Because Amazon was not tied to the limitations of existing HTTP clients, it did not have to bow to the limitations of HTTP Basic or Digest authentication in web browsers when creating S3. The S3 authentication protocol is a thin layer, adding an HMAC signature to each request. After the message is signed, a header is added to the HTTP request as follows:

    Authorization: AWS *AWSAccessKeyId*:*Signature*

The *AWSAccessKeyId* value indicates the ID of the access key that the bucket owner generated; it is tantamount to a user ID. The *Signature* value is the Base64-encoded result of the HMAC calculation.

Alternative authentication options

S3 is a closed system; the owner of a bucket is billed for most operations on it. Therefore, all requests to S3 must be signed or otherwise authorized by the bucket owner, as he is the one ultimately responsible for payment.

However, signing each request can be inconvenient in some situations. A common example is when an organization uses S3 as an asset server; usually the organization would want the corresponding bucket to be world-readable. S3 includes access control lists (ACLs) for this purpose. As long as the owner is comfortable with being charged for operations by anonymous users, he can give READ access to the AllUsers group, which will eliminate the need for a signature.

Another option, which can be incredibly useful, is to delegate access control by including the authentication information in the query string of the object's URI. This is most useful when the object is still private but there are designated users without an AWS account who should be allowed to retrieve it via plain HTTP or BitTorrent. Basecamp uses this approach to store a company's files. The files are kept on S3 with a locked-down ACL, and when an authorized user requests the file, he is sent to a URI including a signature, which is valid for a limited period of time. The format of the URIs is such:

```
/objectkey?AWSAccessKeyId=AWSAccessKeyId&Expires=Expires&Signature=Signature
```

The `AWSAccessKeyId` and `Signature` values are as described previously, while the Expires value is a POSIX-time-formatted value indicating when the authorization expires. The `Expires` value is also signed by the HMAC so that the recipient cannot modify it undetected.

Architecture and Operations

S3 has a truly RESTful HTTP interface, in which the URIs correspond to resources only, the proper HTTP methods are used according to their semantics, and status codes are used appropriately. There are three types of resources in the S3 system:

Service
Represents the Amazon S3 service; its well-known URI is `http://s3.amazonaws.com/`. This resource supports only one HTTP method:

GET service
Returns a list of all buckets owned by the currently authenticated user.

Bucket
Represents one bucket belonging to the authenticated user. Can be accessed through the following URIs:

- `http://s3.amazonaws.com/bucketkey`
- `http://bucketkey.s3.amazonaws.com/`
- `http://bucketkey/` (if the key is a valid DNS name with a CNAME pointing to `s3.amazonaws.com`)

A bucket resource supports the following three methods:

PUT bucket
Creates a bucket with the given name (as the client gets to choose the name, this is accomplished with PUT to the resource itself, rather than POST to the parent). Attempting to create a bucket that already exists will return an HTTP 409 Conflict error code.

GET bucket
Retrieves a list of objects contained in the specified bucket. Takes a `prefix` parameter in the query string to list all keys that begin with a given string.

DELETE bucket

> Deletes the specified bucket. Only the bucket's owner may delete a bucket. A bucket can be deleted only if it is empty; attempting to delete a nonempty bucket will cause an error with an HTTP status code of 409 Conflict.

Object

> Represents an object stored within a bucket. Accessible at the following URIs:
>
> - http://s3.amazonaws.com/*bucketkey*/*objectkey*
> - http://*bucketkey*.s3.amazonaws.com/*objectkey*
> - http://*bucketkey*/*objectkey*

All object keys, as seen above, are qualified with their bucket key. An object resource supports the following four methods:

PUT object

> Stores the given data at the location specified, creating a new object or overwriting an existing object.

GET object

> Retrieves and returns the object at the specified location.

HEAD object

> Returns the headers that would be returned from a GET request on this object, with no body.

DELETE object

> Deletes the object at the given location. By analogy to Unix file permissions, you must have WRITE access on a bucket to delete objects within it. Deleting a nonexistent object is not an error, but is effectively a no-op.

S3 Clients and Servers

Marcel Molina, Jr.'s AWS::S3 library (*http://amazon.rubyforge.org/*) is the most popular client for S3. Its design was inspired by ActiveRecord, and it is simple and elegant:

```
require 'aws/s3' # gem install aws-s3

AWS::S3::Base.establish_connection!(
  :access_key_id     => 'MyAWSAccessKeyId',
  :secret_access_key => 'MyAWSSecretAccessKey'
)

image_bucket = Bucket.create "images.example.com"

S3Object.store(
  'hello.jpg',            # key
  File.read('hello.jpg'), # value
  'images.example.com',   # bucket name
  :content_type => 'image/jpeg',
  :access => :public_read
)
```

The s3fuse project (*http://sourceforge.net/projects/s3fuse/*) is an implementation of an S3 client using FUSE (a Linux filesystem framework that runs in userspace rather than kernel space). This makes it possible to mount an S3 bucket as a Linux filesystem and use it transparently within unmodified applications.

Park Place, by *why the lucky stiff* (*http://code.whytheluckystiff.net/parkplace*), is a nearly complete clone of the Amazon S3 web service. It is perfect for developing and testing S3 applications without requiring an S3 account or payment. It does not support S3's SOAP interface, but it supports most everything else, including distributing objects with BitTorrent.

> Park Place is written using the excellent Camping web microframework, also by *why the lucky stiff* (*http://code.whytheluckystiff.net/camping*). Camping is a very stripped-down Ruby framework modeled after Rails but taking less than 4 kb of source (packed).
>
> Incidentally, the Camping source is a great place to learn Ruby metaprogramming inside and out.

Further Reading

Roy Fielding's dissertation, *Architectural Styles and the Design of Network-Based Software Architectures*, is available online from *http://www.ics.uci.edu/~fielding/pubs/dissertation/top.htm*.

The REST wiki is full of theoretical as well as practical guidance about the principles of REST: *http://rest.blueoxen.net/*.

The HTTP/1.1 specification, RFC 2616, is fairly accessible for the working web developer. Every web application developer should at least be conversant in HTTP. An HTML version of the RFC is available from *http://www.w3.org/Protocols/rfc2616/rfc2616.html*.

Leonard Richardson and Sam Ruby's *RESTful Web Services* (O'Reilly) is a very accessible, yet comprehensive, introduction to the principles of RESTful design. Although it is oriented toward machine-consumable web services, the principles of REST are generally applicable to any network architecture.

Software architecture has a surprising amount in common with building architecture. For a different perspective on software architecture, Christopher Alexander's classic trilogy (*The Timeless Way of Building*, *A Pattern Language*, and *The Oregon Experiment*) is worth a read. The books describe how architecture influences and is influenced by life. Alexander's philosophies on architecture were the inspiration for the modern software design patterns movement.

i18n and L10n

Wer fremde Sprachen nicht kennt,
weiß nichts von seiner eigenen.
(He who ignores foreign languages
knows nothing of his own.)
—Goethe

As the reach of the Web expands, developers find that their web applications must be customized to match the needs of new audiences of different cultures. *Internationalization* is the process of adapting software so that it may be used across many various cultures and locales. *Localization* is the process of actually modifying the product and creating a version customized for a particular language, country, or locale.

The difference between internationalization and localization can be fuzzy, and it can change from situation to situation. As a simplistic example, consider a social networking site. At a minimum, internationalization would involve adapting the application to accept and display data in a wide variety of character sets (say, by using UTF-8 for all input, output, and storage). Localization would at least involve translation of user interface elements to several languages, and possibly much more.

 The term *internationalization* is usually abbreviated *i18n*, short for "*i*, 18 letters, and then *n*." Similarly, "localization" is abbreviated *L10n*. To avoid ambiguity, i18n is always written with a lowercase *i*, while L10n always uses an uppercase *L*. I will use this convention throughout this chapter.

Locale

Although language translation gets the lion's share of attention in this field, it is but one part of i18n. A human language may have significant regional differences or variants between countries where the language is spoken. Dialects aside, there can be large differences in currency, collation (sort order), number and date format, and even writing system across regional or political divisions within a country.

These differences are encapsulated in the concept of *locale*. A locale is usually defined as a language plus a country or region. It includes not only language but also regional and local preferences and possibly a character encoding. A POSIX-style locale identifier looks like en_US.UTF-8 (English, United States, UTF-8 character encoding).

Character Encodings

One of the most fundamental topics in i18n is the concept of a *character encoding* or *character set*.* Computers work with numbers; people work with characters. A character encoding maps one to the other. This is simple enough. The difficulty comes, as it usually does, because of history.

At the time of this writing, ASCII is nearing its 45th birthday; yet we still see its legacy today. This should not surprise anyone; data is usually the most long-lived part of a computing system. As networking protocols and storage formats are built on top of a character encoding, it should not be a surprise that the character encoding would be among the most deeply entrenched and hardest to change parts of a protocol stack.

ASCII

ASCII, the American Standard Code for Information Interchange, was one of the first character encodings to gain widespread use; it was introduced in 1963 and first standardized in 1967. Most encodings in use today descend from ASCII.

The ASCII standard (ANSI X3.4-1986) defines 128 characters. The first 32 characters (with hex values 0 through 1F) and the last character (7F) are nonprinting control characters. The remainder (20 through 7E) are printable. The control characters have largely lost their original meaning, but the printable characters are nearly always the same. The standard ASCII table is as follows.

	x0	x1	x2	x3	x4	x5	x6	x7	x8	x9	xA	xB	xC	xD	xE	xF
0x	NUL	SOH	STX	ETX	EOT	ENQ	ACK	BEL	BS	HT	LF	VT	FF	CR	SO	SI
1x	DLE	DC1	DC2	DC3	DC4	NAK	SYN	ETB	CAN	EM	SUB	ESC	FS	GS	RS	US
2x		!	"	#	$	%	&	'	(	)	*	+	,	-	.	/
3x	0	1	2	3	4	5	6	7	8	9	:	;	<	=	>	?
4x	@	A	B	C	D	E	F	G	H	I	J	K	L	M	N	O
5x	P	Q	R	S	T	U	V	W	X	Y	Z	[	\	]	^	_
6x	`	a	b	c	d	e	f	g	h	i	j	k	l	m	n	o
7x	p	q	r	s	t	u	v	w	x	y	z	{			}	~	DEL

---

* A character set is a collection of characters (such as Unicode), while a character encoding is a mapping of a character set to a stream of bytes. For the older character sets such as ASCII, the two terms can generally be conflated.

Extended ASCII

Although ASCII defines 128 characters and a 7-bit encoding, most computers process data in 8-bit bytes. This leaves room for 128 more characters. Of course, computer vendors each chose their own way to deal with this situation. This led to the development of numerous *extended-ASCII* character sets, each of which used a different interpretation for the upper octets (80 through FF).

The most widely adopted extended-ASCII standard is ISO 8859. This standard adopts the ASCII values for the first 128 characters, and provides 15 different "parts" that each provide a definition for the last 128 characters. In effect, ISO 8859 defines 15 separate character sets.

The most used of these character sets is ISO-8859-1 (Latin-1). This provides nearly complete coverage for most Western European languages. In fact, the 256 characters defined by ISO-8859-1 correspond to the first 256 code points of Unicode. ISO-8859-1 is still in widespread use among languages that use the Latin alphabet.

Problems with ASCII

Though the extended ASCII character encodings were widely successful for years, they only provided a temporary fix. With so many encodings floating around, it is difficult for people to communicate. It is always impossible to look at a sequence of bytes and determine their character encoding; that information must be carried out-of-band. The more potential character sets in use, the worse this problem becomes.

Another problem with the use of ASCII or extended ASCII is that it has no support for bidirectional, or *bidi*, text. Some written languages, such as Hebrew and Arabic, are written primarily right-to-left (RTL). This causes problems in rendering systems that were designed with left-to-right (LTR) text in mind. Bidirectional text, which combines LTR and RTL within a page or paragraph, is usually impossible with ASCII or extended ASCII.

The worst limitation of the extended-ASCII model is that it still only provides support for a maximum of 256 characters. This is not nearly enough for East Asian languages (the so-called *CJK* or *CJKV languages*, for Chinese, Japanese, Korean, and Vietnamese), which are ideographic and can require tens of thousands of characters for adequate coverage. There are several encodings that cover the CJKV languages specifically, but they do not solve the general problem of having too many encodings.

Unicode

The extended-ASCII model was successful for many years, and the ISO-8859 encodings provided a good way to support different world scripts. However, the limitations became increasingly bothersome; multiple languages could not be supported within one document, and the CJKV languages had their own independently developed character sets and encodings. In addition, the Internet began to develop in the 1990s, connecting people and allowing them to exchange digital information with a far greater reach than before.

So, in 1991, the Unicode Consortium published the first Unicode standard. Unicode sought to be the "one true character set" in which all text would eventually be represented. In a large part, that goal is well on the way to being accomplished. Unicode is a widely known, well-supported standard that is used extensively on the Internet and in other forms of data exchange today.

Unicode supports all of the world's writing systems currently in use and many archaic ones, with very few exceptions. There is no "code page" switching as there was under the old character-set systems. All of the scripts can be used interchangeably within a document, and the encodings are universal; they can be exchanged over the Internet without worrying too much about differing encodings.

Unicode deals with the world in Platonic ideals. Rather than representing glyphs (the rendering of a character), each Unicode code point represents a *grapheme* (the character abstracted from its representation).[*] This is consistent with the purpose of a character encoding: to encode text without specifying presentation. For example, the following two characters are the same grapheme and would be represented by the same Unicode code point (U+0061, LATIN SMALL LETTER A), even though they are different glyphs (see Figure 8-1).

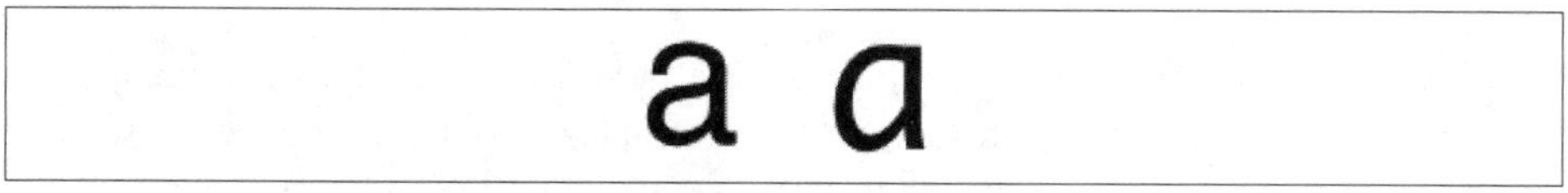

Figure 8-1. Alternative glyphs representing the "a" grapheme

Though the distinction between graphemes and glyphs is relatively easy to make for English, it can be very difficult and occasionally political for Han characters (the ideographs common to CJKV languages).[†]

Unicode Transformation Formats

One of the key factors driving the adoption of Unicode is *UTF-8* (8-bit Unicode Transformation Format). UTF-8 has several clever features (some would call them compromises) that make it attractive to those who are used to working with ASCII or Latin-1 text:

---

[*] In this chapter, I use *grapheme* and *character* synonymously.

[†] See *http://en.wikipedia.org/wiki/Han_unification* for one aspect of this situation.

- In UTF-8, text that only uses standard ASCII characters is byte-for-byte identical to its ASCII encoding. UTF-8 ensures that the encoding of every code point above U+007F begins with a high-ASCII character (with a most significant bit of 1).

- Because of this, a UTF-8 encoded string will never contain the null byte (0x00), except as the encoding of the code point U+0000.

- UTF-8 is somewhat self-synchronizing, which makes it resilient to error. Each type of byte in UTF-8 (single-byte character, first byte of a multibyte character, and subsequent bytes of a multibyte character) can be distinguished by its prefix. Therefore, you can start at any byte point in a string and find the next character without working backward. Similarly, you can find the previous character by only working backward.

- Because of these unique prefixes, no encoding of a character is a substring of another character's encoding. For example, the ASCII character "a" is represented by 0x61 in UTF-8. No other character's encoding will contain the byte 0x61, so if you see that byte, you know that it represents the character "a." This ingenious design decision means that string searching works with standard, non-UTF-8-aware algorithms.

However, UTF-8's similarity to previous encodings can lead to confusion. When working with UTF-8 text, there are more things to think about:

- The number of code points in a string cannot be determined from the number of bytes. The entire string must be read and processed to determine the number of characters.

- Even when the number of code points is known, features such as ligatures, combining characters, bidi text, and control characters make it impossible to determine how much space is needed to display a string without parsing every byte.

- UTF-8 strings cannot be cut at byte boundaries; they must be cut on character boundaries. Due to the design of UTF-8, it is easy to find character boundaries with simple bit operations, but this must still be taken into account.

UTF-8 has largely won out over other encodings, especially on the Internet. Later in this chapter, we will examine the problems encountered when working with UTF-8 text in Rails, and we will look at the solutions we have available.

The Unicode *Basic Multilingual Plane* (BMP), which contains most of the scripts in common use today, covers code points U+0000 through U+FFFF. In UTF-8, code points in the BMP can be expressed in three or fewer bytes. Though Unicode supports up to 17 planes of characters (with 65,536 code points each), only about 10% of the available space has been assigned thus far.

Rails and Unicode

Ruby 1.8 has less-than-ideal Unicode support, when compared to its contemporaries such as Java and the .NET languages. To Ruby, strings are just sequences of 8-bit bytes, while the character and string types of the Java runtime and .NET CLR are based on Unicode code points. While Ruby's approach simplifies the language, most developers at this point in time need Unicode support. Luckily, Ruby is flexible enough that we can tack support for Unicode onto the language in a relatively friendly way.

It is not surprising that Ruby's Unicode support is lacking. During the time of Ruby's genesis in Japan (the mid-1990s), Unicode was first being developed. In Unicode's early stages, its supporters were mainly American and European, with less East Asian involvement.

Many Japanese people opposed the process of *Han unification*, or collapsing most of the Han characters common to CJKV languages into a single set of code points. The unified Han characters tended to appeal more to Chinese speakers than Japanese speakers. The people involved in Han unification (primarily Westerners) tended to collapse characters that were similar, but not identical, across Asian languages. In the early days of Unicode, rendering software would get confused and display similar, but incorrect, glyphs for the Han-unified characters. This was at best disconcerting; at worst, offensive.

There are technical solutions to all of these problems today, but Unicode was a slow starter in Japan. Other character sets such as Shift_JIS gained more currency in Japan at the time, which actually may have contributed somewhat to the problem; having more extant character sets leads to more conversion issues.[*]

Multilingualization in Ruby 1.9

Ruby 1.9 will support multilingualization (*m17n*). Rather than a built-in Unicode assumption, Ruby 1.9 will support interoperability between multiple character sets. This is more flexible than assuming that all string literals are Unicode, and it is a more general approach to character set handling. To use UTF-8 for all string and regex literals, the following pragma can be used:

```
# coding: utf-8
```

---

[*] Matz expresses this sentiment in an interview available at *http://blog.grayproductions.net/articles/the_ruby_vm_episode_iv*.

ActiveSupport::Multibyte

In lieu of complete multibyte character support in Ruby 1.8, Rails has created a workaround. We touched on this solution, ActiveSupport::Multibyte, back in Chapter 2. Here, we will explore it in more detail.

Recall that the global variable $KCODE determines the current character encoding, and thus influences how Ruby treats your strings. In Rails 1.2 and later, Initializer sets $KCODE to 'u', so all processing is assumed to be in UTF-8 unless otherwise specified.

Rails includes a library called ActiveSupport::Multibyte that provides a way to deal with multibyte characters on top of Ruby. At this time, only UTF-8 is supported. The encoding is derived from the current value of $KCODE.

Multibyte adds a String#chars instance method, which returns a proxy (of type ActiveSupport::Multibyte::Chars) to that string. This proxy delegates to a handler, depending on the current encoding. (Right now, the only handlers are a UTF-8 handler for $KCODE = 'u' and a pass-through handler for everything else.) The Chars object uses method_missing to trap unknown calls and send them to the handler. If the handler cannot deal with them, they are sent to the original String.

The most important feature Multibyte provides is the ability to split strings on character boundaries, rather than byte boundaries. All you need to do is call the String#chars method and optionally convert back to a String when you are done:

```
$KCODE = 'u'

str = "résumé" # => "résumé"

str[0..1]        # => "r\303"
str.chars[0..1].to_s # => "ré"
```

Multibyte also provides case conversion, which can differ vastly among languages:

```
str.upcase # => "RéSUMé"
str.chars.upcase.to_s # => "RÉSUMÉ"
```

And method calls to chars can be chained, as the Chars methods return a Chars object rather than Strings. Even methods that are proxied back to the original String have their String return values converted to Chars objects.

```
str.chars[0..1].upcase.to_s # => "RÉ"
```

The implementation of Multibyte is itself fascinating; the tables of composition maps, codepoints, case maps, and other details are generated automatically from tables at the Unicode Consortium web site and stored in *active_support/values/ unicode_tables.dat*. The generator can be found in *active_support/multibyte/ generators/generate_tables.rb*.

Unicode Normalization

As with any increasingly complicated encoding, normalization and canonicalization are important issues with Unicode. One representation on paper (or screen) may map to multiple encodings. In some cases, it may be more desirable to treat those sequences identically, but in other cases we may need to treat them differently.

One complicating issue is *character composition*. Unicode provides multiple versions of some characters, for various reasons. For example, the *ö* in the German word *schön* can be encoded as either *ö* (U+00F6 LATIN SMALL LETTER O WITH DIAERESIS) or as the combination of *o* (U+006F LATIN SMALL LETTER O) and ¨ (U+0308 COMBINING DIAERESIS). The two representations use different byte sequences, and therefore they would not compare as equivalent to a byte-oriented procedure.

Another example is *compatibility characters*, or characters that were introduced into Unicode for compatibility with older encodings. One area where this occurs is typographical ligatures (see Figure 8-2).

Figure 8-2. The "fi" sequence shown without a ligature and with a ligature

The text on the left does not use a ligature. For typographical reasons, the style on the right is usually used for the combination of *f* and *i*. The original intent of Unicode was that a smart rendering system would replace the consecutive code points *f* and *i* with the appropriate ligature. However, many systems turned out not to be capable of this advanced rendering (Mac OS X being a notable exception). Therefore, common ligatures were given their own code points, so that they could be embedded in a body of text and rendered (with a suitable font including those ligatures) with a dumb client. In this case, the ligature "fi" is U+FB01 LATIN SMALL LIGATURE FI.

To support character composition on platforms with less complex rendering systems, Unicode includes *precomposed characters*, such as the *ö* shown earlier (U+00F6 LATIN SMALL LETTER O WITH DIAERESIS). Compatibility characters such as the typographical ligatures are often precomposed. In order to properly compare and collate strings that may include both combining characters and precomposed characters, the strings must be *canonicalized*, or reduced to a well-known form such that two strings that are "the same" (by some definition) will always map to the same sequence of code points.

To canonicalize sequences of code points, we must first determine what our notion of equivalence is. Unicode defines two types of equivalence: the narrow *canonical equivalence* and the broader *compatibility equivalence*. Canonical equivalence is limited to characters that are equal in both form and function—the standard example being the decomposed ö (the two code points *o* and ¨) versus the precomposed character ö (one code point). Two sequences of code points, such as those, that are canonically equivalent are identical in appearance and usage, and can in nearly all cases be substituted for each other.

Compatibility equivalence is a broader concept. Compatibility equivalence includes all canonically equivalent characters, plus characters that may have different semantics but are rendered similarly. Examples include the characters *f* and *i* versus the fi ligature, or the superscript ^{2} versus the ordinary numeral 2.

There are four methods of Unicode normalization: D, C, KD, and KC. (They are also referred to as NFD, NFC, NFKD, and NFKC, with NF standing for *Normalization Form*.) The D forms leave the string in a decomposed form, while the C forms leave the string canonically composed (by first decomposing, and then recomposing by canonical equivalence). The K forms decompose by compatibility equivalence, while those without a K decompose by canonical equivalence. (All composition is done under canonical equivalence to ensure a consistent composition.)

ActiveSupport provides methods on the UTF-8 handler for Unicode normalization, supporting all four forms. The following code shows the differences between the four forms as applied to the string *final piñata*. The first word includes the fi ligature, which is compatibility equivalent (but not canonically equivalent) to the separated characters fi. The second word includes the character *ñ*, which is both compatibility equivalent and canonically equivalent to the code points *n* and ˜.

```
$KCODE = 'u'

str = "final piñata".chars

str.normalize(:d).to_s  # => "final pin˜ata"
str.normalize(:c).to_s  # => "final piñata"
str.normalize(:kd).to_s # => "final pin˜ata"
str.normalize(:kc).to_s # => "final piñata"
```

Filtering UTF-8 Input

Although you may be UTF-8 clean through your entire system (UTF-8 text can be entered anywhere and is displayed identically upon output), you are still at risk of problems if you just accept user-provided strings as UTF-8. Users can provide invalid UTF-8 text (not all byte sequences correspond to valid sequences of UTF-8 code points). Users will even provide maliciously malformed UTF-8 text in an attempt to crash or exploit your string-processing functions.

Paul Battley wrote an article addressing the issue of filtering untrusted UTF-8 strings.[*] As with most other hard problems in Rails, we cheat. In this case, the iconv library can clean up UTF-8 strings for us:

```
require 'iconv'

ic = Iconv.new('UTF-8//IGNORE', 'UTF-8')
valid_string = ic.iconv(untrusted_string + ' ')[0..-2]
```

The `Iconv.new` line creates a new `Iconv` object to translate potentially invalid UTF-8 data into UTF-8 data with invalid characters ignored. The next line works around an `Iconv` bug: it will not detect an invalid byte at the end of a string. Therefore, we add a space (a known-valid byte) and chop it off after performing the conversion.

Ilya Grigorik shows how to use the Oniguruma regular expression engine to filter out control characters (of the Cx classes).[†] Note that the Oniguruma engine is standard in Ruby 1.9, but is also available for Ruby 1.8 (gem install oniguruma).

```
require 'oniguruma'

# Finall all Cx category graphemes
reg = Oniguruma::ORegexp.new("\p{C}", {:encoding => Oniguruma::ENCODING_UTF8})

# Erase the Cx graphemes from our validated string
filtered_string = reg.gsub(validated_string, '')
```

Storing UTF-8

Proper i18n requires that your character set be correctly processed in the application and correctly stored in the database. For most Rails applications, this means setting up the database and connection to be UTF-8 clean. Since Rails 1.2, ActiveRecord correctly processes UTF-8 data and is ready for UTF-8 storage over supported connections. The specifics differ among database engines, so we'll examine MySQL and PostgreSQL here.

MySQL

To properly store UTF-8 data in a MySQL database, two things need to be in place. First, the database and tables need to be configured with the proper encoding. Secondly, the client connection between ActiveRecord and MySQL needs to use UTF-8.

MySQL ships with Latin1 (ISO-8859-1) as the default character set. Thus, all of the string operations are by default byte-oriented. You can change the default character set and collation for the entire database server with the following commands in the MySQL configuration file (*my.cnf*):

```
character-set-server=utf8
default-collation=utf8_unicode_ci
```

[*] *http://po-ru.com/diary/fixing-invalid-utf-8-in-ruby-revisited/*
[†] *http://www.igvita.com/blog/2007/04/11/secure-utf-8-input-in-rails/*

The Rails `create_database` schema definition method will attempt to do the right thing. If you use `create_database` to create your databases, they will default to UTF-8:

```
>> ActiveRecord::Schema.define do
?>   create_database :test_db
>> end
-- create_database(:test_db)
   SQL (0.000585)   CREATE DATABASE `test_db` DEFAULT CHARACTER SET `utf8`
   -> 0.0008s
=> nil
```

However, the `create_table` method does not specify a character set, but you can provide an `:options` parameter that specifies any table creation options, including a character set. (Bear in mind, though, that by specifying DBMS-specific table creation syntax, you lose portability between DBMSs.)

```
>> ActiveRecord::Schema.define do
?>   create_table :test do end
>> end
-- create_table(:test)
   SQL (0.028168)   CREATE TABLE `test` (`id` int(11) DEFAULT NULL
                    auto_increment PRIMARY KEY) ENGINE=InnoDB
   -> 0.1264s
=> nil

>> ActiveRecord::Schema.define do
?>   create_table :test2, :options =>
      'ENGINE=InnoDB DEFAULT CHARSET=utf8' do end
>> end
-- create_table(:test2, {:options=>"ENGINE=InnoDB DEFAULT CHARSET=utf8"})
   SQL (0.028386)   CREATE TABLE `test2` (`id` int(11) DEFAULT NULL
                    auto_increment PRIMARY KEY) ENGINE=InnoDB
                    DEFAULT CHARSET=utf8
   -> 0.0287s
=> nil
```

However, none of these methods will handle preexisting databases. Chances are, if you have created databases and tables without specifying CHARACTER SET utf8, the tables are treating the data as Latin1. If the data is actually Latin1 (and you are now converting the entire application to Unicode at once), the conversion is simple, though it must be done once for each table:

```
ALTER TABLE table_name CONVERT TO CHARACTER SET utf8;
```

If your only need is straight data conversion, this will work. If you are using ActiveRecord migrations, Graeme Mathieson has written a migration that will perform this conversion for every table in your database. It is available from *http://woss.name/2006/10/25/migrating-your-rails-application-to-unicode/*.

Be very careful converting a table that has existing data. If you have been using Rails 1.2 or later (which support UTF-8 by default) and have not converted your tables to UTF-8, you may have UTF-8 data stored in the database as Latin1. If you then convert the table to UTF-8, the conversion will be performed twice, which will corrupt your data. The standard procedure in this case is to dump the data as Latin1, piping the dump through sed to change the output character set to UTF-8:

```
mysqldump -uusername -p --default-character-set=latin1 mydb \
  | sed -e 's/SET NAMES latin1/SET NAMES utf8/g' \
  | sed -e 's/CHARSET=latin1/CHARSET=utf8/g' >mydb.sql
```

Then, load the dump back into MySQL as UTF-8:

```
mysql -uusername -p –default-character-set=utf8 <mydb.sql
```

The last step in this process is to set up the client connection to support UTF-8. Even if all of the data is properly configured and using UTF-8, if MySQL thinks the client wants Latin1 data, that is what it will send. The SQL command to set the client encoding in MySQL is the following:

```
SET NAMES utf8;
```

The Rails MySQL connection adapter has an encoding option that sets the client encoding as well; in lieu of sending the preceding command, just add the following to your *database.yml*:

```
production:
  adapter: mysql
  (...)
  encoding: utf8
```

At this time, MySQL does not support 4-byte UTF-8 characters. This is generally not a problem, as characters in the Basic Multilingual Plane can always be encoded in three or fewer bytes.

PostgreSQL

PostgreSQL is in a similar situation; both the database encoding and client encoding must be specified. The default encoding is SQL_ASCII. This is a special byte-oriented compatibility encoding; the low-ASCII bytes (0x00 through 0x7F) are treated as ASCII characters, and the rest (0x80 through 0xFF) are left alone. Because of the design of UTF-8, the SQL_ASCII encoding is safe to use with UTF-8. However, it is not optimal, as the database server will not validate any input data.

A new database can be created with UTF-8 encoding, using either the -E option to createdb or the SQL WITH ENCODING clause:

```
$ createdb -E UTF-8 new_database
```

-or-

```
=> CREATE DATABASE new_database WITH ENCODING 'UTF-8';
```

Existing databases that were created with another encoding can be dumped and reloaded to convert them, as with MySQL.

The ActiveRecord PostgreSQL adapter also respects the encoding option to control client encoding, so remember to set it to UTF-8:

```
production:
  adapter: postgresql
  (...)
  encoding: UTF-8
```

Serving UTF-8

Properly serving UTF-8 is a matter of telling the browser that you are using UTF-8. This is done in two ways:

HTTP Content-type *header with a charset parameter*
> This is the preferred way to set the encoding. The server should be configured to spit out a header like:
>
> ```
> Content-Type: text/html; charset=UTF-8
> ```
>
> Rails takes care of this for us. As of Rails 1.2, the encoding automatically defaults to UTF-8.

HTML <meta> *tag*
> This method is often used by those who are not able to change their server's configuration to add a proper header. The <meta> tag takes the place of the HTTP header. Put this inside of the <head> tag on your layouts for the same effect as the header specified previously:
>
> ```
> <meta http-equiv="Content-Type" content="text/html; charset=UTF-8" />
> ```
>
> When used by itself, setting a <meta> tag is less than ideal. This is because once a browser reaches this tag, it must re-parse the document from the beginning if its initial assumption about the encoding was incorrect. (This method works because the characters likely to be used in an HTML document before the <meta> tag have the same representation in all of the common encodings—they are the low ASCII characters.)
>
> However, <meta> tags are helpful when used in conjunction with proper server headers. They allow the browser to determine the proper encoding even if the file is saved locally (thus removing the header information).

Note that, in the Content-type header, the name "charset" is misleading, as this parameter really specifies the encoding.

Character Set Conversion

You must consider the issue of data you receive from external sources in non-UTF-8 encodings. If you serve HTML in UTF-8, the data you receive through form posts will be UTF-8. But there are other external sources as well:

- Forms from third-party sites pointed at your server may not be encoded in UTF-8. These forms will post their data in the original character set.

- When interacting with other systems through web services or messaging, a character set and encoding must be agreed upon.

- When retrieving data from the Web (with net/http or open-uri), you must be sure to convert text from its source encoding into your working encoding.

To remedy this situation, you can use the iconv library, which is part of the Ruby standard library. We have seen this earlier; it was used to strip invalid characters out of our UTF-8. To convert a string from one encoding to another, create an Iconv object, providing the source and destination encodings, and call its iconv instance method:

```
require 'iconv'

# Latin-1 (ISO-8859-1) equivalent of "café"
# Latin-1 E9 == "é"
cafe_latin1 = "caf#{"E9".hex.chr}"

ic = Iconv.new("utf-8", "iso-8859-1") # to_encoding, from_encoding
cafe_utf8 = ic.iconv(cafe_latin1)
```

We can play with the $KCODE variable to change how we see the output. If we set $KCODE to "U", the string is interpreted as UTF-8 and we see the properly converted "café." If $KCODE is "A", the string is interpreted as a series of bytes, and so we see the unprintable characters escaped:

```
cafe_latin1 # => "caf\351"

$KCODE = "U"
cafe_utf8    # => "café"

$KCODE = "A"
cafe_utf8    # => "caf\303\251"
```

As usual, we can see the byte length of each string with String#length:

```
cafe_latin1.length # => 4
cafe_utf8.length # => 5
```

JavaScript URI encoding and UTF-8

There is one important thing to remember if you use JavaScript to URI-encode text in a UTF-8 environment: always encode data using encodeURI( ) or encodeURIComponent( ); do not use escape( ). The encodeURI forms follow RFC 3986, converting the text to UTF-8 and percent-encoding each byte. This makes things much easier on the server end.

The escape( ) function, on the other hand, escapes one character at a time, using nonstandard constructs such as %u1234 (corresponding to the code point U+1234). It escapes extended-ASCII characters as Latin-1, even on a page served as UTF-8:

```
>>> document.characterSet
"UTF-8"

>>> escape("café")
"caf%E9"

>>> encodeURI("café")
"caf%C3%A9"
```

Rails L10n

For an application to be truly ready for worldwide visitors, internationalization is just
the beginning. It is vital for an application with global reach to correctly accept, process, and store UTF-8 data. But it is also important, when supporting users from different regions and locales, to localize the interface and any applicable data to the users'
locales. This can involve any of several things, which we will cover in this section.

Interface/Resource Translation

The way the term "localization" is most often used, it refers to translating interface
text and resources into users' languages. The traditional software package used for
localizing interface text is GNU gettext.[*]

gettext

gettext uses literal strings from the program's source as keys; translators write files
that provide translations for each of the strings. There are several steps to using gettext in an application. We will use Ruby-Gettext, which is a mostly compatible Ruby
version of GNU gettext.

First, we install the gettext gem:

```
$ sudo gem install gettext
Successfully installed gettext-1.10.0
```

Next, we create a very basic skeleton application that loads the gettext gem, binds to
the text domain (application name) *hello*, and displays a greeting:

hello.rb

```
#!/usr/local/bin/ruby -w

require 'rubygems'
require 'gettext'

include GetText
bindtextdomain('hello')

puts _("Hello, world!")
```

---

[*] *http://www.gnu.org/software/gettext/*

The _( ) function is gettext's standard method for localization. All literal text that is to be localized should be wrapped in a call to this method. Our locale is set to U.S. English, so upon running the program, we see the default U.S. English version without having to do any localization:

```
$ echo $LC_CTYPE
en_US.UTF-8
$ ./hello.rb
Hello, world!
```

The developer now creates a *.pot* file from the source. This extracts all text to be translated from the program and puts it in a template, which the translator will work from. The GNU gettext program to create *.pot*-files is xgettext; the Ruby-gettext version is called rgettext.

```
$ rgettext hello.rb -o hello.pot
```

The resulting *hello.pot* file has several lines of boilerplate, followed by the extracted strings for translation—in this case, only one:

hello.pot
```
# SOME DESCRIPTIVE TITLE.
# Copyright (C) YEAR THE PACKAGE'S COPYRIGHT HOLDER
# This file is distributed under the same license as the PACKAGE package.
# FIRST AUTHOR <EMAIL@ADDRESS>, YEAR.
#
#, fuzzy
msgid ""
msgstr ""
"Project-Id-Version: PACKAGE VERSION\n"
"POT-Creation-Date: 2007-10-19 12:20-0500\n"
"PO-Revision-Date: 2007-10-19 12:20-0500\n"
"Last-Translator: FULL NAME <EMAIL@ADDRESS>\n"
"Language-Team: LANGUAGE <LL@li.org>\n"
"MIME-Version: 1.0\n"
"Content-Type: text/plain; charset=UTF-8\n"
"Content-Transfer-Encoding: 8bit\n"
"Plural-Forms: nplurals=INTEGER; plural=EXPRESSION;\n"

#: hello.rb:9
msgid "Hello, world!"
msgstr ""
```

This file is ready to be translated. The translator receives *hello.pot* from the developer and copies it into a directory corresponding to the destination locale. Ruby-gettext provides tools for this, but we will use the GNU gettext msginit; the Ruby-gettext documentation recommends using it if it is available.

```
$ mkdir -p locale/es
$ cd locale/es/
$ LANG=es_MX msginit -i ../../hello.pot -o hello.po
(...)
Couldn't find out about your email address.
Please enter your email address.
```

(...)
```
Creado hello.po.
```

Now that the *hello.po* file is created, the translator will work through it and add translations for each string:

locale/es/hello.po
```
# Spanish translations for PACKAGE package.
# Copyright (C) 2007 THE PACKAGE'S COPYRIGHT HOLDER
# This file is distributed under the same license as the PACKAGE package.
# Brad Ediger <translator@example.com>, 2007.
#
msgid ""
msgstr ""
"Project-Id-Version: PACKAGE VERSION\n"
"POT-Creation-Date: 2007-10-19 12:20-0500\n"
"PO-Revision-Date: 2007-10-19 12:27-0500\n"
"Last-Translator: Brad Ediger <translator@example.com>\n"
"Language-Team: Spanish\n"
"MIME-Version: 1.0\n"
"Content-Type: text/plain; charset=UTF-8\n"
"Content-Transfer-Encoding: 8bit\n"
"Plural-Forms: nplurals=2; plural=(n != 1);\n"

#: hello.rb:9
msgid "Hello, world!"
msgstr "¡Hola, mundo!"
```

When all strings have been translated, the translator ships off the *.po* files to the developer. The developer then creates *.mo* files (binary translations of the *.po* files; the binary versions are used directly by the application) using *rmsgfmt* from Ruby-gettext (or msgfmt from GNU gettext). When doing local development, we set the GETTEXT_PATH environment variable to look in our *locale* directory. If we didn't do that, we would have to install our *.mo* files under a shared location such as */usr/share/locale* so that Ruby-gettext could find them at runtime.

```
$ export GETTEXT_PATH=locale
$ mkdir locale/es/LC_MESSAGES
$ rmsgfmt locale/es/hello.po -o locale/es/LC_MESSAGES/hello.mo
```

When we run the script with our locale set to es_MX.UTF-8, gettext searches a series of paths under GETTEXT_PATH (including *locale/es/LC_MESSAGES*) for an appropriate *.mo*-file. Finding the one we just created, it displays the properly localized text:

```
$ LC_ALL=es_MX.UTF-8 ./hello.rb
¡Hola, mundo!
```

This is a very simple example, but it illustrates many of the basic aspects of gettext. There is a document available detailing how to integrate the Ruby bindings to gettext into a Rails application. See *http://manuals.rubyonrails.com/read/chapter/105* for the full explanation and source files. This is essentially a do-it-yourself approach; it is a thin layer on top of gettext, and you have to fill in some of the gaps (such as allowing users to change their locale and dialect) yourself. But there are good examples on that page, and it is a good start. Also see *http://jonathan.tron.name/articles/2007/03/30/gettext-and-rails* for a few miscellaneous concerns if you decide on this approach.

Gibberish

Gettext has a few disadvantages, the primary one being that translated strings are keyed by the original string. Under gettext, even changing "Hello, world!" to "Hello world!" would require updating that entry in every *.po* file and recompiling everything. Even if only the English version changed, every file would require modification, as the strings are keyed on the exact source text.

Gibberish,* by Chris Wanstrath, is a very lightweight Rails localization plugin. Like gettext, it is based on replacing individual strings from a language-dependent resource file. However, it is much simpler (and, correspondingly, somewhat less flexible) than gettext. It is also tailored toward Ruby's style and Rails' needs.

First, install the Rails plugin from Subversion. Its *init.rb* file will load Gibberish and any translation files under the *lang* directory:

```
$ script/plugin install svn://errtheblog.com/svn/plugins/gibberish
```

Unlike gettext, which scans your source files to generate translation files, Gibberish requires you to create translation files yourself. However, they are very easy to create. A sample Gibberish language file looks like this:

lang/es.yml
```
welcome: ¡Hola, mundo!
```

The source syntax is very much like gettext, but with the addition of a symbol tag, used as a key in place of the string itself. Gibberish overrides the String#[] method to provide nice syntax for this:

```
puts "Hello, world!"[:welcome]
# >> Hello, world!
```

The default language is English, so if no language is selected, that statement will output "Hello, world!". We can change the default language:

```
Gibberish.use_language :es

puts "Hello, world!"[:welcome]
# >> ¡Hola, mundo!
```

Interpolation variables are available, and values for them can be passed as positional or keyword arguments. If String#[] is passed non-hash arguments, the second and subsequent arguments are interpolated into the string, in order:

```
puts "Date of birth: {dob} ({age} years old)"[:dob, u.dob, u.age]
# >> Date of birth: 1/1/95 (12 years old)
```

* *http://require.errtheblog.com/plugins/browser/gibberish/README*

Alternatively, the second argument to `String#[]` can be a hash. The keys correspond to the names of the interpolation variables, while the values provide the text to be inserted. The following code is equivalent, but more descriptive and more resilient to change in the translated text:

```
puts "Date of birth: {dob} ({age} years old)"[:dob, {:dob => u.dob, :age => u.age}]
# >> Date of birth: 1/1/95 (12 years old)
```

This example highlights one common problem with localization: it is never straight translation of text. In most nontrivial situations, the translated text has some level of dependence on the data that is more complicated than simple string interpolation ("{age} years"). Later in this chapter, we will see how the Globalize Rails plugin handles these situations.

Gibberish provides good Rails integration. You can automatically set a user's language from a session variable with a simple around filter:

```
class ApplicationController < ActionController::Base
  around_filter :set_language

  private

  def set_language
    Gibberish.use_language(session[:language]) { yield }
  end
end
```

Despite its simplicity, Gibberish has one more trick up its sleeve. If you omit the string key, one will be generated for you:

lang/es.yml
```
hello_world: ¡Hola, mundo!
```
hello.rb
```
Gibberish.use_language :es

puts "Hello, world!"[:hello_world]
# >> ¡Hola, mundo!

puts "Hello, world!"[]
# >> ¡Hola, mundo!
```

This method is resilient to small changes (capitalization, punctuation, and anything else that is removed when folding the string into a symbol), but if this feature is overused, you will run into the same fragility problems that gettext presents.

Globalize

For those with heavy localization needs, the Globalize plugin (*http://www.globalize-rails.org/*) is the best thing since sliced bread. We will first examine the features of

Globalize that compete with gettext, Gibberish, and the other text-based localization libraries commonly used with Rails. Later, we will examine some of the other features that make Globalize so compelling.

As is the custom, Globalize provides a simple method to access translations of a string; it can be called as String#t or Object#_ (the latter is provided for gettext compatibility):

```
<% Locale.set("es-MX") %>

<%=h "Hello, World!".t %>
==> Hello, World!

<%=h _("Hello, World!") %>
==> Hello, World!
```

However, there is a twist. Unlike gettext and Gibberish, which both use text files to store translations, Globalize uses the database. Since we had no Mexican Spanish translation for "Hello, World!", Globalize passed it through, storing the "Hello, World!" tag in the database for future reference when you need to translate. This replaces gettext's harvesting phase and uses the strings themselves from your application to determine what needs to be translated.

When we do add a translation to the database, it works as expected:

```
Locale.set 'es-MX'
Locale.set_translation 'Hello, World!', '¡Hola, mundo!'

puts "Hello, World!".t
# >> ¡Hola, mundo!
```

Globalize also tries to capture all of the Rails error messages and add them to the table, to be localized. When they have been translated, Globalize will intercept them and replace them depending on the current locale.

Globalize includes a collection of data about the world's languages, to minimize the amount rote translation of common data. Data provided includes the following:

- ISO codes, English names, and native names for each language (for example, "FR," "French," and "Français").
- Pluralization rules (for example, is "0 items" inflected the same as "1 item," or the same as "2 items," as in English?).
- Writing direction (left-to-right or right-to-left).
- Date, currency, and number format (for example, "12,345.67" versus "12.345,67") for each locale.
- Translation of date information (weekday and month names) for most languages.

Locale-Specific Settings

Beyond simple translation, there are plenty more locale-specific issues. Different locales, even within the same language, can have vastly different conventions for representing dates, times, currency, and numbers.

Luckily, this is more of a data problem than a programming problem. Globalize provides data to help with all of these issues. The date formatting helpers, Time#localize and Date#localize, serve as a replacement for Time#strftime that translates day and month names (both full and abbreviated):

```
>> Time.now.strftime("%A, %d %B %Y")
=> "Saturday, 02 June 2007"

>> Locale.set 'en-US'
>> Time.now.localize("%A, %d %B %Y")
=> "Saturday, 02 June 2007"

>> Locale.set 'pl-PL'
>> Time.now.localize("%A, %d %B %Y")
=> "Sobota, 02 Czerwiec 2007"
```

The localize method is also available on Integers and Floats, and provides numbers localized to the current locale:

```
>> Locale.set 'en-US'
>> 123456.789.localize
=> "123,456.789"

>> Locale.set 'de-DE'
>> 123456.789.localize
=> "123.456,789"
```

Globalize also provides a Currency class to handle money. It acts like Tobias Lütke's Money class, in that it stores prices as integers in the database. But it is more flexible in handling multiple currencies. Refer to the API documentation for the full story, but here is a sample usage:

```
# app/models/product.rb
class Product < ActiveRecord::Base
  composed_of :price, :class_name => 'Globalize::Currency',
    :mapping => [%w(price cents)]
end
```

Then we can create a product:

```
@product = Product.new :price => Currency.new(1000_00)
puts @product.price.to_s
# >> 1,000.00
```

The Currency#format method formats the currency according to the specifications of the current locale (which, as usual, is set with the Locale.set method):

```
Locale.set 'de-DE'
puts @product.price.format(:code => true)
# >> 1.000,00 EUR
```

Note that unlike the Money library, which handles basic currency exchange, you will need to handle any exchange calculations yourself when using Globalize. The Globalize library only takes care of formatting, not the semantics of the currency.

Model Translation

Model translation is the most complicated, least standardized, and most application-dependent part of localization. *Model translation* or *content translation* refers to the translation of the content stored within an application for multiple locales. This kind of localization is the most difficult because it is application-specific. Often, the translation cycles are much tighter than when only the application itself is localized.

The premier example of an application with a need for content translation is a web content-management system. Often, web pages and documents need to be maintained in parallel in many languages. One of the key selling points of enterprise content-management systems over their open source brethren is rock-solid support for managing translations and their workflow.

In these applications, workflow is the key application-dependent factor. The actual technical practice of selecting and displaying the proper content for a user's locale is dead simple compared to the work of coordinating to make sure the content is translated and available.

On the other hand, it is perfectly possible for an application to require internationalization but not require any content translation at all. Applications with geographically localized clients (such as web-based applications with many small clients located in different countries) may have a need for interface translation, and they certainly need to handle UTF-8 text properly, but they may not need to interchange data between different languages. Again, the need is highly application-dependent.

Globalize provides facilities for model translation, closely integrated with ActiveRecord. There are a few easy steps to follow after installing Globalize:

1. Set a base language, which is the default locale assumed for data without a translation. This is best done in *environment.rb*, after Rails is loaded but before the application serves requests:

   ```
   Locale.set_base_language 'en-US'
   ```

2. Provide a `before_filter` on your localized actions that sets the locale. This part is application-specific; the locale can be provided in the URL, a cookie, the session, or a user preference in the database. Here is a simple `before_filter` that sets the locale based on a `locale` request parameter:

   ```
   class ApplicationController < ActionController::Base
     before_filter :set_locale

     protected

     def set_locale
   ```

```
        Locale.set(params[:locale] || Locale.base_language.code)
    end
  end
```

After this filter is set up, you can specify the locale for any action within the application by adding the appropriate parameter to the URL (http://example.com/posts/show/34?locale=zh-CN). Alternatively, you can specify the locale parameter with a custom route:

```
map.cms_page ':locale/*path_info', :controller => 'pages', :action => 'show'
```

This route would support a multilingual content-management system, where the locale parameter determines the language and the *path_info segment looks up the page in the database: http://example.com/en-US/about-us/contact-us.

3. Declare that the ActiveRecord class in question contains translated data:

```
class Page < ActiveRecord::Base
  translates :title, :body
end
```

4. Find an object that needs translation; set the locale, set the text, and save the object.

```
Locale.set 'es-MX'
@page.reload
@page.update_attributes! :body => "¡Hola, mundo!"
```

5. The ActiveRecord accessors for the attributes specified by the translates method now automatically check the current locale and look for the proper translation:

```
<%= @page.body %>
# >> "¡Hola, mundo!"
```

Globalize Example: An Address Book

To illustrate the use of Globalize for view translation all the way through an application, we will construct a simple database that functions like an address book. First we will develop the address book as an English-only application; later, we will see what is involved in integrating Globalize and adding translations.

We will use a simple SQLite3 database file for storage:

config/database.yml
```
development:
  adapter: sqlite3
  database: db/globalize.sqlite3
  encoding: utf8
```

First, we create the model and migration for the Person model and its corresponding people table:

db/migrate/001_create_people.rb

```ruby
class CreatePeople < ActiveRecord::Migration
  def self.up
    create_table :people do |t|
      t.string :first_name
      t.string :last_name

      t.string :home_phone
      t.string :office_phone
      t.string :mobile_phone

      t.text :address
      t.string :country
    end
  end

  def self.down
    drop_table :people
  end
end
```

app/models/person.rb

```ruby
class Person < ActiveRecord::Base

  def full_name
    "#{first_name} #{last_name}"
  end

  def address_with_country
    "#{address}\n#{country}"
  end

end
```

Running the migration creates the *db/globalize.sqlite3* database file:

```
$ rake db:migrate
== 1 CreatePeople: migrating =====================================================
-- create_table(:people)
   -> 0.0020s
== 1 CreatePeople: migrated (0.0021s) ===========================================

$ ls db/
globalize.sqlite3 migrate          schema.rb
```

Here are the models, views, helpers, and controllers that we create for a very simple first iteration of the address book. For simplicity, we only include the index (list of all people in the address book), new (display a form to create a new entry), and show (display an individual entry's details) actions.

config/routes.rb

```ruby
ActionController::Routing::Routes.draw do |map|
  map.resources :people
end
```

app/controllers/people_controller.rb

```ruby
class PeopleController < ApplicationController

  def index
    @people = Person.find :all, :order => 'last_name ASC, first_name ASC'
  end

  def create
    @person = Person.create params[:person]
    redirect_to person_path(@person)
  end

  def show
    @person = Person.find params[:id]
  end

end
```

app/helpers/people_helper.rb

```ruby
module PeopleHelper
end
```

app/views/people/index.html.erb

```erb
<h1>Address Book</h1>

<% if @people.empty? %>
  <p><em>Address book is empty.</em></p>
<% else %>
  <ul id="people">
    <% @people.each do |person| %>
      <li id="person-<%= person.id %>">
        <%= link_to h(person.full_name), person_path(person) %>
      </li>
    <% end %>
  </ul>
<% end %>

<p><%= link_to 'New person', new_person_path %></p>
```

app/views/people/new.html.erb

```erb
<h1>New Person</h1>

<% form_for :person, @person, :url => people_path,
             :method => :post do |@person_form| %>
  <%= render :partial => "form" %>
  <p>
    <label></label>
    <%= submit_tag "Save" %>
  </p>
<% end %>
```

app/views/people/_form.html.erb

```erb
<p>
  <label for="person_first_name">First name</label>
  <%= @person_form.text_field :first_name %>
</p>
```

```
<p>
  <label for="person_last_name">Last name</label>
  <%= @person_form.text_field :last_name %>
</p>

<p>
  <label for="person_home_phone">Home phone</label>
  <%= @person_form.text_field :home_phone %>
</p>

<p>
  <label for="person_office_phone">Office phone</label>
  <%= @person_form.text_field :office_phone %>
</p>

<p>
  <label for="person_mobile_phone">Mobile phone</label>
  <%= @person_form.text_field :mobile_phone %>
</p>

<p>
  <label for="person_address">Address</label>
  <%= @person_form.text_area :address, :size => '30x5' %>
</p>

<p>
  <label for="person_country">Country</label>
  <%= @person_form.text_field :country %>
</p>
```

app/views/people/show.html.erb

```
<h1><%=h @person.full_name %></h1>

<h2>Phone Numbers</h2>
<dl>
  <% unless @person.home_phone.blank? %>
    <dt>Home</dt>
    <dd><%=h @person.home_phone %></dd>
  <% end %>

  <% unless @person.office_phone.blank? %>
    <dt>Office</dt>
    <dd><%=h @person.office_phone %></dd>
  <% end %>

  <% unless @person.mobile_phone.blank? %>
    <dt>Mobile</dt>
    <dd><%=h @person.mobile_phone %></dd>
  <% end %>
</dl>

<h2>Address</h2>
<%= simple_format(h(@person.address_with_country)) %>

<p><%= link_to "Address Book", people_path %></p>
```

Complete the first iteration with a very simple XHTML layout and stylesheet:

app/views/layouts/people.html.erb
```
<!DOCTYPE html PUBLIC "-//W3C//DTD XHTML 1.0 Strict//EN"
  "http://www.w3.org/TR/xhtml1/DTD/xhtml1-strict.dtd">
<html xmlns="http://www.w3.org/1999/xhtml">
  <head>
    <title>Address Book</title>
    <%= stylesheet_link_tag 'default' %>
  </head>
  <body>
    <%= yield %>
  </body>
</html>
```

public/stylesheets/default.css
```
body {
  font-family: sans-serif;
}

form label {
  display: block;
  float: left;
  width: 130px;
  text-align: right;
  padding: 3px 5px;
}
```

Although this application leaves out many features that you would want in a real address book, it will serve our purposes to demonstrate localization with Globalize. The basic English-only interface is shown in Figures 8-3 through 8-6; the user can create and view address book entries.

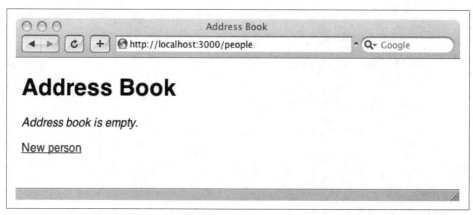

Figure 8-3. Blank state of an empty address book

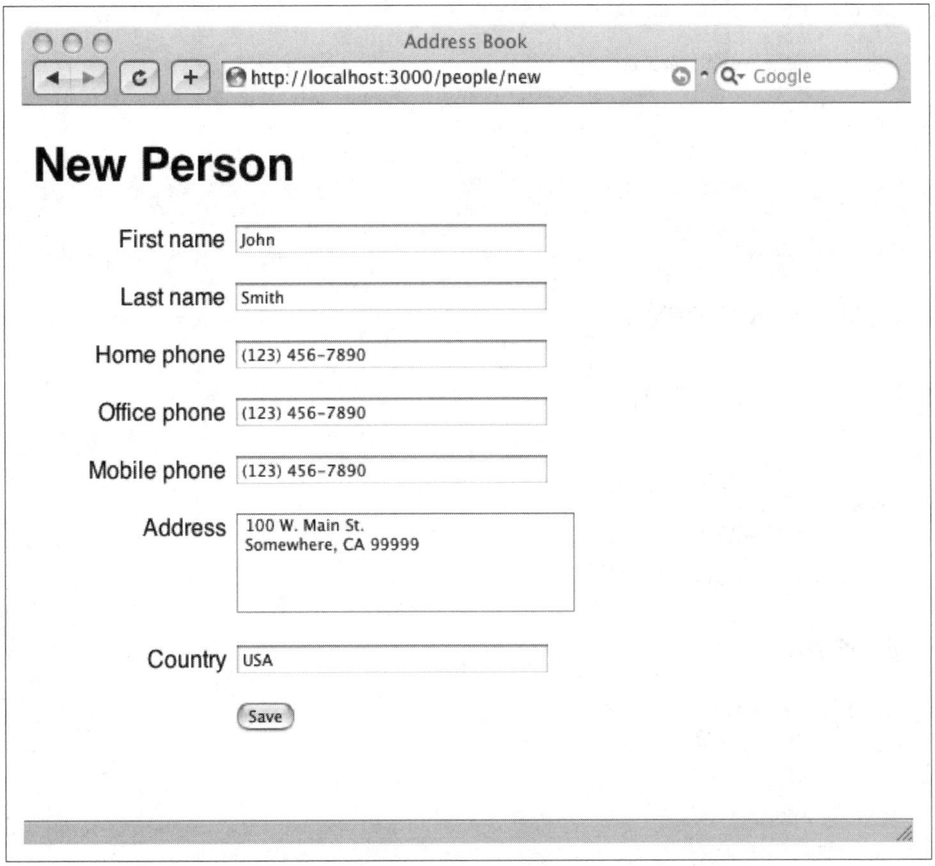

Figure 8-4. Adding a person

Localizing the address book

Now we will localize the address book's interface so that the interface elements appear in the language of the user's choice. First we will install the Globalize plugin. This can be done by any method of your choice (see Chapter 3 for plugin installation options), but we will use svn export:

```
$ svn export svn://svn.globalize-rails.org/globalize/trunk vendor/plugins/globalize
```

Globalize comes with a Rake task to set up the tables. Unfortunately, Globalize trunk is still broken, and it misidentifies user-created translations as built in. To fix this, immediately after we create the translation tables, we will change the built_in column of the globalize_translations table to default to false:

```
$ rake globalize:setup
$ script/console
>> ActiveRecord::Schema.define do
?>   change_column_default :globalize_translations, :built_in, false
>> end
```

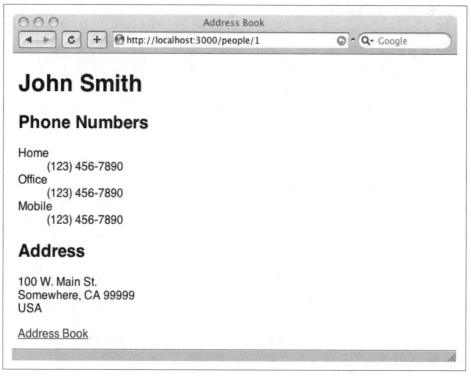

Figure 8-5. Viewing a newly created person

Figure 8-6. Viewing all people; one created

Now, we need to modify the views to use the String#t method, so that the views can be translated. This can be a tedious process; here is one resulting view:

app/views/people/_form.html.erb

```
<p>
  <label for="person_first_name"><%= "First name".t %></label>
  <%= @person_form.text_field :first_name %>
</p>

<p>
  <label for="person_last_name"><%= "Last name".t %></label>
  <%= @person_form.text_field :last_name %>
</p>

<p>
  <label for="person_home_phone"><%= "Home phone".t %></label>
  <%= @person_form.text_field :home_phone %>
</p>

<p>
  <label for="person_office_phone"><%= "Office phone".t %></label>
  <%= @person_form.text_field :office_phone %>
</p>

<p>
  <label for="person_mobile_phone"><%= "Mobile phone".t %></label>
  <%= @person_form.text_field :mobile_phone %>
</p>

<p>
  <label for="person_address"><%= "Address".t %></label>
  <%= @person_form.text_area :address, :size => '30x5' %>
</p>

<p>
  <label for="person_country"><%= "Country".t %></label>
  <%= @person_form.text_field :country %>
</p>
```

Next, we need to integrate Globalize into the controllers. We will use an initializer to set up Globalize and some locale settings for the application.

config/initializers/globalize.rb

```
include Globalize
Locale.set_base_language 'en-US'
LOCALES = {
  'en' => 'en-US',
  'es' => 'es-MX'
  }.freeze
```

The Locale.set_base_language method tells Globalize that our views are in U.S. English, and it need not bother with translation if the user's locale is the same.

The LOCALES hash is a list mapping two-letter language codes to the actual locale names that Globalize uses. The next step is to set up an application-wide filter that will set the user's locale so that Globalize knows which translation to look for.

app/controllers/application.rb
```
class ApplicationController < ActionController::Base
  helper :all

  before_filter :set_locale

  protected

  def set_locale
    # params overrides session, but en-US is only used if both
    # params and session are absent
    session[:locale] = LOCALES[params[:locale]] ||
                          session[:locale] ||
                          'en-US'
    Locale.set session[:locale]
  end
end
```

The set_locale filter will notice anytime a page is requested with a locale in the query string (for example, *http://localhost:3000/people?locale=es*). It will set the locale so the views are translated into the correct language, and then it will store the chosen locale in the session so that the locale will be used again, even if the next request has no locale parameter. The locale defaults to en-US if none can be found in the session or params. An application that required user registration would most likely store the user's locale preference in the user account, but the session will suffice for our needs.

One very nice thing that Globalize does for us is to collect a list of text that needs to be translated. As soon as the String#t method is called, if the appropriate translation is not in place, it is stored away to be translated. We can use Ruby to strip out a list of needed translations and send them to a translator. Alternatively, we could build an administrative interface with Rails that allows our translators to log in, see any text that needs to be translated, and input translations that are used immediately. For now, we will stick with the simple approach.

Before we can enter the translations, we need to generate the list of needed translations. Browse to */people?locale=es* and click around until you have visited all of the pages. (As ActionView doesn't render templates until they are needed, the String#t methods will not be called until the page is actually needed.) This will populate the list of required translations, which we can easily extract at the Rails console. All we need to do is tell Globalize that we are translating into Mexican Spanish, and then find the translations that have no corresponding Spanish text:

```
>> Locale.set 'es-MX'
>> pp ViewTranslation.find(:all, :conditions =>
        ['text IS NULL AND language_id = ?', Locale.language.id]).map(&:tr_key)
["Address Book",
 "New person",
 "Phone Numbers",
 "Home",
 "Office",
 "Mobile",
 "Address",
 "New Person",
 "First name",
 "Last name",
 "Home phone",
 "Office phone",
 "Mobile phone",
 "Country",
 "Save",
 "Address book is empty."]
```

We can take this list to our translator, get the translations back, and use the console (or an administrative interface) to enter translations. This script, run at the Rails console, will set up our translations.

```
Locale.set 'es-MX'

translations = {
 "Address Book" => "Libreta de direcciones",
 "New person" => "Nueva persona",
 "Phone Numbers" => "Números de teléfono",
 "Home" => "Casa",
 "Office" => "Oficina",
 "Mobile" => "Móvil",
 "Address" => "Dirección",
 "New Person" => "Nueva Persona",
 "First name" => "Nombre",
 "Last name" => "Apellido",
 "Home phone" => "Teléfono de casa",
 "Office phone" => "Teléfono oficina",
 "Mobile phone" => "Teléfono móvil",
 "Country" => "País",
 "Save" => "Guardar",
 "Address book is empty." => "Libreta de direcciones está vacía."
}

translations.each do |key, text|
  ViewTranslation.update_all ['text = ?', text],
    ['tr_key = ? and language_id = ?', key, Locale.language.id]
end
```

As a final touch, we will add a language bar that enables the user to switch back and forth between our supported locales. We create a partial for the language bar, and update the master layout to include the language bar at the bottom of each page:

app/views/layouts/_language_bar.html.erb

```
<p>
  <%= LOCALES.keys.map { |code|
    link_to_unless code == Locale.language_code, code, url_for(:locale => code)
  }.join(" | ") %>
</p>
```

 Using url_for( ) in this manner relies on the fact that it will fill in any missing required URL parameters from the URL of the current page. Therefore, url_for(:locale => 'es') will point to the Spanish version of the current page.

app/views/layouts/people.html.erb

```
(...)
    <body>
      <%= yield %>
      <%= render :partial => "layouts/language_bar" %>
    </body>
(...)
```

And with that, the localization is complete. All static resources have been translated into Spanish, and we have added all necessary features to allow users to choose a locale. See Figures 8-7 through 8-10 for screenshots of the completed application.

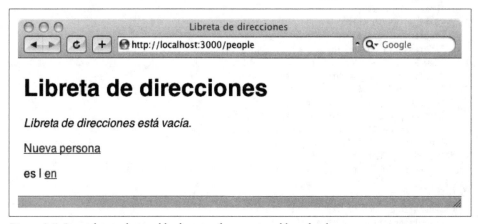

Figure 8-7. Spanish translation: blank state of an empty address book

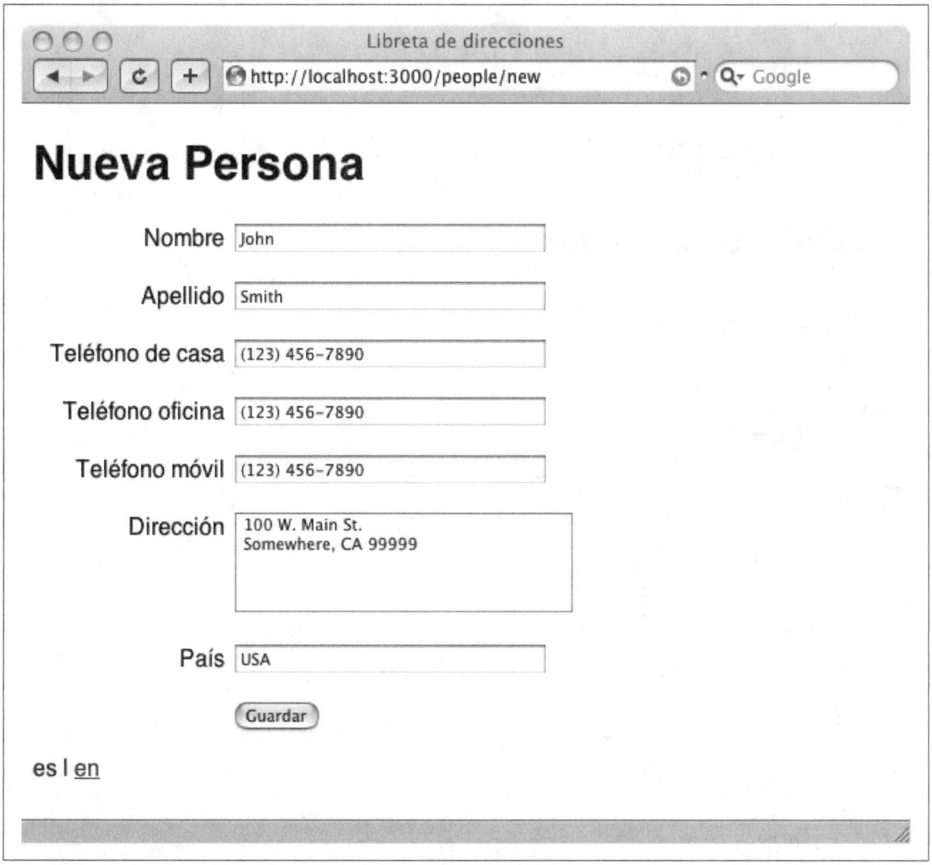

Figure 8-8. Spanish translation: creating a new person

Further Reading

Sven Fuchs has a great write-up about Globalize on his blog (*http://www.artweb-design. de/2006/11/10/get-on-rails-with-globalize-comprehensive-writeup*). The Globalize site (*http://www.globalize-rails.org/*) has plenty of information on setting up Globalize.

There is a mailing list for developers involved with internationalization in Rails. The list information page is available at *http://rubyforge.org/mailman/listinfo/railsi18n-discussion*.

The Ruby on Rails wiki has a page with good coverage of the current i18n options at *http://wiki.rubyonrails.com/rails/pages/InternationalizationComparison*.

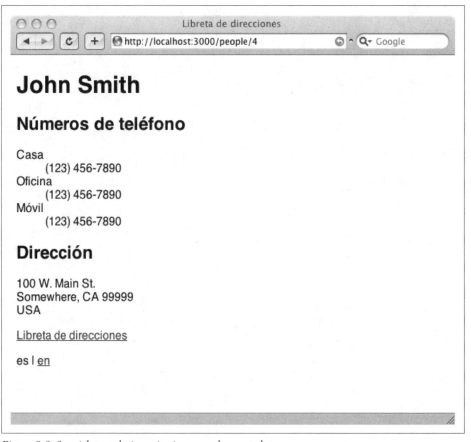

Figure 8-9. Spanish translation: viewing a newly created person

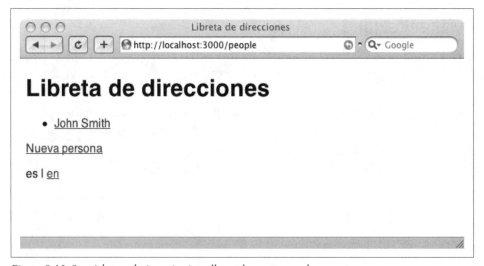

Figure 8-10. Spanish translation: viewing all people; one created

## CHAPTER 9

Incorporating and Extending Rails

The best way to predict the future is to invent it.
—Alan Kay

Ruby on Rails was designed as a loosely coupled set of components (ActionPack, ActiveRecord, ActiveResource, ActiveSupport, and ActionMailer) with some glue to hold them together (RailTies). Although Rails is typically used as a framework (an environment specialized to programming web applications), the components of Rails can be replaced with other components more suitable to a project. Alternatively, the components can be broken out and used apart from the rest of Rails. In this chapter, we will see how these techniques can be used for maximum flexibility in application development.

Replacing Rails Components

Replacing ActiveRecord

ActiveRecord, the Rails object-relational mapper, is one of the best-known parts of the Rails framework. But it represents one of many valid ways to map objects to a database. Martin Fowler identified and defined the Active Record pattern, along with other data-source patterns, in his book *Patterns of Enterprise Application Architecture*. (The Active Record pattern should not be confused with the ActiveRecord library, which is based on that pattern.) Several Ruby libraries have been developed based on other patterns. We will look at DataMapper, based on the pattern of the same name. We will also examine Ambition, an off-the-wall experimental library that maps Ruby statements directly to SQL.

If you are not using ActiveRecord in a Rails application, you can disable it by removing it from `config.frameworks` in *config/environment.rb*:

```
config.frameworks -= [ :active_record ]
```

DataMapper

The DataMapper library (*http://www.datamapper.org/*) is based on Martin Fowler's Data Mapper pattern, which is similar to Active Record but with less coupling. Active Record's chief structural weakness is that it ties the database schema to the object model. We see this happen in Rails when using ActiveRecord. Every structural change we want to make to the objects must be reflected in the database at the same time.

The Data Mapper pattern provides a better balance when the object model and database need to evolve separately. The drawback is that there will be some duplication. Because of the additional layer of indirection, DataMapper cannot infer your object's structure from the database like ActiveRecord can. This is the necessary price of flexibility.

DataMapper confers several other advantages over ActiveRecord:

- DataMapper includes an implementation of the Identity Map pattern, which ensures that each database record is loaded only once. ActiveRecord will happily allow a record to be loaded many times, which can potentially cause conflicts when one becomes stale.

- Empirically, DataMapper is faster than ActiveRecord. The code is also smaller and less complicated. This can be good or bad, depending on whether you need ActiveRecord's more advanced features.

- DataMapper can generate your database tables from their Ruby description:

  ```
  class Person < DataMapper::Base
    # (property definitions)
  end

  # Create the table based on the above properties
  database.save(Person)
  ```

 DataMapper defines a top-level method, database, that returns the current database session. As a top-level method (defined on Object), it can be used anywhere. DataMapper plays nicely, though—the method will not be defined if there is already another top-level method with the same name.

It does not have ActiveRecord's complex migration support, which means that any production schema changes must be done manually. But it does have a convenient task to recreate the entire schema, destroying any data in the process:

```
DataMapper::Base.auto_migrate!
```

DataMapper is very easy to use with Rails. It detects when it is being run under Rails and reads the *config/database.yml* file for a connection specification. So, everything should be ready to go with a gem install datamapper and one line in a Rails initializer:

```
require 'data_mapper'
```

DataMapper uses many of the same constructs as Rails. Start out by defining a model class that inherits from `DataMapper::Base`:

```
class Person < DataMapper::Base
  # ...
end
```

Within the class definition, property methods define fields that should be mapped from the class to the relational database:

```
class Person < DataMapper::Base
  property :first_name, :string
  property :last_name, :string
  property :biography, :text

  # Associations work pretty much like ActiveRecord...
  # belongs_to :company, :foreign_key => 'firm_id'
  # has_many :transactions, :class => FinancialTransaction
end
```

DataMapper comes with a set of convenience methods that behave like ActiveRecord object lifecycle methods. For example, the syntax to create a `Person` is the same as under ActiveRecord:

```
>> p = Person.new :first_name => 'John', :last_name => 'Smith',
                  :biography => 'Something about John'
=> #<Person:0x13ce99c @new_record=true, @first_name="John",
    @last_name="Smith", @biography="Something about John", @id=nil>
>> p.save
=> 1
>> p
=> #<Person:0x13ce99c @new_record=false, @first_name="John",
    @last_name="Smith", @biography="Something about John", @id=1>
```

> Notice that under DataMapper, the attributes of `Person` are directly stored as instance variables of the `Person` object. In ActiveRecord, these attributes would be stored in a hash as the `@attributes` variable. In some ways, DataMapper's approach is cleaner, as it avoids another layer of indirection.

There are many more features behind DataMapper, and the full set of documentation can be found at *http://www.datamapper.org/*. API documentation is also available at *http://datamapper.rubyforge.org/*.

Ambition

Chris Wanstrath's Ambition project (*http://errtheblog.com/post/10722*) is an amazing little experiment that turns Ruby code into SQL almost transparently. Using Ryan Davis's ParseTree library, Ambition walks the Ruby abstract syntax tree and turns various methods into their corresponding SQL queries.

Ambition is not an object-relational mapper (in fact, it requires ActiveRecord), but it is a simple interface on top of an ORM. It allows us to write SQL queries as pure Ruby. It does this using lazy evaluation—putting off SQL queries until the last possible moment.

To try out Ambition, we will check out the latest code and use the test console provided with Ambition (which requires us to create a development database first):*

```
$ git clone git://errtheblog.com/git/ambition
$ cd ambition
$ mysql -uroot -e"create database ambition_development"
$ test/console
(...)
Available models: Admin, Company, Developer, Project, Reply, Topic, and User
>>
```

This is a standard irb console, from which we can interact with any of these models as if from a Rails console. We can start off by finding users with a salary of greater than $50,000:

```
>> User.select{|u| u.salary > 50_000}
=> Query object: call
```

Here we see lazy loading in action. Nothing has been sent to the database; instead, a Query object has been created. Ambition relies on *kicker methods* to actually run the query and return results; right now, all that we have is an object representing the query. (This kind of object is often referred to as a *promise*; it has the ability to perform an expensive calculation, but will not do so unless asked.) We can call one of the kicker methods, map (collect), to run the query and extract the results:

```
>> User.select{|u| u.salary > 50_000}.map(&:name)
# SELECT * FROM users WHERE (users.`salary` > 50000)
=> ["David", "Jamis", "fixture_3", "fixture_4", "fixture_5", "fixture_6",
    "fixture_7", "fixture_8", "fixture_9", "fixture_10", "admin", "Goofy"]
```

Since the Query object being passed around contains all information necessary to run the query, additional methods chained onto it can actually modify the query as needed. For example, asking the Query object for its length changes the query to select only a count instead of a full list of columns:

```
>> User.select{|u| u.salary > 50_000}.length
# SELECT count(*) AS count_all FROM users WHERE (users.`salary` > 50000)
=> 12
```

These methods can be chained, augmenting the query as they progress. For example, the sort_by method adds an ORDER BY clause:

```
>> User.select{|u| u.salary > 50_000}.sort_by{|u| u.name}.map(&:name)
# SELECT * FROM users WHERE (users.`salary` > 50000) ORDER BY users.name
=> ["admin", "David", "fixture_10", "fixture_3", "fixture_4", "fixture_5",
    "fixture_6", "fixture_7", "fixture_8", "fixture_9", "Goofy", "Jamis"]
```

---

* Currently, the only way to fetch the latest Ambition source is using Git, a decentralized version control system. We cover the decentralized paradigm in Chapter 10, but for now you can fetch Git from *http://git.or.cz/*.

The Query object has a to_hash and a (mostly functional) to_sql method, which help debug the SQL queries and conditions being generated:

```
>> User.select{|u| u.salary > 50_000}.sort_by{|u| u.name}.to_sql
=> "SELECT * FROM users WHERE users.`salary` > 50000 ORDER BY users.name"
>> User.select{|u| u.salary > 50_000}.sort_by{|u| u.name}.to_hash
=> {:order=>"users.name", :conditions=>"users.`salary` > 50000"}
```

There are many more features, including some syntactic sugar on the standard Ruby Enumerable methods:

```
>> User.any?{|u| u.salary > 50_000}
# SELECT count(*) AS count_all FROM users WHERE (users.`salary` > 50000)
=> true

>> User.all?{|u| u.salary < 500_000}
# SELECT count(*) AS count_all FROM users
# SELECT count(*) AS count_all FROM users WHERE (users.`salary` < 500000)
=> true
```

Consult the Ambition blog post for an overview of all the useful methods and syntax provided. Ambition is still under heavy development and is certainly subject to change. At this time, the best source of documentation is the README (available from the Git repository at *git://errtheblog.com/git/ambition*), as well as the source itself.

Og

Og (short for ObjectGraph) is yet another object-relational mapping library for Ruby. It is part of the Nitro project, which is a web framework similar to Rails. Like Rails, Nitro is composed of layered components. However, these components take a different approach to solve the same problems as Rails, and so it is much harder to use Og with Rails than with Nitro. In particular, the Rails Dependencies system causes many problems with file loading. We can work around these problems, but this method should still be considered very experimental.

The Og library has less baggage than ActiveRecord, and doesn't try to do as much, so the code is a bit more readable. It uses "magic" just as much as ActiveRecord does, but in a different way. Rather than defining its own set of property accessors (as DataMapper does), Og overrides the standard Ruby attr_accessor method to define properties. It uses ObjectSpace to find objects that represent model classes (based on their use of the new attr_accessor or inclusion of the Og::Model module). This means that the models can look almost exactly like plain-old Ruby objects. The only difference is that the types of the properties must be explicitly specified, so that they can be mapped to SQL types:

```
class Person
  attr_accessor :first_name, String
  attr_accessor :last_name, String
  attr_accessor :dob, Date
end
```

This approach leads to very readable code, but it has a couple of drawbacks:

- All models must be loaded before Og is started, because Og only traverses ObjectSpace when it is first loaded.
- Og's attr_accessor method will mark a class as an Og model. However, if the attr_accessor method is not used first thing in a class declaration, the Og methods will not be pulled in. Consider this example:

```
class Person
  is Og::Model
  has_many :friends, Friend
end
```

  The is method is a Ruby Facets alias for include that more closely reflects the semantics of multiple inheritance. Without this declaration or an attr_accessor, the has_many class method would not exist.

- The process of finding Og models relies on ObjectSpace. ObjectSpace implementation greatly complicates Ruby interpreter implementation; on platforms with managed garbage collection such as the .NET CLR or Java, it takes some special—and comparatively slow—implementation techniques. Because of this, it is possible that some of the Ruby 1.9 virtual machines may have limited or no support for ObjectSpace.

We will now see a highly experimental method of using Og with Rails. This method works around most of the incompatibilities between Nitro and Rails.

Installing Og from source. Unfortunately, the current stable gem version of Og (0.41.0) does not work with Rails. We will download the latest version of the code with Darcs and build a gem ourselves.

 Darcs is a distributed version control system written in Haskell. It is available from *http://darcs.net/*. If you have a working installation of GHC (the Glasgow Haskell Compiler), you can install Darcs from source. Otherwise, there are Darcs binaries available for many platforms.

First, we get the latest Nitro code using Darcs:

```
$ darcs get --partial http://repo.nitroproject.org nitroproject
$ cd nitroproject
```

Next, we find out what version of Ruby Facets this version of Nitro requires and install it. The dependency is contained within the gem specification for Glue:[*]

```
$ grep facets glue/glue.gemspec
  s.add_dependency("facets", "= 1.8.54")
$ sudo gem install facets --version =1.8.54
```

---

[*] Glue is Nitro's library that ties all of the components together, similar to ActiveSupport and RailTies in Rails.

Then we can build the Glue and Og (and, optionally, Raw and Nitro) libraries into gems and install them:

```
$ cd glue/
$ gem build glue.gemspec
$ sudo gem install glue-0.50.0.gem
$ cd ../og/
$ gem build og.gemspec
$ sudo gem install og-0.50.0.gem
$ cd ../raw/
$ gem build raw.gemspec
$ sudo gem install raw-0.50.0.gem
$ cd ../nitro/
$ gem build nitro.gemspec
$ sudo gem install nitro-0.50.0.gem
```

 To update the beta gem to the latest source, you can later run darcs pull from the *nitroproject* directory. Then recheck the Facets dependency, and run the preceding code again to rebuild and reinstall the latest gems.

Verify that the Og gem is correctly installed:

```
$ gem list --local og

*** LOCAL GEMS ***

og (0.50.0)
    State of the art object-relational mapping system
```

Using Og with Rails. We will use a custom Rails initializer to load Og and work around a few of its Rails incompatibilities. All Ruby files in *config/initializers* are loaded automatically on Rails startup, so this is a perfect place to start Og. Here is the initializer:

config/initializers/og.rb
```
# 1. Require our custom edge version of Og
gem 'og', '=0.50.0'

# 2. Work around the RubyGems / Dependencies version of require
class Object
  alias_method :require_with_rubygems, :require
  alias_method :require, :gem_original_require

  require_with_rubygems 'og'

  # Restore the Dependencies require for future require calls
  alias_method :require, :require_with_rubygems
end

# 3. Define autoload path so the model can find the Orderable mixin.
# This is relative to $LOAD_PATH, which includes the lib path in the og
# gem directory.
```

```
Og::Mixin.autoload :Orderable, 'og/model/orderable'

# 4. Models must be loaded before Og starts
Dir[File.join(RAILS_ROOT, 'app', 'models', '*.rb')].each(&method(:load))

# 5. Read in database.yml and start Og
config = YAML.load_file(File.join(RAILS_ROOT, 'config', 'database.yml'))
$og = Og.start(config[RAILS_ENV].symbolize_keys)
```

This does several things to initialize Og:

1. First, as a sanity check, we use the gem method to specify the exact gem version we installed. As long as the gem specification (*og.gemspec*) specifies a version of 0.50.0, that is the version that RubyGems will recognize. Therefore, we can refresh the Og gem from edge for minor changes without updating this line.

2. The class Object block is in place to work around an incompatibility between Ruby Facets and Rails Dependencies. Og's initialization methods load methods in Facets using the require method. However, Dependencies overrides the require method to keep track of the modules and classes being defined by files as they are required. The new version of require causes problems and prevents Og's dependencies from being loaded properly.

   To resolve this, we temporarily disable all special require functionality while loading Og. First, we store away a copy of the fully functional require, with RubyGems and Dependencies, as require_with_rubygems. Then we alias gem_original_require (the no-frills standard Ruby require, which RubyGems helpfully aliases) as require, so that Og doesn't notice any of the sneaky things we are doing. When Og is loaded, we can put the full-featured require_with_rubygems back into place.

   Notice that the actual call requiring Og needs to use require_with_rubygems so that it will find the gem. We do all of this manipulation so that Og's nested calls to require will use the Ruby version, not the RubyGems/Rails version.

3. In this example, we are mixing the Orderable module into our class; Og uses mixins to add behavior to model classes, where ActiveRecord would conventionally use class methods (in this example, acts_as_list). Using Module#autoload, we designate that Og::Mixin::Orderable can be found under Og's source tree at *og/model/orderable.rb*.

4. As mentioned before, Og needs to see all of the models when it starts, so that it can inject them with Og model methods. (This is in contrast to the ActiveRecord and DataMapper method of requiring all models to inherit from a common base class.) But Rails uses Dependencies to lazy-load models; if we do not explicitly load them here, they will not exist until their name is referenced.

(See Chapter 2 for a full explanation of Dependencies.) We load all the Ruby files in *app/models* so that ObjectSpace can find them.

5. We start Og, loading its database adapter configuration from the traditional *config/database.yml*. The Og manager (an instance of Og::Manager) is stored in the global variable $og. We do not typically need to use this manager directly; it finds and injects functionality to ("enchants," in Og lingo) our model classes. The exception is if we need two or more database connections. Each manager is limited to one database connection, so if we need more connections, we need to create more managers.

The database connection syntax is similar to ActiveRecord's, but there are some differences. A basic configuration using SQLite3 and a database file of *todo_list.db* has the following syntax:

config/database.yml
```
development:
    adapter: sqlite
    name: todo_list
```

Now we are ready to create model classes. Like DataMapper, Og requires us to define all attributes to be mapped to the database. Also like DataMapper, Og creates our schema automatically. Here are some model classes for a very simple to-do list:

app/models/todo_list.rb
```
class TodoList
  attr_accessor :name, String

  # Orderable is like ActiveRecord's acts_as_list.
  # Equivalent to:
  #   include Og::Mixin::Orderable
  # or (as Og::Mixin is included at the top level)
  #   include Orderable
  is Orderable

  has_many :todo_list_items, TodoListItem
end
```

app/models/todo_list_item.rb
```
class TodoListItem
  attr_accessor :name, String

  belongs_to :todo_list, TodoList
  is Orderable, :scope => :todo_list
end
```

Now we can open up the Rails console and start playing with the model classes we have created.

To get a better idea of the queries being issued, it is helpful to redirect the Rails logger to standard output when using the Rails console. This code, thanks to Chad Humphries and Tim Lucas, will redirect Rails log activity to the console. Put this block in your ~/.irbrc.

```
script_console_running = ENV.include?('RAILS_ENV') &&
  IRB.conf[:LOAD_MODULES] &&
  IRB.conf[:LOAD_MODULES].include?('console_with_helpers')
rails_running = ENV.include?('RAILS_ENV') &&
  !(IRB.conf[:LOAD_MODULES] &&
  IRB.conf[:LOAD_MODULES].include?('console_with_helpers'))
irb_standalone_running = !script_console_running &&
  !rails_running
if script_console_running
  require 'logger'
  Object.const_set(:RAILS_DEFAULT_LOGGER, Logger.new(STDOUT))
end
```

The first run of *script/console* creates the SQLite database file and our tables.

```
$ script/console
Loading development environment (Rails 1.2.5)
 INFO: Og uses the Sqlite store.
 INFO: Created table ogtodolistitem.
 INFO: Created table ogtodolist.
 INFO: Created table ogtag.
>>
```

All Og-managed tables currently start with og and are simply the downcased, alphanumeric versions of the class names. The primary key defaults to oid, not id. The ogtag table was created because the optional tagging module was loaded; it currently creates a table whether it is in use or not.

Now we can create a to-do list and some items:

```
>> og = TodoList.create_with :name => 'Og', :position => 1
=> #<TodoList:0x33e75bc @validation_errors={}, @name="Og", @oid=1, @position=1>

>> item1 = TodoListItem.create_with \
        :name => "Make Og work with ActiveSupport's Dependencies",
        :position => 1, :todo_list => og
=> #<TodoListItem:0x33dd3b4 @validation_errors={}, @todo_list_oid=1,
    @name="Make Og work with ActiveSupport's Dependencies", @position=1,
    @oid=1>

>> item2 = TodoListItem.create_with \
        :name => "Autoload Orderable so that Ruby can find it",
        :position => 2, :todo_list => og
=> #<TodoListItem:0x33ce1c0 @validation_errors={}, @todo_list_oid=1,
    @name="Autoload Orderable so that Ruby can find it", @position=2,
    @oid=2>
```

Og has finder methods reminiscent of ActiveRecord's, but with slightly different syntax:

```
>> TodoList[1]
=> #<TodoList:0x3562b1c @name="Og", @oid=1, @position=1>

>> TodoList.find_by_name 'Og'
=> #<TodoList:0x356b078 @name="Og", @oid=1, @position=1>
```

The find_with_attributes method (an alias for query_by_example) has some nice syntactic sugar to provide a "pattern" to match the searched-for attributes. We can view the SQL queries being generated by setting the $DBG global variable to true. For example:

```
>> $DBG = true
=> true

>> TodoList.find_with_attributes :name => 'Og'
DEBUG: SELECT * FROM ogtodolist WHERE name = 'Og'
=> [#<TodoList:0x3558784 @name="Og", @oid=1, @position=1>]

>> TodoList.find_with_attributes :name => 'O%'
DEBUG: SELECT * FROM ogtodolist WHERE name LIKE 'O%'
=> [#<TodoList:0x3553874 @name="Og", @oid=1, @position=1>]
```

Associations work very much like in ActiveRecord. The association contents are lazily loaded; the collection is not loaded until something is done with the data.

```
>> list = TodoList[1]
DEBUG: SELECT * FROM ogtodolist WHERE oid=1
=> #<TodoList:0x33e6608 @name="Og", @oid=1, @position=1>

# Note that this statement issues no query.
>> list.todo_list_items
=> #<Og::HasManyCollection:0x33e23c8 @loaded=false (...)>, oid1, position1

# Sending the collection a message such as #to_a or #map forces it to load.
>> list.todo_list_items.to_a
DEBUG: SELECT * FROM ogtodolistitem WHERE todo_list_oid = 1
=> [#<TodoListItem:0x35033d8
      @name="Make Og work with ActiveSupport's Dependencies",
      @todo_list_oid=1, @oid=1, @position=1>,
    #<TodoListItem:0x3501c7c
      @name="Autoload Orderable so that Ruby can find it",
      @todo_list_oid=1, @oid=2, @position=2>]

>> list.todo_list_items.map(&:name)
DEBUG: SELECT * FROM ogtodolistitem WHERE todo_list_oid = 1
=> ["Make Og work with ActiveSupport's Dependencies",
    "Autoload Orderable so that Ruby can find it"]
```

Alternative Template Engines

The standard Rails template engine uses Ruby's ERb (embedded Ruby), which is a very powerful template system. However, it may be too powerful for some applications. The PHP-like free embedding of code within views can encourage placing too much logic in a view, which the MVC architecture frowns upon. Writing HTML code through ERb can be a painful process, as the developer must switch back and forth between thinking in HTML and thinking in Ruby.

There are some other options on the continua of power and uniformity, and Rails has a flexible extension system that allows different handlers to be simply registered for different view file types. We will look at three markup languages, available as Rails plugins: Markaby, Liquid, and Haml.

Markaby

Markaby (*http://redhanded.hobix.com/inspect/markabyForRails.html*) is a markup language for HTML, by *why the lucky stiff* (Rails plugin due to Tim Fletcher). Its advantage is that it is pure Ruby. All tags have a corresponding Ruby method, similar to Ruby's Builder library. The markup looks like this:

```
h1 'Users'

ul do
  @users.each do |user|
    li do
      user.name
      link_to 'edit', user.edit_url
    end
  end
end
```

Markaby can be installed as a Rails plugin from *http://code.whytheluckystiff.net/svn/markaby/trunk*. Once installed, you can create templates that use Markaby by giving them a *.mab* extension.

Liquid

Liquid (*http://www.liquidmarkup.org/*), by Tobias Lütke, is another alternative Rails template engine. Its main advantage is that it is secure. It does not eval any of its input; it only substitutes provided values into a template with some optional filters. This division of labor has several advantages:

Simplicity

There are only a few basic constructs in Liquid: the simple ones are literal HTML code, variable interpolation, filters, conditionals, and loops. This makes the templates clean and easy to understand, which is an advantage when the designer is not a developer.

Logical separation

The inability to execute code in the views forces model- and controller-related code into the models and the controllers. This helps encourage good boundaries and separation of concerns appropriate for a web application.

Security

Because the Ruby environment is protected against dangerous or malicious code in the templates, you can use Liquid to give customers or users access to templates without security concerns.

To get started with Liquid and Rails, install the Liquid plugin from *http://liquid-markup.googlecode.com/svn/trunk*. The plugin registers a template handler for all view files with an extension of `.liquid`. You can mix and match your Liquid views with standard Rails views, and the Liquid views get all of the assigned instance variables from the controller. The following is an example of Liquid code:

```
<h1>Users</h1>

<ul>
  {% for user in users %}
    <li>{{ user.name }} ({{ 'edit' | link_to: user.edit_url }})</li>
  {% endfor %}
</ul>
```

Haml

Haml is a very terse markup language designed to concisely represent HTML. Haml was created by Hampton Catlin and is available from *http://haml.hamptoncatlin.com/*. The Haml philosophy is summarized on the tutorial page: "Every character means something." We see this in several ways in Haml:

- There are no closing tags; indentation denotes nesting.
- The verbose id and class attributes are shortened to their CSS equivalents # and ., respectively.
- The commonly used div tag can be omitted altogether.
- Rails HTML output is expressed by a single = sign instead of ERb's <%= %> tags.

Haml's terseness can make it a bit difficult to understand at first, but many people find it useful and less intrusive than ERb markup. Our example can be coded in Haml as follows:

```
%h1 Users

%ul
  - @users.each do |user|
    %li
      = user.name
      = link_to('edit', user.edit_url)
```

Notice that we do not need to close anything. The HTML tags are all closed for us, but so is the each iterator we opened. This style of code has a learning curve, but it has less duplication overall than comparable template systems such as ERb.

The stable version of Haml can be installed as a Rails plugin from *http://svn. hamptoncatlin.com/haml/tags/stable*. As with the other template language plugins, it registers a template handler, so all you need to do is install the plugin and start writing views with an extension of *.haml*.

Incorporating Rails Components

As Rails is built up of many modular components, these components can be used individually just as they can be used as a framework. Here we will see how the pieces that make up Rails can be used in other Ruby code. We will walk through two modular components of Rails, ActiveRecord and ActionMailer, and see how to use them in standalone applications.

ActiveRecord

ActiveRecord is perhaps the easiest component to decouple from the rest of Rails, as it fulfills a purpose (object-relational mapping) that can be used in many different places. The basic procedure for loading ActiveRecord is simple; just define the connection, and then create the classes that inherit from `ActiveRecord::Base`:

```
require 'rubygems'
require 'active_record'

ActiveRecord::Base.establish_connection(
  # connection hash
)

class Something < ActiveRecord::Base # DB table: somethings
end
```

The `establish_connection` function takes a hash of parameters needed to set up the connection. This hash is the same one that is loaded from *database.yml* when using Rails, so you could just pick up that file and load it:

```
require 'yaml' # Ruby standard library
ActiveRecord::Base.establish_connection(YAML.load_file('database.yml'))
```

If you are used to the features of edge Rails, you may not want to stick with the latest gem version of ActiveRecord. To use the latest edge, first check out ActiveRecord's trunk from Subversion:

```
$ svn co http://svn.rubyonrails.org/rails/trunk/activerecord \
        vendor/activerecord
```

Then, just require the *active_record.rb* file from that directory:

```
require 'vendor/activerecord/lib/active_record'
```

ETL operations

ActiveRecord can be a useful tool to load data into and extract data from databases. It can be used for anything from one-off migration scripts to hourly data transformation jobs. The following is a representative example, using James Edward Gray II's FasterCSV library:

```
require 'rubygems'
require 'fastercsv' # gem install fastercsv
require 'active_record'

# Set up AR connection and define User class
ActiveRecord::Base.establish_connection(
  # (connection spec)...
)

class User
  # The table we're importing into doesn't use Rails conventions,
  # so we'll override some defaults.
  set_table_name 'user'
  set_primary_key 'userid'
end

FasterCSV.foreach('users.csv', :headers => true) do |row|
  # The CSV header fields correspond to the database column names,
  # so we can do this directly, with no mapping.
  User.create! row.to_hash
end
```

Schema operations

ActiveRecord's migration methods can be used as a portable abstraction for SQL data definition language (DDL). The ActiveRecord::Schema.define function allows you to use the ActiveRecord schema definition statements within a block to perform operations on a database. The full set of DDL operations is documented in ActiveRecord::ConnectionAdapters::SchemaStatements.

```
require 'rubygems'
require 'active_record'

ActiveRecord::Base.establish_connection(
  # (connection spec)...
)

ActiveRecord::Schema.define do
  create_table :sites do |t|
    t.string :name, :null => false
    t.string :city
    t.string :state
  end

  add_column :users, :site_id, :integer
  add_index :users, :site_id
end
```

Standalone data store

Often, a console or desktop application needs to store persistent data, whether it be preference data or application data itself. A common solution is to use YAML, which can marshal and unmarshal most Ruby objects (round trip), while also being human-readable. However, YAML is verbose compared to binary data formats, which may be an issue when storing larger amounts of data. SOAP::Marshal from Ruby's standard library is similar; it can serialize objects into an (often quite verbose) XML representation. This approach has similar benefits and drawbacks to YAML.

Another option is to use Ruby's Marshal module, which dumps Ruby objects into a more concise byte stream. This uses less space, but it can be brittle. Though efforts are made to maintain backward compatibility across major Ruby versions, Ruby 1.9 has a new Marshal format that is not completely interoperable with Ruby 1.8.

For a more structured approach to persistent data storage, SQLite and ActiveRecord can provide a helpful balance. The data schema must be defined first and acted upon by a constrained set of operations (those permitted by SQL DML). But these constraints pay off; as the data store is completely separated from the application, the two halves can evolve separately. There is no need to recode data when an application is upgraded, save for application-level data changes.

Using ActiveRecord for this purpose is simple; just open a connection to a SQLite file (which will be created if it does not exist), and define the appropriate ActiveRecord classes.

```ruby
require 'rubygems'
require 'active_record'

ActiveRecord::Base.establish_connection(
  :adapter  => :sqlite3,
  :database => "db.sqlite3"
)

class Client < ActiveRecord::Base
  has_many :conversations
end

class Conversation < ActiveRecord::Base
  belongs_to :client
end

# Sample usage:
def time_log
  Client.find_all_by_active(true).each do |client|
    # this uses ActiveRecord::Calculations to grab the sum
    # in one SQL query
    hours = client.conversations.sum('hours')

    # format string gives us a nice table:
    # First Client      5.00
    # Another Client    12.40
```

```
      printf "%-20s%5.2f", client.name, hours
    end
  end
```

Other Ruby applications

ActiveRecord can be used as a library in any Ruby application, and it is great for rapidly prototyping simple interfaces to a database. The database interface can be self-contained, which makes it easy to integrate with existing applications; it will coexist with other libraries such as Ruby-DBI.

The rapid prototyping aspect is key; ActiveRecord provides a consistent interface to many database management systems, and you can use this interface to abstract away the database details while building an application. An application can theoretically be developed on a laptop with SQLite and deployed on a big-iron server running Oracle (in practice, this is not a perfect transition, but it is somewhat easier than working with the individual database libraries).

Gregory Brown wrote an article that walks through the process of building a to-do list console application from the ground up with Ruby and ActiveRecord, without using code generation. The article is available from *http://www.oreillynet.com/pub/a/ ruby/2007/06/21/how-to-build-simple-console-apps-with-ruby-and-activerecord.html*.

ActionMailer

Using ActionMailer to send emails from outside of Rails is a simple process as well. It requires slightly more configuration, but not by much. First, load the framework, either using RubyGems or a newer Subversion checkout:

```
# gem version
require 'rubygems'
require 'action_mailer'

# or edge version
require 'vendor/actionmailer/lib/action_mailer'
```

Next, set the outgoing mail server settings. All settings are optional.

```
# Default is :smtp; also accepts :sendmail or :test
ActionMailer::Base.delivery_method = :smtp

ActionMailer::Base.server_settings = {
  :address        => 'localhost',
  :port           => 25,
  :domain         => 'example.com', # HELO example.com
  :authentication => :cram_md5,
  :user_name      => 'me',
  :password       => 'secret'
}
```

ActionMailer needs a template directory in which to look for email templates:

```
ActionMailer::Base.template_root = 'views'
```

Mailer classes and their email templates are defined just as they are in Rails:

```
class Mailer < ActionMailer::Base
  def quota_exceeded_notification(user)
    from       "System Administrator <root@example.com>"
    recipients name_and_email(user)
    subject    "Your account is over the quota"
    body       {:user => user}
  end

  private

  # "John Smith <jsmith@example.com>"
  def name_and_email(user)
    "#{user.full_name} <#{user.email}>"
  end
end
```

The template follows the usual pattern, and is located under our template root, in *views/mailer/quota_exceeded_notification.erb*:

```
Dear <%= @user.name %>,
Your account is over its storage quota. You are currently using
<%= human_size(user.storage_used) %>, and your limit is
<%= human_size(user.account.quota) %>.

Please reduce your usage within 5 days or we will reduce it for you.

Regards,
The Management
```

Now, this Mailer class can be used just as if it were inside a Rails application. We'll look at one possible application for this next.

Custom Rake tasks

Rake is best known in Rails for its purposes in testing. Rake is used to kick off Rails tests, but also to perform administrative functionality (database maintenance and migrations, managing temporary files and sessions, and the like). We can easily extend Rake to handle any application-specific maintenance we need to do; in this case, to find users who are over their quota and send them a nasty email. (For simplicity, we will abstract away some of the details of finding those users.)

Here is a custom *Rakefile* that provides the email functionality:

```
require 'rake'

# Mailer setup commands from above
require 'mailer_config'

# ActiveRecord setup, not shown
require 'ar_users'
```

```
# User administration tasks go in a separate namespace
namespace :users do
  desc "Send a nasty email to over-quota users"
  task :send_quota_warnings do
    users = User.find(:all).select{|u| u.storage_used > u.account.quota }
    users.each do |user|
      Mailer.deliver_quota_exceeded_notification(user)
    end
  end
end
```

We can now kick off the email with one command from the project's directory:

```
rake users:send_quota_warnings
```

Receiving email

The ActionMailer documentation includes instructions on how to receive incoming email using Rails and ActionMailer. This method involves having your MTA pipe incoming mail to a command such as this:

```
script/runner 'Mailer.receive(STDIN.read)'
```

Do not do this except in the absolute simplest of cases. Using `script/runner` is very computationally expensive, because it loads the entire Rails environment on each invocation. Loading a Ruby interpreter with all of Rails for each incoming email is ridiculous.

The standard method for processing incoming mail is to batch email in a mailbox and have a process retrieve that mail at a regular interval. The mail can be retrieved using `Net::POP3` or `Net::IMAP` from the Ruby standard library.

If mail really needs to be processed immediately upon receipt, a custom solution, even using Ruby and ActionMailer, will still be much faster than the preceding example that loads all of Rails. But if you need immediate delivery, you should probably first consider a solution like SMS or Jabber rather than SMTP.

Contributing to Rails

Rails, as an open source framework, benefits greatly from contributions from the community. Rails incorporates code from hundreds of developers, not just the dozen or so on the core team. Writing code to expand, extend, or fix Rails is often the best way to learn about its internals.

Of course, not all functionality belongs in Rails itself. Rails is an opinionated framework, so there are some defaults that may not be useful to everyone. The plugin system was designed so that Rails would not have to incorporate every feature that is useful to someone. Refer to Chapter 3 for information on writing plugins to extend Rails; it is only minimally more work than patching the Rails codebase.

There are several reasons that useful features are rejected from Rails in favor of being plugins. The primary reason for rejection is that the feature is too specific; it would not be useful to most Rails developers. Alternatively, it may be contrary to the "opinion" of the framework. However, features may be rejected simply because there are many valid ways of accomplishing one goal, and it does not make sense to default to one. Some common areas of functionality that have been repeatedly discussed and rejected from Rails core are the following:

Engines

> David Heinemeier Hansson's rejection of high-level components in Rails is a topic that has generated much more heat than light. Rails engines (*http://rails-engines.org*) are full-stack (model, view, and controller) components that can be incorporated into larger applications; in effect, they augment the plugin system to structure the sharing of model, view, and controller code.

> The trouble with engines comes when they are treated as high-level components, as if dropping a content-management-system engine into an application will accomplish 90% of the CMS functionality a particular project needs. In many cases, the work required to integrate such a high-level component into an existing application outweighs the benefits of not writing the component from scratch.

> In short, engines are best seen as a way to structure plugins that need controller and view code, rather than a drop-in replacement for high-level features. In this respect, engines are amazingly powerful; they allow plugins to augment an application's models, views, controllers, helpers, and even routes and migrations.

Internationalization and localization

> There are many valid approaches to the problems of internationalization and localization. We discuss several solutions in Chapter 8. ActiveSupport's Multi-Byte standardizes the low-level operations on Unicode text, but there are still many valid ways to localize an application at the high level.

Authentication and authorization

> Again, there are many application-specific ways to authorize users that authorization does not belong in Rails. Authorization can range from a simple "admin" Boolean flag on a user's record to a complete role-based access control system, and there are plenty of plugins available for authorization in Rails.

> Similarly, there are many valid ways to authenticate users. The only authentication method in Rails proper is HTTP Basic authentication, because it is very simple. However, the most popular authentication solutions descend from the acts_as_authenticated plugin by Rick Olson (which has its roots in Tobias Lütke's original Login Generator). The newer version of acts_as_authenticated is restful_authentication, which is the same logic molded into Rails 2.0's RESTful paradigm.

Complex scaffolding

Scaffolding is another misunderstood issue in Rails. Like high-level components, scaffolding can be overapplied. Developers who see scaffolding as a substitute for writing complex application code will be disappointed.

Still, there are many valid uses for simple CRUD features, especially on an application's administrative interface. Streamlined (*http://streamlinedframework.org*) is a way to quickly build CRUD interfaces on top of Rails. Additionally, AjaxScaffold (*http://www.ajaxscaffold.com/*) is a scaffolding system with a richer interface than the built-in Rails scaffolds.

There is another reason for starting a feature as a plugin, though. Plugins are often a testing ground for experimental or risky features before they are rolled into the main distribution. As an example, the RESTful features of Rails 2.0 were a plugin, `simply_restful`, before they were pulled into Rails trunk.

Contributing Patches

There is a new process for contributing Rails bug reports and patches, to help deal with the large volume of tickets and contributed patches. The process is as follows:

Write a patch

Bug reports are always welcome, but patches get more attention. Fixing problems that you experience, even if they are problems with Rails itself, has some advantages. It gives you greater familiarity with the Rails source, which is very well written. It also helps you verify and prove that the problems you are experiencing are actually problems with Rails.

Most patches should include tests. Especially for bugfixes, test-driven development is a good philosophy to use. A test-driven methodology would incorporate the following basic steps:

1. Before writing any application code, write a test that verifies the correct functionality. Run the test; it should fail.

2. Write code to fix the bug until the test passes.

3. Verify that all other tests pass, not just the test in question.

Most areas of Rails are well-tested; however, there are some components (such as the generators and CGI processing code) that are not very easy to test. When writing nontrivial patches for those areas, the burden of proof is higher to ensure that there are no regressions of other functionality.

The basic procedure to create a patch against Rails is simple:

1. svn up to grab the latest version of Rails.

2. Make the appropriate changes to the source.

3. Run rake to ensure all of the tests pass.

4. Check the output of svn st as a sanity check for missing files, merge conflicts, or other junk.

5. svn diff > my_patch.diff to create a unified diff of the changes.

6. Manually inspect the generated diff to verify that there are no extraneous changes and that all necessary changes are included.

File a ticket

Rails uses the Trac issue-tracking system, which is set up at *http://dev.rubyonrails.org/*. You need an account to use the system, due to excessive spam in the past. Once you have an account, click "New Ticket" to create a ticket.

If you have a patch for the issue you are reporting, use [PATCH] at the beginning of the ticket summary, and remember to check the "I have files to attach to this ticket" button.

There are a few points of basic ticket-creation etiquette. Leave the "Keywords" field blank unless you know better. The "Assign to" and "Cc" fields should in most cases be left blank as well; if other developers want to be added to the Cc list, they will add themselves.

At this point, there may be a good deal of back-and-forth, or there may be no activity. Be prepared to defend your decisions and your code, and you may be sent back for rewrites or additions. Make sure to keep the patch current; if the Rails trunk changes significantly in the meantime, you should rebase your patch so that it still applies cleanly (with no fuzz). If a patch is well-tested, it can be rebased and verified simply by repeating the preceding steps (updating, running tests, and creating a new diff).

Get reviewed

Every month, the Rails Trac system sees thousands of actions (tickets opened, closed, or commented on). In order to manage this flow, there is a barrier to entry for contributors so that the core team doesn't have to deal with patches that are outdated, untested, or that break obvious functionality.

Generally, to get attention for a patch, you have to find three reviewers to assert that the patch applies cleanly, passes the automated tests, and "works" for them. They do this by making an appropriate comment (as simple as "+1 for me") in the ticket's comments. Once you have three reviewers, it is up to you to add the verified keyword to the ticket to indicate that review is complete.

Be available

At this point, your ticket will show up in the "verified" report (*http://dev.rubyonrails.org/report/12*). Patches in this queue are usually acted upon quickly, whether the action is acceptance, rejection, or sending it back for more discussion.

Rails contributors use ticket status and resolutions as a way to deal with the large volume of incoming tickets. It is common for a ticket to be opened and closed a few times before being accepted or rejected. Don't worry if your ticket is closed as untested; that just means it needs tests (or, alternatively, a very good reason why it can't or shouldn't be tested). Then it can be sent back.

Also, don't be discouraged if your patch is ultimately rejected. There are many features that used to be in core Rails that have been removed or turned into plugins in Rails 2.0. The Rails core team is focusing on keeping Rails smaller and more agile; most frameworks tend to accumulate features without limit unless their growth is kept in check. The Rails plugin system was designed so that almost anything in Rails can be changed at runtime. In this way, the core can be kept simple without hampering the development of new features.

Many Rails contributors spend time in the #rails-contrib IRC channel on *irc. freenode.org*, and there is good discussion about Rails internals there. Most contributors also subscribe to the rubyonrails-core mailing list at Google Groups (*http:// groups.google.com/group/rubyonrails-core*), which has more visibility and permanence than the IRC channel. Both are good places to look for patch reviewers, and it is a good idea to ask around on IRC and the mailing list before diving into any major new feature work; there may be people who have started (or even completed) similar work, and it is good to find other developers who may have ideas about your plans.

Rails Unit Tests

The Rails framework is built in a modular fashion; Rails 2.0 comprises ActionPack, ActiveRecord, ActionMailer, Active Resource, ActiveSupport, and RailTies. As such, each component is tested separately. This causes a few minor issues (as the full functionality of one module may depend partially on another, so they can never be completely independent), but for the most part it increases flexibility, and the benefits outweigh the drawbacks.

Unit tests for most components are self-contained. Each component has a Rakefile defining its testing strategy and any other Rake tasks it requires. With the exception of ActiveRecord, all Rails components can be tested by changing to their directory and executing rake. If all is well, you will see a large number of periods (representing successful tests), and it will end with no failures or errors:

```
Finished in 1.444231 seconds.

704 tests, 5475 assertions, 0 failures, 0 errors
```

ActiveRecord is a bit more difficult to test, due to its dependency on many external databases. The default task, if no task is provided to rake, is to run the tests for MySQL, PostgreSQL, SQLite (version 2), and SQLite3.

In Rails 2.0, the lesser-used connection adapters have been moved out of Rails trunk and into gems so that they can be installed if needed. The connection adapters for Firebird, FrontBase, OpenBase, Oracle, Microsoft SQL Server, and Sybase now live under /adapters in the Rails repository.

The gems for these connection adapters are hosted at the Rails gem server (*http://gems.rubyonrails.org*) and are named activerecord-*dbname*-adapter (for example, activerecord-oracle-adapter or activerecord-sqlserver-adapter), so they can be installed with a command such as the following:

```
$ gem install activerecord-sybase-adapter –source \
        http://gems.rubyonrails.org
```

Incidentally, IBM maintains its own DB2 adapter for ActiveRecord, so the old ActiveRecord DB2 connection adapter is gone in Rails 2.0.

In order to run the ActiveRecord unit tests, you will need to create test databases. Thankfully, there are some Rake tasks that automate this process. For a full test of the "big four" connection adapters from the ground up, follow these steps:

1. Install and configure the database servers: MySQL, PostgreSQL, SQLite, and SQLite3. The client libraries also need to be installed; these are installed with the server binaries but can be installed separately if the server is on a remote machine.

   For MacPorts users, SQLite 2 can be installed with sudo port install sqlite2 (even though its files are named sqlite for historical reasons, the port name is now sqlite2). If you have previously installed the sqlite port, you should uninstall it before installing sqlite2 and sqlite3.

2. Install the Ruby database libraries with RubyGems:

   ```
   $ sudo gem install mysql
   $ sudo gem install postgres
   $ sudo gem install sqlite-ruby
   $ sudo gem install sqlite3-ruby
   ```

Installing the mysql library is not strictly necessary; Rails includes a pure-Ruby MySQL library in *activerecord/lib/active_record/vendor/mysql.rb*. This implementation will be used if no native mysql extension is found, which is useful on systems like Windows, where a Ruby interpreter can be more accessible than a C compiler. Additionally, the postgres gem can be replaced by the postgres-pr gem, which is also pure Ruby.

MacPorts users may have some difficulty with these steps; the default configuration scripts look in the /usr and /usr/local trees for the client libraries installed in step 1, while MacPorts installs into /opt/local. This can be fixed by passing configuration parameters into gem, which are preceded by -- so they are not parsed as options to gem itself:

```
$ sudo gem install sqlite3-ruby -- --with-sqlite-dir=/opt/local
```

3. Verify the database connection information for the unit tests. ActiveRecord tests require two database connections per adapter, to verify that ActiveRecord is able to properly manage multiple simultaneous connections. If needed, modify the connection specifications in *activerecord/test/connections/native_adaptername/ connection.rb*.

4. Create the unit test databases for MySQL and PostgreSQL. The SQLite and SQLite3 databases will be automatically created upon first run, as they are backed by a single file per database. For a default configuration (no modifications to the above connection specifications), run the following Rake tasks from the *activerecord* directory:

```
$ rake build_mysql_databases
$ rake build_postgresql_databases
```

For more complicated configurations, create the databases specified in the preceding connection files, and ensure that the user specified in those files has full access to those databases, or you will get permission errors.

5. Change to the *activerecord* directory and run rake. The tests should run on all four connection adapters with no failures or errors. Tests for individual adapters can be run with separate Rake tasks such as test_mysql; run rake -T for a list of all recognized tasks.

Further Reading

Railscasts has produced a screencast detailing the process of contributing to Rails. It is available at *http://railscasts.com/episodes/50*.

Notes from Josh Susser's talk on contributing to Rails are posted at *http://edgibbs.com/ 2007/04/23/josh-susser-on-contributing-to-rails/*.

## CHAPTER 10

Large Projects

Fools ignore complexity. Pragmatists suffer it.
Some can avoid it. Geniuses remove it.
—Alan Perlis

This chapter introduces several concepts that are related to deploying large applications in general, and Rails applications in particular. These are valuable concepts for any project, regardless of the framework being used.

Version Control

For all but the tiniest of projects, version control is non-negotiable. Version control is like a time machine for a project; it aids in collaboration, troubleshooting, release management, and even systems administration. Even for a solo developer working on a small project on one workstation, the ability to go back in time across a codebase is one of the most valuable things to have.

There are two primary models for version control systems: centralized and decentralized. Though the former is the most widely known, the latter is steadily gaining in popularity and has some amazing capabilities.

Centralized Version Control

Centralized version control is the most popular model, and perhaps the easiest to understand. In this model, there is a central repository, operated by the project administrators. This repository keeps a virtual filesystem and a history of the changes made to that filesystem over time.

Figure 10-1 illustrates the typical working model used for centralized development.

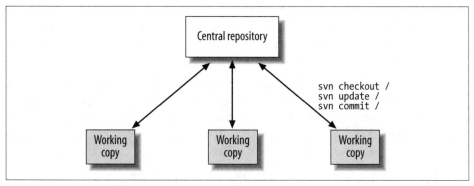

Figure 10-1. Centralized version control

A developer follows this basic procedure to work with a version control system:

1. Create a *working copy* (a local copy of the code for development) by performing a checkout. This downloads the latest revision of the code.

2. Work on the code locally. Periodically issue update commands, which will retrieve any changes that have been made to the repository since the last checkout or update. These changes can usually be merged automatically, but sometimes manual intervention is required.

3. When the unit of work is complete, perform a commit to send the changes to the repository. Repeat from step 2, as you already have a working copy.

CVS

The Concurrent Versions System (CVS, *http://www.nongnu.org/cvs/*) is the oldest version control system still in common use. Although Subversion is generally favored as its replacement, CVS pioneered several features considered essential to centralized version systems, such as the following:

Concurrent access

Previous version control systems such as RCS required a developer to "check out" a file, locking it for update, and then check it in to release the lock. CVS introduced the *copy-modify-merge* model for text files. Under this model, many developers can work on different parts of the same file concurrently, merging the changes together upon commit.

Repository hooks

The ability to run external scripts upon commit—to run tests, notify a team, start a build, or anything else.

Branches and modules

CVS allows multiple concurrent branches for development. Vendor branches can pull code from unrelated projects; modules map symbolic names to groups of files for convenience.

One often-cited drawback to CVS is that it does not guarantee *atomic commits*. If interrupted while in process, commits can leave the working copy and repository in an inconsistent state. Most other version control systems provide an atomicity guarantee: commits are applied to the repository either in full or not at all.

In practice, this is more of an annoyance than a critical flaw. Important repositories should be backed up regularly, regardless of what version control system they are backed by. Still, this and other limitations make some developers uncomfortable. In response, many other version control systems have evolved out of the CVS model, and CVS is not used very much anymore for new projects.

Subversion

Subversion (*http://subversion.tigris.org/*) is currently the most popular version control system among Rails developers. It was designed to be a replacement for CVS, and it has been very successful. Developers used to CVS will feel at home with Subversion's commands.

As a centralized version control system, Subversion uses one primary server that keeps a master repository. Developers check out a working copy, make their changes, and check them back in. By default, Subversion uses the *copy-modify-merge* model for concurrent development. Multiple people can check out the same file, make concurrent changes, and have their work merged. Non-overlapping changes will be merged automatically; conflicting changes must be merged by hand.

Files that cannot be merged (such as image files) can be locked for serialized access:

```
$ svn lock images/logo.png -m "Changing header color"
(work with logo.png...)
$ svn ci images/logo.png -m "Changed header to blue"
```

You can also use the svn:needs-lock property to designate that a file should be locked before editing. If a file marked with that property is checked out without a lock, the working copy version will be set as read-only to remind the developer to lock the file before changing it.

Subversion was designed as a replacement for CVS, and it improves on CVS in many ways:

- Subversion has truly atomic commits; interrupted commits are guaranteed to leave the repository in a consistent state (though they may leave outstanding locks in the working copy).

- Subversion supports constant-time branching using copy-on-write semantics for copies. Branches and tags are simply directories; they are not separate objects as in CVS.

- Directories are tracked independently of the files they contain. Directories and files can be moved while retaining their version history.

- Symbolic links can be stored in the repository and versioned as links.

Subversion provides the best fit for many developers, especially in the open source world. Many projects have migrated from CVS to Subversion over the past few years. Subversion is successful in a large part because it strikes a good balance between features and ease of use.

One drawback of Subversion is that it can be difficult to build the server from source because of its dependencies. It is built on top of APR (the Apache Portable Runtime), a portability layer for network applications. Although the basic dependencies are included for a svnserve installation, you may run into difficulty if you want to use Apache as a Subversion server. However, once you have the dependencies in order, building the server is straightforward.

Decentralized Version Control

Centralized version control has some drawbacks, especially when working in larger teams. The central server and repository can become a bottleneck, especially when dealing with many developers, as in large open source projects. A new paradigm, *decentralized version control*, is attempting to fix some of these issues. Though it is not widely used among Rails developers, it is worth knowing about, as it is extremely useful for certain situations.

In contrast to the hierarchical structure of centralized versioning systems, decentralized systems provide a more egalitarian approach. (It's the cathedral versus the bazaar, if you will.) Rather than having many working copies that all must communicate their changes back to the repository, each working copy is in fact a full repository. Any of the local repositories can pull and push changes to and from each other, and changesets destined for production will ultimately be pushed back to the authoritative repository.

In fact, the only thing that designates a repository as authoritative is community support: project administrators set up a repository as the master and publish its network address. Developers can pull changes from any repository that decides to publish them. Interestingly, this parallels the meritocracy inherent in open source software: your worth is measured by how much you contribute and how many people listen to you.

The decentralized development model can be more complicated to learn, but it is much more flexible, especially with large projects that have many contributors. The Mercurial wiki gives an example of distributed development best practices based on the development style of the Linux kernel.*

At first glance, a distributed workflow might look fairly similar to a centralized one. In fact, a decentralized version control system can be used as a centralized system; its functionality is a superset of that of centralized systems. Using Mercurial, a developer

---

* *http://www.selenic.com/mercurial/wiki/index.cgi/KernelPractice*

can "check out" a codebase (hg clone), make modifications, update from the repository (hg pull; hg merge), and check in (hg commit). This process is illustrated in
Figure 10-2.

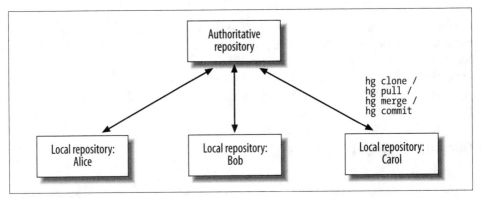

Figure 10-2. Decentralized version control

There is a slight difference here from the centralized paradigm, in that the pull and
merge steps are second. Mercurial gives the developer complete control over the
local repository and working copy, so merges do not take place unless requested.

The real power comes from the ability to synchronize repositories. Changesets can
be pulled from any repository, not just the master. So, if Bob developed a feature that
Alice needs to test, Alice can pull it directly from him, merge it into her repository,
and test it before committing it to the master. This is most commonly done today
with centralized systems using diff and patch, but distributed systems formalize this
method. The process looks something like Figure 10-3.

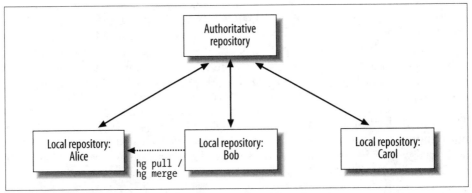

Figure 10-3. A repository can pull from or push to any other repository

One of the most compelling features of decentralized version control is its compatibility with offline development. With a centralized system, the developer must be

able to contact the server whenever he wants to check code in. Under the decentralized model, a developer can check in code to his local repository on his laptop in the Bahamas, and then push all of the changesets at once to the authoritative repository when he has an Internet connection. This keeps the changesets clean and focused, while not requiring a connection to the main repository on every commit. In effect, this method creates a hierarchy of repositories (see Figure 10-4).

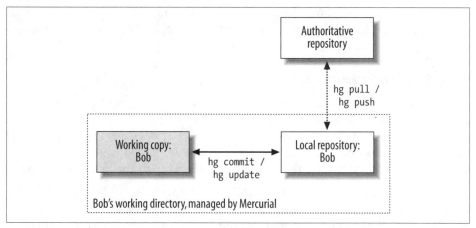

Figure 10-4. Disconnected or offline development with decentralized version control

The primary technical drawback to distributed systems (other than their complexity) is that each working copy is a full repository. Because each repository contains a full change history, a checkout of a large or often-changing system can be quite large. As an example, the Linux kernel source code is around 50 MB (bzipped), but a `git clone` checkout of the same source (with history) transfers hundreds of megabytes across the network.

Branching and Merging

In large software development projects, there is usually a need to keep multiple lines of development separate. This need exists for a few reasons:

- Ongoing feature development will take place almost immediately after a release is issued. If the release is buggy, the developers need a mechanism to fix the version that was released without introducing any of the changes that were introduced since the release.

- A development team will often work on multiple features concurrently. It would be a nightmare if each developer had to ensure that his half-developed, half-tested feature worked with another developer's half-developed, half-tested feature every time he checked in code.

- When creating a release for public consumption, there is often a period of testing and evaluation. If the entire development team were frozen during this test period, it would be very hard to get anything done.

- A team may offer support for multiple versions of the software at the same time, in effect making public their branching system. Bugfixes and occasionally features must be backported to old releases of the software.

Most version control systems offer flexible branching and merging support. A branch is an independent line of development that can be developed on its own and merged back into the trunk.

Subversion branching and merging

Subversion does not actually have a built-in branching or tagging mechanism as such; all branches and tags are simply copies of part of the directory tree. Subversion creates *cheap copies* using copy-on-write semantics; data is written to disk only when the copy is actually changed. The amount of extra information required to maintain a branch is roughly proportional to the difference between the branch and its parent.

This characteristic has some drawbacks, though. Subversion 1.4 has very primitive merging support. It does not keep track of when branches were created or merged, and does not prevent a change from being applied twice. Most developers who do at least a moderate amount of merging use *svnmerge.py,*[*] which keeps track of this metadata in Subversion properties.

There are many different paradigms for how branches are used. Here are some of the most common ones for web development:

Production branch

The trunk is used for ongoing development. When a feature is fully developed and tested, it is merged into the production branch and deployed. This style is well suited to web applications, which tend to have a single development team working on one feature package at a time. Urgent production defects can be fixed in the production branch without disturbing feature work, and later can be merged into the trunk.

For typical web applications, there is only one release branch, as there is only one version of the software running at a time. When multiple release versions must be supported, the production-branch model is strong, as multiple branches can be created. This can be useful on occasion even in web applications; for example, a large feature release can be staged as a "beta" to a subset of users. If the beta is long-lived, it is useful to create a branch so that development can continue independently.

---

[*] *http://www.orcaware.com/svn/wiki/Svnmerge.py*

This model is a slight deviation from the ordinary non-web software development model. In that model, features are developed in the trunk, stable work toward a release is kept in a branch, and finished releases are tagged by copying them to the *tags* directory. The Rails framework itself uses that model.

Feature branches

This is essentially the opposite of the production-branch model. One branch is created for each new feature to be deployed. The trunk is always expected to be stable and represents the latest stable version of the software.

Some prefer the feature-branch model over the production-branch model for web applications, as it compartmentalizes features and isolates them from one another during development and testing. It supports the single-deployment-environment paradigm, but it is difficult to support multiple releases under this model.

Developer branches

Again, the trunk is a stable codebase. Each developer has his own branch that he can use as his "sandbox" for developing and testing features. He will either merge code into the trunk himself or submit the changesets to be integrated by one person. Often, this is found in large teams, as it integrates well with a formal code review process.[*]

If you have a large enough team that developer branches are necessary, you may find yourself passing around and manually applying patches way too often. In that situation, it may be worthwhile to consider moving to a distributed version control system such as Mercurial or Bazaar.

Of course, the appropriate model will vary from project to project. Do not feel constrained by these models. The *trunk*, *branches*, and *tags* directories are only the traditional conventions used by Subversion developers. You could just as easily set up *features*, *production*, and *snapshots* if it suited your fancy.

Mercurial branching and merging

Branching under distributed version control systems such as Mercurial is much more natural. Any Mercurial repository is automatically a branch, because any repository can pull changes from and push changes to any other repository, even between two different directories on the same filesystem. Thus, the standard branching method under Mercurial is to clone an entire project to a new directory, make the changes, and then use hg pull to retrieve and merge the changes from a branch when needed.

As an example, suppose we are changing an application's color scheme and want to branch to keep the color-related changes together while doing other development. First, we clone the trunk to a new feature branch:

```
$ hg clone trunk trunk-newcolors
47 files updated, 0 files merged, 0 files removed, 0 files unresolved
```

---

[*] Google uses a similar method, without explicit developer branches, for its internal development. They use NFS, Perforce, and a code review tool called Mondrian developed by Guido van Rossum.

Now *trunk-newcolors* contains an identical copy of the trunk, including all history. We are going to make changes to *trunk-newcolors*, preview them, and then merge them back into *trunk*. We now make the appropriate changes to *trunk-newcolors* and commit them:

```
$ cd trunk-newcolors/
$ sed -ie 's/color: red/color: blue/g' public/stylesheets/main.css
$ hg ci -m "Changed red to blue in main stylesheet"
$ hg tip
changeset:   1:18bb8b07ec40
tag:         tip
user:        Brad Ediger <brad.ediger@madriska.com>
date:        Fri Oct 26 13:08:01 2007 -0500
summary:     Changed red to blue in main stylesheet
```

We can preview this line of development for as long as we like, and then merge it back into trunk. To merge, we first pull the changes from *trunk-newcolors* into the *trunk* repository:

```
$ cd ../trunk/
$ hg pull ../trunk-newcolors
pulling from ../trunk-newcolors
searching for changes
adding changesets
adding manifests
adding file changes
added 1 changesets with 1 changes to 1 files (+1 heads)
(run 'hg heads' to see heads, 'hg merge' to merge)
```

This indicates that there have been changes to the trunk since the branch, so we will need to merge.

 Mercurial requires an explicit merge step, even if the merge turns out to be trivial. In some cases, when you pull, you do not want to merge. An extension called FetchExtension provides an hg fetch command to automate the pull/merge/commit process in the case of trivial merges.

We use the hg heads command to see the two *heads* (two branches of development), one from our local repository at *trunk* and the other from *trunk-newcolors*. The merge step using hg merge is simple, and in this case, it is a trivial merge (without any conflicts). Had there been conflicts, hg merge would have attempted to find a three-way merge tool such as FileMerge or kdiff3 to help us resolve the changes. When the merge is complete and we have approved it, we need to commit the merge.

```
$ hg heads
changeset:   2:18bb8b07ec40
tag:         tip
parent:      0:65aca7b5860a
user:        Brad Ediger <brad.ediger@madriska.com>
date:        Fri Oct 26 13:08:01 2007 -0500
summary:     Changed red to blue in main stylesheet
```

```
changeset:   1:800424c888ed
user:        Brad Ediger <brad.ediger@madriska.com>
date:        Fri Oct 26 13:08:57 2007 -0500
summary:     added another CSS class

$ hg merge
merging public/stylesheets/main.css
0 files updated, 1 files merged, 0 files removed, 0 files unresolved
(branch merge, don't forget to commit)
$ hg ci -m "Merged"
```

Mercurial Revision Numbers

Note the changeset identifiers in this example; in particular, the changeset we pulled from *trunk-newcolors* into *trunk* has the same hexadecimal ID in both repositories (18bb8b07ec40), but a different numeric ID (1 versus 2).

Because changesets can be copied somewhat arbitrarily between repositories, their numeric IDs (which simply reflect the order in which they were added to the repository) will differ. But the hex IDs, which are SHA-1 hashes of the content of the changeset and its history, remain the same.

Mercurial shows both identifiers, and either of them can be used to identify a revision, as can tags (hg update 2, hg update 18bb8b07ec40, and hg update tip are all the same thing in the preceding example). But the hex IDs are the only ones that are valid when talking with another developer, or even when working between repositories on the same machine, as we see here.

The newly committed merge shows the two changesets from earlier as its parents:

```
$ hg tip
changeset:   3:5f98ca15ccbc
tag:         tip
parent:      1:800424c888ed
parent:      2:18bb8b07ec40
user:        Brad Ediger <brad.ediger@madriska.com>
date:        Fri Oct 26 13:10:00 2007 -0500
summary:     Merged
```

Often, cloning a repository in this way can be difficult. Rails applications can accumulate a good deal of configuration files (in particular, *database.yml*) that are not version controlled, and so must be recreated on each clone. There are a few ways around this:

- hg clone is basically an atomic recursive copy when working between two repositories on the same filesystem. So, if you can be sure that the source repository will not change during the copy, the following two commands are roughly equivalent:

    ```
    $ hg clone trunk trunk-newcolors
    $ cp -R trunk trunk-newcolors
    ```

Of course, the latter has the advantage of preserving files that are not kept under revision control.

- Mercurial keeps all of its revision control metadata, including the entire repository, in a single *.hg* directory under the project root. You can recursively copy this *.hg* directory over the *.hg* directory of another repository and then perform an `hg update --clean` from the target repository to update the working copy (which may contain extra, non-version-controlled files).

Mercurial also has support for *named branches*, which are separate branches of development within one repository. This support has been mature since version 0.9.4. However, named branches complicate certain aspects of using Mercurial, and they are a somewhat advanced feature. Named branches are preferable for long-lived development branches, while branching by cloning is still preferred for feature branches. Chapter 8 of *Distributed Revision Control with Mercurial* goes into detail about branching and merging (*http://hgbook.red-bean.com/hgbookch8.html*).

Database Migrations

When working with large Rails projects, especially those with multiple developers or feature branches, an issue that frequently comes up is synchronizing database migrations. Since Rails migrations are numbered sequentially in the order in which they are generated (with respect to the current project), the generate script will happily use a number that may have been in use elsewhere, in other versions of the project. This causes difficulty upon merging. The typical workflow is this:

1. The current migration version number in the trunk is 123. You branch the project for a new feature, and in the branch you generate a migration for the database support:

   ```
   [branches/feature]$ script/generate migration AddNewFeature
           exists  db/migrate
           create  db/migrate/124_add_new_feature.rb
   ```

2. You need to fix an issue in the trunk, so you create and apply a migration to trunk. It is created with version number 124, because the other version 124 is not visible yet:

   ```
   [trunk]$ script/generate migration BugFix
           exists  db/migrate
           create  db/migrate/124_bug_fix.rb
   ```

3. Upon merging, there are two migrations with version 124. These must be manually renumbered, which can be difficult if there were many migrations. The database must then be migrated down to the lowest migration common to both branches, and migrated back up. If the migrations are not fully reversible, the changes may have to be applied manually.

This situation can also happen when there are multiple developers generating their own migrations. The solution for that situation is good communication: developers should always pull the *db/migrate* directory from the version control system immediately before generating a migration. Conversely, these migrations should be checked in as soon as is practical after generation, so all developers have access.

Unfortunately, when using branches, it is not generally possible to publish every schema change across all branches. If it were, a simple solution would be to set up a shared migrations directory in the version control repository, and import it via a svn: externals (or equivalent) declaration. In most cases, schema changes to separate branches must be kept separate; at the least, production databases should not be polluted with database changes for new features. So, another solution must be found. There are several schools of thought on how this should work.

The simplest solution, which is probably the most popular, is Courtenay's Independent Migrations plugin (*http://blog.caboo.se/articles/2007/3/27/independent-migrations-plugin*). The basic assumption is that migrations which are created in different branches or working copies are logically independent of each other. (If this assumption doesn't hold, you will have problems when merging, no matter how you slice it.)

After installing the plugin, simply tag your independent migrations as such by inheriting from `ActiveRecord::IndependentMigration` rather than `ActiveRecord::Migration`.

```
class AddFeature < ActiveRecord::IndependentMigration
  # ...
end
```

Multiple independent migrations will then be applied concurrently, so migrations can be merged without renumbering. However, this does not eliminate the need to migrate down and back up when several migrations have been applied to a database; the plugin will not search old version numbers (older than the current version) for new migrations.

My solution, Subverted Migrations,[*] is more complicated, but it aims to be as transparent as possible once you understand it. As the name suggests, it only works with Subversion. The intent is to synchronize version numbers across all branches. That way, all developers and all branches have the same view of the migrations that have been applied project-wide. It applies two changes to the Rails version-numbering mechanism:

- It serializes version numbers across all branches by scanning the Subversion repository for all branches to find a free version number.
- It changes the semantics of the schema_version table: rather than being the number of the latest-applied migration, the schema version is a list of migrations that have been applied to the database. When older changes from other branches are merged in, a simple `rake db:migrate` applies them without the need to migrate down and up.

---

[*] *http://www.bradediger.com/blog/2006/11/subverted_migrations.html*

Of course, this only works if all developers promptly check in their new migrations, and if the migrations are truly independent from each other in the first place. The multiple-developer scenario always requires good communication. Another drawback of Subverted Migrations is that it requires access to the Subversion repository every time a migration is generated. The other solutions operate only with the working copy.

The last solution is François Beausoleil's Timestamped Migrations patch. This patches Rails to use UTC timestamps rather than simple version numbers. Like Subverted Migrations, this method changes the semantics of the schema_info table to reflect exactly which migrations have been applied. Timestamped Migrations is not available as a plugin, but only as a patch against edge Rails (*http://blog.teksol.info/ articles/search?q=timestamp*).

Issue Tracking

Issue-tracking systems are essential to any large or long-lived project. The term "issue" is broad enough to encompass things that may not be thought of as bugs or defects: feature requests, work orders, support requests, or even planning documents for future changes to an application.

The difference between products called "issue trackers" and those called "bug trackers" is largely one of focus; the two typically implement similar sets of features. Issue trackers tend to be customer-oriented; even if only used by employees, each ticket represents a customer problem. Bug trackers tend to be focused more on the product; they collect bugs, feature requests, or other issues regarding the project. One distinguishing factor is that under a bug tracker, multiple tickets representing the same issue will usually be folded into one ticket, even if the tickets affect different customers.

One powerful feature that some issue trackers offer is integration with a version control system. This allows the history of each issue to be correlated with the development of the code. Patches intended to fix an issue can reference the issue number directly. Conversely, issues can reference version control changesets (for example, "fixed in r1843"), and the issue-tracking system provides the changesets in a friendly format (such as HTML diff).

Some of the most popular issue-tracking systems are listed here.

Product	Platform	Description
Bugzilla	Perl, Apache or IIS	Mozilla project's bug tracker. Oriented toward open source software development. Flexible workflow.
Collaboa	Rails	Newcomer to the industry; development trunk is still fairly unstable. Takes the best features from Trac and cleans them up a bit. Looks very promising.
RT (Request Tracker)	Perl, Apache	Email-based workflow. More suited to customer support than issue tracking, but can be used for either or both.

Product	Platform	Description
Trac	Python, Subversion	Great Subversion integration. Very nice workflow. Based on modular architecture, so many plugins are available. However, it can be difficult to install. Currently used to manage Rails development (*http://dev.rubyonrails.org/*).
Lighthouse	Rails (*Hosted*)	New subscription-based issue-tracking service by Active Reload (Rick Olson and Justin Palmer). Very slick interface, good extensibility, and integration with email.

Project Structure

There are several decisions that must be made about how to structure a large Rails application. Issues arise with how to manage multiple branches of development, a team of developers, and external or vendor software. In this section, we cover some of the most common choices.

Subversion Configuration

Subversion usually needs a little bit of configuration to work with Rails. There are some "volatile" files that change from development to production or within a deployment. These files should be kept out of version control. In Subversion, a file is ignored within a directory by setting a pattern matching the file as the value of the svn:ignore property on the parent directory. For most Rails applications, the following ignores are typically used:

```
$ svn propset svn:ignore database.yml config/
$ svn propset svn:ignore "*" log/ tmp/{cache,pids,sessions,sockets}
```

There is a Subversion client configuration that sets up many of these settings, and will ignore those volatile files without the need for svn:ignore. It also sets up *autoprops*, which sets the MIME type on files in the repository automatically. If you work mainly with Rails projects, this can be a good choice. The config file is available from *http://3spoken.wordpress.com/rails-subversion-tng-config-file/*.

As a rule, configuration specific to a particular Rails environment (excluding database connection specifications, which are more specific to the developer and his environment) should not be ignored, but rather should be placed in environment-specific blocks. This allows the configuration to be versioned while still remaining environment-specific.

Importing existing applications

The svn import command is designed to place a directory (and its subdirectories) under version control. Unfortunately, it is only an import, not a checkout. It does not turn the imported directory into a working copy, which is usually the behavior you want when importing a project that is already under development.

There is a neat Subversion trick to add an existing directory tree "in place" to an empty repository. You can use this when putting an existing application under version control:

```
$ svn mkdir svn://repo/my_app/trunk

$ cd my_app
$ svn co svn://repo/my_app/trunk .
$ svn add *
$ svn ci
```

To add only certain directories without their contents, pass the -N (--non-recursive) flag to svn add. This is very useful when setting contents of certain directories to be ignored; for example, these commands will add the *public/attachments* directory while ignoring its contents:

```
$ svn add -N public
$ svn add -N public/attachments
$ svn propset svn:ignore "*" public/attachments
```

Subversion Externals and Piston

Subversion has an *externals* facility for pulling in code from other repositories. When a folder is designated as an external, it is paired with a remote repository. When updating the working copy, code will be pulled from that repository in addition to the main project repository.

In Rails, there are two reasons you would want to do this. The first is to lock Rails to a certain version (or to track edge Rails). The second is for plugins: you may want to follow updates to a plugin's Subversion repository, so you can lock *vendor/plugins/plugin_name* to the plugin's development repository. The script/plugin command even provides a flag that adds the plugin as an external rather than downloading it:

```
$ script/plugin install -x some_plugin
```

This works for small-scale applications, but the dependencies can quickly become a mess. Most of the time, you will not want to follow the bleeding edge of Rails or a plugin, but instead lock to a known-stable version. Although svn:externals has a feature to do that, it can get messy. The biggest problem is that any local changes you make to the external code are not versioned. In addition, updates are slow as they must query each external server.

The best solution at this point is François Beausoleil's Piston (*http://piston.rubyforge. org/*). Rather than pulling a copy of the code from the remote Subversion server, Piston stores a copy locally, in your project's own Subversion repository. It uses properties on the folder to track the current version at the remote repo. To Subversion, the directory is just another set of files in your project. This means that updates are fast, as they only talk to one server. You also only get external updates when you ask for them (piston update).

First, install Piston and convert your existing `svn:externals` to Piston-locked directories:

```
$ sudo gem install --include-dependencies piston
$ piston convert
```

You can now lock to edge Rails:

```
$ piston import http://svn.rubyonrails.org/rails/trunk vendor/rails
```

Installing plugins is simple if you know the repository URL:

```
$ piston import \
  http://activemerchant.googlecode.com/svn/trunk/active_merchant \
  vendor/plugins/active_merchant
```

Remember to manually execute the commands in *install.rb* if it does anything special; `script/plugin` would do this for you, but Piston doesn't know or care that you are installing a Rails plugin.

Piston-controlled directories can be updated all at once with `piston update`, or one at a time with `piston update vendor/plugins/active_merchant`.

Rails Version

If a Rails distribution is unpacked in *vendor/rails* under the application root, it will be used. If *vendor/rails* is not present, Rails will look for an installed `rails` gem matching the specified `RAILS_GEM_VERSION` (usually specified in *config/environment.rb*). It is usually best, for the sake of predictability, to have the Rails code unpacked in *vendor/rails*. Although it takes up a little more room in the repository and on the server, it ensures that everyone is on the same page and developing against the exact same version.

Nothing says that you have to use edge Rails; for the stable branch of Rails 1.2, use Piston to lock *vendor/rails* to *http://svn.rubyonrails.org/rails/branches/1-2-stable*.

Environment Initialization

As Rails has matured, the *environment.rb* configuration file has been shifting in purpose and style. Originally, it started out as a procedural language where every little bit of configuration was included, and you would just "throw something at the bottom" to have it run upon Rails initialization. Now, its purpose is more focused, to the point that it almost seems to be a domain-specific language for configuring Rails. The mechanics of starting up Rails have been moved to *boot.rb*, and what is left has been cleaned up.

However, sometimes we just need a place to put initialization routines. In edge Rails, these have been given a new place. If you have (or create) a *config/initializers* directory, any Ruby files there will be executed after the environment is configured.

Having a separate place for initializers helps you to separate them by function. Here is a sample file for custom inflections:

```
# config/initializers/inflections.rb

# inflect.uncountable(["data"]) doesn't catch "something_data"
Inflector.inflections do |inflect|
  inflect.plural(/(data)$/i, '\1')
  inflect.singular(/(data)$/i, '\1')
end
```

The last trick for initialization is the `after_initialize` block. Included as part of the configuration, it will be run at the end of initialization (immediately before the initializers mentioned previously). The block is specified thus:

```
config.after_initialize do
  # some initialization code...
end
```

Unfortunately, you only get one `after_initialize` block per initialization—you can't have one in *environment.rb* and another in *production.rb*. So, choose wisely where you need it. My recommendation: use it in your environment-specific configuration files, and use the initializers directory for your generic initialization.

Including Gems

When deploying to a new machine, it can be frustrating to make sure all of the dependencies are in order. RubyGems are typically the main culprit here. One way to ensure you have gem dependencies under your control is to include them in the project tree. This idea, from Chris Wanstrath,[*] is the natural extension of keeping Rails and plugins within the project.

To include gems in the project, we will create a directory to hold them, then unpack a gem there using the `gem unpack` command (you may need to update RubyGems for this command to work):

```
$ mkdir vendor/gems
$ cd vendor/gems
$ gem unpack hpricot
Unpacked gem: 'hpricot-0.4'
```

Now we need to ensure that the directory we have created is added to the load path. In the environment.rb file, inside the `Rails::Initializer.run` block, add the following:

```
config.load_paths += Dir["#{RAILS_ROOT}/vendor/gems/**"].map do |dir|
  File.directory?(lib = "#{dir}/lib") ? lib : dir
end
```

[*] *http://errtheblog.com/post/2120*

There are plenty of nuances to this trick, so be sure to check the aforementioned blog post and its comments for the full story.

Multi-Application Projects

For large projects, sometimes multiple Rails applications need to be grouped together. Multiple applications that need to share code can be grouped in the same version control tree. This is a good use for Subversion externals; externals can point to other parts of the repository that they live in.

Under this setup, bits of shared code are kept in the repository at the top level of their branch or trunk (at the same level as the Rails applications). Subversion externals are used to pull shared folders into each of the Rails projects. A typical directory structure looks like Figure 10-5.

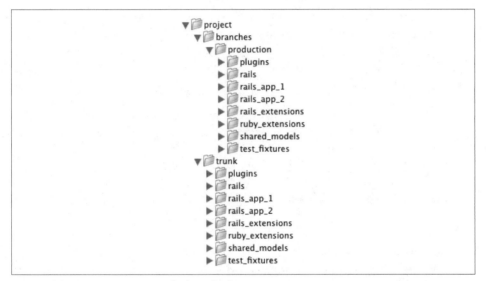

Figure 10-5. Directory structure of a large Rails project

Under this directory layout, you would issue commands like the following to import each directory from the shared tree:

```
$ cd project
$ svn propset svn:externals "models (repo)/trunk/shared_models" \
    trunk/rails_app_{1,2}/app
```

That command tells Subversion to source *trunk/rails_app_1/app/models* and *trunk/rails_app_2/app/models* from *trunk/shared_models*. When you update either of the Rails applications, they will grab code from *shared_models*. When you commit code into the applications' model directories, Subversion will push the code into *shared_models*.

There is one caveat to this approach. Subversion will not commit to two repositories at once, and it sees an external as a separate repository. So, if you make changes to both the models and some other part of an application at the same time, you must check those changes in separately. This can take some getting used to, but it quickly becomes second nature.

Depending on your situation, you may want to keep any or all of these shared between two or more Rails applications:

Rails codebase

> Usually, you want all of the applications within a project to be locked to the same version of Rails. With a project maintained under Subversion, using Piston to source the vendor code offers an advantage; you can maintain local changes to the Rails tree independently of what happens upstream. Using Piston, you can lock Rails to a certain branch (stable or edge) and update when you feel like it.
>
> You can pull changes from the upstream Rails repository and sync them throughout trunk with the following commands:

```
$ cd project/trunk
$ piston update rails
$ svn up
```

Plugins

> Like the Rails source, plugins usually come in from an upstream repository. Often you will need them synchronized across projects. Here, Piston is a great help again, as you can update across your project and only pull changes from upstream when you are ready. You have two options for structuring the source tree: you can either pull the plugins directory as a whole (into *vendor/plugins*), or you can cherry-pick the plugins you need for each application.

RubyGems

> Maintaining gem dependencies between development environments, staging, and production servers can be a hassle. The most consistent solution is to "vendor everything"—create a *vendor/gems* directory, carry your gem dependencies around with the project code, and modify Rails to look there before your installed RubyGems.
>
> Chris Wanstrath came up with this solution (*http://errtheblog.com/post/2120*), and Dr. Nic Williams packaged it into a gem itself, gemsonrails (*http://gemsonrails.rubyforge.org/*). Kyle Maxwell has a Rails plugin that allows the "vendor everything" approach to be used for gems that require building native extensions (*http://svn.kylemaxwell.com/rails_plugins/vendor_everything_extensions/*).

Ruby and Rails extensions

Any project of reasonable size usually accumulates a series of extensions, annotations, and utility functions that supplement the Ruby and Rails core. Examples of Ruby extensions:

```ruby
class String
  # "Frequently - Asked Questions!" => "frequently_asked_questions_"
  def to_slug
    self.downcase.gsub(/[^a-z0-9]+/, "_")
  end

  # 12345678.to_s.with_commas => "12,345,678"
  def with_commas
    self.reverse.gsub(/\d{3}/,"\\&,").reverse.sub(/^,/,"")
  end
end
```

Because these utility functions are usually widely applicable, it is useful to share them between projects. I usually keep them under *lib/extensions* and require them from an initializer.

ActiveRecord models

Some situations call for two or more separate applications sharing the same data. While this is usually accomplished with one Rails application and judicious separation of concerns, occasionally the purposes for the applications will diverge and it will make sense to split them up. In that case, the models can be placed in a *shared_models* directory and shared out among the applications.

Test fixtures

If you share a data model between applications, you will usually want to share any test fixtures you have between those applications as well.

Rails Deployment

As a full-stack web framework, Rails can require some work to deploy an application from the ground up. Rails, unfortunately, has a bad reputation for being hard to deploy, mainly due to problems with the preferred deployment environments when Rails was young (2004–2005). But Rails has grown up, and Mongrel came along in 2006 and made things much easier. There are now good sets of best practices for deploying Rails applications, from the smallest development environments to huge multi-data-center worldwide clusters.

Shared-Nothing Scalability

One of the most basic concerns when deploying any web application is scalability: how well the underlying architecture can respond to increased traffic. The canonical Rails answer to the scalability question is *shared-nothing* (which really means shared-database): design the system so that nearly any bottleneck can be removed by adding hardware. The standard architecture looks like Figure 10-6.

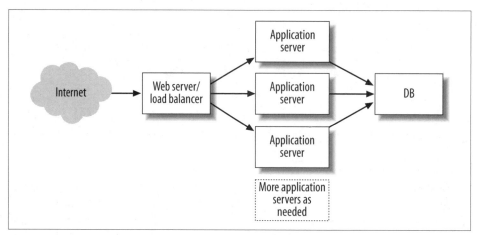

Figure 10-6. Simple shared-nothing deployment environment

The interface to the application is either a light web server (operating as a reverse proxy balancer*) or a hardware load balancer. A small web server is usually used to handle the static files (images, JavaScript, static HTML, stylesheets, and the like) because a single-purpose static file server is much faster than an application server at serving static files. This front end box delegates dynamic requests to one of the application servers, selected either randomly or based on load.

For redundancy in large setups, two front end servers can be used, on separate machines, proxying to the same set of application servers (see Figure 10-7).

If high availability is required, the load balancers must use a VIP-/VRRP-based solution to ensure that the cluster will always respond to all of its IP addresses even under the failure of one load balancer. If high availability is not a requirement, primitive load balancing will suffice, by giving each load balancer its own IP address and exposing them all through a DNS RR (round-robin) record.

---

* A *forward proxy* sits in front of users and accelerates content that those users request. A *reverse proxy* sits in front of web servers and accelerates the content requested of that server. A *proxy balancer* is a reverse proxy that balances requests among its member servers.

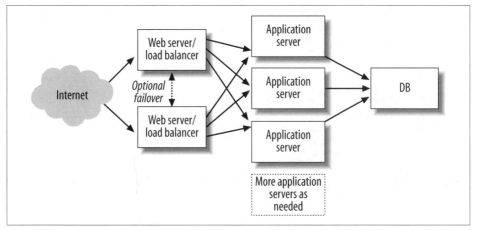

Figure 10-7. Shared-nothing deployment with redundancy for load balancing or high availability

One drawback of this architecture is that once the database becomes the bottleneck, things can get difficult. Database scalability is a hard problem, and we examine this issue in Chapter 4.

Front End Web Server

The front end web server has several purposes. Depending on the application, these may be mission-critical or not even needed. Consequently, the concrete systems architecture will look very different from application to application. The most common functions of the front end server are the following:

Reverse proxying and load balancing
> The front end server balances and distributes requests between the application servers. It also acts as a reverse proxy so that the requests to the application servers appear to be coming from the client, rather than the balancer.

Static file serving
> The front end web server (which may or may not be the same software as the load balancer) serves static files much faster than the application servers.

Compression
> If HTTP compression is to be used, the front end web server can handle this to reduce CPU load on the application servers.

SSL wrapping
> The front end server can handle SSL encryption so that the application server does not have to do it (SSL encryption and decryption are CPU hogs). The front end server usually adds a header such as X-Forwarded_Proto: https to indicate that SSL was used.

Common choices for a front end web server and proxy balancer are as follows.

Apache (http://httpd.apache.org)

> Of these servers, Apache is definitely the heaviest. Administrators who have a choice usually select one of the lighter options. But Apache has some advantages: it is well-known and relatively easy to configure, it is very flexible, and it integrates well with its environment.
>
> If you have a choice, use Apache 2.1 or higher, as it supports `mod_proxy_balancer`. Otherwise, you will need to proxy to a balancer such as pen or pound in order to load balance between application servers.
>
> Apache can actually directly serve Rails applications over FastCGI, using `mod_fastcgi` and the Rails FastCGI dispatcher. However, this approach has mostly been superseded by the reverse-proxy/Mongrel method for new deployments.

Lighttpd (http://www.lighttpd.net)

> Lighttpd (usually just pronounced "lighty") is a powerful, light web server. It supports reverse proxying and load balancing with the `mod_proxy` module. It is one of the preferred front end servers today.
>
> Like Apache, lighttpd can directly serve Rails with FastCGI. This is still not recommended, as the Mongrel approach is more robust and scalable.

Pen (http://siag.nu/pen/)

> Pen is a standalone proxy balancer. It does not serve static files; it only proxies to a list of servers and balances between them. Pen has SSL-wrapping support.
>
> If high availability is needed, Pen can be clustered using the VRRP protocol for failover.

Pound (http://www.apsis.ch/pound/)

> Pound is another reverse proxy balancer. Like Pen, it can proxy, balance between servers, and unwrap SSL. It is also not a web server, so you may have to set up a static file server.
>
> However, Pound has some X-Forwarded-For problems when being used as a reverse proxy between Apache and Mongrel,[*] so you should consider Pen instead for this configuration.

nginx (http://nginx.net)

> One of the newest but most promising contenders is nginx ("engine X"). Like Apache and lighttpd, nginx is a web server with comprehensive load balancing, rewrite, and proxy features. While the featureset is comparable to Apache, the performance characteristics and memory footprint are more like lighttpd. At the moment, nginx seems to be the best front end for Rails applications.

---

[*] *http://blog.codahale.com/2006/11/07/pound-vs-pen-because-you-need-a-load-balancing-proxy/*

Asset hosts for static files

There is yet another way to serve static files. Rather than intercepting requests for static files at the proxy, you can define an *asset host*, or another server from which static files will be served. The Rails image_path and similar helper methods will then use that host to reference files in the public directory. Configuration is simple:

```
config.action_controller.asset_host = "http://assets.example.com"
```

But this can be inefficient: browsers limit the number of concurrent connections to one host, so the download speed can actually be limited by the connection rate, which is often governed by the user's upload speed.* This can be solved by increasing the number of DNS names from which assets are served, as the restrictions operate based on names, not IP addresses. In Rails 2.0, the configuration looks like this:

```
config.action_controller.asset_host = "http://assets-%d.example.com"
```

This will distribute asset requests across *assets-0.example.com*, *assets-1.example.com*, *assets-2.example.com*, and *assets-3.example.com*. Just point all of those DNS names at your asset server, and you gain the benefit of increased concurrency without changing any client settings.

Application Server

With the other pieces in place, we now need the biggest piece of the puzzle: the application server that handles all of the dynamic requests. Right now, the best solution is Mongrel.†

Prior to Mongrel, Rails applications were best served using the CGI protocol or some variation thereof (FastCGI or SCGI). The basic idea behind this is that the front end web server would talk to the application server using a special protocol, with one connection per request (see Figure 10-8). CGI has the limitation that one new process is created for each request, which is extremely slow for interpreted languages such as Ruby. Therefore, the FastCGI and SCGI protocols were created. They have the advantage that they can work with persistent interpreters—one interpreter can serve many requests over the lifetime of the process. This solution can be scaled by adding more workers.

However, the front end server is still a limiting factor here. The front end server handles every request from start to finish, something we can actually eliminate with a load-balanced setup. In addition, using two different protocols confuses things: the application servers speak FastCGI, and the web servers speak HTTP. To top it off, Apache's mod_fastcgi has had a reputation for crashing after being up for a while.

---

* See *http://www.die.net/musings/page_load_time/* for a full explanation.

† *http://mongrel.rubyforge.org/*

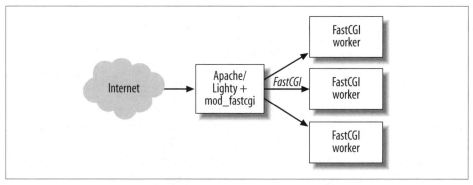

Figure 10-8. Serving a Rails application with FastCGI

Enter Mongrel: an HTTP application server. It supports several frameworks, the most prominent being Rails. Instead of having your application servers speak FastCGI, they can natively speak HTTP. This means, among other things, that you can put them behind a hardware or software load balancer, and the dynamic requests may not even need to hit a web server other than Mongrel. Alternatively, you can proxy to them from a web server, as described previously.

Mongrel is very easy to install and control:

```
$ sudo gem install mongrel
$ cd my_rails_app
$ mongrel_rails start -d

(mongrel is running as a daemon)

$ mongrel_rails stop
```

Mongrel can be run as a service on the Win32 platform, using the mongrel_service gem.

Remember: as an HTTP server, Mongrel will happily serve static files in its docroot, but it will be slower than a server optimized for static files. This is fine in development mode (script/server defaults to Mongrel, even in development mode), but it will be slow in production. For situations where performance matters, set up a front end web server and check the logs to be sure it is serving all of the static assets.

Of course, managing several Mongrels in parallel can get tiring. That's why Bradley Taylor created mongrel_cluster. It is a small library that manages parallel Mongrel application servers. It takes a configuration file, which specifies how many Mongrels to run, with a range of port numbers to expose to the load balancer. The cluster servers can then be started and stopped at once with the simple commands:

```
mongrel_rails cluster::start
mongrel_rails cluster::stop
mongrel_rails cluster::restart
```

Capistrano

Once you have a server set up and running smoothly, you need a way to deploy your application from the repository to the server. The naïve process of sshing into the server, updating the code, and restarting the server process gets old very quickly, and it is error-prone.

Enter Capistrano (*http://capify.org/*): a framework for scripting interaction with remote machines. Capistrano started out as a deployment framework (it was originally called SwitchTower). As people started using it for wider and more varied purposes, it evolved into a general framework for executing commands in parallel on a set of remote servers. In version 2.0, deployment is only a subset of the functionality available through Capistrano, and the deployment tools must be explicitly loaded.

Capistrano, like the rest of Rails, follows the *convention over configuration* paradigm. In general, the more "mainstream" your situation, the less configuration you will have to write. The framework gives you enough power to do most things you would want to do, but tries to make the simple situations simple.

The Capistrano 2.0 source code is an excellent example of well-structured Ruby code. It is hosted in the Rails Subversion repository (*http://svn.rubyonrails.org/rails/tools/capistrano/*).

Vlad the Deployer

Of course, as Capistrano grows larger and becomes more general, some people just want a simple deployment tool. The Ruby Hit Squad released Vlad the Deployer (*http://rubyhitsquad.com/Vlad_the_Deployer.html*) as a reaction against Capistrano's complexity. It does one thing: application deployment. It uses native programs (ssh and rsync), as opposed to Capistrano, which depends on the Net::SSH library.

Because Vlad is focused on deployment only, the configuration file can be simpler. It defaults to one server; Capistrano assumes a large setup—the default deployment tasks assume separate web, app, and db roles. Either solution works well; generally, Vlad is easier to get started with, and Capistrano will be more flexible for large projects or those with unusual requirements.

Continuous Integration

Another powerful tool for software development, especially in large teams, is *continuous integration*. As a principle, continuous integration comes from the Extreme Programming discipline. It usually involves a build/test process that happens either just before or just after each version control commit. If tests fail, an email is typically sent to the entire team, shaming the offending developer and providing an incentive to fix the code.

The most popular continuous integration framework is CruiseControl, which started as a Java project. It has since been ported to .NET and Ruby. ThoughtWorks maintains the Ruby port, CruiseControl.rb (*http://cruisecontrolrb.thoughtworks.com/*). It runs in the background and monitors the repository every 30 seconds for commits (the interval is configurable). When a new version is detected, it checks it out into a working directory and runs the tests with Rake. If there are failures or errors, a failure email is sent out. (Likewise, if the build was broken but is now fixed, a "fixed" email is sent.) CruiseControl.rb also provides a neat web interface to view test progress and results for the latest and previous builds.

Closely related is the ZenTest suite of tools by Ryan Davis.[*] ZenTest consists of five tools that help with test coverage, especially under Rails applications. The documentation tells the full story, but the most compelling part of this suite is *autotest*. This allows an even shorter cycle time than continuous integration tools. Although the method is similar to continuous integration, the AutoTest tools are used more for development (to shorten the cycles between writing code and testing it) than for continuous integration (which is more of a safety net to prevent obviously bad code from being deployed).

AutoTest sits in the background and watches the files in a Rails project. When any file is changed, AutoTest runs the appropriate tests immediately. It is pretty smart about which tests need to be run, and even watches test fixtures and other dependencies for changes. If you follow the test-driven development methodology, running AutoTest is a great way to force yourself to stay green. Get started with the following:

```
$ sudo gem install ZenTest
$ cd my_rails_app
$ autotest -rails
```

Further Reading

There are many resources, both free and paid, for learning the version control systems mentioned in this chapter. For Subversion, there is Version Control with Subversion (*http://svnbook.red-bean.com/*), which is available both for free online and as a print book from O'Reilly. Also available is Pragmatic Version Control Using Subversion (*http://pragmaticprogrammer.com/titles/svn2/index.html*), which is more of a tutorial than a reference.

CVS has similar options available. The book Open Source Development with CVS is available under a GPL license online at *http://cvsbook.red-bean.com/*. The print book is also distributed by O'Reilly. The Pragmatic Programmers' offering is Pragmatic Version Control Using CVS (information available at *http://pragmaticprogrammer.com/starter_kit/vcc/index.html*).

---

[*] *http://www.zenspider.com/ZSS/Products/ZenTest/*

Similarly, the best book about Mercurial is free. It can be downloaded from *http://hgbook.red-bean.com/*.

Matt Pelletier and Zed Shaw have written a book on Ruby application deployment with Mongrel; it can be purchased and downloaded as a PDF from *http://www.awprofessional.com/bookstore/product.asp?isbn=0321483502&rl=1*.

Ezra Zygmuntowicz is writing the book on Rails deployment. Information is available at *http://www.pragmaticprogrammer.com/titles/fr_deploy/index.html*.

Index

We'd like to hear your suggestions for improving our indexes. Send email to *index@oreilly.com*.

P

page caching, 177
ParseTree library, 2
partition method, 38
partitioning data, 115
passwords
    hashing, 128, 129
    recovery, 129
patches, contributing, 291
pen, 318
perf_run command, 163
performance
    ActiveRecord, 165
        1+N problem, 166
        indexing, 167–171
        SQL, 165
    architecture, scalability, 173–181
    benchmarking, 161–164
    caching, 176
        action, 177
        fragment, 178
        page, 177
        sweepers, 180
    databases, 171
        query plans, 171–173
    measurement tools, 148–155
        black-box analysis, 148–151
        code timing, 151–153
        Rails Analyzer Tools, 153–155
    profiling, 155–161
    sessions
        ActiveRecordStore, 174
        CookieStore, 176
        management, 176
        MemCacheStore, 175
        scalability, 174
pg_autovacuum daemon, 171
PGCluster, 124
Piston, 81
    Subversion externals and, 310
plain text, password recovery, 129
plugins, 79, 314
    about.yml file, 83
    account_location, 85–87
    attachments, 107
    Deadlock Retry, 93
    examples of, 85–90

Ferret library, 170
Gibberish, 253–254
Globalize, 254, 257
    example of, 258–268
    HTTP Authentication, 89
    Independent Migrations, 307
    installing, 80–83
    Liquid, 283
    loading, 79
    restfully_yours, 221
    ssl-requirement, 87
    testing, 90–95
    whitelists, 141
    writing, 83–85
    (see also applications)
POST method, 190
PostgreSQL, 97
    8-bit Unicode Transformation Format
        (UTF-8), 247
    high availability, 123
    large/binary objects, 102
.pot files, 251
pound, 318
precomposed characters, 243
predicates, 37
privileges, DROP TABLE, 144
Proc method, 48
Proc#binding method, 28
processing
    forms, 132
    upload, 108
procs, 20–23
production branches, 302
Production Log Analyzer, 153
profiling
    Action Profiler, 153
    actions, 155–157
programming
    ActiveSupport, 57
        Core Extensions, 60–75
        dependencies, 57
        deprecation, 58
        Inflector, 59
        JSON, 59
        Whiny Nil, 60
    aspect-oriented programming (AOP), 32

About the Author

Brad Ediger is the CTO of Tasman Labs, a real-estate technology company. He and his wife, Kristen, a web designer, own Madriska Media Group, a firm specializing in custom application development. When not programming, Brad enjoys playing various musical instruments and watching obscure films.

Colophon

The animal on the cover of *Advanced Rails* is a common, or Burchell's, zebra (*Equus burchellii*). Members of the horse family (equids), common zebras grow to a height of 45–55 inches at the shoulder and weigh 485–550 pounds. They have excellent hearing and eyesight (their night vision is comparable to that of cats or owls), and can run as fast as 35 miles per hour. Common zebras inhabit East African savannas, from treeless grasslands to open woodlands; tens of thousands of them can be found in migratory herds on the Serengeti plains. They are herbivores and feed mostly on grasses and occasionally leaves or stems. They graze for many hours each day; a zebra's teeth grow throughout its lifetime to counteract the wearing that occurs from this near-constant feeding.

Zebras are social herd animals, and the social system of the common zebra is based on a "harem" of females led by a stallion. Stallions compete for fillies that have come into their first estrus, and the filly will stay permanently with the stallion that succeeds in mating with her. Foals are dark brown and white at birth, and can walk a mere 20 minutes after birth and run within an hour. This allows them to keep up with the rest of the herd as it searches for food and water. Family groups stay together within the larger group. Communication plays a key role in the herd as well; the zebras communicate with a variety of sounds, such as barking and snorting, and with facial expressions and ear position. They even greet each other with a "smile"— a bared-teeth grimace that discourages aggression. Shared grooming further reinforces the bonds between them; they nibble at one another to remove loose hair or to help scratch those hard-to-reach spots.

Of course, the most prominent and recognizable feature of a zebra is its black and white stripes. The pattern of stripes on a zebra is as distinct as a human's fingerprints; in fact, scientists can identify individual zebras by comparing patterns, stripe widths, coloring, and scars. The stripes help serve as protection against predators in the wild such as leopards and lions; when the herd is grouped together, it is hard for the cats to discern a specific zebra to pursue. Interestingly, zebras are attracted to black and white stripes; even if the stripes are painted on a wall, a zebra will tend to migrate to them.

The cover image is from Wood's *Illustrated Natural History*. The cover font is Adobe ITC Garamond. The text font is Linotype Birka; the heading font is Adobe Myriad Condensed; and the code font is LucasFont's TheSans Mono Condensed.

Related Titles from O'Reilly

Web Programming

ActionScript 3.0 Cookbook

ActionScript 3.0 Design Patterns

ActionScript for Flash MX: The Definitive Guide, *2nd Edition*

Advanced Rails

AIR for JavaScript Developer's Pocket Guide

Ajax Design Patterns

Ajax Hacks

Ajax on Rails

Ajax: The Definitive Guide

Building Scalable Web Sites

Designing Web Navigation

Dynamic HTML: The Definitive Reference, *3rd Edition*

Essential ActionScript 3.0

Essential PHP Security

Flash Hacks

Head First HTML with CSS & XHTML

Head Rush Ajax

High Performance Web Sites

HTTP: The definitive Guide

JavaScript & DHTML Cookbook, *2nd Edition*

JavaScript Pocket Reference, *2nd Edition*

JavaScript: The Definitive Guide, *5th Edition*

Learning ActionScript 3.0

Learning PHP and MySQL, *2nd Edition*

PHP Cookbook, *2nd Edition*

PHP Hacks

PHP in a Nutshell

PHP Pocket Reference, *2nd Edition*

PHP Unit Pocket Guide

Programming ColdFusion MX, *2nd Edition*

Programming Flex 2

Programming PHP, *2nd Edition*

Programming Rails

Rails Cookbook

Upgrading to PHP 5

Web Database Applications with PHP and MySQL, *2nd Edition*

Web Scripting Power Tools

Web Site Cookbook

Webmaster in a Nutshell, *3rd Edition*

The O'Reilly Advantage

Stay Current and Save Money